Jesus' Resurrection and Apparitions

Jesus' Resurrection and Apparitions

A Bayesian Analysis

JAKE H. O'CONNELL

RESOURCE *Publications* • Eugene, Oregon

JESUS' RESURRECTION AND APPARITIONS
A Bayesian Analysis

Copyright © 2016 Jake H. O'Connell. All rights reserved. Except for brief quotations in critical publications or reviews, no part of this book may be reproduced in any manner without prior written permission from the publisher. Write: Permissions, Wipf and Stock Publishers, 199 W. 8th Ave., Suite 3, Eugene, OR 97401.

Resource Publications
An Imprint of Wipf and Stock Publishers
199 W. 8th Ave., Suite 3
Eugene, OR 97401

www.wipfandstock.com

PAPERBACK ISBN: 978-1-4982-2559-5
HARDCOVER ISBN: 978-1-4982-2561-8
EBOOK ISBN: 978-1-4982-2560-1

Manufactured in the U.S.A.   OCTOBER 26, 2016

Contents

Preface | vii

1   Introduction | 1
2   Bayes' Theorem | 32
3   The Reality of Apparitions | 68
4   1 Corinthians 15 and the Gospels | 119
5   The Reliability of the Resurrection Narratives | 151
6   Objections | 166
7   Analyzing the Data with Bayes' Theorem | 198

Appendix: Can the Historian Affirm that a Miracle Occurred? | 265

Preface

IN THE PRESENT BOOK, I set forth the argument that the hypothesis Jesus rose physically from the dead is superior to the hypothesis that the resurrection appearances should be construed as appearances of a non-bodily apparition. A secondary purpose of the book, as I explain in chapter 1, is to serve as an introduction to Bayes' Theorem. Bayes' Theorem is a quite interesting subject, and I believe I present here a clear introduction to it and a fine application of it; and I would be quite interested to see Bayes' Theorem more widely used by religion scholars, even though, as I say at the end of the book, it is not necessarily going to lead to a major boon.

Chapter 3 constitutes in some ways a third purpose of the book. In that chapter, I examine the case for the reality of apparitions of the dead. It is a stand-alone chapter which will be the primary chapter of interest to those reading the book for the parapsychology element.

In addition to these three primary aspects of the book, I address along the way matters such as the possibility of intentional fiction in the Gospels, the reliability of 1 Corinthians 15:3-8, the historicity of the empty tomb, the accuracy of eyewitness testimony, and the issue of alleged contradictions in the resurrection narratives.

And before we begin, it is time for acknowledgments. First of all, let me thank the following individuals for reading portions of the manuscript prior to publication: Keith Augustine, Richard Carrier, William Lane Craig, Alan Gauld, Hugh Gauch Jr., Gary Habermas, Craig Keener, Michael Licona, and Richard Levine. And let me thank Jodi Magness for answering questions of mine regarding the practice of burial in Jesus' time.

I would like to thank the library of Hartford Seminary for access to their resources.

I would like to thank Wipf and Stock for publishing the manuscript.

I would like to thank David Cornell for permission to reprint material from Tony Cornell, *Investigating the Paranormal* (New York: Helix Press, 2002). And I would like to thank the Society for Psychical Research for permission to reprint material from Ian Stevenson, "The Blue Orchid of Table Mountain," *Journal of the Society for Psychical Research* 42 (1964): 401-409; and Andrew MacKenzie, "A Case of Haunting in Kent," *Journal of the Society for Psychical Research* 44 (1967): 131-49.

All quotations from the Bible in this book are taken from the New American Standard Bible.

1

Introduction

AFTER SURVEYING OVER 2,200 publications on Jesus' resurrection from 1975-2005, Gary Habermas came to a conclusion which has surely not changed since then: "The substantially unanimous verdict of contemporary critical scholars is that Jesus' disciples at least believed that he was alive, resurrected from the dead."[1] But though there is widespread agreement that the disciples had experiences which they believed were appearances of the resurrected Jesus, there have always been divergent opinions as to the nature of these appearances. The traditional position is of course that Jesus was physically raised from the dead. Those who have defended this view have had to contend with a myriad of alternative explanations, such as that the disciples lied, or that they hallucinated, or that Jesus faked his death on the cross, or that all of the New Testament material is legendary.

The present work is written not to consider all of these alternative hypotheses, but only one particular alternative: the hypothesis that the New Testament accounts of the resurrection appearances are reports of real, non-physical apparitions, just like the many reports of apparitions which have been published in the parapsychological literature in contemporary times. Since the late 1800s, the literature of parapsychology has collected thousands of cases of apparitions of the dead, and if at least some of these cases are not susceptible to any naturalistic explanation (lies, hallucinations, and so forth), then it is a documented fact that real apparitions of the deceased are sometimes seen. If this is so, we must consider the possibility that the resurrection appearances were neither any form of naturalistic phenomena, nor appearances of Jesus physically raised from the dead, but that they were appearances of a real, non-bodily apparition. In this work, I will examine this hypothesis and conclude that it is unconvincing. For I will argue that the resurrection hypothesis—that is, the hypothesis that Jesus was raised physically from the dead—provides a better explanation of the data.

---

1. Gary R. Habermas, "Experiences of the Risen Jesus: The Foundational Historical Issue in the Early Proclamation of the Resurrection," *Dialog* 45 (2006): 288-97 (289).

Proponents of the Apparition Theory

Surveys have found that approximately 10% of the population has seen an apparition,[2] and as we will see shortly, there is strong reason to believe that many of these apparitions are real. Thus we would be remiss if we did not consider the possibility that apparitions may be what happened to the disciples in the first century.

But this will not be the first work to consider the apparition hypothesis, and so I must begin by putting my treatment in context. Quite a number of scholars have said that they consider it at least plausible that real apparitions are the best explanation for the resurrection appearances. (Unless it is otherwise clear from the context, when I use the term "apparition," I henceforth mean a real apparition.) I have come across nineteen such scholars, some from the world of theology and some from the world of parapsychology, who have indicated that they think the apparition hypothesis is either probable or plausible. ("Plausible" is a term I will use often throughout this work. By "plausible" I mean a reasonable possibility; i.e., not exceedingly improbable.) The parapsychologists in question are Frederick W.H. Myers, James Hyslop, Sir Oliver Lodge, Hereward Carrington, C.H. Broad, George Zorab, H.H. Price, and Kenneth R. Vincent. From the theology side, there is Kirsopp Lake, Cyril Emmet, B.H. Streeter et al., Cecil Cadoux, Sir Alister Hardy, Paul Badham, John A.T. Robinson, Michael Perry, Leslie Weatherhead, Hugh Montefiore, and Dale Allison Jr.[3] One cannot help but be

---

2. The 10% figure was the result found by the 1894 Census of Hallucinations, which we will discuss in chapter 2. Professor Sidgwick's Committee, "Report on the Census of Hallucinations," *Proceedings of the Society for Psychical Research* 10 (1894): 25-422. (By "hallucination" the study meant to refer to any apparition experience, whether real or imaginary.) Two later studies by D.J. West found results of 14% and 11% respectively (D.J. West, "A Mass-Observation Questionnaire on Hallucinations," *Journal of the Society for Psychical Research* 34 (1948): 187-96; D.J. West, "A Pilot Census of Hallucinations," *Proceedings of the Society for Psychical Research* 57 (1990): 163-207). In a later article, West explained why a survey by the BBC television network which found a result of 22% probably overestimated the frequency of hallucinations: the study did not make any attempt to sort through the accounts to see in how many cases real objects might have been mistaken for apparitions, and since it was a telephone survey, the participants did not have much time to reflect on the nature of their experience (D.J. West, "Note on a Recent Psychic Survey," *Journal of the Society for Psychical Research* 60 (1995): 168-71).

3. Frederick W.H. Myers, *Human Personality and its Survival of Bodily Death* (vol. 2; London: Longmans, 1903), 288; James H. Hyslop, *Psychical Research and the Resurrection* (Boston: Small, Maynard, and Company, 1908), 382-84; Sir Oliver Lodge, *Science and Immortality* (New York: Moffat, Yard, and Company, 1908), 268-69; Hereward Carrington, *Loaves and Fishes* (New York: Scribner's Sons, 1935), 175-78; C.H. Broad, *Religion, Philosophy, and Psychical Research: Selected Essays* (New York: Harcourt, 1953), 230-31; George Zorab, "The Resurrection—A Psychical Analysis," *Tomorrow* (New York: Garrett Publications) 2.4 (1954): 4-14; H.H. Price, *Essays in the Philosophy of Religion* (London: Oxford University Press, 1972), 120. Kenneth R. Vincent, "Resurrection Appearances of Jesus as After Death Communication," *Journal of Near Death Studies* 30 (2012): 137-48; Kenneth R. Vincent, "Resurrection Appearances of Jesus as After Death Communication: Rejoinder to Gary Habermas," *Journal of Near Death Studies* 30 (2012): 159-66. Kirsopp Lake, *The Historical Evidence for the Resurrection of Jesus* (London: Williams and Norgate, 1907), 272-76; Cyril W. Emmet, *The Eschatological Question in the Gospels: And Other Studies in Recent New Testament Criticism* (London: T&T Clark, 1911), 124-27; B.H. Streeter et al., *Foundations: A Statement of Christian Belief in Terms of Modern Thought: By Seven Oxford Men* (London: MacMillan, 1912), 136; Cecil John Cadoux, *The*

impressed not only by the number of scholars who have entertained this hypothesis, but also by the fact that many of these scholars have had quite a bit of influence in their respective disciplines. For example, Myers was one of the founders of parapsychology, and James Hyslop was the leading American parapsychologist during the early part of the 1900s. Hardy was a winner of the Templeton Prize for his work on religious experience. Robinson is perhaps the most well-known liberal theologian of the twentieth century with the exception of John Hick.

Before we proceed, let us quote some of these scholars, so we can see how they have put the matter themselves:

George Zorab:

> As the Resurrection problem deals quite definitely with the apparition of a deceased person collectively perceived, and such cases are a specialty, so to say, of psychical research, I suggest that the solution to the problem can only be found if we are willing to approach it parapsychologically.[4]

Michael Perry:

> We saw that the most promising approach might be to compare these appearances with apparitions of the dead. . . . If our investigation shows that we can reasonably place the Resurrection in the same class as phantasms of the dead, we can go on to see what each tells us about the other. The differences are likely to be as informative as the similarities, though it will be the latter we shall especially stress. . .[5]

Alister Hardy:

> These examples of apparitions, seen by responsible citizens of the present day, show us that we can accept the stories of the appearances of Jesus to those who

---

Life of Jesus (West Drayton: Penguin, 1948), 164-66; Sir Alister Hardy, *The Biology of God: A Scientist's Study of Man, the Religious Animal* (London: Cape, 1975), 216-221; Paul Badham, *Christian Beliefs About Life After Death* (New York: Barnes and Noble, 1976), 30-33; John A.T. Robinson, *Can We Trust the New Testament?* (Grand Rapids, MI: Eerdmans, 1977), 126; Michael C. Perry, *The Easter Enigma: An Essay on the Resurrection with Special Reference to the Data of Psychical Research* (London: Faber & Faber, 1959); Leslie D. Weatherhead, *The Resurrection of Christ: In The Light of Modern Science and Psychical Research* (London: Hodder & Stoughton, 1959), 57-92; Hugh Montefiore, *The Miracles of Jesus* (London: SPCK, 2005), 105-14; Dale C. Allison Jr., *Resurrecting Jesus: The Earliest Christian Tradition and its Interpreters* (New York: T&T Clark, 2005), 269-99; Dale C. Allison Jr., "The Resurrection of Jesus and Rational Apologetics," *Philosophia Christi* 10 (2008): 315-35 (329-35). We should also mention John J. Heaney, who argues that apparitions can somehow enlighten our understanding of the resurrection appearances, but it is unclear to me from his treatment whether or not he thinks the resurrection appearances were apparitions (John J. Heaney, *The Sacred and the Psychic: Parapsychology and Christian Theology* (New York: Paulist, 1984), 149-74). For an earlier review of those scholars who have suggested the apparition hypothesis as well as some similar hypotheses which we will mention below, see Perry, *Easter Enigma*, 158-73.

4. Zorab, "Psychical Analysis," 11.
5. Perry, *Easter Enigma*, 174.

Jesus' Resurrection and Apparitions

had been close to him, and felt his love when he was alive, without any damage to our intellectual integrity.[6]

Frederick Myers:

> I venture now on a bold saying; for I predict that, in consequence of the new evidence [cases of real apparitions], all reasonable men, a century hence, will believe the Resurrection of Christ, whereas, in default of the new evidence, no reasonable men, a century hence, would have believed it.[7]

Paul Badham:

> I suggest therefore that the apparitions of Jesus, seen by his disciples, can best be understood as veridical hallucinations [this means real apparitions, not "hallucinations" in the ordinary sense of the word], revealing truthfully the fact of Jesus' continued aliveness to the disciples' minds. I suggest that the source of this information was Jesus himself, communicating telepathically to his disciples.[8]

Thus this hypothesis has attracted a good deal of attention, including the attention of influential scholars. However, there are three peculiar things to note about the way this hypothesis has been treated in the literature. First, of the long list of scholars just mentioned, only five have treated the topic in any substance. These are Perry (a whole book), Weatherhead (35 pages), Zorab (10 pages), Montefiore (9 pages), and Allison (30 pages). None of the others have devoted more than five pages to the subject (and most not more than one or two pages).[9] Hence, though many scholars have been intrigued by this hypothesis, not many have advocated it in detail. The second peculiar fact is the hesitance with which the hypothesis has been advocated. I have distinguished between the terms probable and plausible for a good reason: the large majority of scholars on this list have indeed merely expressed the opinion that the hypothesis is plausible.[10] It is not typically the case that a hypothesis will have many

---

6. Hardy, *Biology*, 220.
7. Myers, *Human Personality*, 351.
8. Badham, *Christian Beliefs*, 32.

9. The title of James Hyslop's book (*Psychical Research and the Resurrection*) is somewhat deceptive in that it implies the entire book is concerned with the resurrection, whereas he only discusses the resurrection on three pages.

10. With regard to why I think most of these authors have only considered the hypothesis plausible, they have not of course all used the word "plausible," but here are some quotations which are representative of the sorts of things some of these authors have said which has led me to think they only regard the hypothesis as plausible (italics mine): Streeter et al., *Foundations*, 136: "Only if the possibility of personal immortality be dogmatically denied can there be any real difficulty in supposing that the Master would have been able to convince His disciples of His victory over death . . . *possibly* by some psychological channel similar to that which explains the mysterious means of communication between persons commonly known as telepathy." Sir Oliver Lodge, *Science and Immortality*, 269: "The Appearances during the Forty Days *are not inconsistent* with the legends of apparitions the world over." Dale Allison, *Resurrecting Jesus*, 284: "I also disbelieve that, if only we knew enough about

INTRODUCTION

advocates who think it is plausible (if advocate is not too strong a word for one who only thinks something is plausible), but few who think it is probable. The third peculiar fact is that though many scholars have suggested this hypothesis, the hypothesis has not left much of a mark, so to speak, in the literature on the resurrection. If one consults a typical overview of explanations for Jesus' resurrection, one will find mention of the hypothesis that the disciples lied, the hypothesis that they hallucinated, the hypothesis that Jesus faked his death, as well as a variety of other alternative hypotheses, but chances are high there will be no mention of the apparition hypothesis.[11] This is not to say there have been no responses to the apparition hypothesis by those favoring a physical resurrection (there have been—for example, from William Lane Craig, Gary Habermas, and Gerald O'Collins),[12] but this hypothesis is typically missing from scholarly overviews of hypotheses for the resurrection.

What all three of these peculiarities indicate is that there is a general uncertainty among scholars with regard to how to evaluate this hypothesis. This uncertainty calls for an explanation, and I believe the uncertainty stems largely from scholars' lack of familiarity with the parapsychological literature on apparitions. For if one does not know very much about apparitions, it will be difficult to make a judgment on the two questions which must be answered in order to evaluate this hypothesis: 1) Are apparitions real? (For if they are not, the hypothesis can be dismissed a priori.) 2) If apparitions are real, how do we go about determining whether the resurrection appearances were apparitions? It is not obvious how one ought to go about arguing for this hypothesis, and if one is not familiar with the apparition literature, one will not be

---

apparitions of the dead in general, we would necessarily know enough about the appearances of Jesus in particular. I make no claim to having some grand, reductionist theory that presumes to cover all the facts." Montefiore, *Miracles of Jesus*, 114, "a paranormal explanation *is consistent* with a critical examination of their [the Gospels] contents."

11. Consider some prominent works dealing with explanations for Jesus' resurrection which do not mention the apparition hypothesis: Norman Anderson, *A Lawyer Among the Theologians* (London: Hodder & Stoughton, 1973); Paul L. Maier, *In the Fullness of Time: A Historian Looks at Christmas, Easter, and the Early Church* (San Francisco: HarperSanFrancisco, 1991); Gary R. Habermas and Michael R. Licona, *The Case for the Resurrection of Jesus* (Grand Rapids, MI: Kregel, 2004); Richard Swinburne, *The Resurrection of God Incarnate* (Oxford: Oxford University Press, 2003); N.T. Wright, *The Resurrection of the Son of God* (Minneapolis: Fortress, 2003). The hypothesis is dealt with in William Lane Craig, *Assessing the New Testament Evidence for the Historicity of the Resurrection of Jesus* (rev. ed.; Lewiston: Edwin Mellen, 2002 [1989]), 290-93; and Michael R. Licona (largely in response to Allison's work), *The Resurrection of Jesus: A New Historiographical Approach* (Downers Grove, IL: IVP Academic, 2010), 623-41; and see also, in response to Allison's work, William Lane Craig, "Dale Allison on the Resurrection of Jesus," http://www.reasonablefaith.org/site/News2?page=NewsArticle&id=5781.

12. The other sources I have found which rebut the apparition hypothesis, in addition to those of Craig and Licona (in the works cited in the immediately preceding footnote), are as follows: James Orr, *The Resurrection of Jesus* (London: Hodder & Stoughton, 1908), 227-31; S.H. Hooke, *The Resurrection of Christ as History and Experience* (London: Darton, 1967), 141; George Eldon Ladd, *I Believe in the Resurrection of Jesus* (Grand Rapids, MI: Eerdmans, 1975), 139; Gary R. Habermas, "Dale Allison's Resurrection Skepticism: A Critique," *Philosophia Christi* 10 (2008): 303-13; Gerald O'Collins, *Christology: A Biblical, Historical, and Systematic Study of Jesus* (2nd ed.; Oxford: Oxford University Press, 2009), 93-100.

sure how to do so. (Lack of familiarity with the apparition literature does not entirely explain why parapsychologists themselves have not dealt with the hypothesis in much depth (though it does to some extent, since apparitions are one of the less popular research topics in parapsychology today). In parapsychologists' case, the most significant problem is likely the opposite: lack of expertise in New Testament scholarship and thus uncertainty as to which portions of the New Testament can be considered historically reliable. For if we do not know how much of the New Testament is historically reliable, we do not know how much data we have to explain, and thus we do not know if the apparition hypothesis adequately explains the data.) Regarding the first question, one of the two contributions I intend to make to this issue is to present a rigorous case for the reality of apparitions, so that the reader will come away convinced that it is at least plausible apparitions are real, and thus that this hypothesis is worth taking seriously. (The only other theology writer to have presented a sustained case for the reality of apparitions is Michael Perry,[13] though he leaves much to be desired, since he does not deal very much with potential alternative explanations of the cases he presents, and as we will see, refuting alternative explanations is the most important part of making a case for the reality of apparitions.) The second contribution concerns the second essential question, that of method:

Method

Even if we know apparitions are real, we have only taken the first step in asking the question of whether the resurrection appearances were apparitions. The next step is to ask the question: If there are such things as real apparitions, how do we determine whether the resurrection appearances were real apparitions? If one consults the sources mentioned above, along with their critics, one will find that a certain popular method has arisen for attempting to answer this question, and this method is to look for similarities or differences between apparitions and the resurrection appearances (this is evidenced by the quote from Michael Perry above). A number of the proponents of the apparition hypothesis have made their case by explicitly citing similarities between apparitions and the resurrection appearances, and a number of those who have argued against the hypothesis have made their case by explicitly citing differences between apparitions and the resurrection appearances. This includes the last five writers to have addressed the hypothesis (Allison, Montefiore, Licona, Habermas, and O'Collins).[14]

---

13. Perry, *Easter Enigma*, 137-57.

14. Here are quotations from those five writers in which they cite either similarities or differences as support for their argument: Allison, *Resurrecting Jesus*, 277, 278: "it is simply not true that the events in the Gospels are 'utterly without analogy'"; "to protest the parallel is to recognize it." Montefiore, *Miracles*, 111: "There are also similarities." Licona, *Resurrection*, 634: "Allison appeals to the canonical Gospels and Acts in order to show similarities between the resurrection appearances of Jesus and apparitions. Therefore, it is right to note the differences between them as well." Habermas,

INTRODUCTION

The thought process on the part of proponents of the apparition hypothesis is that if two things have a large number of similarities, they are probably the same thing. The reason we believe a bulldog and a German shepherd are both the same thing, both dogs, is because they have a sufficient number of similarities. (For example, they both have four legs, both have tails, and both bark.) Thus the reasoning is that if the resurrection appearances and apparitions also have a large number of similarities, perhaps they are the same thing. Dale Allison provides the longest list of parallels, and his list includes the following:[15]

> The resurrection appearances and apparitions are both seen and heard
>
> Are seen now by one person and later by another
>
> Are seen by more than one percipient at the same time
>
> Appear to individuals who did not know them in life
>
> Create doubt in some percipients
>
> Offer reassurance and give comfort
>
> Give guidance and make requests or issue imperatives
>
> Are overwhelmingly real and indeed seemingly solid

The thought process on the part of those who have cited differences between the resurrection appearances and apparitions as a mark against the apparition hypothesis is that if two things have a lot of differences then they must be two different things. Analogously, a dog and a cat have certain differences (different types of faces, different fur, one purrs and the other barks), and we regard them as two different things. Differences between the resurrection appearances and apparitions include the following:

Jesus' disciples concluded he was physically raised from the dead, whereas witnesses of apparitions conclude the person is a disembodied spirit.[16]

Jesus predicted his resurrection, whereas apparitions do not make such predictions.[17]

Jesus made great claims to personal authority, but people who appear as apparitions do not.[18]

"Resurrection Skepticism," 308: "there are significant differences that emerge in a comparison of both sorts of reports." O'Collins, *Christology*, 98: "detailed comparison shows serious differences." It is also worth citing Perry since he is the one to have devoted the most space to this hypothesis: *Easter Enigma*, 174: "The differences are likely to be as informative as the similarities, though it will be the latter we shall especially stress in this chapter." Most of the proponents of the apparition hypothesis, since they have dealt with it only very briefly, have not presented any substantial arguments, and have not done much more than simply state that one can see a parallel between Jesus appearing after his death and apparitions appearing after their deaths, and so perhaps the resurrection appearances were apparitions.

15. Allison, *Resurrecting Jesus*, 278-82.
16. Habermas, "Resurrection Skepticism," 309; Licona, *Resurrection*, 635.
17. Habermas, "Resurrection Skepticism," 308.
18. O'Collins, *Christology*, 98.

Jesus died a violent death, whereas people who appear as apparitions usually died a normal death.[19]

The disciples proclaimed the resurrection, but those who see apparitions usually do not tell anyone about it.[20]

Jesus' tomb was discovered empty, but the tombs of those who appear as apparitions are not.[21]

While this approach may seem to make sense, the problem with this way of arguing is brought out by Dale Allison (who, like many in the list above, considers the apparition theory only plausible, and so recognizes the limitations of the evidence he presents for it) who explains that any two phenomena will be similar in some ways and different in other ways, and thus seeing that two things have certain similarities or certain differences does not do enough as far as telling us whether the two things are the same phenomenon.[22] A parallel between a dog and a cat is that they both have four legs, but that does not mean a dog is the same kind of thing as a cat. On the other hand, one will find differences between two dogs, even two dogs within the same species (e.g., one bulldog might have a spot on his tail that another bulldog does not have), but that does not mean the dogs are not both the same kind of thing.

Yet though the problem with this approach is clear, one cannot help but feel that scholars have been on the right track. After all, similarities and differences do help us to tell one thing from another. If I want to know if the car in my driveway is a Rolls Royce, I will probably look for similarities and differences between it and the other Rolls Royces I am familiar with. If I want to know whether the creature before me is a frog, I will look for similarities and differences between it and other frogs. And I will have a kind of intuitive sense as to which similarities and differences matter and which do not. I know that if two animals both bark, that is a better indication of the fact they are both dogs than the fact they both have a tail.

To illustrate how our intuition works in this regard, consider the following analogy. Suppose this fellow shows up at our house claiming to be a police officer. We notice some differences between him and a typical police officer. First, he is not wearing a uniform; typical police officers wear uniforms. Second, the badge he shows us is not the same kind of badge as the badge typical police officers have. Third, he has a different kind of car than typical police officers; he has an ordinary looking car rather than a typical police car. Hence we start to think he is not a real police officer.

But now suppose this other police officer shows up and he has some other differences. He has a moustache whereas all the other police officers we know do not. He is shorter than the other police officers. He speaks with a foreign accent whereas the other police officers do not. But despite these differences, we do not suspect he is a

19. O'Collins, *Christology*, 98.
20. O'Collins, *Christology*, 99.
21. Habermas, "Resurrection Skepticism," 308-9; O'Collins, *Christology*, 99-100.
22. Allison, "Resurrection and Rational Apologetics," 333.

fake police officer. We see the similarities between him and real police officers (that he does have a uniform, and the type of badge we expect, and the type of car we expect) and we believe he is a real police officer.

So similarities and differences clearly do help us distinguish one type of thing from another. But as the example of the fake police officers shows, there must be more to this process than simply noting a given similarity or a given difference. Some similarities and differences matter and some do not, but the question is how to tell which ones matter (and of those that matter, which ones matter the most). I suspect that though the reader agrees with the above analysis as to which differences matter in the hypothetical case of the fake police officer, the reader cannot quite put his finger on just why he feels this way. Likewise, I suspect the reader feels as if some of the similarities and differences enumerated above between the resurrection appearances and apparitions matter more than others, though he cannot quite put his finger on why.

Bayes' Theorem

Thus we have a dilemma: We can see that similarities and differences will help us determine whether the resurrection appearances were or were not apparitions, but we can also see that if we are going to get very far, there must be something more to this. I propose that the way to resolve this dilemma, the way to determine which similarities and differences matter and which do not, is to use Bayes' Theorem (BT). BT is a mathematical theorem used for determining the probability that a hypothesis is true. It has been invoked before in discussions of the resurrection, and I will review those sources at the end of the following chapter, after I have thoroughly explained BT. But I ought to state the most essential point upfront, which is as follows. One of the basic principles behind BT is what is called consequent probability, a concept which is difficult to grasp at first. We are always used to asking: Given that we have some piece of evidence (e.g., a murder weapon), what is the probability our hypothesis is true? (E.g., What is the probability Bob committed murder given that we found a knife?) But BT tells us that to answer this question, we must turn the question around and ask two questions: Given that the hypothesis is true, what is the probability of getting the evidence we have, and given that the hypothesis is false what is the probability of getting the evidence we have? (E.g., given that Bob committed the murder, what is the probability we would find a knife? And given that Bob did not commit the murder, what is the probability we would find a knife?)

For reasons I will explain, this matter of consequent probability is the key to being able to see which differences matter and which do not. When we use similarities and differences to distinguish one thing from another, we are subconsciously using consequent probability. It is because you were subconsciously using consequent probability that you were able to understand the analogy of the fake police officer, and it is also why some of the similarities and differences between apparitions and the resurrection appearances struck you as more significant than others. But given that you are unsure exactly why this is, we will be able to analyze our topic much better if we use the principle of consequent probability consciously. But we cannot use it consciously until we fully understand BT, and thus in the next chapter I will explain BT, and at the end of that chapter I will explain more fully why consequent probability holds the key to this issue.

Preliminaries

But before I explain BT, there are three preliminary matters that need to be dealt with. First, in order to avoid confusion, I need to explain how the apparition hypothesis differs from two other hypotheses: the hallucination hypothesis and the objective vision hypothesis. Second, a general overview of the rest of the book will be given, so that the reader understands the general plan I intend to follow. And third, I must explain certain premises which I will assume throughout the book.

The Apparition Hypothesis in Relation to Other Hypotheses

The apparition hypothesis has the potential to be confused with two other hypotheses: the hallucination hypothesis and the objective vision hypothesis. Thus it is necessary to explain how these hypotheses differ from the apparition hypothesis.

By the term "apparition hypothesis" I mean to designate the hypothesis that the resurrection appearances were real apparitions, not the hypothesis that they were hallucinatory apparitions. The hallucination hypothesis will not be addressed in this book (unlike the apparition hypothesis, the hallucination hypothesis has already been addressed to a considerable extent in the literature).[23] This distinction between the two hypotheses, real apparitions vs. hallucinatory apparitions, probably seems clear, but the potential for confusion arises from the fact that proponents of the hallucination hypothesis have cited the same data (the fact that it is common for people to see apparitions of the dead) as support for the argument that the resurrection appearances were hallucinations.[24] The argument in their case is that if apparitions are hallucinations, and apparitions are common, then it is common to hallucinate a deceased loved one, and hence it would not be a surprise if the disciples hallucinated Jesus.

---

23. For an overview, see Gary R. Habermas, "Explaining Away Jesus' Resurrection: The Recent Revival of Hallucination Theories," *Christian Research Journal* 23.4 (2001): 26-31, 47-49. I cite over a dozen proponents of the hallucination hypothesis in Jake H. O'Connell, "Jesus' Resurrection and Collective Hallucinations," *Tyndale Bulletin* 60 (2009): 69-105 (70).

24. See e.g., Gerd Ludemann, *What Really Happened to Jesus?* (Louisville, KY: Westminster John Knox, 1995), 80; Jack Kent, *The Psychological Origins of the Resurrection Myth* (London: Open Gate, 1999); Richard C. Carrier, "The Spiritual Body of Christ and the Legend of the Empty Tomb," in Robert M. Price and Jeffrey Jay Lowder eds., *The Empty Tomb: Jesus Beyond the Grave* (Amherst, NY: Prometheus, 2005), 105-231 (186-87).

Introduction

Now whether the apparition literature shows that real apparitions are common or that hallucinations are common depends on whether we think apparitions are real or hallucinatory (and if we think some are real and some hallucinatory, then the apparition literature documents the occurrence of both). I will argue in chapter 3 that at least some apparitions are real, and readers should know that I am dealing in this book only with those scholars who have used the apparition literature to argue that the resurrection appearances were real apparitions, not with those scholars who have used it to argue the resurrection appearances were hallucinations.

Regarding my statement that the apparition hypothesis has not been addressed very much, some readers may be thinking that this is not correct—for haven't there been many scholars who have argued that the resurrection appearances were appearances of a real non-bodily apparition? In fact, there have been. Such readers have in mind the objective vision theory, the theory that God supernaturally caused non-bodily apparitions of Jesus. This theory is indeed often to be found in the literature on the resurrection.[25] But when I have referred to proponents of the apparition theory, I have meant scholars who have used the apparition literature to argue that Jesus was an apparition. Proponents of the objective vision theory, though they believe Jesus

---

25. The objective vision theory was popularized by Theodor Keim, *The History of Jesus of Nazara* (vol. 6; London: Williams and Norgate, 1883), 364-65. For a review of its history, see Gary R. Habermas, "Mapping the Recent Trend Towards the Bodily Resurrection Appearances of Jesus in Light of Other Prominent Critical Positions," in Robert B. Stewart ed., *The Resurrection of Jesus: John Dominic Crossan and N.T. Wright in Dialogue* (Minneapolis: Fortress, 2006), 78-92 (87-89). For criticisms, see e.g., Ladd, *I Believe in the Resurrection of Jesus*, 138-39; Habermas and Licona, *Case for the Resurrection*, 112; Timothy and Lydia McGrew, "The Argument From Miracles: A Cumulative Case for the Resurrection of Jesus of Nazareth," in William Lane Craig and J.P. Moreland eds., *The Blackwell Companion to Natural Theology* (Oxford: Wiley-Blackwell, 2009), 593-662 (627). One point should be made concerning exactly what the objective vision theory is. I have defined it as the theory that Jesus appeared as an apparition after his death (and that his appearing was due either to God's activity or to Jesus' supernatural powers). But it seems to me that some of the scholars whom Habermas cites (in the essay I just referred to) as proponents of the objective vision theory may not think that Jesus appeared as an apparition but may only think that he appeared in such a way that he was not perceptible to neutral observers (e.g., if Pilate or Caiaphas had been present at the resurrection appearances, they would not have been able to see Jesus). Now the idea that the resurrection appearances were not perceptible to neutral observers does not necessarily entail the idea that Jesus appeared as an apparition; he could have appeared with a physical body which was nevertheless not perceptible to neutral observers. Likewise, if the resurrection appearances were apparitions, that is, objective visions, that does not necessarily entail the idea that they were not perceptible to neutral observers. For there is no reason why a non-bodily Jesus could not still be seen by all present (the angel who rolls back the stone in Mt 28:2 is seen by neutral observers, the guards, but is still a spirit, not a physical being). Stephen Davis, in an essay arguing that the resurrection appearances were indeed perceptible to neutral observers, refers to the theory that they were not perceptible to neutral observers as the objective vision theory ("Seeing the Risen Jesus," in Stephen T. Davis, Daniel Kendall, and Gerald O'Collins eds., *The Resurrection: An Interdisciplinary Symposium on the Resurrection of Jesus* (Oxford: Oxford University Press, 1997), 126-47). But that is not what I mean by the objective vision theory. I do think there is a strong correlation between those who hold the objective vision theory as I have defined it, and those who think the resurrection appearances were not perceptible to neutral observers; however, the two views are not exactly the same.

was an apparition, have not cited the apparition literature as a way of illuminating this idea. The question will then be asked as to why I draw a distinction here—why, if you are using the apparition literature to argue that Jesus was an apparition, are you advocating a different theory than if you simply made the argument without appealing to this literature? The reason why I draw a distinction is because of what is implied by an appeal to the apparition literature. When scholars argue that such and such is true for apparitions and therefore if the resurrection appearances were apparitions it was also true for the resurrection appearances (e.g., apparitions are sometimes collective and so were the resurrection appearances, apparitions are sometimes solid and so were the resurrection appearances), they clearly assume that the resurrection appearances followed the same laws that other apparitions follow. Now if this is the argument, then it is implied that the resurrection appearances were a paranormal but not a supernatural phenomenon. By "paranormal," I mean something which goes beyond the bounds of conventional scientific understanding. By "supernatural," I mean something having to do with God. A paranormal phenomenon could have something to do with God (e.g., miraculous healings), but it need not necessarily (e.g., if ESP is real, there is no reason to think it has anything to do with God; reading someone's mind is not related to God—unless God gave you the ability to do it, which could be the case, but is not necessarily).

Regarding the resurrection appearances as apparitions implies that they are paranormal rather than supernatural, because the data indicates that apparitions, if they are real, are not related to God at all. For apparitions never come bringing a religious message, as we would expect them to do if God was involved. Thus to argue that the resurrection appearances are the same phenomenon as typical apparitions is to imply that the resurrection appearances were a paranormal but not a supernatural phenomenon, and we should expect that whatever laws typical apparitions follow (e.g., their likelihood of lasting a long time, their likelihood of being solid, their likelihood of being able to eat) were followed by the resurrection appearances. The objective vision theory proposes the opposite: It proposes that God was the cause of the resurrection appearances. However, it is also possible to combine the two ideas, and since some of the proponents of the apparition hypothesis have invoked both the apparition literature and God in their treatment of this hypothesis, this is what some of them actually do.[26] If we combine the two, we have the hypothesis that the resurrection appearances generally followed the laws of apparitions, but that God occasionally circumvented these laws. (Or that Jesus circumvented the laws by his supernatural powers, but that amounts to the same thing as saying God circumvented the laws, since Jesus' supernatural powers were given him by God.) For example, Michael Perry discusses many of the parallels between the resurrection appearances and apparitions, but after noting the differences (such as the number of people to whom Jesus appeared, the length of

---

26. E.g., Perry, *Easter Enigma*, 189-90; Weatherhead, *Resurrection*, 84; Montefiore, *Miracles of Jesus*, 111.

Introduction

the appearances, and the amount of conversation Jesus engaged in), he proposes that these differences were likely due to the fact that Jesus had a greater command of the laws.[27]

Thus there are three possible theories. The first is a straight paranormal theory, according to which God had nothing to do with the apparitions. We will call this the apparition theory. The second is a straight supernatural theory, according to which God caused the apparitions of Jesus entirely by his own power (or that Jesus caused the apparitions entirely by his supernatural power; whenever we refer to God's activity in conjunction with the objective vision theory, this will be shorthand for God and/or Jesus acting by his supernatural power), and so since the cause is entirely supernatural, we should not expect the resurrection appearances to be bound by the laws of apparitions. We will call this hypothesis what it has been called, the objective vision theory. The third is a combination paranormal/supernatural theory according to which the resurrection appearances generally followed the laws of apparitions, but which proposes that God in some instances intervened so that the appearances did not always follow these laws. We will call this the apparition/objective vision theory. We will consider all three of these theories, but, for reasons that will become clear, there is much more to say in the case of the apparition theory.[28] The other two theories can be dealt with quite quickly.[29]

Overview of the Book

The general purpose of this book is to use BT to determine whether the resurrection hypothesis or apparition hypothesis is more probable. That task requires a certain logical plan, and that plan is as follows.

Since we cannot use BT to analyze hypotheses unless we first understand what BT is, I will provide an explanation of BT in chapter 2. A secondary purpose of this book is to explain how BT works, and thus the book will be of use even to those who are not especially interested in the resurrection. Once BT has been explained, I will explain at the end of that chapter why BT is the key to assessing our hypotheses.

---

27. Perry, *Easter Enigma*, 189-90.

28. In regard to explaining the resurrection appearances as paranormal we should note that two of the proponents of the apparition theory mentioned above, Carrington and Montefiore, devote their books to arguing that not just the resurrection appearances but all of Jesus' miracles can be explained paranormally rather than supernaturally.

29. I am also not considering in this work two other hypotheses which are related to the apparition hypothesis, but which are so wildly speculative that they do not warrant more than a brief mention. The first is the idea that Jesus' appearances were séance-type materializations in which the apostles acted as mediums, and the second is the idea that Jesus not merely communicated to the disciples in the way spirits in séances allegedly do, but actually took control of the minds of the disciples and caused them to see visions. The theories are discussed and refuted in Perry, *Easter Enigma*, 162-71. The essential problem with these theories is that there is nothing in the New Testament to indicate the witnesses to the appearances served as mediums.

But there is no point in analyzing the apparition hypothesis if there are no real apparitions. For if there are not, the apparition hypothesis cannot be taken seriously. Thus in chapter 3, I will present an overview of the evidence that apparitions are real. Although I myself think the evidence indicates it is probable apparitions are real, the reader only needs to come away from chapter 3 convinced that it is plausible (i.e., not exceedingly improbable) apparitions are real in order to agree that it will not be an unproductive use of our time to examine the apparition hypothesis. (I ought to make one clarification as to what I mean when I say that apparitions are "real." Those unfamiliar with the parapsychological literature, when they hear of a "real" apparition, will automatically think a real apparition means a disembodied spirit. But this is only one of the two general views which a parapsychologist might have reference to in speaking of the reality of apparitions. The other is the view that apparitions are consciousless images which result from ESP. If that view is correct, then although apparitions are not actual persons, they are real in that they are not an imaginary construct of the percipient's mind; they incorporate information from outside the percipient's mind, information which the percipient could not know by normal means. This theory will be discussed in more detail at the end of the chapter on apparitions. But the way in which we approach the question of whether the resurrection appearances were real apparitions will not vary very much depending upon which of the two theories of the reality of apparitions we endorse. Thus we do not need to spend a great deal of space addressing this question. In any event, a real apparition is an apparition which is either a disembodied spirit or an ESP projection.)

Once we have explained BT and demonstrated that it is plausible apparitions are real, we will be ready to use BT to analyze the data to see whether the apparition hypothesis is more probable than the resurrection hypothesis. However, we have a complication: Scholars dispute how much of the New Testament is historically reliable, and thus there is dispute over how much data we have to analyze. Thus chapters 4, 5, and 6 will examine the reliability of the New Testament.

In order to understand the layout of chapters 4-6, we must first understand the current state of scholarship on the resurrection. The obvious place to start for data on Jesus' resurrection would seem to be the resurrection narratives of the Gospels. However, for the last 200 years or so, the majority of scholars have doubted whether the Gospels are what can be called "generally reliable." If a source is generally reliable, that means it has the same status we would give to a witness in a courtroom: We assume what they say is correct until we have evidence to the contrary, and though we will not be surprised if they make errors concerning minor details, the presence of minor errors will not cause us to question the reliability of their testimony as to the major elements of the event (e.g., if the witness was wrong about whether Bob shot the man at 8:00 p.m. or 8:30 p.m., that will not cause us to question the witness's testimony that Bob did shoot the man). And even in the case of minor details, the burden of proof is still on the other side to show that even a minor error is present (e.g., though we would not be surprised if the witness was mistaken on a minor detail, such as whether the victim was shot at 8:00 or 8:30, we still assume they are correct when they tell us the victim was shot at 8:00 until there is evidence the victim was actually shot at 8:30). (What I have just described is the common sense view of eyewitness testimony, according to which eyewitness testimony is very reliable. This view has been questioned, and I will address objections to the accuracy of eyewitness testimony in chapter 6.) Thus if the Gospels are generally reliable, that means we accept that what they say is true until there is evidence to the contrary, and even if there is evidence to the contrary on minor matters, that will not cause us to question their reliability on major matters (e.g., even if the Gospels disagree on exactly which women discovered the empty tomb, that will not cause us to question the fact that an empty tomb was discovered). And even in the case of minor matters, we still assume the Gospel writers correct until there is evidence to the contrary (e.g., if a Gospel writer tells us a certain group of women went to the tomb, we will accept that this is so until we have evidence to the contrary). Now for a source to be considered generally reliable, there must be some reasons for thinking it is generally reliable. In the case of a witness in court, the reason is usually that the witness was an eyewitness. In the case of the Gospels, the most common argument for their general reliability has been the argument that they were written by the traditional authors and thus come from eyewitness or near eyewitnesses.[30] However, most modern scholars have rejected the traditional authorship of the Gospels,[31] as well as any other reasons to accept the Gospels as generally reliable. If the Gospels are not generally reliable, that leaves us with two other options for gathering data about Jesus' resurrection:

First, we may rely on Paul's list of resurrection appearances in 1 Corinthians 15:3-8. In contrast to the Gospels, no one doubts Paul wrote 1 Corinthians, and it is also not doubted that Paul was very close to the events, being a first or secondhand source for the appearances (or possibly a third or fourthhand source for the appearance to the 500). Hence 1 Corinthians 15:3-8 usually serves as the starting point for

30. This is one of the arguments used by Craig L. Blomberg, *The Historical Reliability of the Gospels* (2nd ed.; Downers Grove, IL: InterVarsity, 2007,); Craig L. Blomberg, *The Historical Reliability of John's Gospel: Issues and Commentary* (Downers Grove: InterVarsity, 2002). An argument for the general reliability of the Gospels does not necessarily depend on establishing the traditional authorship of the Gospels. There is also the argument that the Gospels should be thought generally reliable because the amount of time in between Jesus' life and the writing of the Gospels was not sufficient for any substantial legendary accrual. I mention this argument in chapter 5. There is also Birger Gerhardsson's argument that the Gospels should be considered generally reliable because of the careful manner in which the disciples passed on oral tradition: Birger Gerhardsson, *The Reliability of the Gospel Tradition* (Peabody, MA: Hendrickson, 2001). And there are other arguments, such as the argument from external confirmation.

31. Though perhaps with the exception of Luke. Craig Keener, after doing a thorough survey of the relevant literature as part of the research for his Acts commentary, comes to the conclusion that a majority of modern scholars accept the traditional authorship of Luke and Acts (Personal conversation between Craig Keener and Michael R. Licona, cited in Michael R. Licona, "Review of Bart Ehrman's Book Forged: Writing in the Name of God," http://www.risenjesus.com/articles/52-review-of-forged).

contemporary discussions of the historicity of the resurrection, since scholars are in much greater agreement as to the reliability of this material than the material of the Gospels.

Second, those scholars who do not accept the Gospels as being reliable on the whole are largely agreed that we can still demonstrate that certain particular things in the Gospels are reliable. For example, a popular argument for the historicity of the empty tomb is that women are said to have discovered it, and since women's testimony was not considered reliable in Jesus' culture, it is unlikely anyone would invent a story which relied on women's testimony. Thus no one would have invented the story of the empty tomb, and therefore the story is historical. Or consider the argument that if Jesus' tomb had not actually been empty the enemies of Christianity would have produced the body and stopped the spread of Christianity; since they did not produce the body, the empty tomb must be historical. If these types of arguments succeed, we can establish that certain facts in the Gospels (such as the empty tomb) are historical even if we cannot establish that the Gospels are generally reliable.[32] (Arguing for the reliability of certain facts in the Gospels does not have to be mutually exclusive of arguments for the Gospels' general reliability. If we think the Gospels are generally reliable, we can still welcome further confirmation of their reliability by looking for evidence to support some of their particular statements. Analogously, if we think a witness is generally reliable, and so we believe him when he tells us he saw Bob fire the gun, we will still be happy if we find other evidence which supports this claim (for example, if we find Bob's fingerprints on the gun).)

Hence, the plan for chapters 4-6 is as follows. In chapter 4, I will explain why the material of 1 Corinthians 15:3-8 can be accepted as reliable, and I will also try to determine what data can be garnered from the Gospels if we do not accept their general reliability, but have to produce the kinds of arguments I mentioned above in the example of the empty tomb. I will conclude that the only fact from the resurrection narratives which we can accept as historical, if we do not accept their general reliability, is the historicity of the empty tomb (though we cannot be as confident that Jesus' *tomb* was empty as we can that his *burial place* was empty).

---

32. The attempt to argue that certain facts in the Gospels are reliable even if the Gospels as a whole are not reliable is closely equivalent to the use of the so-called criteria for authenticity. The distinction is that not every argument which could be used to establish that something in the Gospels is reliable would be considered part of the criteria for authenticity. The "criteria for authenticity" only refers to those arguments which are commonly used; for example, the argument that if something in the Gospels is embarrassing then it is historical is commonly used and is therefore considered one of the criteria ("the criterion of embarrassment"), whereas the argument that Jesus' tomb must have been empty because otherwise the Jewish leaders would have produced the body is not considered one of the criteria, because it is not commonly used (for it cannot be, since it is an argument which clearly applies only to the question of the empty tomb). On the criteria for authenticity, see e.g., John P. Meier, *A Marginal Jew: Rethinking the Historical Jesus* (vol. 1; New York: Doubleday, 1991), 167-95; Robert H. Stein, "Criteria for the Gospels' Authenticity," in William Lane Craig and Paul Copan eds., *Contending with Christianity's Critics: Answering New Atheists & Other Objectors* (Nashville: B&H Academic, 2009), 88-103.

Introduction

In chapter 5, I will argue that the Gospels, or more exactly, not the entirety of the Gospels, but the resurrection narratives, are generally reliable. I will not do this by arguing for the traditional authorship of the Gospels, but by making an argument based on the significance with which the resurrection appearances were regarded by the early church. I will argue that the resurrection appearances were regarded as very significant by the early church, and that if they were regarded as very significant, we should expect that they were passed down accurately from the time of their occurrence to the time of the Gospels, *if* we accept a premise which most scholars accept, which is that the Gospels are what can be called "fairly reliable." Fairly reliable is not the same as generally reliable. By fairly reliable, I mean a source which contains a good amount of accurate information, but which does not contain so much accurate information that we are prepared to believe whatever it says until there is evidence to the contrary. If we have a generally reliable witness, that means we accept what they say until there is evidence to the contrary. But if we have a fairly reliable witness, that means that though we know they are often accurate, we still take what they say with a grain of salt until we have some way to confirm what they say. I will argue that if we accept the premise that the Gospels as a whole are fairly reliable, and if we add the premise that the resurrection appearances were considered significant, we should conclude that the resurrection narratives are generally reliable. That is, those scholars who treat the Gospels on the whole as they would a fairly reliable witness ought to treat the resurrection narratives in particular as they would a generally reliable witness.

(Perhaps the best way to understand the distinction between fairly reliable and generally reliable is to consider the analogy of the Boy Who Cried Wolf. If the wolf was always there, or nearly always there, when the Boy called, the Boy would be generally reliable. If the wolf was often there but also often not, the Boy would be fairly reliable. If the wolf was rarely if ever there, the Boy would be unreliable. Most scholars think the wolf is often there, but also often not, when the Gospels call. Some think he is always or almost always there. A few think he is rarely if ever there.[33])

Although I will not here defend in detail the idea that the Gospels are fairly reliable (it is a premise which I will assume, and I admit that if you do not accept this premise, you will not be persuaded by the argument in chapter 5), it may be helpful to here mention some of the reasons why most scholars consider the Gospels fairly reliable. 1) Archeology and various extra-Biblical sources confirm that the Gospels and Acts accurately reflect the world of pre-70 Palestine.[34] 2) Most historical Jesus scholars think that quite a number of facts can be established about Jesus' life by arguing for the historicity of particular facts in the Gospels in the same way as we did for

---

33. Having written this, I see that Thomas R. Yoder Neufeld, *Recovering Jesus: The Witness of the New Testament* (Grand Rapids, MI: Brazos, 2007), 41-43 lays out the same kind of threefold division which I have.

34. See e.g., John McRay, *Archeology and the New Testament* (Grand Rapids, MI: Baker Academic, 1991); James H. Charlesworth, *Jesus and Archeology* (Grand Rapids, MI: Eerdmans, 2006).

the empty tomb above. When these facts add up, we are left with the conclusion that there is much historically reliable information in the Gospels and thus the Gospels are fairly reliable. Criteria which are often used to establish the historicity of particular facts in the Gospels include embarrassment (we used this criterion above when we argued the empty tomb is likely historical because women discovering it is embarrassing), dissimilarity (if something in the Gospels is dissimilar to the practices of the early church, it is likely historical), and multiple attestation (if something is attested by more than one Gospel, it is likely historical). 3) The time in between Jesus' life (30 CE) and the writing of the Gospels (70-100 CE) is not especially vast; we should not expect legends to have thoroughly corrupted the truth in such a short time period.[35] 4) The Gospels are largely in agreement with Paul, and Paul, as we have said, and as we will see in greater detail in chapter 4, was very close to the events.[36]

If we have a witness who seems to be generally reliable, major errors in the witness's testimony will cause us to change our mind and regard them as unreliable. Hence in chapter 6 I will consider objections to the general reliability of the resurrection narratives.

Finally, in chapter 7, I will use BT to analyze the data; the data being the material of the New Testament which is relevant to Jesus' resurrection. But in analyzing the data, I will divide the data up into three categories: The data which comes from 1 Corinthians 15; the data which we can get from the resurrection narratives if their general reliability is not accepted; and the data we can get from the resurrection narratives if their general reliability is accepted. By dividing the data up in this way, the reader will be able to see how the probability of the hypotheses vary depending on how much data we have to work with, for we will arrive at one probability after considering only the data of 1 Corinthians 15, another probability after considering the data we get from the resurrection narratives if their general reliability is not accepted, and another probability after considering the data we get from the resurrection narratives if we do accept their general reliability. To state my conclusion upfront, the resurrection hypothesis will end up more probable than the apparition hypothesis after each of the three stages, and the probability of the resurrection hypothesis will increase as the amount of data from the New Testament which we accept as historical increases. In chapter 7, we will primarily focus on the apparition hypothesis itself, and the objective vision and combination apparition/objective vision theory will be dealt with briefly at the end of that chapter because, as I said, it will become clear that these two theories can be dealt with much more briefly than the apparition hypothesis itself.

---

35. This argument, the argument that the time gap in between Jesus' life and the writing of the Gospels is short enough that we ought to regard to the Gospels as *fairly reliable*, is not the same as the argument I mentioned before, which is that the time gap is short enough that the Gospels ought to be regarded as *generally reliable*.

36. It is sometimes argued that there was a large disconnect between Paul's beliefs and the beliefs of the other apostles. For a refutation of this, see David Wenham, *Paul: Follower of Jesus or Founder of Christianity?* (Grand Rapids, MI: Eerdmans, 1995).

INTRODUCTION

Premises

Parapsychology and the Academy

Parapsychology is a legitimate academic enterprise. Because of its controversial subject matter, parapsychology is sometimes unfairly criticized as being a pseudoscientific endeavor. However, the large majority of academics agree that this is not the case. Since 1930, five surveys about parapsychology have been conducted on various groups of academics, such as professors in general, psychologists belonging to the American Psychological Association, and the leaders of the American Association for the Advancement of Science, and one of the questions put to them has been "Is ESP a legitimate scientific undertaking?"[37] Depending on the group surveyed, anywhere from 69%-94% have answered yes. Although the question does not ask about other types of paranormal phenomena besides ESP, it is difficult to believe there is a vast disparity between academics' position on the scientific legitimacy of the study of ESP and their position on the scientific legitimacy of the study of paranormal phenomena in general. Thus these surveys indicate that the large majority of academics regard parapsychology as a legitimate academic discipline.

Another important indication of the academic legitimacy of parapsychology is the fact that the Parapsychological Association, which is the leading professional organization of parapsychologists, has over a hundred members who possess doctorates, and is an affiliate member of the American Association for the Advancement of Science, the leading scientific organization in the US.[38]

The Meaning of "Resurrection"

When the early Christians spoke of "resurrection" (*anastasis*), they meant physical resurrection, that is, the idea of a dead body coming physically back to life. It has been argued that this is not the case: that the term resurrection could refer to entering the afterlife as a disembodied spirit, or that it could mean Jesus rose in the disciples' hearts, that is, that the disciples were inspired to continue Jesus' movement. However, if one examines the Jewish sources from in and around Jesus' time, one will find that the term "resurrection" always meant the physical raising to life of a dead body. This has been thoroughly demonstrated by N.T. Wright's 500 page evaluation of the sources.[39] Examples of Jewish sources from Jesus' time which affirm a belief in physical resurrection include the following:

---

37. For an overview of these surveys, see "Surveys of Academic Opinion Regarding Parapsychology," http://en.wikademia.org/Surveys_of_academic_opinion_regarding_parapsychology. Most of the surveys were published in the Journal of Parapsychology.

38. See the Parapsychological Association's website at http://www.parapsych.org/.

39. N.T. Wright, *Resurrection*, 32-552. Other helpful surveys of texts about resurrection in ancient Judaism are Hans Clemens Caesarius Cavallin, *Life After Death: Paul's Argument for the Resurrection*

> But when now all things shall have been reduced
> To dust and ashes, and God shall have calmed
> The fire unspeakable which he lit up,
> The bones and ashes of men God himself
> Again will fashion, and he will again
> Raise mortals up, even as they were before
> (Sibylline Oracles 4:231-36)

> Hear, Baruch, this word,
> And write in the remembrance of your heart all that you shall learn.
> For the earth shall then assuredly restore the dead,
> [Which it now receives, in order to preserve them].
> It shall make no change in their form,
> But as it has received, so shall it restore them,
> And as I delivered them unto it, so also shall it raise them.
> (2 Baruch 50:2)

The New Testament is no exception to this rule, for when the New Testament writers speak of resurrection, they clearly mean physical resurrection. This is obvious in the case of the Gospel writers, since all of them mention Jesus' empty tomb. The only question posed by scholars has been whether Paul (and by implication, other Christians in Paul's time) believed in a physical resurrection. But that Paul did believe in physical resurrection is clear from the following passages. In Romans 8:11, Paul states that the Holy Spirit will give life to our mortal bodies. If it is our mortal bodies that will be given life to, it must be our mortal bodies that rise. In Romans 8:23, Paul states that at the eschaton we will experience the redemption of our bodies. If they are to be redeemed, they must rise. In 1 Corinthians 15:36-44, Paul uses the analogy of a seed and a plant to explain the resurrection, saying that our pre-resurrection body is like a seed, and the resurrection body is like the plant which arises from the seed. This analogy clearly implies that the body which we are buried in is numerically identical to the body that rises, for a plant is numerically identical to the seed from which it arose. And in 1 Corinthians 15:42 Paul refers to our present body as corruptible and our resurrection bodies as incorruptible, and in 15:53-54 he tells us that what is corruptible must put on incorruptibility. Since put on (*endyo*) means "get into" (in the sense of getting into clothes), the clear meaning is that our corruptible, pre-resurrection body becomes our incorruptible, resurrection body.[40]

---

of the Dead in I Corinthians 15: An Enquiry into the Jewish Background (Lund, Sweden: Gleerup, 1974); Ladd, *I Believe in the Resurrection of Jesus*, 44-73.

40. Two passages in Paul which have been interpreted by many to mean that he did not believe in physical resurrection (1 Cor 15:44 where he refers to the resurrection body as a "Spiritual body" and 1 Cor 15:50 where he says that flesh and blood cannot inherit the kingdom of God) will be addressed

Introduction

Thus when the disciples expressed belief in Jesus' resurrection, they meant physical resurrection.[41] Hence when I refer to the "resurrection hypothesis" in this work, I mean the hypothesis Jesus was physically raised from the dead. If Jesus' appearances were those of an apparition, this is not a different version of the resurrection hypothesis; this is a different hypothesis, and I appropriately label it the "apparition hypothesis."

Which Sources To Use?

Paul and the canonical Gospels are primarily the only sources which need to be considered in a study of the resurrection appearances, or for that matter, in a study of any aspect of Jesus' life. We have discussed above why most scholars think the Gospels are fairly reliable, and Paul is an even better source than the Gospels are (presuming the Gospels are only fairly reliable, rather than generally reliable; if the Gospels are generally reliable, then they are equal to Paul), because Paul was personally acquainted with a number of the people who knew Jesus, including Peter and James (we will address Paul's proximity to those who knew Jesus in detail in chapter 4). The rest of the New Testament does not help us very much in reconstructing Jesus' life because the rest of the New Testament does not tell us very much about Jesus' life (since the focus of the rest of the New Testament is not on Jesus' life but on the beliefs of the early Christians and on the issues which were being faced by the churches of the first century). And the apocryphal sources, (the Gospel of Thomas, the Gospel of Mary Magdalene, and so forth) will not help us at all.[42] The essential problem with these sources is that they

---

in chapter 7.

41. I also assume that physical resurrection meant one body resurrection, that is, it meant that the person was raised in the same body they were buried in. A few scholars have argued that the early Christians (or Paul at least) believed in a two body form of resurrection, that is, the idea that the person was raised in a different physical body from the one they were buried in, while the first body remained in the ground (e.g., C.F. Moule, "St. Paul and Dualism: The Pauline Conception of the Resurrection," *New Testament Studies* 12 (1966): 106-23; Carrier, "Spiritual Body"). But the same passages that prove Paul believed in a physical resurrection also prove he believed in a one body resurrection. 1) All of the Jewish sources which say anything one way or the other attest not only that resurrection is physical, but that it is the same physical body that is raised. 2) In 1 Cor 15:42 Paul refers to the present body as corruptible and in 15:53-54 he says what is corruptible must put on incorruptibility. Put on means to "get into" (as in getting into clothes), thus clearly the present body is transformed into an incorruptible body; if it was replaced by an incorruptible body, it would not be putting incorruption on. 3) In Rom 8:23 Paul speaks of the redemption of our bodies. For our bodies to be redeemed, they must be the same bodies we possess at the resurrection. 4) In Rom 8:11 Paul refers to the transformation of our present bodies at the resurrection. Clearly, they cannot be transformed unless they are the same bodies. 5) Paul's use of the sowing reaping analogy (15:44) indicates he believed it was the same body that is raised, for the grain of wheat transforms into the plant; it is not replaced by the plant. For more on all this, see "On Paul's Theory of Resurrection: The Carrier-O'Connell Debate" http://www.infidels.org/library/modern/richard_carrier/carrier-oconnell/.

42. On the unreliability of the apocryphal sources, see Darrell L. Bock, *The Missing Gospels: Unearthing the Truth Behind Alternative Christianities* (Nashville: Nelson, 2006); Craig A. Evans,

date to a very long time after the events of Jesus' life, and there is therefore no reason to think they are at all close to the original witnesses.[43] (I would make an exception here for the Odes of Solomon, which I will discuss in chapter 6.) And the arguments which have convinced most scholars that the Gospels are fairly reliable do not work for the apocryphal sources—for example, there is no archeological confirmation for the apocryphal sources, and the criteria for authenticity have not been shown to work on them. Further, many of these sources have obviously legendary features, such as the Gospel of Peter's account of Jesus' resurrection, in which Jesus is so tall he reaches up to the sky, or the Arabic Infancy Gospel in which the child Jesus turns the other children into goats because they are hiding from him.[44] In addition, these Gospels often contradict Paul, who as we said, knew some of the eyewitnesses, and who is thus a reliable source, whereas the canonical sources are in harmony with Paul.[45] And while there are some instances in which it can plausibly be argued that a non-canonical source preserves an authentic saying of Jesus which is not recorded in the canonical Gospels, or preserves a more original form of a saying which is also found in the canonical Gospels,[46] even this situation is not common, and it has no significant impact on our understanding of Jesus' life.

The Honesty of Our Sources

As Gary Habermas says in the quote at the beginning of this chapter, it is the nearly unanimous consensus of scholars that the early Christians honestly believed Jesus had been raised from the dead. The fact that they honestly believed this, and that they honestly believed Christianity in general to be true, is clear from the fact that they did not renounce Christianity even though they were persecuted.[47] (It is of course hypothetically possible that a group which honestly believes its essential message might on occasion lie about this or that fact (perhaps in the case of Christianity, this or that

---

Fabricating Jesus: How Modern Scholars Distort the Gospels (Downers Grove, IL: IVP, 2006); Licona, *Resurrection*, 257-75.

43. Some scholars argue that some of these sources (particularly the Gospel of Thomas) do date to the first century, but for the arguments against early dates, see the sources just mentioned.

44. Gospel of Peter 39-40; Arabic Infancy Gospel 40.

45. We have already referred to David Wenham's book *Paul: Follower of Jesus or Founder of Christianity?* in support of the contention that Paul was in harmony with the original disciples.

46. So e.g., Bart D. Ehrman and Zlatko Plese, *The Apocryphal Gospels: Texts and Translations* (Oxford: Oxford University Press, 2011), 307.

47. That the early Christians were persecuted is widely attested. For example, Peter and John are imprisoned (Acts 5:18), Paul persecutes the Christians (Acts 9:1-3; Gal 1:1-13), James the brother of John was killed by Herod (Acts 12:2), and Josephus tells us James the brother of Jesus was killed during the early 60s (*Antiquities of the Jews*, 20.9.1). The Gospels also attest to persecutions (e.g., Mt 5:11-12; Mt 10:17-18), and Paul attests that he was later persecuted by Jews himself (2 Cor 11:25). And of course, Christians throughout the Roman Empire were persecuted during the Neronian persecution of 64 CE.

Introduction

miracle) in order to promote what they think is overall a good cause. But though this is hypothetically possible, the burden of proof is on the skeptic to show that this is so in any given case, since the Gospel writers, like any other witness whom we have no specific reason to suspect of lying, must be assumed to be telling the truth unless there is evidence to the contrary.)

Our Sources Do Not Contain Any Intentionally Fictitious Events

The Gospels do not contain any intentionally fictitious events (and neither does the rest of the New Testament, but one does not find the hypothesis of intentional fiction argued except in the case of the Gospels and Acts, since they are the only New Testament documents which fall under the genre of narrative). By "intentional fiction," I mean not lies, but events which the author knew to be unhistorical and which he also expected his readers to know were unhistorical. Shakespeare, for example, obviously knew the events related in Macbeth were unhistorical, and he expected his audience to realize this as well. It is sometimes argued that the Gospels are intentional fiction, either in whole (for example, Dennis MacDonald argues that the Gospels are fictional creations based on the writings of Homer),[48] or in part (e.g., one can find a fair number of scholars who think the race to the tomb between Peter and the Beloved Disciple is fictional).[49] Now the view that the Gospels are intentional fiction in their entirely has few advocates—the vast majority of scholars believe the Gospels are documents which either in total, or, with a few exceptions here and there, relate what their authors believed actually happened. However, the view that the Gospels for the most part relate actual events, but on occasion create an event or two, is fairly common.

To address these issues, let me first present the arguments against the idea that the Gospels are fiction in their entirety and then consider the hypothesis that only some events in the Gospels are fictional.[50]

---

48. Dennis R. MacDonald, *The Homeric Epics and the Gospel of Mark* (New Haven, CT: Yale University Press, 2000); *Does the New Testament Imitate Homer? Four Cases From the Acts of the Apostles* (New Haven, CT: Yale University Press, 2003). And see also Randel Helms, *Gospel Fictions* (Buffalo, NY: Prometheus, 1988); John Shelby Spong, *Liberating the Gospels: Reading the Gospels with Jewish Eyes: Freeing Jesus From Two Thousand Years of Misunderstanding* (San Francisco: HarperSanFrancisco, 1996).

49. E.g., Willi Marxsen, *The Resurrection of Jesus of Nazareth* (Philadelphia: Fortress, 1970), 59; Reginald H. Fuller, *The Formation of the Resurrection Narratives* (Philadelphia: Fortress, 1980), 135; James M. Somerville, *Jesus: A Man for Others: How He Interacted with the People who Knew Him* (Scranton, PA: University of Scranton Press, 2004), 152. Other events in the Gospels which have been argued to be intentional fiction are: the angel's presence at the tomb (Raymond E. Brown, *The Virginal Conception and Bodily Resurrection of Jesus* (New York: Paulist, 1973), 122); Matthew's account of the guards (Daniel A. Smith, *Revisiting the Empty Tomb: The Early History of Easter* (Minneapolis: Fortress, 2010), 120); and Matthew's claim that when Jesus died, many people rose from the dead and appeared in Jerusalem (we will examine this event in detail in chapter 6).

50. For another critique of the intentional fiction theory, see Dale C. Allison Jr., *Constructing Jesus: Memory, Imagination, and History* (Grand Rapids, MI: Baker Academic, 2010), 435-58.

1. It is a basic epistemological principle that when we encounter words which in our past experience have had one particular meaning in the large majority of instances in which we have heard those words, then, barring evidence to the contrary, we should assume that the words mean the same thing that they have meant in the large majority of other instances in which we have encountered those words. If we do not follow this principle, communication will completely break down. For example, suppose someone asks me if I want to "go bowling." In the large majority of instances in which I have heard someone utter those words (in fact, as far as I can recall, in every instance in which I have heard someone utter those words) the words have meant that the person uttering them is asking if I want to go pick up a ball and knock down pins. Hence when I hear this question, I assume that the person asking it is asking me if I want to go pick up a ball and knock down pins. Now conceivably, he might mean something else. I have not asked him to define "go bowling," so maybe he is using those words to ask me if I want to play poker. But I am not going to ask him to define "go bowling"; I am simply going to assume that the words have the same meaning they have had in the vast majority of other instances in which I have heard them used.[51]

Hence, Norman Anderson, a lawyer who has studied the resurrection, notes that it is a basic principle of law that the words in a document should be assumed to have their literal sense (that is, their ordinary sense; the sense which they typically have) until there is evidence to the contrary. He quotes one prominent law textbook, "Rule Three declares that 'Words are to be taken in their literal meaning' wherever this is possible or appropriate,"[52] and Sir George Jessel, a famous British judge, "The grammatical and ordinary sense of the words is to be adhered to, unless that would lead to some absurdity, or some repugnance or inconsistency with the rest of the instrument. . ."[53]

Now in the case of the Gospels, we have what are ostensibly historical narratives (they certainly look like historical narratives, and at least in the case of Luke, the author appears to tell us quite explicitly that it is a historical narrative).[54] Our past experience is that when people have used words in the way the Gospel writers use them (when they have presented us with what appear to be historical narratives), they

---

51. I have made this point in "On Paul's Theory of Resurrection: The Carrier-O'Connell Debate," http://www.infidels.org/library/modern/richard_carrier/carrier-oconnell. I first came across the general idea in Swinburne, *Resurrection*, 10-12.

52. Norman Anderson, *A Lawyer Among the Theologians* (Grand Rapids, MI: Eerdmans, 1973), 17, quoting Charles E. Odgers, *Construction of Deeds and Statutes* (London: Sweet & Maxwell, 1967), 36.

53. Anderson, *Lawyer*, page 18, quoting Sir George Jessel in the legal document "Re Levy ex. P. Walton (1881) 17 C.D. 746 17 p. 751."

54. "Inasmuch as many have undertaken to compile an account of the things accomplished among us, just as they were handed down to us by those who from the beginning were eyewitnesses and servants of the word, it seemed fitting for me as well, having investigated everything carefully from the beginning, to write it out for you in consecutive order, most excellent Theophilus; so that you may know the exact truth about the things you have been taught." (Lk 1:1-4)

have meant that they are trying to tell us about actual events which they believe took place. Thus when we see the Gospel writers using words in this way, we should assume they are trying to relate actual events until we have evidence to the contrary.

2. Josephus and Philo, and other first century Jewish authors, accept the Old Testament as a narrative of actual events. Josephus, for example, notes other historians who mentioned the Flood, and he even goes so far as to say that he has seen the very pillar of salt which Lot's wife was turned into.[55] If first century Jews understood the Old Testament to be a record of actual events, we should assume the early Christians understood the New Testament to be a record of actual events as well, since they believed Jesus' life was the climax of the story of the Old Testament.

3. In the case of the Gospels and Acts there is a remarkable amount of archeological confirmation. While it is true that a fictional document could hypothetically include many details which are confirmed as historically accurate, in fact, this is not the case for fictional writings from around the time of the Gospels.

4. The Gospels are written in the style of ancient biography. For they parallel Greco-Roman biographies in features such as their size, structure, and the amount of space they devote to Jesus' death.[56] If they are biographies, then, since the intent of a biography was to give an actual account of a person's life, we can conclude the Gospels are an attempt to give an actual account of Jesus' life.

5. There is of course the fact that by the time of the Church Fathers the Gospels were universally interpreted as historical accounts. Thus if one wishes to propose that the accounts were originally intended as fiction, one will have to explain how the authors' original intent was so completely and massively misinterpreted. But there is no good explanation for this, and in fact, I do not think any proponents of the fiction theory have even attempted to offer one.

Now what of the possibility that though the Gospels are not intentional fiction in their entirety, there are a few intentionally fictitious events here and there? Although this is hypothetically possible, it would be difficult in practice to prove that any given event in the Gospels is intentional fiction. For if the hypothesis is that there are only occasional intentionally fictitious events in the Gospels, that means the number of passages in the Gospels which are not intentional fiction vastly outnumber the texts which are, and thus in the case of any given text, we should assume it is meant historically until there is evidence to the contrary. (In Bayesian terms, the initial probability is very high that a given text is meant historically; this statement will make more sense once we have examined the concept of initial probability in chapter 2.) But how do we get evidence to the contrary? To demonstrate that a given event was not meant

---

55. Josephus mentions the other writers who mention the Flood in *Antiquities of the Jews*, 1.3.6. He mentions the pillar of salt still being visible in 1.11.4.

56. See Richard Burridge, *What Are the Gospels? A Comparison with Greco-Roman Biography* (2nd ed.; Grand Rapids, MI: Eerdmans, 2004); Craig S. Keener, *The Historical Jesus of the Gospels* (Grand Rapids, MI: Eerdmans, 2009), 73-83.

historically, we would have to demonstrate that 1) the event is unhistorical, and 2) the author knew the event was unhistorical (if the event is unhistorical, but the author did not know this, he has not written intentional fiction, but simply mistaken history). While it is hypothetically possible that this can be demonstrated, I have yet to encounter any cases where one can actually show it, and unless we get such cases we should simply assume that all of the events recorded in the Gospels are meant to be understood as actual events. When a particular case of this kind is proposed, so far as I recall from my general knowledge of the literature, it seems that the reason cited for thinking the event is fictional is typically that the event supports some interest of the Gospel writer. For example, the race to the tomb between Peter and the Beloved Disciple is thought to be invented, because since it has the Beloved Disciple getting to the tomb first, it demonstrates the superiority of the Beloved Disciple over Peter. However, the fact that an event serves some interest of the Gospel writer does not lead to the conclusion that the event is intentional fiction; for obviously a real event can support the opinion of the Gospel writer, and even if one thinks the event unhistorical, it could be that the Gospel writer thinks it is historical even though it is not. Since we have many cases in ancient literature in which a historian includes in support of his opinion an event which actually did happen, and also many other cases in which he includes an event which he thinks happened though it actually did not, but no clear cases of a historian inventing an intentionally fictional event, then in any given case in which our only relevant datum is that the historian includes some event which supports his interests, it is much more likely that either the event actually happened or that the historian thinks it actually happened though it did not, than that the historian is writing intentional fiction. Moreover, since our general knowledge of the world tells us that people lie more often than they add intentional fiction into an otherwise historical account, even the hypothesis that the historian lied has a higher initial probability than that he wrote intentional fiction. To put the matter in Bayesian terms, (terms which will not make sense until after chapter 2), if we have the datum that a given event supports the interests of a historian, that datum has an equally high probability on the hypothesis that the event actually happened, on the hypothesis that the historian mistakenly thought the event actually happened, on the hypothesis that the historian lied, and on the hypothesis that the historian wrote intentional fiction. And so we must ask which hypothesis has a higher initial probability, and since historians record actual events, record events which they mistakenly think are actual, and lie more often than they write intentional fiction, the initial probability is decidedly against the intentional fiction theory.

Are Miracles Possible?

In this work I obviously take it for granted that it is at least hypothetically possible to establish that miraculous (i.e., supernatural) phenomena have taken place (and also

Introduction

that paranormal phenomena have taken place). But some dispute this—one sometimes finds the argument that it is impossible even in theory to affirm that a miracle occurred, that claims of the miraculous should simply be dismissed a priori. For my answer to this objection, see the appendix at the end of this book.

Are Our Sources Divinely Inspired and/or Inerrant?

Not only the events recorded in our sources, but the sources themselves are believed by many to be supernatural. The Bible is widely believed to be divinely inspired (that is, the belief that God aided the writers of the Bible as they wrote), and is also believed by many to be inerrant (that is, the belief that God aided the writers to such an extent that he prevented them from making any errors). Inerrancy may come in one of two forms. Full inerrancy: the belief that the writers did not make any errors at all. Or partial inerrancy: the belief that the writers did not make any errors in regard to faith or morals, but did make errors in regard to other matters, such as history and science. I personally believe in the full inerrancy of the Bible, a belief which is the traditional belief of the church.[57] It has been argued that this belief will bias one in such a way that one will not be able to look at the sources objectively, and so I want to consider this question upfront.[58]

---

57. For some reason, the misconception has arisen that the doctrine of inerrancy is a modern day invention of the "Old Princeton" theologians (the theologians at Princeton Theological Seminary during the late 1800s and early 1900s). But on the fact that it has been believed throughout the church's history, see John D. Hannah ed., *Inerrancy and the Church* (Chicago: Moody, 1984); John D. Woodbridge, "Evangelical Self Identity and the Doctrine of Biblical Inerrancy," in Andreas Kostenberger and Robert W. Yarbrough eds., *Understanding the Times: New Testament Studies in the 21st Century* (Wheaton, IL: Crossway, 2011), 104-40. Augustine stated his belief in inerrancy quite explicitly: "For I confess to your Charity that I have learned to yield this respect and honour only to the canonical books of Scripture: of these alone do I most firmly believe that the authors were completely free from error. And if in these writings I am perplexed by anything which appears to me opposed to truth, I do not hesitate to suppose that either the manuscript is faulty, or the translator has not caught the meaning of what was said, or I myself have failed to understand it" (Augustine, Letter 82, 1.3). That it cannot have been an invention of the Old Princeton theologians is also clear from the fact that Pope Leo XIII affirmed it as the traditional teaching of the Catholic Church: "But it is absolutely wrong and forbidden, either to narrow inspiration to certain parts only of Holy Scripture, or to admit that the sacred writer has erred. . . For all the books which the Church receives as sacred and canonical, are written wholly and entirely, with all their parts, at the dictation of the Holy Ghost; and so far is it from being possible that any error can co-exist with inspiration, that inspiration not only is essentially incompatible with error, but excludes and rejects it as absolutely and necessarily as it is impossible that God Himself, the supreme Truth, can utter that which is not true. This is the ancient and unchanging faith of the Church, solemnly defined in the Councils of Florence and of Trent, and finally confirmed and more expressly formulated by the Council of the Vatican"("Providentissimus Deus: Encyclical Of Pope Leo XIII on the Study Of Holy Scripture," paragraph 20).

58. Examples of the charge that inerrancy makes one biased: Kathleen C. Boone, in a discussion of the history of inerrancy, tells us that two prominent critics of inerrancy, James Barr and Dewey Beegle, argued that holding the belief necessarily results in biased interpretations (Kathleen C. Boone, *The Bible Tells Them So: The Discourse of Protestant Fundamentalism* (Albany, NY: SUNY Press, 1989, 34). And see Bart Ehrman in William Lane Craig and Bart Ehrman, "Is There Historical Evidence for

Jesus' Resurrection and Apparitions

My response is that though I am indeed biased in the sense of wanting certain beliefs to be true, I am not biased in the sense of distorting the evidence to fit those beliefs. But in being biased in this first sense of the word, I am not alone, for everyone who studies religion is biased in the same sense that I am. If a person does not believe in Christianity, they will want their investigation of the evidence to show that the Bible is largely unreliable. For what skeptic wants to admit that miracle accounts rest on eyewitness testimony? Likewise, the liberal Christian will want to find what is favorable to liberal Christianity. For example, he will not want to find that the Pentateuch rests on eyewitness testimony and that we therefore have eyewitness testimony to miracles which place a divine stamp of approval on a mission which included destroying the Canaanites and various other groups. But the liberal Christian will also not want to uncover anything which is too far in favor of the skeptic. If, for example, the historical evidence indicates that Jesus did not exist, there will be no Jesus to follow, and thus no liberal Christianity.

But despite the fact that we are all biased in this sense when it comes to studying religion, that does not mean we are all biased in the second sense of distorting the evidence to fit our beliefs. Though this may sometimes happen consciously, and more often subconsciously, it will not always happen. Medical research sponsored by drug companies furnishes an analogy here. It has been found that when a drug company sponsors research, this makes it more likely that the research will come out in a way favorable to the drug company.[59] Hence in some cases, consciously or subconsciously, the fact that the drug companies are supporting the research makes it so the researchers do not evaluate the data as objectively. Hence medical journals now require that if an author's research was sponsored by an organization, the author reveal this when submitting the article. But this does not mean research sponsored by drug companies is always or even usually wrong. Most of the time it is not. Thus religious scholarship will not necessarily go wrong simply because certain scholars want certain beliefs to be true. It is simply a possibility we need to be aware of.

But it might be objected that belief in the inerrancy of the Bible biases one in a way that other religious beliefs do not. For how can we look at the Bible objectively if we start out with the presumption that it has no errors? However, once we understand the process by which one arrives at a belief in inerrancy, it becomes clear that belief in inerrancy does not impede our ability to look at the sources objectively any more

---

the Resurrection of Jesus? A Debate between William Lane Craig and Bart D. Ehrman," College of the Holy Cross, Worcester, MA, March 28, 2006, p. 31, transcript available at http://www.reasonablefaith.org/site/DocServer/resurrection-debate-transcript.pdf?docID=621. Ehrman tells us that since Craig believes in inerrancy, "he can't critically evaluate these sources, and the one thing that historians have to do is be able to critically evaluate the sources that they base their claims on."

59. G. Schott et al., "The Financing of Drug Trials by Pharmaceutical Companies and Its Consequences: Part 1. A Qualitative, Systematic Review of the Literature on Possible Influences on the Findings, Protocols, and Quality of Drug Trials," *Deutsches Aerzteblatt International* 107 (2010): 279-85, doi: 10.3238/arztebl.2010.0279.

Introduction

so than any other religious belief does. The most common type of argument for inerrancy is as follows:[60]

First, we begin by looking at the Bible just as we would any other historical document. By using the same criteria we would use for any other historical document (e.g., considering issues of authorship, date, and confirmation from other sources), we establish that certain portions of the Bible are historical (in some cases, perhaps a whole book, in some cases, perhaps only specific passages within the book). From those portions which we establish as historical, we are able to conclude that Jesus claimed to be the Messiah, and also that there is evidence in support of this claim (the evidence comes from miracles and prophecies; the parts of the Bible which we show to be historical must include narratives of miracles and/or accurate prophecies). At this point in the process, we are confident Jesus is the Messiah and therefore that we can trust his teachings, but there is still quite a lot in the Bible which we do not know one way or the other to be true, because the historical evidence has only been able to establish the truth of certain parts of the Bible. However, we then show that in some of the portions of the Bible which we have shown to be historical, Jesus taught the inerrancy of the Bible. Once we have demonstrated this, all of the passages which we cannot show to be accurate on the basis of historical evidence, we can now believe to be accurate because of the fact that Jesus taught that the entire Bible is accurate. To give an analogy, suppose I hear a voice claiming to be God, and I ask for evidence, and this voice performs miracles and predicts the future. I am now justified in believing this is really the voice of God, and therefore I will believe whatever he tells me even if I have no other evidence than the fact that he has told me. If God tells me there was a car crash yesterday, I will believe it without checking it for myself. If God tells me a tree has fallen in my yard, I will believe it without checking it for myself.

It is the same situation as regards inerrancy. Jesus claiming to be God (or God's agent) is analogous to the voice claiming to be God. Jesus' claim to be God is verified by miracles and prophecies just as the voice's claim is (although in the case of Jesus I must evaluate historical evidence to see that there have been miracles and prophecies, rather than seeing these things personally). And my believing, for example, that Jonah was swallowed by a whale for no other reason than that Jesus says so (Jesus says so indirectly by saying that the body of writings in which this claim is found is inerrant) is analogous to believing there was a car crash or that a tree fell for no other reason than that God has told me.

Thus this is the process for coming to believe in inerrancy, and it is not difficult to see how this is consistent with approaching the Bible as a historical document. There are some things in the Bible which I believe only because Jesus has said they are true, and there are some things which I believe because there is also historical evidence for them. For example, though I have no historical evidence that Jonah was swallowed by

---

60. For a fuller argument of this kind, see John W. Wenham, *Christ and the Bible* (Downers Grove, IL: InterVarsity, 1972).

a whale, I do have historical evidence the temple was destroyed in 587 BCE. And if I am asked to make an argument based only on those things in the Bible for which I have historical evidence, and not to appeal to anything which I believe only because it is in the Bible, I can easily do so. For example, if I am trying to reconstruct the Babylonian destruction and I want to present the results of my investigation to an audience that does not accept the inerrancy of the Bible, there will be some facts I can use because there is historical evidence for them (such as that the temple was destroyed, and that the people were deported), and other facts which, though I believe them because they are in the Bible, I will not use because I have no independent evidence for them (such as that Ezekiel traveled in spirit to Jerusalem, or that he saw a vision of God). Hence someone who believes in inerrancy can still evaluate the sources in the same manner as anyone else.

It should be added that a commitment to the inerrancy of the Bible does not mean that one must interpret everything in the Bible literally. How a passage should be interpreted is dependent on the author's intent. If an author did not intend for a passage to be understood as historical narrative, then the fact that the passage is not historical does not mean there is an error. Only if the author did intend to narrate historical events, is the fact some of those events did not happen an error.

And of course, the fact that someone believes in inerrancy does not mean they are not open to finding an error in the Bible. They are still open to doing so, but if they do so, they will have to renounce inerrancy. They will of course, not want to have to do this, but this only means that their evaluation of alleged errors in the Bible is biased in the first sense of that word. But I have explained why everyone else who is studying the Bible is also biased in this sense (if not with regard to finding errors, then with regard to something else).

A Word About Ancient Apparitions

In addition to the many accounts of apparitions which have been reported in our own time, there are many accounts of apparitions to be found in ancient literature, and since in a book entitled *Jesus' Resurrection and Apparitions*, one might expect to see ancient apparitions discussed, I should explain why I will not address them very much.[61] The reason their role will be limited is because our concern is with the reality of apparitions, and ancient accounts do not help us much with this question, since few, if any, of the accounts are firsthand, or even close to firsthand. Thus though comparative treatments between ancient apparitions and the resurrection appearances may be

---

61. For sources on ancient apparitions, see Ronald C. Finucane, *Ghosts: Appearances of the Dead and Cultural Transformation* (Amherst, NY: Prometheus, 1996); D. Felton, *Haunted Greece and Rome: Ghost Stories from Classical Antiquity* (Austin, TX: University of Texas Press, 1999); Sarah Iles Johnston, *Restless Dead: Encounters Between the Living and the Dead in Ancient Greece* (Berkeley: University of California Press, 1999); Daniel Ogden, *Magic, Witchcraft, and Ghosts in the Greek and Roman Worlds: A Sourcebook* (Oxford: Oxford University Press, 2002).

helpful in other contexts,[62] they will not help us much with our present task, which is to determine whether the resurrected Jesus was a real apparition.

---

62. For discussions of ancient apparitions in relation to the resurrection of Jesus, see Deborah Thompson Prince, "The 'Ghost' of Jesus: Luke 24 in Light of Ancient Narratives of Post-Mortem Apparitions," *Journal for the Study of the New Testament* 34 (2007): 287-301; Jake H. O'Connell, "Did Greco-Roman Apparitional Models Influence Luke's Resurrection Narrative? A Response to Deborah Thompson Prince," *Journal of Greco-Roman Christianity and Judaism* 5 (2008): 190-99; Jason Robert Combs, "A Ghost on the Water? Understanding an Absurdity in Mark 6:49-50," *Journal of Biblical Literature* 127 (2008): 345-58.

2

Bayes' Theorem

BAYES' THEOREM (BT) IS a mathematical theorem which takes its name from Thomas Bayes, a minister and mathematician of the seventeenth century.[1] The purpose of BT is to determine the probability that a hypothesis is true. It has a special status over other mathematical theorems because it is the theorem which underlies all logical thought about the probability of hypotheses; whenever we evaluate any hypothesis, we use Bayes' Theorem subconsciously. (This claim is contested by objectivists, who contend that BT's application is much narrower, but I will address their arguments below.) Sharon Bertsch McGrayne tells us something of the storied history of this theorem:

> The defenders of Captain Dreyfus used it to demonstrate his innocence; insurance actuaries used it to set rates; Alan Turing used it to decode the German Enigma cipher and arguably save the Allies from losing the Second World War; the U.S. navy used it to search for a missing H-bomb and to locate Soviet subs; RAND Corporation used it to assess the likelihood of a nuclear accident; and Harvard and Chicago researchers used it to verify the authorship of the Federalist Papers.[2]

We should begin by presenting the theorem, or rather one version of the theorem, the one which I think makes it easiest to explain how BT encapsulates logical thinking. This particular form of BT is called the "odds form."[3] (There are different versions of BT, but they are all mathematically equivalent—that is, they will all give you the same answer as long as you put in the same numbers. This is analogous to how ¼ and 0.25 are mathematically equivalent ways of expressing the same idea.)

---

1. The clearest introduction to Bayes' Theorem (other than the present one) is Richard C. Carrier, *Proving History: Bayes's Theorem and the Quest for the Historical Jesus* (Amherst, NY: Prometheus, 2012). Other useful sources include: Richard Swinburne, *An Introduction to Confirmation Theory* (London: Methuen, 1973); Colin Howson and Peter Urbach, *Scientific Reasoning: The Bayesian Approach* (La Salle, IL: Open Court, 1989); Eliezer S. Yudkowsky, "An Intuitive Explanation of Bayes' Theorem," http://yudkowsky.net/rational/bayes. For many further sources, see Timothy McGrew, "Bayesian Reasoning: An Annotated Bibliography Compiled by Timothy McGrew," http://homepages.wmich.edu/~mcgrew/bayes.htm .

2. Sharon Bertsch McGrayne, *The Theory that Would Not Die: How Bayes' Rule Cracked the Enigma Code, Hunted Down Russian Submarines, and Emerged Triumphant from Two Centuries of Controversy* (New Haven, CT: Yale University Press, 2011), 3.

3. For the different versions of BT, see Carrier, *Proving History*, 283-85.

$$\frac{p(h|e)}{p(\sim h|e)} = \frac{p(h)}{p(\sim h)} \times \frac{p(e|h)}{p(e|\sim h)}$$

We should also begin with two notes on terminology. First, most people are used to seeing probability expressed on a scale of 1-100 (60%, 70%, etc). But in the literature on BT one will often find probability expressed on a scale of 0-1 (e.g., 0.6 instead of 60%, 0.7 instead of 70%). I have used both forms of expression in this chapter. Second, I have used the terms "probability" and "odds" interchangeably throughout the chapter. However, readers should know a technical distinction is often made between the two. In that case, "probability" is used when we express the chances either on a scale of 1-100, or 0-1; "odds" is used when we express the chances as a ratio (e.g., 4:1, 8:1, 10:1, etc). There is a bit more to this technical distinction, though, and I explain that in n5.

Seeing a mathematical equation like the one above can seem intimidating, but it will not seem so intimidating once we realize that BT is not math in the sense in which most people think of math. What likely comes to most people's minds when they hear the word "math" is the solving of complicated calculations. But it is exceedingly simple to solve the BT equation once the numbers have been put into the equation. The challenge of BT is not to perform the calculation, but to understand the ideas behind the equation, to understand how we get the numbers in the first place, and why we would want to do what the equation tells us to do with the numbers. The equation is really not as mysterious as it seems, because it does not do anything other than describe the logical thought process of human beings. The equation is a shorthand way of expressing that thought process, since it is quicker to express the thought process by means of the equation than by means of words. But this chapter is written because the words must be used first in order to understand what the equation is shorthand for. (And in fact, the matter can be addressed entirely with words, for as I will explain, you can use BT by doing a 3 step process which does not involve using an equation.)

Concerning the formula, the essential facts are these. The numerator on the left side of the equation, p (h|e), means the probability of a hypothesis (h) given the evidence (e). The p is for "probability," the h is for "hypothesis," the slash sign (|) is for "given" (as in "assuming"), and the e is for "evidence" (and the evidence can also be called a datum; hence some versions of BT use d instead of e). It is asking, given that we have some piece of evidence, what is the probability our hypothesis is true? In the denominator of the left side of the equation we have p (~h|e). This means the probability our hypothesis is not true ("~" is read as "not") given the evidence. Once we have solved the equation, we will have numbers here, for example, if $\frac{p(h|e)}{p(\sim h|e)}$ is replaced with $\frac{2}{1}$, that means that the hypothesis (h) is two times as likely as the alternative (~h), or in other words, the odds are 2:1 in favor of our hypothesis. The question being asked here is a question we ask everyday: we get evidence for some hypothesis and ask how likely our hypothesis is, given the evidence we have. The equation tells us that this is the number on the left side of the equation, and that this number equals the information on the right side of the equation; that means the way we figure out whether our hypothesis is true given the evidence we've got is to do what is on the right side of the equation. And the right side of the equation tells us we do three things. First, there is the matter of consequent probability. We are always used to asking what is on the left hand side of the equation, that is, we are used to asking: given that we have such and such a piece of evidence, what are the odds our hypothesis is true? The right hand side of the equation tells us that to answer this question we have to turn the question around and ask two questions: first, assuming our hypothesis is true, what are the odds of getting this piece of evidence, (p (e|h))? And second, assuming our hypothesis is false, what are the odds of getting this piece of evidence (p (e|~h))? On the right side of the equation there is also h; this is the initial probability (also called the prior probability), that is, the probability our hypothesis was true before we even examined the piece of evidence in question; and there is ~h, the probability our hypothesis was not true before we examined the evidence. Thus BT tells us that if we want to know the probability a hypothesis is true (say the hypothesis Bob committed murder) given a certain piece of evidence (ultimately we must consider all the evidence, but in the case of any hypothesis we must necessarily start with one piece of evidence, in this case, say it is the fact that the murder weapon was a knife) we must determine three things: the probability of getting the piece of evidence in question if our hypothesis is true (the probability of getting a knife if Bob committed murder), the probability of getting the piece of evidence if our hypothesis is not true (the probability of getting a knife if Bob did not commit murder), and the initial probability (the probability that our hypothesis was true before we examined the evidence). And we must also determine the initial probability our hypothesis was false, but this is necessarily simply the opposite of the initial probability it was true (e.g., if the initial probability it is true is 0.7, the initial probability it is false is 0.3). (For example, most people would say the resurrection has a low initial probability because resurrections happen rarely, if ever, and thus we should be quite skeptical as we approach the evidence (though others have contested whether the resurrection really has a low initial probability).)

Why we ought to do all of this will not become clear until BT has been fully explained. But let me first show what an example of a final solution to the equation would look like:

What was once:

$$\frac{p(h|e)}{p(\sim h|e)} = \frac{p(h)}{p(\sim h)} \times \frac{p(e|h)}{p(e|\sim h)}$$

May become:

$$\frac{20}{1} = \frac{10}{1} \times \frac{2}{1}$$

Bayes' Theorem

The Principles of BT

There are three basic principles behind BT, and we should lay out these principles before we examine the equation in detail:

1. *The lower the initial probability of a hypothesis, the more strongly the specific evidence must support the hypothesis for us to be convinced that the hypothesis is true.* Specific evidence means evidence directly relevant to that hypothesis; this is in contrast to general evidence; general evidence is evidence which comes from our background knowledge. This principle states that the less likely we think a claim is based on our background knowledge, the more strongly the evidence must support it in order for us to believe it is true. This accords with our common sense; we require stronger evidence for an extraordinary claim than for an ordinary one. If someone claims they were abducted by aliens, we will require stronger evidence than if they claim they got a flat tire, because, quite apart from the evidence specific to those claims, our background knowledge of the world tells us alien abductions are much rarer than flat tires.

2. *The way to determine the probability that a hypothesis is true given the evidence, is to turn the question around and ask: What is the probability of getting the evidence given that the hypothesis is true, and what is the probability of getting the evidence given that the hypothesis is not true?* For example, if we have found a knife, and we want to know the probability Bob committed the murder given this piece of evidence, we have to turn the question around and ask: What is the probability of getting a knife if Bob committed the murder and what is the probability of getting a knife if Bob did not commit the murder? This is called consequent probability, and it is the most difficult of these three concepts to grasp. If we think that the probability of getting a knife is higher if Bob committed the murder than if he did not commit the murder, we will conclude that this piece of specific evidence favors the hypothesis that Bob is the murderer.

However, whether the hypothesis is true depends not just on this one datum, but also on the initial probability, and on the rest of the specific evidence. Which leads into the third point:

3. *We update the probability of a hypothesis in light of new evidence.* We may assign a hypothesis a certain probability at one point, but as we get more evidence, we may have to alter our original judgment.

Thus BT tells us to do three things to determine the probability that a hypothesis is true: 1) consider the initial probability, 2) consider the question of consequent probability, and 3) adjust our evaluation each time we get new evidence. The first and third of these points seem like common sense. The second is more difficult to explain, and it is now time to explain it, along with all of the other intricacies of BT.

Explaining BT

The best way to explain BT is to consider various hypothetical cases. To begin with, suppose we live in a city in which two fellows, Bob and Joe, commit all the murders. Suppose space aliens have used advanced technology to program everyone's brains so that Bob and Joe commit murder but no one else commits murder. Suppose we find a person who was murdered with a knife, and suppose we somehow know (this is of course a hypothetical case) that when Bob commits murders he uses a knife 90% of the time and that when Joe commits murders he uses a knife 45% of the time. And suppose that, at this point in the investigation, the fact that the murder weapon was a knife is the only datum we have relevant to the question of which person committed the murder. Now our question is: What are the chances Bob committed the murder? That is, h is "Bob committed the murder" and ~h is "Bob did not commit the murder," which in this case is equivalent to "Joe committed the murder" (to keep the example simple, we are limiting it to two suspects. In a real case, there may of course be various ~h hypotheses).

One can easily see that to determine this probability we have to somehow put the numbers 90% and 45% together. But the question is how? For numbers can of course be added, subtracted, multiplied, or divided. But to discover the answer to our question, we simply have to imagine what the scenario would look like over a long run of trials. For when we say that something occurs a certain percentage of the time, we mean it occurs a certain number of times over the course of a large number of trials. If Bob uses a knife 90% of the time, that means he uses a knife 90[4] out of every 100 times. If Joe uses a knife 45% of the time, that means he uses a knife 45 out of every 100 times. Now suppose that Bob and Joe have each committed 100 murders. That means there are 200 murdered bodies. Since we know that Bob uses a knife 90% of the time, that means 90 of the bodies Bob murdered will have died by a knife. And since we know Joe uses a knife 45% of the time, that means 45 of the bodies Joe murdered will have died by a knife. Hence in our collection, there are 200 murdered bodies; 90 of them have knife wounds from Bob and 45 of them have knife wounds from Joe. Thus of the bodies with knife wounds, there are twice as many bodies killed by Bob as there are bodies killed by Joe (90 versus 45). Hence if we take a random body with a knife wound, the odds are 2:1 (90/45) that Bob is responsible for that murder. And the odds will be 2:1 so long as the proportion is 2:1; the numbers do not have to be 90 and 45; they could be 60 and 30, 80 and 40, 100 and 50, etc.

So if it is the case that Bob uses a knife 90% of the time he commits a murder and Joe uses a knife 45% of the time he commits a murder, and we know the murder

---

4. More exactly, he uses a knife 90 out of every 100 times over the course of a large series of trials. If he uses a knife 90% of the time in the long run, there is no guarantee that in a given series of 100 trials he will use it exactly 90 times; he might use it 87, or 88, or 91 times. But since in the long run, we will find him using it 90 out of every 100 times, for illustrative purposes, it is simplest to state that he uses it 90 out of every 100 times.

victim died by a knife, and Bob and Joe are the only two suspects, the odds are 2:1 Bob committed the murder. The odds of h are 2:1 (67%) and the odds of ~h are 1:2 (33%).

To take another example, suppose we find a hot dog with mustard on it in Bob and Joe's house, and suppose we want to know the odds it is Bob's hot dog or Joe's hot dog. Suppose we know that when Bob eats a hot dog, he uses mustard 60% of the time, and when Joe eats a hot dog, he uses mustard 20% of the time. Again, to see the answer we simply have to imagine what the situation would look like over a long series of trials. If Bob and Joe each eat 100 hot dogs, that means there will be 60 hot dogs with mustard on them from Bob, and 20 hot dogs with mustard on them from Joe. Hence there are 3 times as many hot dogs with mustard from Bob as there are from Joe. Thus if we find a random hot dog with mustard on it, the odds are 60/20=3:1 that the hot dog is Bob's.

However, there is a hidden assumption in our above calculations. We have implicitly assumed that Bob and Joe commit the same number of murders and eat the same number of hot dogs. To use Bayesian terms, we have assumed a neutral initial probability; we have assumed that prior to our examination of the datum (the murder weapon in the first case, the hot dogs in the second) both hypotheses are equally likely to be true. If this assumption is not correct, our above calculations will not be correct. Consider how the question of initial probability affects the murder example. We imagined a set of 100 murders by Bob, of which 90 involved a knife, and 100 murders by Joe, of which 45 involved a knife, and we concluded that since there are twice as many knife murders by Bob as there are by Joe, then if we come across a random knife murder, we should conclude the odds are 2:1 Bob was responsible. But suppose Bob commits 10 times as many murders as Joe. In that case, we will not find 100 murders by Bob for every 100 murders by Joe. We will find 1000 murders by Bob for every 100 murders we find by Joe. So suppose we have gone around the city looking for murder victims, and we have found 1000 murders by Bob and 100 by Joe, and it is still the case that we know that when Bob commits a murder he uses a knife 90% of the time and when Joe commits a murder he uses a knife 45% of the time. Now let us again ask: If we come across a random murder victim who died by a knife, what are the odds Bob committed the murder?

To answer this, imagine again a large series of trials. There are 1000 murders by Bob for every 100 murders by Joe. We have found 1000 murders by Bob, and since Bob uses a knife 90% of the time, 900 of those 1000 murder victims died by a knife. We have found 100 murders by Joe, and since Joe uses a knife 45% of the time, of those 100 murder victims, 45 died by a knife. We have grabbed a random knife victim and we want to know the odds he died by Bob. Well, in our collection there are 900 knife victims by Bob and 45 knife victims by Joe. 900 is 20 times greater than 45; there are 20 times as many people who were killed by a knife by Bob than were killed by a knife by Joe. Thus if we find a random knife victim, the odds are 20:1 in favor of Bob as the murderer.

Notice how much of an effect the initial probability can have. When the initial probability was neutral, when we had no reason in advance to think Bob committed the murder rather than Joe, the odds were only 2:1 in Bob's favor. But once we see the initial probability is 10:1 in Bob's favor, the odds become 20:1. We can see that the initial probability plays a very significant role in determining the odds a hypothesis is true.

The Theorem Itself

Thus far we have calculated a probability by counting up the outcomes of large numbers of trials. But mathematical formulas make this process easier. For example, suppose we wanted to know the odds a coin will come up heads 15 times in 20 tosses. One method of discovering this is to do lots of series of 20 coin flips and count up how many times we get heads 15 times. For example, if we do 100 series of 20 flips, and the coin comes up heads 15 times in only 2 of these series, we can conclude the odds are 20:2 (10:1) against a coin coming up heads 15 times in a series of 20 tosses. But that method will take a lot of time. It is quicker to use the binomial formula to arrive at the answer:

$$(a+b)^n = \sum_{k=0}^{n} \binom{n}{k} a^{n-k} b^k$$

If we put the numbers into this formula we can learn our odds of getting 15 heads in 20 tosses, without actually having to perform any tosses.

Our arriving at a probability that Bob committed murder by counting up the results of a large number of trials is like flipping a coin lots of times and counting up the results. But Bayes' Theorem gives us a formula to simplify the process. We can use Bayes' Theorem to get the same answer we got by counting up the results of a large number of trials; and that means Bayes' Theorem passes the test of whether a formula is accurate. That test being whether the formula gives you the same answer you would get if you counted up the results of a large number of trials.

We can arrive at the same answer of 20:1 if we do the following. First, we divide the odds that the victim will have died by a knife if Bob committed the murder (0.9) by the odds that the victim will have died by a knife if Joe committed the murder (0.45). This gives us odds of 2:1. Next, we see that Bob commits ten times as many murders as Joe. That means the probability Bob had committed the murder before we had the evidence of the knife was already 10:1 in Bob's favor. The evidence of the knife is 2:1 in favor of Bob by itself, and if we multiply 10:1 by 2:1 we will arrive at 20:1, the same answer we got by hypothetically performing a large series of trials and counting up the results. We can see that the method of BT is a three step process:

First, determine the probability of getting the data if the hypothesis is true vs. the probability of getting the data if the hypothesis is not true. (In the case of the murder example, this was 90% and 45%. If Bob committed the murder, there is a 90% chance the victim will have died by a knife, and if Joe committed the murder, there is a 45% chance the victim will have died by a knife. So if h is true, the odds of getting the data are 90%; if ~h is true the odds are 45%.)

Second, determine the odds ratio by dividing the two numbers. For example 90/45 gives us odds of 2:1. 75 and 25 would give us odds of 3:1. 100 and 10 would give us odds of 10:1, etc.[5]

Third, multiply these odds by the odds of the initial probability (2:1 x 10:1=20:1).

However, since BT is traditionally done by using a theorem instead of this process, it is time to see why all of this is expressed in the BT formula.

$$\frac{p(h|e)}{p(\sim h|e)} = \frac{p(h)}{p(\sim h)} \times \frac{p(e|h)}{p(e|\sim h)}$$

Recall that our hypothesis is that Bob committed the murder (h), and the negation of that hypothesis is that Bob did not commit the murder (~h) (and since Joe is the only other candidate, that means that in this particular case, the hypothesis that Bob did not commit the murder is equivalent to the hypothesis Joe did commit the murder). Thus we have a hypothesis (h), the negation of that hypothesis (~h), and a piece of evidence ("e"; the victim in question died by a knife). We want to know the odds our hypothesis is true given the evidence we have; we want to know the information on the left hand side of BT, which is: in the numerator of the equation, the probability of the hypothesis given the evidence, p (h|e), and in the denominator, the probability of the alternative hypothesis given the evidence, p (~h|e). We concluded that this was 20:1, the 20 representing p (h|e), and the 1 representing p (~h|e). But how did we arrive at that answer? By solving the right side of the equation. The top of the first part of the right side, p (h), means the initial probability of h, and the bottom

---

5. This is a convenient point at which to further explain the technical distinction between "probability" and "odds." When that distinction is made, "odds" is not used until we reach this second step of BT, where we compare h to ~h; prior to that, "probability" is used. That is, when we are performing the first step of BT, which I just explained in the second to last paragraph, we use the term "probability." Once we get those numbers, and we perform the second step—what I just referred to as determining the odds ratio—we use the term "odds." And "probability" is expressed on a scale of 0-1 (e.g., 0.1, 0.8) or 1%-100% (e.g., 10%, 80%), whereas "odds" are expressed as a ratio (e.g., 10:1, 4:1). Personally, I think the distinction is confusing, and so I simply use the two terms interchangeably, as all lay people do, and I do not reserve the colon notation for "odds" in the technical sense, since there is no reason to do so.

One other point to note is that some distinguish between odds in favor and odds against based on whether the larger number is on the left side of the colon or the right side. If the larger number is on the left side, that means odds against, whereas if the larger number is on the right side, that means odds in favor. For example, 4:1 means odds against; 1:4 means odds in favor. But I do not use the colon notation this way. If I mean the odds are 4 to 1 in favor, I will say 4:1 in favor, and if I mean the odds are 4 to 1 against, I will say 4:1 against.

of the first part of the right side, p (~h), means the initial probability of ~h. We said this was 10:1, the 10 for p (h) and the 1 for p (~ h). This information is to be multiplied by the information on the second half of the right side: p (e|h) (the probability of getting the evidence given that the hypothesis is true) on the top, and p (e|~h) on the bottom (the probability of getting the evidence given that the hypothesis is not true). (The second half of the right side is referred to as a "likelihood function.") We said this was 2:1, the 2 corresponding to the information on the top, p (e|h), and the 1 corresponding to the information on the bottom, p (e|~h). Hence we multiplied 10:1 by 2:1 and got an answer of 20:1. To put this in equation form:

$$\frac{20}{1} = \frac{10}{1} \times \frac{2}{1}$$

A Note on "b"

Before we proceed, it should be noted that some versions of BT include "b." Hence the equation would read:

$$\frac{p(h|e.b)}{p(\sim h|e.b)} = \frac{p(h|b)}{p(\sim h|b)} \times \frac{p(e|h.b)}{p(e|\sim h.b)}$$

As a matter of fact, "b" is an essential part of BT. Whenever it is not included, it is implied to be there. "B" stands for "background knowledge" (or "background evidence") and it refers to all of our knowledge other than the specific datum in question. The specific datum in question, as I have said, is "e." Thus if the datum is the fact that the murder weapon was a knife, b means all of our knowledge other than the fact that the murder weapon was a knife. The period sign (.) means "and." Thus, for example, "e.b" is read as "the specific evidence and the background knowledge." The point of b is that there are many other facts which affect our evaluation of the hypothesis other than the specific datum under examination at the moment. In the first place, b is the sole factor which determines the initial probability of the hypothesis, because since the initial probability is the probability our hypothesis is true before we examine the specific datum in question, the initial probability obviously cannot be based on the specific datum in question; it must be based on other data. And second, b also affects our evaluation of the specific datum in question (e), because our idea of the probability of e given the hypothesis, and the probability of e given ~h, does not come from out of nowhere; it comes from our knowledge. Suppose we think p (e|h) is high; suppose we think that if Bob committed murder, there is a high probability he would have used a knife. This thought did not come from out of nowhere; it came from those aspects of our knowledge relevant to determining the probability that if Bob committed murder he would use a knife. (In this case, the aspect of our knowledge which is relevant is the percentage of the time Bob has used a knife when he has committed murder.) Hence, p (e|h) is actually p (e|h.b). And if we think there is a low probability that if Bob did not commit the murder (~h) a knife would have been used, this thought did not come from out of nowhere; it came from those aspects of our knowledge relevant to determining that question. (In this case, the aspect of our knowledge which is relevant is the percentage of the time Joe has used a knife when he has committed murder.) Hence p (e|~h) is actually p (e|~h.b).

It should also be realized that since b means all of our knowledge other than the specific datum in question, there are many things in b which are relevant neither to establishing the prior probability nor to establishing the values for p (e|h.b) and p (e|~h.b). For example, the fact that there is a telephone pole outside my house will not help us establish either the prior probability that Bob committed murder, or either of the likelihood functions.

In conclusion, b means all of our knowledge other than the specific datum in question, and this knowledge can be divided into three categories: knowledge which helps us establish the prior probability, knowledge which helps us establish the values for p (e|h) and p (e|~h), and knowledge which does not help us in evaluating our hypothesis. The reason why b is often omitted is because we can take for granted what b tells us. We can take for granted that the prior probability does not come from out of nowhere, but comes from things in our knowledge other than the specific datum in question. We can take for granted that the values we assign to p (e|h) and p (e|~h) do not spring from out of nowhere, but come from things in our knowledge which cause us to think these probabilities are either low or high. And we can take for granted that we have some things in our knowledge which will not help us to evaluate the hypothesis.

BT in an Actual Case

Now that we understand BT, it will be helpful to see how it applies to an actual case instead of a hypothetical one. BT is often used in medicine to diagnose diseases. One example is heart disease. Suppose a doctor administers a test to see whether a patient has heart disease. It is not as simple as simply giving the patient the test, getting a positive result, and concluding he has the disease. No medical test is 100% accurate; it could tell us the patient has the disease, or tell us the patient does not have the disease, and could be wrong. The test's accuracy is determined by considering three essential quantities: the odds of getting a positive result on the test if the person has the disease (in BT terms, the odds of getting the evidence (the evidence in this case is a positive result on the test) given that the hypothesis is true), the odds of getting a positive result on the test if the person does not have the disease (the odds of getting the evidence given h is false), and the odds the patient has the disease prior to the administration of the test (the initial probability; the probability h is true before examining the specific evidence). Suppose the patient is a man in his sixties, and 10%

of men in their sixties have heart disease. The initial probability this patient has heart disease is thus 0.1; those are the odds he has heart disease prior to the administration of the test. Suppose the patient takes the test and there is a positive result, and suppose the odds of getting a positive result given that the person has the disease are 0.95 (95% of people with the disease test positive), and the odds of getting a positive result given that the person does not have the disease are 0.1 (10% of people without the disease test positive). The physician will take these three numbers, and put them into the BT equation to determine the odds the patient has the disease.[6]

We can also use this medical example to understand the third principle behind BT: that we update our beliefs in the light of new evidence. The doctor started with an initial probability of 0.1. He takes into account the results of the test, and arrives at a new probability (in this case, we had 0.1, 0.95, and 0.1, and that would give us 0.51). If he were to perform another test, the initial probability would no longer be 0.1, it would be 0.51. If he arrived at a final probability of 0.75 after the next test (a hypothesis's final probability is also called its epistemic probability), and he wanted to run yet another test, the new initial probability would be 0.75. The probabilities are updated each time there is new information.

(If you have the values for p (h), p (e|h), and p (e|~h) you can determine the solution without actually having to write out the theorem. You can simply use the calculator at: http://psych.fullerton.edu/mbirnbaum/bayes/BayesCalc.htm.)

Subjective Probability

So far we have demonstrated what everyone who is an expert on BT agrees with: If we can determine the values for p (e|h), p (e|~h), and the initial probability of h, BT will tell us the probability of h. But the disagreement lies in the question of whether we can always determine these probabilities. If we cannot, then BT cannot be applied every time we are evaluating a hypothesis, and so it cannot serve as the basis for all our logical thinking about hypotheses. Thus we need to consider the question of how widely BT applies.

The essential question in the debate is whether BT applies only when we are dealing with frequencies or whether it also applies when we are dealing with degrees of belief. If it only applies to frequencies, it can only apply to those hypotheses which are based on frequencies. If it applies to degrees of belief, then it applies to all hypotheses, since all hypotheses involve degrees of belief. Those who contend that it applies only to frequencies are called objectivists. Those who contend that BT also applies to degrees of belief are called Bayesians. (But see the appendix to this chapter for other definitions of "Bayesian" and "objectivist.")

---

6. For a more detailed explanation of the use of BT in medical evaluation, see Harold C. Sox, Marshal A. Blatt, Michael C. Higgins, and Keith I. Martin, *Medical Decision Making* (Philadelphia: American College of Physicians, 2006), 67-101.

In order to understand what the two sides are talking about, we must of course understand what frequencies are and what degrees of belief are. A frequency means how often an event happens. The examples we considered above all involved frequencies, because I wanted to begin by using examples that everyone would agree with. In the murder example, we had the frequency that Bob and Joe commit murder, and the frequency that they commit murder with knives. In the hot dog example, we had the frequency with which they eat hot dogs and the frequency with which they put mustard on their hot dogs. In the heart disease example, we had the frequency with which a person has heart disease, the frequency with which a person with the disease gets a positive result on the test, and the frequency with which a person without the disease gets a positive result on the test. In each case, we determined the probability by asking how frequently an event happens. But when probability is used in reference to degrees of belief we mean something different. We mean not how frequently an event happens, but how much confidence we have in the truth of a proposition. For example, if I say it is probable that God exists, or that it is improbable the Earth is flat, I am expressing different degrees of confidence. And my belief is not based on frequencies—how frequently God exists or how frequently the Earth is flat—it is based on other kinds of evidence.

Now according to Bayesianism, we can do more than simply express degrees of confidence in terms of words such as high, low, very high, very low, and so on. According to Bayesianism, we can put numbers on these degrees of confidence, and say for example that I am 80% sure Harry stole the ice cream, or that I am 20% sure Sally took the car out. Objectivists contend that you cannot do this with degrees of belief; degrees of belief don't work like frequencies. Intuitively, we can feel the force of both sides. On the one hand, we have all probably had at least one experience where someone asked us to put a number on our degree of belief by asking, "what percent sure are you?" and we have probably obliged by offering at least an approximate percentage. On the other hand, we probably recall that our estimates in such cases were never very exact. What I will show is that the Bayesians have it right; we can put numbers on our degrees of belief, even though we may not have great confidence in a specific number (but I will also show that the objectivists have it right in a way too).

The Principles of BT

Before we show that the BT formula itself applies to degrees of belief, I first want to show that the three principles behind the formula apply. These principles are, again: 1) The value of initial probability—the lower the initial probability of h, the more strongly the specific evidence must support the hypothesis; the higher the initial probability of h, the less strongly the specific evidence needs to support the hypothesis. 2) The force of the specific evidence is determined by asking: What are the odds you would get the data if h is true vs. what are the odds you would get the data if h is false (consequent probability). 3) The fact that the probability of h is updated each time you acquire new evidence. If it is admitted that these three principles all apply to degrees of belief, we have taken a significant step towards admitting that BT itself applies to degrees of belief. For if the principles apply, the only remaining questions are whether numbers can be applied to degrees of belief and whether the numbers relate to each other in the same way they do when BT is used for frequencies (e.g., whether we multiply the same things we multiplied and divide the same things we divided). Thus I will here consider various hypotheses, hypotheses whose values cannot be determined by frequencies, and show how these three principles are what human beings subconsciously use to determine whether their hypotheses are true.

Initial Probability

This is the degree of confidence we have that Bob committed the murder before we examine the evidence. In our original example, we pretended we knew Bob commits 10 times as many murders as Joe and thus our odds were 10:1 in Bob's favor. In real life, we are not likely to know the total number of murders that Bob and Joe have committed; neither of them may have committed any murders. However we may have other reasons for thinking it is likelier that one of them committed the murder before we examine the evidence. Suppose we know Bob has a history of violent behavior whereas Joe has no such history. Or suppose we can think of a motive as to why Bob would want to commit the murder, but we can think of no such motive for Joe. In such cases, our estimate of the odds Bob committed the murder will be higher in advance of examining the evidence. Thus our judgment of murder cases depends not just on the evidence actually adduced, but also on our estimate of the odds prior to examining the specific evidence.

To take another example, it is easy to see how the principle of initial probability applies to an alleged case of alien abduction. If we hear a claim of something extraordinary, such as an alien abduction, we will certainly require stronger evidence than for an ordinary claim. For example, suppose a child misses school, and claims he missed it because he was sick, and he produces a note from his mother saying he was sick. We would accept this as sufficient evidence. However, suppose that instead of claiming he was sick, he claims he missed school because he was abducted by aliens, and he produces a note from his mother saying this is so. Here we have the exact same evidence—a note from his mother. But though we believed him on the basis of this evidence in the first case, we will not believe him in the second. Why? Because the initial probability is lower. There are plenty of cases of people getting sick but there are no clear cases of abduction by aliens. Since the initial probability is lower, stronger evidence is required; a higher initial probability means less strong evidence is required.

Bayes' Theorem

Consequent Probability

According to BT, in order to answer the question "what are the odds h is true given the data we have?" p (h|e), we have to turn it around and ask "what are the odds of getting the data we have if h is true?" p (e|h), and "what are the odds of getting the data we have if h is false?" p (e|~h). This is consequent probability, and it strikes us as counterintuitive, but it is clearly what human beings do for every hypothesis they test. Take for example, the hypothesis Bob committed murder. Suppose we are evaluating the following piece of evidence: Bob's fingerprints were found at the scene of the crime. If h is true (Bob committed the murder) it is likely we will find Bob's fingerprints at the scene of the crime. But if h is false (if Bob did not commit the murder), it is highly unlikely we will find Bob's fingerprints at the scene of the crime (presuming Bob does not have some good explanation for why his fingerprints were at the scene of the crime). There is a vast difference between the probability of getting the datum if h is true vs. the probability of getting the datum if h is false. If the defense lawyer wants to rebut this argument, he will do so by trying to narrow the gap between the probability of getting the datum on h vs. ~h. For example, suppose Bob lives in the house in which the murder took place. In that case, we would expect to find Bob's fingerprints at the scene of the crime even if h is false. If that is so, the datum is highly likely given both h and ~h.

Or take the hypothesis of alien abduction. Perhaps the child who claims he was abducted will argue that there are strange indentations in the ground at his house, and thus a UFO probably landed there. He is implicitly arguing that: if h is true (if he was abducted by aliens) we should expect to find strange indentations in his yard, but if h is false (if he was not abducted by aliens) we should not expect to find such indentations. Now suppose the skeptic combats this argument by pointing out that a wheelbarrow was used in the yard that day and that this could account for the strange indentations. The skeptic is arguing that the datum is just as likely on ~h as on h: we are just as likely to get the datum in question (the indentations) if aliens did not land as we are if they did land. Since the datum is equally to be expected on either hypothesis, we are right back where we were when we had only the initial probability, which means the alien hypothesis is improbable.

In these two examples, we have seen how a piece of data can be more expected on h than not h, and that when this happens the data favors h. We should lay out all of the hypothetical relationships between h and ~h.

The probability of getting the evidence may be higher on h than on ~h. This happens when we have a good argument for h. For example, suppose Bob was seen at the scene of the crime. This is expected if h is true (if Bob committed the murder), but unexpected if h is false (presuming Bob has no good explanation for why he was at the house). Hence the evidence supports h. The greater the disparity between the odds of getting the evidence if h is true and the odds of getting the evidence if h is false, the more strongly the evidence supports h. For example, suppose Bob visited the house where the murder took place once every few months. In this case, the evidence of Bob being at the house is more likely given h than given ~h (if he committed the murder he certainly should have been at the house, but if he did not commit the murder there is only a slight chance he would have been at the house), so the datum supports h. But suppose Bob had never visited the house before. Here, ~h would require us to suppose that the day of the murder just happened to correspond not just with one of the few days Bob happened to visit the house, but with the only day Bob ever visited the house. Bob's being at the house is even less likely on ~h in this scenario than in the previous one, hence there is a greater disparity between how probable the datum is on h vs. how probable it is on ~h, and therefore the datum more strongly supports h than in the previous scenario.

The probability of getting the evidence may be higher on ~h than on h. This happens when we have a good argument against h. For example, suppose Bob presents a plane ticket showing he was in another country on the day the murder occurred. This is much more likely if h is false (if Bob did not commit the murder) than if h is true. As with the first example, the greater the disparity between ~h and h, the greater the probability is on behalf of ~h.

The probability of getting the evidence may be high on both h and ~h. This happens when the evidence is to be expected if h is true but also if h is false. In such a case, the evidence supports neither hypothesis. For example, suppose the defense argues that Bob was seen at the scene of the crime because the crime took place at his house. If this is true, the evidence of Bob being seen at the scene of the crime is equally to be expected on h and ~h (we should expect him to have been there if he committed the murder and we expect him to have been there if he did not commit the murder). Or suppose the prosecution argues that though Bob has a plane ticket allegedly showing he was in another country, it is not clear whether the ticket was actually used. In this case, the evidence is to be expected on both h and ~h (if Bob was really in another country like he says, we should expect him to have a plane ticket for that day; but if he was trying to cover up a murder we should also expect him to lie about this).

The probability of getting the evidence may be low on both h and ~h. This happens when neither hypothesis predicts the data in question very well. For example, suppose Bob and Joe both belong to a gang, and this gang despises blue handkerchiefs. But the murder weapon was wrapped in a blue handkerchief. This is unlikely if Bob committed the murder and also unlikely if Joe committed the murder. In such a situation, we would be tempted to look for a third hypothesis which explains the datum better, but of course, in our hypothetical case, we have determined Bob and Joe are the only viable suspects, and thus we are stuck with the fact that either Bob or Joe did something which it would seem improbable for them to do. (Of course, if we were not convinced on other grounds that Bob and Joe were the only two conceivable suspects, the presence of the blue handkerchief, something which is not predicted well on either hypothesis, would lead us to look for other suspects.)

The Distinction Between Absolute Probability and Relative Probability

An important point needs to be noted here: The disparity between the values of p (e|h) and p (e|~h) is more important than the values of p (e|h) and p (e|~h). One could easily commit the mistake of thinking that the higher is the probability of the datum given h, the better off the hypothesis is, and the higher is the probability of the datum given ~h, the worse off the hypothesis is. For example, if the probability of getting the datum given h is 0.9, we might be tempted to think that the datum strongly supports h. Or if the probability of the datum given h is 0.1 we might be tempted to think the datum does not support h. By contrast, we might be tempted to think that if the probability of the datum given ~h is 0.9, this strongly supports ~h, and if the probability of the datum given ~h is 0.1, this does not support ~h. But in fact, none of this is the case. The key question with regard to how much a datum supports a hypothesis is not the probability of the datum given h, or the probability of the datum given ~h, *but the disparity between the probability of the datum given h and the probability of the datum given ~h*. For example, suppose the probability of the datum given h is 0.1; suppose the probability is 0.1 that if Bob committed murder he would use a knife. But suppose the probability Joe would use a knife if he committed murder is 0.01. Even though the odds are low Bob would use a knife, we have a knife, and so we know one of them must have used a knife, and since the odds are 100 times lower Joe would use a knife, this datum favors h by odds of 100:1. Thus a low number for p (e|h) will still support h very much if the number for p (e|~h) is even lower (and the converse is necessarily true, a low number for ~h still supports ~h if the number for h is even lower). Likewise, a high number for h does not necessarily support h (and the same is true for ~h). For example, suppose the probability of getting a datum given h is true is high: suppose the probability Bob would use a knife if he committed murder is 0.9. If the probability Joe would use a knife if he committed murder is also 0.9, h is not any better off than it was before we had the datum.

Because of this issue, one should be aware that in a discussion of probability, the terms "high" and "low" may mean different things depending on the context. A high probability may mean high relative to a value of 100%. Thus if p (e|h) is 0.9 and p (e|~h) is 0.9, we might say that in each case the probability is high. Likewise, a low probability may mean low relative to 100%. Thus if p (e|h) is 0.1 and p (e|~h) is 0.1, we might say that in each case the probability is low. If this is how we are using the terms, we are referring to the "absolute probability" of getting a datum given a hypothesis (100% being an absolute standard). However, if p (e|h) is 0.1 and p (e|~h) is 0.01, we might also say that the probability of the evidence given h is high. For though 0.1 is not high when it is compared to 100%, it is high when it is compared to ~h's value of 0.01. Likewise, if p (e|h) is 0.95 and p (e|~h) is 0.85, we might say the probability of the evidence given ~h is low. For though 0.85 might seem rather high compared to 100%, our point is that the evidence is lower given ~h than given h. If we are using the terms in this sense, we are referring to a datum's "relative probability." That is, the probability of getting a datum given one hypothesis relative to the probability of getting the datum given another hypothesis. (I will elaborate on this point in chapter 7.)

We should also note concerning the initial probability and the relationship between p (e|h) and p (e|~h), that we can see not only that they relate to each other, but that they relate to each other at least in the general way BT says. The lower the initial probability, the more convincing the specific evidence must be. The greater the disparity between p (e|h) and p (e|~h), the stronger or weaker the hypothesis is.

We Update Our Beliefs with New Evidence

This is the most obvious point. In the case of Bob and Joe's murder, we would not consider only the first piece of evidence we come across. We may believe on the basis of the first datum, say the fact that the murder was committed with a knife, that Bob committed the murder, but this is surely not the end of the case. More evidence may arise in support of the hypothesis Bob committed the murder (such as that Bob's fingerprints were found at the scene of the crime, that a witness saw Bob going into the house, etc), or more evidence may arise which may make us change our original judgment about Bob's guilt (we may find that the witness who thought they saw him does not have very good vision, or that Bob can prove he was in another state on the day the murder took place). And this same procedure applies not only to murder hypotheses, but to every other hypothesis.

Can Numbers Be Put on Degrees of Belief?

Clearly, the principles behind BT do apply to our everyday probability assessments of hypotheses. But we still have to settle the question of whether numbers can be put on degrees of beliefs, and the question of whether those numbers relate to each other in the way BT says they do. There are two strong arguments for the fact that numbers can be put on degrees of belief.

First, in the case of the large majority of our beliefs, we can indisputably say that the probability of the belief being true is either more probable than not, or less probable than not, or exactly equal. If you are presented with a proposition, you will likely say that you think the proposition is more probable than not, less probable than not, or that the probability is exactly equal. (The only type of proposition for which this is arguably not the case is a proposition the probability of which you think is unknown, though some contend that in this case, the probability is not unknown because an

BAYES' THEOREM

"unknown" probability actually equals 50%.) But this admission necessarily means that numbers apply to degrees of belief. For if you say your hypothesis is more probable than not, you are saying its probability is between 51%-99%. If you say it is less probable than not, you are saying its probability is between 1%-49%. If you say the probability is equal, you are saying its probability is exactly 50% Thus at the very least, it is clear that a broad range of numbers can be put on your degrees of belief, and it then becomes a question of to what extent you can narrow the range.

Second, consider the matter of laying odds. Suppose you are asked to accept bets on a game between the Bobbers and Whips. Suppose the Bobbers are much better than the Whips, and so an even money bet would not be fair. An even money bet means both sides put up the same amount: Both bet $10 and if you win, you win $10, and if you lose, you lose $10. But since the Bobbers are the favorites, it wouldn't be fair for the bettors to place even money bets, since the Bobbers are much more likely to win. In this situation the bets have to be weighted so that the people betting on the favorites put up more money than those betting on the underdogs. Thus we will see that someone is a 5:1 favorite, a 10:1 favorite, etc. To understand how this process of determining fair odds works, let us first consider a case where it occurs with frequencies rather than with subjective probabilities.

Consider the poker machines at casinos where you play the machine and try to get a poker hand, and if you win, the machine pays out a certain amount of money based on which type of hand you get. For example, the odds of getting a royal flush are 649,740:1. If you bet $1 and the machine paid out $649,740:1, both sides would be getting a fair bet, for they would both come out even in the long run. If you played it 649,740 times you would lose a dollar 649,739 in a row, but then win it all back on the 649,740th time.[7] In fact, casinos don't pay out this way. The payout for such a game is always less than the fair one (in this case less than 649,740:1), so the player would surely lose in the long run. (Although the payout would probably be large, say 200,000:1, so that the excitement of big payouts will deceive the players into thinking they have a chance. For example, a player loses one dollar 649,740 times in a row, but does not keep track of how much he has lost. He then wins $200,000 on the next play, and thinks he has won a lot, not realizing he is out $449,740.) But though casinos do not pay out with fair odds, we can see how it would work if the odds were fair. Now to return to subjective probability, ask yourself, if you had to lay odds on the basketball game, what odds would be the fairest odds to lay? Suppose you, unlike the casino, want to make the bet fair for both players. And suppose you decide that the fairest odds are 10:1 on the favorite. That means you think the probability is 90% the favorite will win. Thus you are admitting that probabilities do apply to beliefs.

---

7. This statement is simplified for illustrative purposes. You will not necessarily lose the first 649,739 times and win the 639,740th time. You will in the long run win 1 out of every 639,740 times, but the one win could come at any point during the 639,740 trials; it will not necessarily come on the very last trial.

Now you may object that you are not very confident in your belief, and this lack of confidence means that probability cannot apply to it. But this is not the case. There is no problem with greater or lesser amounts of confidence applying to subjective beliefs, since greater or lesser amounts of confidence apply to calculations based on frequencies too. This is what confidence intervals are. We have all probably seen the results of a poll which stated that the results were, for example, 53% with a margin of error of 3% and a 95% confidence interval. This means the pollsters think the likeliest number is 53%, but they are not absolutely certain of this single number; they are 95% sure the answer lies between 50-56%. In the same way, while you may not be 95% sure the odds are 10:1, you may think 10:1 is the likeliest number and, just like in a poll, you may be able to specify a range. You may be able to say, for example, that you are 90% sure the true odds are somewhere between 10:1 and 100:1. You may often have to specify a very broad range, but you will be able to specify some sort of range.

Further, there is definite empirical proof both that numbers can be applied to degrees of belief and that human beings can be successful at specifying subjective probabilities more specific than 51-99%. The way sports betting works, bettors have to win 53% of their bets in order to make a profit in the long run.[8] This is because bets are always laid at odds of 11:10 (52%-48%) in favor of the bookie. Bettors thus have to make subjective judgments on the odds each time they place a bet; the odds are not gotten from frequencies. So if bettors just guess, or if their subjective belief somehow cannot be translated into numbers, they will not win in the long run. And for them to place the bet, they must be confident they are going to win at least 53% of the time. So for them to win: 1) it must be possible to translate degrees of confidence into numbers, and 2) they must be able to narrow their confidence interval from 51%-99% to at the very least 53%-99%, since they need to get to 53% in order to win. And since some sports bettors actually are successful in the long run,[9] we can conclude that these people are able to accurately narrow their range of subjective probability from 51-99% to at least 53%-99%. And if it is possible to narrow your range to 53%-99% it is possible to narrow it still further. And if this is possible in the case of your beliefs about who will win a sports contest, it is possible in the case of your beliefs about anything else. Of course, some people are better at this than others; some people win at sports betting more often than others do. This is because some people have better judgment than others. Some people win more of their "bets" on things in life than others do.

So for these reasons, numbers can be put on degrees of belief.

---

8. This is so for the most common type of bet, the "spread bet." But there are various other types of bets.

9. See for example the website: http://www.professionalgambler.com/. They place their predictions on their website before the games are actually played, and if you examine their record, you will find that they have won over 53% of the time in the long run.

Bayes' Theorem

Do the Numbers Relate in the Way BT Says?

We have seen that the principles behind BT apply to degrees of confidence, and that degrees of confidence can be expressed in numbers. Thus the only remaining question is whether degrees of confidence, when they are expressed in numbers, fit together as frequencies do, that is, whether they fit together in the way BT proposes. Now we have already seen above that degrees of confidence do fit together in the way BT proposes in a general sense. We have looked at initial probability, the relationship between p (e|h) and p (e|~h), and the fact that we update our beliefs in light of new evidence, and we saw that we do these things in real life just as we do them with BT. The question is now simply whether the numbers fit together in exactly the way BT proposes—whether we can take the numbers and put them into the BT equation.

That degrees of confidence do indeed fit together in this way is clear once we realize the following fact: *Degrees of confidence are frequencies.*[10] They are frequencies of the number of times beliefs that are supported by the same amount of evidence as the belief in question have proven right in the past. To understand this, suppose you think a certain belief has a 75% chance of being true. What you mean when you say this, is that the amount of evidence for this belief has made you 75% sure the belief is true. But why has that amount of evidence made you 75% sure it is true? It must surely be because, as best you can tell with your sense of judgment, beliefs supported by the amount of evidence which that belief has, have been right 75% of the time in the past.

I submit that this explanation is the only way of making sense of why you would believe a belief is 75% likely to be true. For a belief which you begin to hold will be supported by a certain amount of evidence, and there will have been other beliefs which you have encountered in the past which were supported by the same amount of evidence; and what other rational way is there of deciding the odds that this belief is true other than to look at how often beliefs of that sort have been right in the past? For all sides agree that if a frequency can tell you how often a certain event occurs, then that frequency is the probability of that event. For example, if a test has in the past correctly diagnosed 95% of the people with the disease, then you assume the probability that the person in question has the disease is 95%, because you assume the frequencies that applied in the past will apply in the future. Thus once we see that we are being presented with a possible belief with a certain amount of evidence, and we know that beliefs with that amount of evidence have been right a certain frequency of the time in the past (e.g., 75%), it would be foolish not to accept this frequency as the probability that that belief will be right in the future.[11]

---

10. Carrier, *Proving History*, 265-80.

11. I would allow for the possibility that some of the probabilities we assign may be based on our innate feelings rather than our past experience of frequencies. For example, why would a young child, upon seeing the ocean for the first time, run towards it, implicitly assigning a low probability to the hypothesis that the ocean will harm him? Perhaps because he has an innate sense that this is so. But if some of the probabilities we assign are of this nature, not very many of them are. Further, such

Jesus' Resurrection and Apparitions

To understand this matter further, let us again pretend to count up the results of a large number of trials. Suppose we consider again the hypotheses that Bob or Joe committed murder. We again have the datum that a knife was used, and so have to ask again, what is the probability Bob would use a knife if he committed murder (h), and what is the probability Joe would use a knife if he committed murder (~h)? Except this time, we have no frequencies to tell us the probability; Bob and Joe have never to our knowledge committed murder with a knife before, so we cannot count up the past occurrences Bob used a knife and the past occurrences Joe used a knife. We need to analyze the evidence and make a subjective judgment as to the probability that Bob would use a knife if he committed a murder and that Joe would use a knife if he committed a murder. Suppose we look at the evidence and we judge that there is a 60% chance Bob would use a knife and a 30% chance Joe would use a knife. (Our evidence in this case could be, for example, that the knife has a picture of a cartoon character on it, and we know Joe is fairly fond of cartoon characters, so the probability is not especially low Joe would have such a knife, but Bob is fonder of cartoon characters, so the probability is higher Bob would have such a knife.) Our beliefs are frequencies because we are saying that of beliefs supported by the amount of evidence as the belief "Bob would use a knife," 60% of those beliefs have turned out to be correct in the past; and of the beliefs which are supported by the amount of evidence in support of the belief "Joe would use a knife," 30% have turned out to be correct in the past. We can understand this by imagining the results of a large number of trials, just as we did when we were dealing with ordinary frequencies. Suppose we have 100 beliefs supported by the same amount of evidence that we have in support of our belief Bob would use a knife, and 100 beliefs supported by the same amount of evidence we have in support of our belief Joe would use a knife (take any belief, and we can find 100 beliefs in our minds somewhere supported by approximately the same amount of evidence). When we say we are 60% sure Bob would use a knife, we mean that of those 100 beliefs we have which are supported by the same amount of evidence, 60 of them have turned out to be true in the past. And when we say we are 30% sure Joe would use a knife, we mean of those 100 beliefs which are supported by the same amount of evidence as this belief, 30 of them have turned out to be true in the past. Hence in our collection of 200 beliefs—100 supported by the same amount of evidence as our belief Bob used a knife and 100 supported by the same amount of evidence as our belief Joe used a knife—60 of those supported by the same amount of evidence as our belief Bob would use a knife have turned out to be true and 30 of those supported by the same amount of evidence as our belief Joe would use a knife have turned out to be true. Hence there are twice as many beliefs in category 1 that have turned out to be true as there are in category 2 (60 versus 30). Hence if we take a random belief from

---

probabilities would still be based upon frequencies of things which have happened to other people. The young child's belief that it is safe to run towards the ocean has its basis in the fact that when other people have done this, only a low frequency of the time has this resulted in danger.

this collection, the odds are 60:30 (2:1) we will get a belief in category 1 than that we will get a belief in category 2.

But how does initial probability fit in here? Now it is time to explain more exactly how we update our beliefs in the light of new evidence. Let us suppose the initial probability is neutral. We have no more reason to suspect Bob committed the murder than that Joe committed it. Hence, the odds at this point, before we consider any evidence, are exactly 50%. Now consider our first datum: the evidence of the knife. We have determined there is a 60% chance that if Bob committed the murder he would use a knife and a 30% chance that if Joe committed the murder he would use a knife, because we have said, of hypotheses in the past which have been supported by the same amount of evidence as "if Bob committed the murder he would use a knife," 60% have proven right in the past, and of hypotheses supported by the same amount of evidence as "if Joe committed murder he would use a knife," 30% have proven right in the past. Thus we multiply the initial probability, in this case 50%, that is, 1:1, by the probability of h in proportion to ~h (60/30=2:1). Thus, 1:1 x 2:1 = 2:1. Now suppose there is another datum: Bob's fingerprints were found at the scene of the crime. Suppose we think that if Bob committed the murder, his fingerprints should certainly have been there. We assign the odds of getting this datum if h is true (if Bob committed the murder) as being nearly 100%. We are confident that if we take a look at beliefs supported by the same amount of evidence as the belief "if Bob committed the murder his fingerprints would be on the knife," we will be right 99 out of 100 times. Now suppose we assign a probability of getting this on ~h as 10%, because Bob was able to convince us he had a decent reason why he could have been there; he does sometimes visit there, though not very often. We are convinced that of other hypotheses we have seen with that amount of evidence, about 10% have turned out right. Imagine again: We have 100 beliefs supported by the same amount of evidence as "if Bob committed murder, his fingerprints would be on the knife," and 99 of 100 of them have proved accurate in the past; we have 100 beliefs supported by the same amount of evidence as "if Bob did not commit the murder, his fingerprints would be on the knife" and 10 of those have proved to be right in the past. Thus we have one collection of 60 and 30, and another collection of 99 and 10. Our odds are 2:1 and 10:1 (more exactly, 9.9:1). For h to be true, we must win on a bet of 2:1 and a bet of 10:1. For ~h to be true, we must do the opposite and win on bets of 1:2 and 1:10. Thus far, 1:1 x 2:1 x 10:1 =20:1. The odds thus far are 20:1 in favor of h.

Then we get another datum: we find out Bob had a personal vendetta against the murdered man. We judge that if Bob committed the murder there is around a 0.80 chance he would have previous feelings of hostility against the man (people do not usually commit murder from out of the blue). But since a person is also likely to also feel hostility against people whom they have no intention of murdering, we judge that if Bob did not commit the murder there is a 0.1 chance he would have hostility towards the murdered man, since Bob is hostile towards a fairly low percentage of people whom he will not murder. Now, 0.8 and 0.1 gives us 8:1. So far we have 2:1 and 10:1, and 8:1 in favor of Bob. That's 160:1.

But now suppose we get some evidence in favor of Joe. Suppose we find out Joe also had feelings of hostility towards the murdered man. This gives us some reason to think Joe committed the murder. Previous feelings of hostility we said is 8 times as likely if the person committed murder, so that gives us 8:1 in favor of Joe. That means we now have three arguments in favor of Bob (10:1, 2:1, 8:1, giving us 160:1), and one in favor of Joe, 8:1. We multiply $\frac{160}{1} \times \frac{1}{8}$ and get 20:1 in favor of Bob. It is as if we have two poker players who are going to play four hands of poker, and we have to bet on who will win the most chips. The first hand, Bob has a 2:1 advantage, the second hand, Bob has a 10:1 advantage, the third hand, Bob has an 8:1 advantage. The fourth hand, Joe has an 8:1 advantage. Overall, Bob has a 20:1 advantage. Thus we should bet on Bob.

(The only aspect of this analogy which may not make sense is that it seems as if we are assuming either Bob will win all his hands, or Joe will win all his hands. Now in a real poker game, it is of course possible Bob could win on some hands and lose on others. But in this case, we know the propositions which the "hands" support are mutually exclusive. Either Bob committed the murder or Joe did. If, for example, we won on Bob for the bets of 2:1 and 10:1 and lost on the bets of 8:1 and 1:8, we would discover that Bob both had and had not committed the murder, which is impossible. Thus the closer analogy is not to imagine we are betting on each hand, but to imagine we are betting, as I said, on who will win the most chips over the course of all five hands; for the question of who will win the most chips presents us with a mutually exclusive proposition (either Bob will win the most chips or Joe will) and thus we have a closer analogy to the question of murder, where either Bob committed the murder or Joe did.)

A Note on Dependence

In all of the examples we have considered above, we have assumed that the factors in question are independent of each other. That is, we have assumed the probability of getting one datum is not affected by the probability of getting another datum. But we should note that this is not always the case. For example, suppose Bob commits murder every 30 days and Joe commits murder every 20 days, and suppose we ask the question: what are the odds Bob and Joe will both commit murder on the same day? If the factors are independent—if when Bob commits murder is not affected by when Joe commits murder, and if when Joe commits murder is not affected by when Bob commits murder—then the odds would be 20:1 x 30:1 = 600:1. However, let us suppose that half the time Joe commits murder he does so without knowing whether Bob committed one, and half the time Joe commits murder he intentionally chooses a day on which Bob has committed one. That means that if Bob committed a murder, the odds are 2:1 Joe committed one. Thus the odds Bob and Joe will both commit murder on the same day are not 30:1 x 20:1, but 30:1 x 2:1 = 60:1.

Objections

Though what I have said so far may seem persuasive, there are a number of objections to Bayesianism which need to be considered. These are as follows.[12]

Objection 1: The whole notion of subjective probability is . . . too subjective. People will not agree on which numbers to put into the equation. Different people will pick different numbers, and if different numbers are put in we will of course get different answers. Thus the use of BT will simply result in subjective chaos.

Response: The essential point to make in response is that subjective is not the same as arbitrary. Although the numbers are subjective, in the sense of relying on a person's judgment, that does not mean the person can make up whatever numbers they want. They are supposed to have reasons for choosing the numbers they do. If people disagree on these numbers it is because they disagree on the reasons for the numbers, and since we have shown that the process of BT underlies our rational thought, this objection only shows that people disagree on what reasons there are to think certain things true.

However, lying behind this objection is an important point which we must admit: It is not possible for us to put exact numbers on our degrees of belief; we must be satisfied with approximations. I cannot say that I am 51.7% sure that a given basketball team will win the championship this year; I can only say that I do not have much of an idea, and so the probability is somewhere around 50%. Likewise, I cannot say that I am 99.96% sure the Earth is round; I can only say that my belief in this is exceptionally strong and thus very near 100%.

But this limitation on the use of BT does not invalidate its use. It only means that when we assign probabilities to propositions we will have to be content with the fact that the probabilities we assign are approximations, and hence our final conclusion will also be an approximation. But an approximate answer is still an acceptable answer; and since BT underlies logical thought, even if we do not use BT consciously, we are still assigning approximate probabilities as we work out the probability of a

---

12. Objections to Bayesianism can be found in both the literature specifically concerned with Bayes' Theorem (e.g., Clark N. Glymour, *Theory and Evidence* (Princeton: Princeton University Press, 1980), 63-93; Richard W. Miller, *Fact and Method* (Princeton: Princeton University Press, 1987), 267-345)) and in the literature on the resurrection (William Lane Craig in William Lane Craig and Bart Ehrman, "Is There Historical Evidence for the Resurrection of Jesus? A Debate between William Lane Craig and Bart D. Ehrman," College of the Holy Cross, Worcester, MA, March 28, 2006, p. 32, transcript available at http://www.reasonablefaith.org/site/DocServer/resurrection-debate-transcript.pdf?docID=621; Michael R. Licona, *The Resurrection of Jesus: A New Historiographical Approach* (Downers Grove, IL: IVP Academic, 2010), 114-120).

hypothesis subconsciously. Thus refraining from using BT consciously will not solve the limitation of not being able to put exact numbers on our subjective probabilities. This limitation is simply one of the limitations of human thinking.

But if someone is not comfortable using numbers, we should say that it is possible to use BT without consciously using numbers, though you should be aware that you are still using numbers subconsciously. If you do not feel comfortable assigning numbers to the initial probability, the probability of the evidence given h, and the probability of the evidence given ~h, you can simply use the words "high" and "low" with appropriate qualifiers (e.g., "very high," "very low," "pretty high," pretty low"). The essential questions are the highness or lowness of p (e|h), and of p (e|~h), and of the initial probability. If you think the initial probability of h is low, the question is whether the probability of the evidence given h is so much higher than the probability of the evidence given ~h, that the lowness of the initial probability can be overcome. If you think the initial probability of h is high, the question is whether the probability of the evidence given h is so much lower than the probability of the evidence given ~h, that the high initial probability of h is not enough for h to remain probable. Thus you can do BT by simply asking the following questions. First, the three preliminary questions: 1) What is the probability of the datum given h? 2) What is the probability of the datum given ~h? 3) What is the initial probability of h? And once these three questions have been answered, you can use your answers to those questions to answer the following questions: 4) How great is the disparity between the probability of the datum given h and the probability of the datum given ~h? 5) How much does the disparity between the probability of the datum given h and the probability of the datum given ~h raise or lower the initial probability of h? You can answer these questions without using numbers, but since we have explained that the numerical calculation is the subconscious process which underlies our logical thinking, you should know that you are using numbers subconsciously.

Objection 2: Some events of history are unique, and in that case there is no initial probability. If there is no initial probability BT cannot be applied.

Response: If an event is unique, this does not mean that there is no initial probability. It only means the initial probability cannot be determined from frequencies, since if an event is unique, there have been no previous occurrences of it and thus the frequency of the event cannot be established. But as we have seen, probability is not dependent only on frequencies. Initial probability is determined from whatever facts form our background knowledge prior to our examination of the evidence. For example, if Bob has never committed murder before, and thus this event is unique, we cannot use the frequency with which Bob commits murders to determine the initial probability. But there might be other facts in our background knowledge relevant to whether Bob would commit the murder. For example, if we knew of a motive for him to commit the murder, or if we knew he had talked of murder.

Objection 3: Subjective probability has been explained by imagining people placing bets. But suppose someone refused to place a bet.

Response: Although you could refuse to place a literal bet on a literal gambling proposition (if my friend asks me to bet on a basketball game, I could refuse), you can never actually refuse to "place bets" when it comes to choosing beliefs. For when we have spoken of placing bets, we have not meant actual monetary wagers, but choosing which beliefs to accept. When we spoke of betting on a belief, we meant choosing to regard a belief as probable, and we have considered what is the best way of determining whether a belief is probable. The only way to refuse to do this is to refuse to make a judgment on whether the belief is probable, which is to say, refuse to examine the evidence for the belief.

Objection 4: BT cannot be used to evaluate the probability that a person with free will would commit a certain action, because it is not possible to know how a person with free will will exercise their free will, and thus the probability is inscrutable.

Response: There is no reason why a probability cannot be assigned to the odds that a free will action will be performed. Simply because a person with free will could exercise their free will in any way they wish, that does not mean every possible way in which they may exercise their free will is equally likely to happen. For example, suppose every Saturday for the last two years Bob has played poker. Suppose I am considering the hypothesis that he is going to play poker this Saturday. Now this involves a free will action (Bob must freely choose to play poker), but clearly the probability is not inscrutable. From the fact that Bob has played poker every Saturday, I am justified in saying that there is a high degree of probability he will play poker this Saturday. Likewise, consider sports betting. If I am going to bet on a basketball game, for me to win my bet, I must be confident that a variety of free will actions are likely to happen. The players must of their own free will arrive at the game. They must freely choose to play in the game. They must freely choose to play the game in the way that I am expecting them to play for me to win (e.g., they cannot intentionally mess up all the plays).

Conclusion

To repeat the most essential point, BT involves a three step process which is as follows:

First, determine the odds of getting the datum if the hypothesis is true vs. the odds of getting the datum if the hypothesis is not true. (In the case of the murder example, this was 90% and 45%. If Bob committed the murder, there is a 90% chance the victim will have died by a knife, and if Joe committed the murder, there is a 45% chance the victim will have died by a knife. So if h is true, the odds of getting the data are 90%, if ~h is true the odds are 45%.)

Second, determine the odds ratio by dividing the two numbers. For example 90/45 gives us odds of 2:1. 75 and 25 would give us odds of 3:1. 100 and 10 would give us odds of 10:1, etc.

Third, multiply these odds by the odds of the initial probability (2:1 x 10:1=20:1).

In conclusion, we have seen that the subconscious use of BT is what underlies all our logical thought about the truth of hypotheses. Thus, though using BT may seem difficult, as Donald A. Berry says, "Bayesian statistics is difficult to the extent that thinking is difficult."[13] But since our thinking generally works just fine without using BT consciously, we must explain why it is prudent to use BT consciously in order to analyze the resurrection and apparition hypotheses.

Bayes' Theorem and the Resurrection

We have explained that the question of whether the resurrection appearances were apparitions has centered around the issue of the similarities and differences between the resurrection appearances and apparitions. But this has led us to a paradoxical situation. On the one hand, any two things will have some similarities. Thus simply because there are similarities between two things, that does not necessarily mean they are the same thing. But on the other hand, we have seen that similarities and differences do help us to tell one thing from another. I have said that consequent probability holds the key to this paradox, and it is now time to explain why.

Similarities and differences help us to tell one thing from another, because when we note similarities and differences between two things in an effort to tell whether the two things are the same thing, we are subconsciously using the principle of consequent probability. By a similarity, we mean a characteristic which the thing we are examining has in common with the class which we suspect it belongs to. By a difference, we mean a characteristic which the thing we are examining does not have in common with the class we suspect it belongs to. When we see a similarity between the thing in question and the class to which it belongs, the reason we take this as indicating that the thing in question belongs to this class is because we are subconsciously reasoning, "if it is given that the thing in question belongs to the class in question, it is probable the thing would have the characteristic in question." This is clearly to ask the question of consequent probability, for we are saying: "if it is given h is true (if it is given the thing in question belongs to the class in question), it is probable we would get the datum in question (it is probable we would find the characteristic in question)."

For example, suppose someone's dog has gotten lost in the woods, and we have been asked to go look for it. And suppose we see an animal some distance away from us, and though we cannot see it clearly, we can see that it has four legs and that it has fur. These are similarities to a dog, and seeing these similarities increases our

---

13. Donald A. Berry, "Teaching Elementary Bayesian Statistics with Real Applications in Science," *American Statistician* 51 (1997): 241-46 (242).

confidence that it is the dog. This is because we are subconsciously reasoning that: if it is given that the animal in question is a dog, the probability is high it will have four legs, and if it is given that the animal in question is a dog, the probability is also high it will have fur.

But suppose that as the animal gets closer, we can see some differences between it and a dog. We see that it has fangs, and we know that dogs do not have fangs (except perhaps for some rare breeds of dogs). And we hear it make a howl which sounds like the howl of a wolf; we know of course that dogs do not make a howl like a wolf (again, except perhaps for some rare breeds of dogs). Thus we conclude that the animal in question is not a dog but a wolf. This is because we are subconsciously reasoning that: If the animal in question is a dog, the probability is low that it will have fangs, and if the animal in question is a dog, the probability is low that it will howl like a wolf; whereas if the animal is a wolf, the probability is high it will have fangs and high it will howl like a wolf. Thus we conclude that the animal is not a dog but a wolf.

Now let us return to the analogy of the fake police officer we used in the first chapter in order to understand this matter further. We first considered a case in which the differences between an alleged police officer and an actual police officer leads us to suspect he is not a real police officer. First, he is not wearing a uniform; typical police officers wear uniforms. Second, the badge he shows us is not the same kind of badge as the badge typical police officers have. Third, he has a different kind of car from typical police officers; he has an ordinary looking car rather than a typical police car.

Now clearly, it is consequent probability which is the reason why we regard these differences as indicating that this fellow is not a real police officer. If he is a real police officer it is probable he would be wearing a uniform, but if he is not a real police officer, it is improbable he would be wearing a uniform. If he is a real police officer it is probable he would have a badge like the other police officers, but if he is not a real police officer it is improbable he would have this badge, since it would be difficult to acquire such a badge. And if he is a real police officer it is probable he would have a typical police car, but if he is not a real police officer, it is improbable he would have a real police car, because it would be difficult for an impostor to acquire one.

But consider our other scenario, in which another police officer arrives and has some other differences. He has a moustache whereas all the other police officers we know do not. He is shorter than the other police officers. And he speaks with a foreign accent whereas the other police officers do not. But in spite of these differences, we do not suspect he is a fake police officer. Once again we are clearly using the principle of consequent probability. If he is a police officer, it is improbable he would have a moustache (since we do not know any other police officers who have moustaches), but if he is a fake police officer it is also improbable he would have a moustache (since a low percentage of the population has a moustache, and there is no reason to think the rate of moustaches among fake police officers is any higher than among the general population). If he is a real police officer it is improbable he would be as short as he is (since the other police officers we know are taller than him), but if he is a fake police officer it is also improbable he would be as short as he is (since if he is shorter than all the other police officers, then he must be unusually short, and a fake police officer being unusually short is just as improbable as a real police officer being unusually short, since there is no reason to think the rate of unusually short people is any higher among fake police officers than among real police officers). And if he is a real police officer it is improbable he would have a foreign accent (since we do not know any police officers with foreign accents), but if he is a fake police officer it is also improbable he would have a foreign accent (since a low percentage of the population has a foreign accent, and there is no reason to think the rate of foreign accents among fake police officers is any higher than the rate among the general population).

Thus we can see that looking for similarities and differences is a method which can help us distinguish one thing from another. It is a heuristic, a shortcut. But it is not an infallible heuristic. For though we have an intuitive sense of which similarities and differences are more probable given h or more probable given ~h, this intuitive sense can sometimes be mistaken. I believe that this is what has happened in the case of the debate on whether the resurrection appearances were apparitions. In order for similarities to support the apparition hypothesis, they must be not just any similarities, but similarities which are more probable given that the resurrection appearances were apparitions. And for differences between the resurrection appearances and apparitions to support the resurrection hypothesis, they must be not just any differences, but differences which are more probable given that the resurrection appearances were appearances of a physically resurrected person rather than apparitions. But in many cases, those on one side or the other have cited similarities or differences which are not more probable on one hypothesis or the other. Thus since the heuristic of looking for similarities and differences is failing us, we need to cease using this shortcut method, and instead consciously ask the question: what data is more probable given the resurrection hypothesis, and what data is more probable given the apparition hypothesis? Thus in chapter 7 when we analyze the data, I will explain why the data is more probable given that Jesus rose from the dead than given that Jesus was an apparition.

It may be asked how arguments which have been presented for or against the apparition hypothesis but which have not been cited as a similarity or a difference fit in here. For though many of the arguments have taken the form of "this is a similarity" or "this is a difference," this is not true of every argument. For example, the fact that 1 Peter 4:16 refers to Jesus as a spirit (or so it seems) has been cited by Paul Badham as an argument favoring the apparition hypothesis,[14] though he did not say that it is a similarity. Likewise, William Lane Craig has argued that if Jesus was an apparition this would require deception on the part of God,[15] though he did not refer to this fact as a

---

14. Paul Badham, *Christian Beliefs About Life After Death* (New York: Barnes and Noble, 1976), 41.

15. William Lane Craig, *Assessing the New Testament Evidence for the Historicity of the Resurrection of Jesus* (rev. ed.; Lewiston: Edwin Mellen, 2002 [1989]), 291-92. He cites this as an argument against

difference. The answer is that those arguments which have not been cited as similarities or differences can also be evaluated in terms of consequent probability, because every argument can be evaluated in terms of consequent probability, since consequent probability is an aspect of BT and BT underlies all our logical thought (thus to make our statement more exact, every argument not only can be but *is* evaluated in terms of consequent probability subconsciously, and can be evaluated in terms of consequent probability consciously). And it will be prudent to evaluate these other arguments in terms of consequent probability (consciously) because if there are a good number of arguments relevant to this hypothesis for which there is a pressing need to evaluate in terms of consequent probability (I have reference to those arguments which take the form of citing a similarity or difference), then it makes sense to also evaluate the remaining arguments in terms of consequent probability, lest our Bayesian analysis seem unfulfilled.

(We should say, however, that any argument for or against the apparition hypothesis could be understood as a similarity or a difference—in fact, it is possible for *any* argument for or against *any* hypothesis to be understood as a similarity or a difference. The fact that 1 Peter refers to the risen Jesus as a spirit could be understood as a similarity if we say that the datum makes the resurrected Jesus similar to an apparition, in that apparitions are usually referred to as spirits. Deception by God could be considered a difference if we say that it makes the resurrection appearances different from apparitions, in that apparitions do not usually involve deception by God. Likewise, if Bob's fingerprints are found on the gun, this makes him similar to other murderers. If Bob had a motivation to commit the murder, this makes him similar to other murderers. If Bob can prove he was in another country on the day of the murder, this makes him different from other murderers. But in most cases, the statement of an argument does not take the form of saying "this is a similarity" or "that is a difference." Usually an argument is formulated by saying something which gets us much closer to the idea of consequent probability. If, for example, we say that Bob's fingerprints being on the gun supports the murder hypothesis because if Bob committed murder it is not difficult to explain why his fingerprints are on the gun, but if Bob did not commit the murder, it is more difficult to explain why his fingerprints are on the gun, we have come much closer to saying "if h is true, it is probable Bob's fingerprints would be on the gun, but if h is false, it is improbable Bob's fingerprints would be on the gun," than we would if we said "Bob's fingerprints being on the gun makes him similar to other murderers." The fact that the arguments for or against the apparition hypothesis are so frequently being stated as similarities or differences indicates that our subconscious use of consequent probability is not taking us as far as it usually does, and thus there is a need to use consequent probability consciously.)

Before we proceed, I would like to address two preliminary matters concerning the resurrection and Bayes' Theorem. First, I will review the previous literature on BT

---

the supernatural version of the hypothesis, not the paranormal version.

and the resurrection so the reader is familiar with how BT has been used in previous studies of the resurrection. Second, I wish to make a point concerning what light BT sheds on how our theological beliefs affect our judgment of the probability of the resurrection.

BT and the Resurrection in Previous Literature

A number of other scholars have used Bayes' Theorem to analyze the probability of the resurrection, though none have been specifically concerned with the apparition hypothesis. Michael Martin, in an article in the journal *Philo*, and in an essay which incorporates some material from that article, and which responds to Richard Swinburne's argument (which we are about to mention), presents a number of reasons for thinking the initial probability of the resurrection is low, his two primary arguments being: 1) miracles rarely if ever happen and 2) there is no persuasive explanation for why God would want to bring about a resurrection.[16]

Stephen Davis responds to Martin's arguments, arguing that Martin's argument based on the rarity of miracles is unsound, and arguing that the concept of atonement, which Martin criticizes as an explanation for why God would raise Jesus, actually does make sense.[17]

Richard Swinburne provides the most thorough Bayesian analysis, since his entire book is devoted to a Bayesian argument.[18] Swinburne's primary focus is the initial probability of the resurrection; thus he spends most of his book discussing evidence which does not constitute part of the specific evidence. That is, he discusses evidence other than the historical evidence for the resurrection. His explanation for focusing so much on evidence which does not directly pertain to the resurrection is that this other evidence is what determines the initial probability, and the initial probability is just as essential to determining the epistemic probability of a hypothesis as the specific evidence is, and thus typical discussions of Jesus' resurrection, which focus only on the specific evidence, are missing a crucial part of the evidence. Swinburne's argument is that even without the New Testament, we can deduce from reason alone that it is likely God would want to become incarnate in order to atone for sins, to identify with our suffering, and to provide us with an example of how to live a good life. And that if

---

16. Michael Martin, "Why the Resurrection is Initially Improbable," *Philo* 1 (1998): 63-74; Michael Martin "Reply to Davis," *Philo* 2 (1999): 62-76; Michael Martin, "The Resurrection as Initially Improbable," in Robert M. Price and Jeffrey Jay Lowder eds., *The Empty Tomb: Jesus Beyond the Grave* (Amherst, NY: Prometheus, 2005), 43-54.

17. Stephen T. Davis, "Is Belief in the Resurrection Rational? A Response to Michael Martin" *Philo* 2 (1999): 51-61. Davis and Martin exchanged two further articles: Stephen T. Davis, "The Rationality of Resurrection for Christians: A Rejoinder," *Philo* 3 (2000): 41-51; Michael Martin, "Christianity and the Rationality of the Resurrection," *Philo* 3 (2000): 52-62.

18. Richard Swinburne, *The Resurrection of God Incarnate* (Oxford: Oxford University Press, 2003).

God became incarnate, we should expect him to lead a perfect moral life, to tell us he is God incarnate, and to perform an astounding miracle such as a resurrection. Since these reasons give us reason to expect that God will become incarnate, lead the sort of life Jesus is supposed to have led, and rise from the dead, when we come across the New Testament's account of these alleged events, we should not think the initial probability of the story it tells us is very low, and therefore the specific evidence does not need to be incredibly strong to convince us the resurrection is true. After addressing the issue of initial probability, Swinburne then proceeds to evaluate the data of the New Testament.

One will notice that all three of these authors have focused more on the initial probability of the resurrection than on the specific evidence. But the fourth work, an essay by Timothy and Lydia McGrew, is more focused on the specific evidence.[19] They explain how one can analyze the specific evidence for the resurrection without considering the initial probability and still come to an intelligible conclusion (though this may sound paradoxical since the initial probability is essential in determining an epistemic probability, it can be done), and they proceed to analyze the resurrection hypothesis in comparison to a variety of alternative hypotheses. The specific evidence is also our concern, since I have said that consequent probability is the key to this issue and consequent probability is a concept which pertains to the specific evidence rather than the initial probability. Thus in chapter 7, we will (for the most part) adopt the McGrews' method of discussing only the specific evidence.

In addition, Richard Carrier has published an essay in which he argues for a low initial probability for the resurrection, and an essay in which he makes the lack of evidence for the resurrection part of a more general Bayesian argument against Christianity.[20] And Hugh Gauch Jr. has written an article in which he reviews the efforts of Swinburne and the McGrews.[21]

We can also mention two books by Richard Carrier in which he uses BT to analyze hypotheses about the historical Jesus more generally, and an article by Randy Ingermanson and Jay Cost in which they use BT to analyze the probability that the "Jesus Tomb" is actually Jesus' tomb.[22]

19. Timothy and Lydia McGrew, "The Argument From Miracles: A Cumulative Case for the Resurrection of Jesus of Nazareth," in William Lane Craig and J.P. Moreland eds., *The Blackwell Companion to Natural Theology* (Oxford: Wiley-Blackwell, 2009), 593-662.

20. Richard C. Carrier, "Why the Resurrection is Unbelievable," in John W. Loftus ed., *The Christian Delusion: Why Faith Fails* (Amherst, NY: Prometheus, 2010), 291-315; Richard C. Carrier, "Christianity's Success was not Incredible," in John W. Loftus ed., *The End of Christianity* (Amherst, NY: Prometheus, 2011), 53-74.

21. Hugh G. Gauch Jr., "Natural Theology's Case for Jesus' Resurrection: Methodological and Statistical Considerations," *Philosophia Christi* 13 (2011): 339-55.

22. Richard C. Carrier, *Proving History: Bayes' Theorem and the Quest for the Historical Jesus* (Amherst, NY: Prometheus, 2012); Richard C. Carrier, *On the Historicity of Jesus* (Sheffield: Sheffield Phoenix Press, 2014); Randy Ingermanson and Jay Cost, "Bayes' Theorem and the 'Jesus Family Tomb,'" http://www.ingermanson.com/jesus/art/stats2.php.

Bayes' Theorem and the Supernatural

I said in chapter 1 that after explaining BT I wanted to make a further point about how one's theological beliefs will affect an investigation of the historical evidence for the resurrection. And that point is this: As is evident from the literature we have just reviewed, BT tells us that since the prior probability is an essential part of any hypothesis, it is not possible to determine the epistemic probability of the resurrection by considering only the specific evidence (the specific evidence in this case being the historical evidence given us by the documents of the New Testament). It is possible, as the McGrews do, to discuss the specific evidence without discussing the initial probability, but it is not possible to arrive at an epistemic probability without also considering the initial probability, for we have seen that the initial probability can have a dramatic effect on the epistemic probability. This means it is not possible to arrive at an epistemic probability for the resurrection by a "purely historical" investigation, an investigation which considers only the historical facts about Jesus' resurrection without regard to issues such as the existence of God, the coherence of Christian doctrine, and all other issues bearing on the truth of Christianity. A purely historical investigation means a consideration of only the specific evidence, but in order to arrive at an epistemic probability for the resurrection we will have to consider the initial probability, and thus BT is telling us that our judgment as to the epistemic probability of the resurrection will be affected by our judgment of the probability of the existence of God, and of our various other religious beliefs, because these are the things which establish the prior probability. But in telling us this, BT is only telling us something which many have already recognized. For example, Dale Allison says, "the resurrection is not a topic unto itself, and we cannot evaluate it independently of our evaluation of Christianity and the nature of the world."[23] Likewise, Michael Perry:

> This is the point where the purely historical approach needs to be supplemented by theological insights. It would, for example, have been quite an irrational incident if the person to have been raised was one of the thieves who were crucified with Jesus. But the One who was raised was he who had claimed to be God's Son and who had predicted his own rising again from the dead. The Resurrection fits into a pattern which makes theological sense.[24]

Finally, we should explain exactly why it is not possible to arrive at an epistemic probability by considering only the specific evidence and not the initial probability. The reason is that there are no absolute boundaries between the evidence which establishes the prior probability and the evidence we consider the "specific evidence." Since we update the probability with each piece of data, what is the specific evidence

---

23. Dale C. Allison Jr., *Resurrecting Jesus: The Earliest Christian Tradition and its Interpreters* (New York: T&T Clark, 2005), 342.

24. Michael C. Perry, *The Easter Enigma: An Essay on the Resurrection with Special Reference to the Data of Psychical Research* (London: Faber and Faber, 1959), 27.

at one moment will become part of the evidence which establishes the prior once we move on to the next piece of evidence. If the initial probability is 2:1 that Bob committed the murder, and we consider the next datum, say the evidence of a knife, and conclude that the new probability is now 5:1, and then move on to our next piece of evidence (say the fact that Bob was seen at the scene of the crime), the evidence of the knife has moved from being the specific evidence to being part of the evidence which establishes the prior. The question may then become why, if whatever is in the specific evidence will soon go into the evidence establishing the prior, we bother to distinguish between specific evidence and evidence which establishes the prior. The reason we do so is simply a matter of prudence. It would not be prudent, when there is a vast amount of data to consider, to try to consider all of the data at once. We must distinguish between the evidence as a whole and the evidence which we are specifically concerned with. This is clearly the prudent course of action, but since any piece of data will find itself in both categories at some point in time, it would clearly not make sense to base our final judgment on whatever data happens to constitute the specific evidence at the moment.

Appendix: A Note on Terminology

In this chapter, I have used the term "Bayesianism" to refer to the idea that it is legitimate to quantify degrees of belief as probabilities, and the term "objectivism" to refer to the idea that it is not legitimate to quantify degrees of belief as probabilities, but that probabilities can only be applied to frequencies. However, readers should know that these terms, as well as a number of related terms, can mean a number of different things. Let us examine the terminological issues.

The term *Bayesianism* has three distinct meanings. 1) The meaning which I have just referred to: the idea that it is legitimate to quantify degrees of belief as probabilities.[25] 2) The idea that it is legitimate to quantify degrees of belief as probabilities *when performing a statistical analysis of the results of a scientific experiment*. This idea is in contrast to the idea that though quantifying degrees of belief as probabilities is legitimate in some contexts (and hence Bayesianism in the first sense of the word is true), it is not legitimate when analyzing the results of a scientific experiment. This meaning is the common one in the statistics literature, as opposed to the philosophy literature,[26] for there is little support among statisticians for the idea that it is never legitimate to quantify degrees of belief as probabilities (though given the quotations from Leonard Savage in the footnotes below, there evidently used to be). 3) The idea that degrees of belief may legitimately be quantified as probabilities, *whether those beliefs form part*

---

25. "At present, perhaps the most philosophically influential view of probability understands it to be degrees of belief. The subjectivist Bayesian (hereafter, for brevity, simply Bayesian) view of probability..." (Glymour, *Theory and Evidence*, 67).

26. This was explained to me by Richard Levine, a statistics professor at San Diego State University.

of the prior probability or the likelihood functions. This idea is in contrast to *likelihoodism*. According to likelihoodism, only those beliefs which are used to determine the likelihood functions may be legitimately quantified as probabilities; it is not legitimate to quantify degrees of belief in order to form a prior probability.[27] This third meaning is found only in the philosophy literature, for there is little to no support for likelihoodism among statisticians. (Given the point I made above that there is no absolute distinction between the data relevant to establishing the prior and the data relevant to establishing the likelihood functions, likelihoodism is clearly an incoherent idea.)

Objectivism can mean, as I have said, the idea that it is not legitimate to quantify degrees of belief as probabilities, but that probabilities only apply to frequencies.[28] But the second definition of objectivism occurs when it is used as a synonym for *objective Bayesianism*, a position which is contrasted with *subjective Bayesianism* (also called *subjectivism*). Subjective Bayesianism refers to the idea that the probabilities which a person assigns to degrees of belief will be rational so long as the probabilities appear rational in light of that person's personal belief system. Objective Bayesianism contends that the probabilities assigned to degrees of belief are only rational if they appear rational in light of all objective evidence.[29] However, subjectivism also bears another meaning: it can refer to our first definition of Bayesianism.[30]

Frequentism refers to: 1) The idea that probabilities *are* frequencies.[31] Note that this is not the same as objectivism, which contends that probability calculations can

27. On Bayesianism in this sense, and likelihoodism, see Branden Fitelson, "Likelihoodism, Bayesianism, and Relational Confirmation," *Synthese* 156 (2007): 473-89.

28. "Objectivistic views hold that . . . evidence . . . for the magnitude of the probability that applies (in case any does), is to be obtained by observations of some repetitions of the event, and from no other source whatever. . . In any objectivistic view, probabilities can apply fruitfully only to repetitive events, that is, to certain processes; and (depending on the view in question) it is either meaningless to talk about the probability that a given proposition is true, or this probability can be only 1 or 0, according as the proposition is in fact true or false. Under neither interpretation can probability serve as a measure of the trust to be put in a proposition. . . Holders of objectivistic views have, therefore, no recourse but to argue that it is not reasonable to assign probabilities to the truth of propositions. . ." (Leonard J. Savage, *The Foundations of Statistics* (2nd ed.; New York: Dover, 1972), 3-4). Savage uses the term "objectivistic" rather than "objectivism" or "objectivist," but these terms are used for the same position, in commenting upon Savage's work, by D.H. Mellor, *The Matter of Chance* (Cambridge: Cambridge University Press), 50.

29. "According to the objectivist view, the rules of Bayesian statistics can be justified by requirements of rationality and consistency and interpreted as an extension of logic. According to the subjectivist view, the state of knowledge measures a 'personal belief'" (Mark Chang, *Paradoxes in Scientific Inference* (Boca Raton, FL: CRC Press, 2013), 360).

30. "At present, perhaps the most philosophically influential view of probability understands it to be degrees of belief. The subjectivist Bayesian (hereafter, for brevity, simply Bayesian) view of probability. . ." (Glymour, *Theory and Evidence*, 67).

31. "Gamblers, actuaries and scientists have long understood that relative frequencies bear an intimate relationship to probabilities. Frequency interpretations posit the most intimate relationship of all: identity." Alan Hájek, "Interpretations of Probability," *The Stanford Encyclopedia of Philosophy* (Winter 2012 Edition), Edward N. Zalta ed., plato.stanford.edu/archives/win2012/entries/probability-interpret/.

only legitimately be applied to frequencies. One can, as I have done in the text, admit that probabilities are frequencies (because I think degrees of belief are frequencies) and yet contend that probability calculations can be applied to degrees of belief. Thus this definition of frequentism is compatible with either Bayesianism (in the first sense of the word) or objectivism (in the first sense of that word). 2) But frequentism can also be used as a synonym for the first sense of the word objectivism.[32] 3) In statistics, frequentism typically refers to the opposite of what Bayesianism typically refers to in that discipline. Whereas Bayesianism refers to the idea that it is legitimate to quantify degrees of belief as probabilities when performing a statistical analysis of the results of a scientific experiment, frequentism refers to the idea that it is not legitimate to do this (though frequentists in this sense of the word allow that quantifying degrees of belief is legitimate in other contexts).[33]

The terms *subjective probability* and *objective probability* each bear two meanings. First, subjective probability can be used as a synonym for the subjective Bayesian interpretation of probability and objective probability can be used as a synonym for the objective Bayesian interpretation of probability.[34] Second, subjective probability may be used in reference to the Bayesian (in the first sense of the word) interpretation of probability (according to which BT can be applied to degrees of belief), and this can also be called *Bayesian probability, evidential probability*[35] or *epistemic probability*[36]; and objective probability may be used in reference to probabilities based on frequencies.[37]

---

32. Savage, *Foundations of Statistics*, comments, "Keynes, writing in 1921 of what are here called objectivistic views, complained, 'The absence of a recent exposition of the logical basis of the frequency theory by any of its adherents has been a great disadvantage to me in criticizing it.'" The term here (from John Maynard Keynes, *A Treatise on Probability* (London: Macmillan, 1921)) is "frequency theory," but the position is referred to as "frequentist" in a discussion of Keynes's work (Bruno Ventelou, *Millennial Keynes: An Introduction to the Origin, Development, and Later Currents of Keynesian Thought* (Armonk, NY: M.E. Sharpe, 2005), 89). Savage also uses the term "frequentistic" (*Foundations*, iv).

33. My source for this is again Richard Levine.

34. Didier Sornette, *Critical Phenomena in Natural Sciences: Chaos, Fractals, Selforganization and Disorder: Concepts and Tools* (2nd ed.; New York: Springer, 2006), vii refers to "Objective and subjective (Bayesian) probabilities."

35. Glynis M. Breakwell, *The Psychology of Risk* (2nd ed.; Cambridge: Cambridge University Press, 2014), 33 states: "Evidential probability, also called Bayesian probability (or subjectivist probability), can be assigned to any statement whatsoever, even when no random process is involved, as a way to represent its subjective plausibility, or the degree to which the statement is supported by the available evidence."

36. Richard Swinburne, *Confirmation Theory*, 2 states: "Often a proposition makes a second proposition probable... A similar relation to the one analyzed above as holding between propositions, holds between the events or states of affairs reported by the propositions... These relations, whether between propositions or states of affairs, I will term relations of epistemic probability."

37. "Physical probabilities, which are also called objective or frequency probabilities, are associated with random physical systems such as roulette wheels, rolling dice and radioactive atoms... Evidential probability, also called Bayesian probability (or subjectivist probability), can be assigned

3

The Reality of Apparitions

A Brief History of Apparition Research

SYSTEMATIC INVESTIGATION OF APPARITIONS, and in fact, of paranormal phenomena generally, began with the founding of the Society for Psychical Research in London in 1882.[1] The society attracted scholars from a wide variety of fields, and had among their number such noted individuals as Henry Sidgwick (a prominent philosopher), Lewis Carroll (the creator of Alice in Wonderland), and William James (philosopher and psychologist). The primary goal of the organization was twofold: first, to assess the evidence for the reality of paranormal phenomena. And second, if the reality of paranormal phenomena could be demonstrated, to determine the nature of the paranormal phenomena (we may call this second goal the development of theories of the paranormal). Comparable organizations soon arose in other countries, the most prominent one being the American Society for Psychical Research in the US. In addition to apparitions, the primary subjects with which the early parapsychologists were concerned were ESP, mediumship, out-of-body experiences, and hypnotism (hypnotism was not yet accepted as a normal phenomenon).

Since our primary concern is with the reality of apparitions, rather than theories of them, we can omit for now any commentary on the theories the early researchers developed and instead focus on their efforts to establish the reality of apparitions. The following five types of evidential cases were frequently published in the early parapsychological literature: collective apparitions, crisis apparitions, informational apparitions, recurring apparitions, and apparitions recognized from a photograph. In all cases, it was desired that the evidence be firsthand and that testimony be obtained from as many of the witnesses as possible.

Collective apparitions are apparitions which are seen simultaneously by two or more people. One can easily see why these apparitions would appear to be convincing

---

to any statement whatsoever, even when no random process is involved, as a way to represent its subjective plausibility, or the degree to which the statement is supported by the available evidence" (Breakwell, *Psychology of Risk*, 33).

1. On the history of the SPR, see Alan Gauld, *The Founders of Psychical Research* (New York: Schocken Books, 1968); Renee Haynes, *The Society for Psychical Research 1882-1982: A History* (London: MacDonald, 1982).

evidence: the most popular naturalistic explanation for apparitions is that they are hallucinations, but how can a hallucination be seen simultaneously by two or more people? (Since hallucinations are the most popular naturalistic explanation for apparitions, there will be somewhat more focus in this chapter on hallucinations than on other naturalistic explanations.)

Crisis apparitions are apparitions which appear at approximately the same time that the person whose apparition it is dies. For example, suppose Bob sees an apparition of Sally who, so far as Bob knows, is still alive. But Bob later finds out that Sally died at approximately the same time he saw an apparition of her. For an apparition to coincide with a death in this way certainly seems like a startling coincidence, and so the argument is that it is no coincidence, but that the apparition and the death must be somehow related.

An informational apparition is an apparition which conveys to the witness information which the witness did not already know. For example, suppose an apparition tells a person that an object is hidden in a certain place and the person then finds that the object is indeed hidden in that place. If an apparition can provide a person with factual knowledge which that person did not previously have, there certainly must be something paranormal about the apparition. (The apparitions which I am referring to as "informational" have often been referred to as "veridical" in the literature on apparitions. But "veridical" is a confusing term to use, because the same term has also been used in reference to any apparition that is real.)

Recurring apparitions are apparitions which appear to more than one person, though not simultaneously. For example, suppose Bob sees an apparition of Sally, and the apparition is later seen by Joe, and later seen again by Harry. The argument is that a hallucinatory apparition should not be seen by so many people. This argument is especially strong when the appearances are of a person whom no one was in grief over (for if no one is in grief, hallucinations are less likely), or when (in the best cases), people see the same apparition without knowing anyone else saw it. (For example, Bob sees an apparition in a house without knowing who it is an apparition of, and Joe later sees the same apparition in the same house but without knowing Bob saw it. We would not expect they would coincidentally hallucinate the same apparition in the same house.)

By an apparition recognized from a photograph I mean an apparition which the witness did not recognize at the time he saw it, but which he later recognized after seeing a photograph. For example, suppose Bob is in a house and he sees an apparition which he has never seen before, and he wonders who it is, and suppose he is later shown a photograph of the previous owner of the house, and he finds that the apparition he has seen looks just like the previous owner (or even better yet, Bob might be presented with a set of photographs and successfully pick out the owner's photograph from the set). Since Bob is not likely to have a hallucination which coincidently happens to look like the previous owner of the house, this suggests the apparition is real.

Skeptical alternative explanations for these cases were certainly offered (I have already touched on hallucinations), and we will consider these below when we come to analyze the evidence in depth. But for now, we can note that at least prima facie, cases of the above types do look like strong evidence for the reality of apparitions.[2]

Phantasms of the Living

Although numerous journal articles were published on apparitions during the late 1800s and early 1900s, two studies stand out as warranting special attention. The first is *Phantasms of the Living* and the second is *The Census of Hallucinations*.

Phantasms of the Living was a two volume work of approximately 800 pages authored by Edmund Gurney, Frederick W.H. Myers, and Frank Podmore, and published in 1886.[3] Although all three were credited with authorship, the work was primarily Gurney's. Myers wrote only the introduction, and Podmore did not actually write any of the work, though he was an investigator for many of the cases. The book is primarily concerned with crisis apparitions, but it also presents other cases of spontaneous telepathy, as well as the results of some telepathy experiments. (Spontaneous telepathy refers to incidents of telepathy which occur spontaneously, that is, which do not occur as part of an experiment; in Gurney's opinion, crisis apparitions were examples of spontaneous telepathy.)

Gurney realized that if crisis apparitions were to be accepted as paranormal, high evidential standards had to be met. Consequently, his evaluation of the evidence was very thorough. His first step was to attempt to raise the initial probability of the reality of crisis apparitions by discussing the evidence for experimental telepathy and for cases of paranormal phenomena which are similar to crisis apparitions (cases of apparitions of the living, and cases of impressions, dreams, and apparitions which corresponded with some traumatic event other than death). The reasoning was that if ESP is real, and if phenomena similar to crisis apparitions are real, then we should not be surprised if we find that crisis apparitions themselves are real.[4] As for the actual cases of crisis apparitions, Gurney recognized that the main objection would be that the witness misremembered—that the witness thought the apparition appeared at the

---

2. Since the purpose of this book is to consider whether the resurrection appearances were apparitions, and since if they were apparitions, they were certainly apparitions of the dead, I am not going to address the reality of apparitions of the living, that is, cases in which an apparition of a living person is seen. If apparitions of the living are real, that means that such apparitions, in at least some cases, are not hallucinations caused by the percipient, but projections caused by the consciousness of the one who appears. Apparitions of the living are discussed at various points in *Phantasms of the Living*; and see also the article by Hart and Hart I refer to in n15 and the sources on OBEs referred to in n112.

3. Edmund Gurney, Frederic William Henry Myers, and Frank Podmore, *Phantasms of the Living* (2 vols.; London: Trubner & Co., 1886). I have used the 2007 Elibron Classics edition, which is an unabridged facsimile of the original edition.

4. Gurney spends most of the first 450 pages of *Phantasms* discussing other phenomena before coming to the subject of apparitions.

same time the person died, when in fact the correspondence between the appearance of the apparition and the time of the person's death was not so close. Thus he devoted a considerable amount of space to discussing the faults of human memory, and laid out a stringent criterion for accepting crisis apparition cases: in order for a case to be accepted, the witness must have either written down an account of the apparition, or must have told someone else about the apparition, before he found out that the person whose apparition it is died.[5] For example, if Bob says he saw an apparition of Sally and that Sally died the same day[6] he saw the apparition, the only way to be sure Bob did not misremember is to find a written account that Bob made after he saw the apparition, but before he found out that Sally died, or to find a witness whom Bob recounted the experience to before he found out that Sally died.

Besides dealing with the misremembering hypothesis, Gurney also gave due consideration to just about every other skeptical hypothesis: lies, hoaxing, chance, and so on, and we will consider all of these ourselves below when we analyze the evidence for apparitions.

The Census of Hallucinations

The SPR's second major project was a survey called the *Census of Hallucinations*, the purpose of which was to determine the prevalence of hallucinations/apparitions in the general population and to collect accounts of evidential apparitions. (By "hallucination" they meant to designate any experience of an apparition, whether real or not real. Thus they were not using the term "hallucination" in the sense in which it is typically used today.) The results were published in a 400 page article in 1894.[7] The survey involved 17,000 people, and the question put to them was:

> Have you ever, when believing yourself to be completely awake, had a vivid impression of seeing or being touched by a living being or an inanimate object, or of hearing a voice; which impression, so far as you could discover, was not due to any external physical cause?[8]

---

5. Gurney discusses the issue of misremembering and other potential faults of human testimony, on pp. 114-150. He presents the criterion of getting confirmation as to the date from another source on pp. 142-44.

6. I have said above that a crisis apparition is an apparition which appears to someone at approximately the same time that the person whose apparition it is dies. While there are no absolute boundaries as far as what constitutes "approximately," Gurney set the boundary by considering cases in which the apparition appeared within twelve hours of the death (either twelve hours before or twelve hours after). Though there is nothing magical about the twelve hour mark, Gurney needed to set some sort of boundary in order to present the statistical argument of his which I mention below.

7. Professor Sidgwick's Committee, "Report on the Census of Hallucinations," *Proceedings of the Society for Psychical Research* 10 (1894): 25-422.

8. Sidgwick, "Census," 33.

The *Census*, like *Phantasms*, was concerned with finding evidential cases of apparitions, but its scope was wider than *Phantasms* in two ways. First, the *Census* did not have as central a focus on crisis apparitions as *Phantasms* did; the *Census* was also very concerned with presenting other types of evidential apparitions. Second, since it was the first survey addressing the prevalence of hallucinations in the general population, its results were of interest not only to parapsychologists, but also to the wider world of psychology.

The project unfortunately had to be carried out without the help of Edmund Gurney, who had in fact conceived it. Gurney suffered an untimely death in 1888. The principal investigator for the project was Eleanor Sidgwick (the wife of Henry Sidgwick), and the other authors were Alice Johnson, Henry Sidgwick himself, Frank Podmore, and A.T. Myers. Parallel censuses were also carried out in the US, France, Germany, Russia, and Brazil, but none were nearly as extensive as the one in England.[9] The project did indeed succeed in its goals of finding evidential cases (for example, twenty-eight pages are devoted to collective apparitions), and of educating the wider psychology community (the results of the study were presented at the meeting of the International Congress of Psychology).

Whether or not *Phantasms* and the *Census* proved apparitions are real, they were certainly enormous tasks of research which are testaments to the commitment and work ethic of the early SPR researchers.

Apparition Research Since the Early 1900s

As historian of psychical research Alan Gauld notes,[10] beginning around 1910 or so, there was a sharp decline in the number of parapsychology publications devoted to apparitions. Gauld attributes this to the fact that the main concern of the early parapsychologists was to prove that there is life after death, and since apparitions failed to do this (researchers could not agree on whether apparitions were disembodied spirits, or the result of ESP), researchers lost interest in them. (While that was likely one factor, there were other factors as well, but to address all of these would take us too far afield from our main purpose.) In any event, the state of apparition research today is actually not a great deal different than it was in 1910, with no substantive advance in consensus on the two issues which the first parapsychologists were primarily concerned with: the reality of apparitions, and what paranormal theory best accounts for them. While more cases of the five types discussed above have been published, there is no more consensus now than there was then on whether alternative explanations can be ruled out. And the consensus is also no greater on the question of which

---

9. See Gauld, *Founders*, 182.
10. Gauld, *Founders*, 198-99.

paranormal theory best explains apparitions (a question which of course can only be entertained by those who are persuaded that apparitions are paranormal).[11]

We can also note that though there has been little progress on these two central questions, there have been some interesting developments on other aspects of apparition research. The literature of ordinary psychology and medicine has given us many studies which have found that seeing apparitions may occur as part of the bereavement process.[12] There are now many more popular level books devoted to apparitions—a body of literature has arisen which can be dubbed the ADC literature, since it typically refers to apparitions as ADCs ("After-Death-Communications").[13] And there has been progress made with regard to understanding the psychology of those who experience haunting experiences, and with regard to identifying naturalistic explanations for them (though the explanations put forward simply do a better job of explaining the types of haunting cases which were already acknowledged to be evidentially ambiguous; they do not explain the five types of cases enumerated above, and their proponents have not attempted to apply them to these types of cases).[14] But our review of the literature has been sufficient for us to see what our task is if we want to argue for the reality of apparitions: we must produce cases of the five types enumerated above, and we must rule out alternative explanations for them.

---

11. For sources addressing theories of apparitions, see the footnotes below under the section "Theories of Apparitions."

12. The most often cited study in this regard is W. Dewi Rees, "The Hallucinations of Widowhood," *British Medical Journal* 4 (1971): 37-41. Other studies include Agneta Grimby, "Hallucinations Following the Loss of a Spouse: Common and Normal Events Among the Elderly," *Journal of Clinical Geropsychology* 4 (1998): 65-74; Richard Olson et al., "Hallucinations of Widowhood," *Journal of the American Geriatric Society* 33 (1985): 543-47. For other studies, see those cited in Dale Allison, *Resurrecting Jesus: The Earliest Christian Tradition and its Interpreters* (London: T&T Clark, 2005), 273-74. This literature typically assumes apparitions are hallucinations, and has dubbed them "bereavement hallucinations" or "grief hallucinations." It is often asserted that such studies have established the normality of these hallucinations. However, the fact that so many of the studies have focused solely on the elderly makes me hesitant to conclude that this is so. Christopher Baethge, "Grief Hallucinations: True or Pseudo? Serious or Not?" *Psychopathology* 35 (2002): 296-302 states that "[n]early all studies focus on grief hallucinations among elderly, widowed people (297)."

13. Some examples include Bill Guggenheim and Judy Guggenheim, *Hello From Heaven! A New Field of Research—After Death Communication—Confirms that Life and Love are Eternal* (New York: Bantam, 1996); Louis E. LaGrand, *After Death Communication: Final Farewells* (St. Paul, MN: Llewellyn, 1997); Emma Heathcote-James, *After Death Communication: Hundreds of True Stories from the UK of People Who Have Communicated with Their Loved Ones* (London: Metro, 2003). For more sources, see the extensive list of books on Bill and Judy Guggenheim's website: http://www.after-death.com/Pages/Books/List.aspx?category=ADC.

14. For an overview of the recent research bearing on these two points, see James Houran and Rense Lange eds., *Hauntings and Poltergeists: Multidisciplinary Perspectives* (Jefferson, NC: McFarland, 2001).

Collective Apparitions

Collective apparitions are cited as evidence for the reality of apparitions because, as noted above, the most popular alternative explanation for apparitions is that they are hallucinations, but the conventional view in psychology is that collective hallucinations are impossible.[15] Consider the words of Gary Collins, a clinical psychologist:

> Hallucinations are individual occurrences. By their very nature only one person can see a given hallucination at a time. They certainly are not something which can be seen by a group of people. . . . Since an hallucination exists only in this subjective, personal sense, it is obvious that others cannot witness it.[16]

This view has been challenged by some writing in the parapsychological and religious literature, and I will comment on the possibility of collective hallucinations shortly. But before discussing alternative explanations, it will be best to present the cases themselves, so the reader can see just what exactly needs to be explained. Thus what follows are four cases of collective apparitions which I do not think are susceptible to any of the alternative explanations to be considered below.

Case 1: An Apparition in a Bedroom (SPR 1885)[17]

In the first case, a husband and wife, Mr. and Mrs. P, were laying in bed one night when the wife saw a figure which appeared to be a naval officer standing near the bed. The husband then noticed the figure too, and the apparition spoke the husband's name ("Willie, Willie!"). The husband then got up to approach the apparition, but it disappeared into the wall. The husband then searched the house to try to find the figure, but could find it nowhere (which was unsurprising, given that the apparition had been seen to disappear into the wall, and given that the husband had to unlock the bedroom door to leave the room himself). Mrs. P tells us:

> I [was] just pulling myself into a half sitting posture against the pillows, thinking of nothing but the arrangements for the following day, when to my great astonishment I saw a gentleman standing at the foot of the bed, dressed as a naval officer, and with a cap on his head having a projecting peak. The light being in the position which I have indicated, the face was in shadow to me, and the more so that the visitor was leaning upon his arms which rested on

---

15. For a literature review of collective apparitions, see Hornell Hart and Ella B. Hart, "Visions and Apparitions Collectively and Reciprocally Perceived," *Proceedings of the Society for Psychical Research* 41 (1933): 205–249. This was a comprehensive review of cases published up till 1933.

16. Gary R. Collins in a personal letter to Gary Habermas, quoted in Gary R. Habermas, "Explaining Away Jesus' Resurrection: The Recent Revival of Hallucination Theories," *Christian Research Journal* 23.4 (2001): 26-31, 47-49 (48).

17. Anonymous [Society for Psychical Research], "Cases Received by the Literary Committee," *Journal of the Society for Psychical Research* 2 (1885): 272-280 (274-279).

the foot-rail of the bedstead. I was too astonished to be afraid, but simply wondered who it could be; and, instantly touching my husband's shoulder (whose face was turned from me), I said, "Willie, who is this?" My husband turned, and, for a second or two, lay looking in intense astonishment at the intruder; then lifting himself a little, he shouted "What on earth are you doing here, sir?" Meanwhile the form, slowly drawing himself into an upright position, now said in a commanding yet reproachful voice, "Willie! Willie!"

I looked at my husband and saw that his face was white and agitated. As I turned towards him he sprang out of bed as though to attack the man, but stood by the bedside as if afraid, or in great perplexity, while the figure calmly and slowly moved towards the wall at right angles with the lamp in the direction of the dotted line. As it passed the lamp, a deep shadow fell upon the room as of a material person shutting out the light from us by his intervening body, and he disappeared, as it were, into the wall. My husband now, in a very agitated manner, caught up the lamp and turning to me, said, "I mean to look all over the house, and see where he is gone."

I was by this time exceedingly agitated too, but remembering that the door was locked, and that the mysterious visitor had not gone towards it at all, remarked, "He has not gone out by the door!" But without pausing, my husband unlocked the door, hastened out of the room, and was soon searching the whole house. Sitting there in the dark, I thought to myself, "We have surely seen an apparition! Whatever can it indicate—perhaps my brother Arthur (he was in the navy, and at that time on a voyage to India) is in trouble: such things have been told of as occurring." In some such way I pondered with an anxious heart, holding the child, who just then awakened, in my arms, until my husband came back looking very white and miserable.

Sitting upon the bedside, he put his arm about me and said, "Do you know what we have seen?" And I said, "Yes, it was a spirit. I am afraid it was Arthur, but could not see his face"—and he exclaimed, "Oh! No, it was my father!"

Mr. P's father, who had been dead for some time, had served in the navy during his life. Some weeks after the apparition appeared, Mr. P told his wife that at the time of the apparition, he was having financial problems, and was headed towards taking a course of action that would have been detrimental to him.

The husband confirmed Mrs. P's account.[18]

---

18. Anonymous, "Cases," 279.

Jesus' Resurrection and Apparitions

Case 2: The Apparition of Walt Whitman (Prince 1928)[19]

The second case involves a type of apparition known as a deathbed vision.[20] Deathbed visions are apparitions which are seen by a person who is close to death. (They should not, however, be confused with Near Death Experiences. A Near Death Experience occurs when someone has suffered some near fatal event and slips into unconsciousness. For example, a person may have a heart attack and when they return to consciousness, report that while they were unconscious they floated above their bodies, saw apparitions, and went to heaven. A deathbed vision, by contrast, occurs when a person is still conscious and aware of their surroundings. The person does not go to heaven to see the apparitions, but sees the apparitions there in the room with him, and if others are in the room at the time, he will have no trouble describing the apparitions to them.)

In the following case, Horace Traubel, a friend of the famous poet Walt Whitman (and first author of a nine-volume biography about him),[21] was near death. During the days leading up to his death, he was continually seeing Walt Whitman and telling others about the appearances. But, in a development that was unexpected to say the least, shortly before Traubel's death, Col. Cosgrave, one of those who was staying with Traubel, saw the apparition as well. He wrote:

> During this long watch, Horace Traubel, who was suffering from paralysis and debility, was without visible pain, and semi-conscious, unable to articulate owing to paralysis of the tongue. His eyes, however, which were remarkably brilliant and expressive, gave us the clue to the majority of his needs. On the last night, about 3 A. M., he grew perceptibly weaker, breathing almost without visible movement, eyes closed and seemingly comatose, he stirred restlessly after a long period, and his eyes opened, staring towards the further side of the bed, his lips moved, endeavoring to speak, I moved his head back, thinking he needed more air, but again it moved away, and his eyes remained riveted on a point some three feet above the bed, my eyes were at last drawn irresistibly to the same point in the darkness, as there was but a small shaded night lamp behind a curtain on the further side of the room. Slowly the point at which we were both looking grew gradually brighter, a light haze appeared, spread until it assumed bodily form, and took the likeness of Walt Whitman, standing upright beside the bed, a rough tweed jacket on, an old felt hat upon his head and his right hand in his pocket, similar to a number of his portraits, he was gazing down at Traubel, a kindly, reassuring smile upon his face, he

---

19. Walter Franklin Prince, *Noted Witnesses for Psychic Occurrences* (New Hyde Park, NY: University Books, 1963 [1928]), 144-50.

20. On deathbed visions, see Sir William Barrett, *Deathbed Visions* (London: Methuen, 1926); Karlis Osis, *Deathbed Observations by Physicians and Nurses* (New York: Parapsychology Foundation, 1961); Karlis Osis and Erlendur Haraldsson, *At the Hour of Death* (New York: Avon, 1977); and the series of recent journal articles by Peter Fenwick listed at: http://www.researchgate.net/researcher/16176469_Peter_Fenwick.

21. Horace Traubel et al., *With Walt Whitman in Camden* (Boston: Small, 1906).

nodded twice as though reassuringly, the features quite distinct for at least a full minute, then gradually faded from sight. My eyes turned back to Traubel, who remained staring for almost another minute, when he also turned away, his features remarkably clear of the strained expression they had worn all evening, and he did not move again until his death, two hours later. I reported the occurrence to Mrs. Denison, who entered the facts in her diary at once, as she had records of several other psychic phenomena to date. I am thoroughly convinced of the exactness of the above statements, and did not regard it as extraordinary, owing to the fact that I had experienced similar phenomena at crucial moments during heavy casualties in France.[22]

Traubel confirmed to Mrs. Denison that he had also seen the apparition at this time.[23]

In response to Prince's inquiry concerning some details which Mrs. Denison had mentioned in an earlier written account of the incident but which Cosgrave had not mentioned in his account, namely, that the apparition had passed through the bed and that it had touched Cosgrave and caused him to feel an electric shock, Cosgrave wrote back to confirm that these details were indeed accurate:

> Walt Whitman, towards the end of his appearance, while Horace and I were gazing at him, moved closer to Horace from the further side of the bed, as Horace from weakness was forced to allow his head to roll back to a frontal position, and said, 'There is Walt.' At the same moment, Walt passed apparently through the bed towards me, and appeared to touch my hand, as though in farewell, I distinctly felt it, as though I had touched a low electric charge, he then smiled at Horace, and passed from sight.[24]

Case 3: The Seen and Unseen Ghost (Cornell 2003)[25]

The following case, a case dubbed the Seen and Unseen Ghost by its main investigator, is probably the most interesting case of a collective apparition, and perhaps of any apparition, ever published. One afternoon, Tony Cornell, one of the most well-known parapsychology researchers of the last fifty years, received a phone call from a woman, Mrs. M, who had seen him on TV. She told him she had a problem involving a ghost, but did not tell him any of the details. Cornell told her he would come to the house the following day at 3:30 p.m. and that a colleague (called P.D.) would also come and would meet him there. Cornell arrived at the house first, and the woman took him into the sitting room and described the apparition. The apparition, she said, was of a

---

22. Prince, *Noted Witnesses*, 148-49.
23. Prince, *Noted Witnesses*, 149.
24. Prince, *Noted Witnesses*, 149.
25. Tony Cornell, *Investigating the Paranormal* (New York: Helix Press, 2002), 79-82.

man of about sixty with red hair, who repeatedly appeared in that sitting room, and "always sat in the same chair, wore a green corduroy smoking jacket, grey flannel trousers and slippers, and held a large pipe in his hand which he never smoked."[26] Mrs. M said that a maid who used to work there had also seen him, and that another employee, though he had never seen the ghost, said Mrs. M's description of the apparition matched that of the previous owner of the house. Mrs. M was confident that since Cornell was so interested in the apparition, the apparition would soon make his presence known. At this point, we will pick up the narrative in Cornell's own words:

> It was about 3:40 p.m. when, teacup in hand, she said, "Look! There he is in the chair." I turned my head in the direction indicated but could see nothing. Mrs. M. continued calmly that I must be able to see him and then described him getting up and walking over to the fireplace. She looked at me in complete disbelief when I asked what was he doing. She insisted that he was standing near the fireplace, had turned around and was looking at me. She put down her teacup and stood up to peer at the middle of the fireplace. I also stood up and walked towards where she was staring. Nothing further was said while I paced the length of the fireplace and back again to my chair. I then turned to look at Mrs. M., who swung on her heel and said "Hello there." I thought she was addressing the ghost, or had seen another one but, upon following her towards the open double door, I saw P.D. walking towards us halfway down the hallway. He stopped when he saw the two of us approaching him.
>
> I started to introduce him to Mrs. M. but he seemed more interested in the room from which we had just come out. "Come in and have a cup of tea," Mrs. M. said, "I was just showing Mr. Cornell. . ." but got no further as P.D. walked past her and stood in the middle of the room looking a little perplexed. My reaction at the time was that he was behaving rather impolitely and I was about to say something to him when he asked me where the man had gone. "What man?" I said. Mrs. M. offered to get more tea. She was about to say something else when I cut her short with the comment that more tea was a good idea. I asked her if I could show P.D. the garden and steered him towards the open French windows. Mrs. M., looking a little bewildered, followed us but then thought better of it and went into the kitchen.
>
> When I had got P.D. out into the garden he wanted to know what was going on.
>
> "What were you doing barging into the room like that?" I asked.
>
> "Well," he said, "I wondered where the husband had got to."
>
> "What husband?" I asked.
>
> "The bloke," P.D. said, "the one with the green jacket who beckoned me into the room."
>
> I was a little taken aback at this and asked him to explain what he meant. He looked at me as if I was being stupid.

---

26. Cornell, *Investigating*, 79.

> "Look here, when I arrived here," he said in a labored tone, "I found the front door open but knocked and got no answer, so I walked in because I could see you and the lady moving around in the room at the end of the hall. When I got some way towards you I saw the husband standing in front of you and he beckoned to me to join you but then you and the woman came out into the hall, and he seemed to just vanish when I looked over your shoulder at him."
>
> I then asked P.D. to give me a description of the man. He said he had ginger hair, a green jacket, light-colored trousers, and was holding something in his hand as he was beckoning. I made him repeat it all again, which he did just before Mrs. M. reappeared with the tea. When we reentered the sitting room through the French windows I told Mrs. M. that P.D. had seen the man.
>
> "Oh," she said, "well he has gone now. I think he got frightened off." She then told P.D. how just before he arrived she had seen the ghost but I had not, and how she could not understand how I could miss seeing him. I told P.D. to tell her what he had seen. His story puzzled her, as she had not seen the figure beckon anyone but simply look at me and walk over to the side window from the fireplace.[27]

Thus P.D. saw the apparition at the same time the woman saw it, even though he did not know the woman was seeing the apparition at the time or even what the apparition was supposed to look like. It is certainly interesting that Cornell could not see the apparition, and that P.D. saw the figure beckon him though Mrs. M did not see this. In any event, this appears to be the only case on record in which an investigator saw an apparition for himself.

Case 4: An Apparition in Iceland (Haraldsson 2009)[28]

This case was collected by Erlendur Haraldsson, a professor at the University of Iceland, as part of a survey of apparition experiences in Iceland. Although it does not contain as many interesting details as the other cases, we will quote it because, as it is part of Haraldsson's collection, it is among the most recently published cases of collective apparitions.

> I was around twenty. My father and I sat in the kitchen around noon. Then I see clearly a woman coming towards us. I was not going to mention it but notice that my father also sees this. I asked him what he was looking at and he replied, "Surely the same as you." Then he said he knew this woman. She had died a while back. Three or four hours later there was a phone call for my

---

27. Cornell, *Investigating*, 80-81.
28. Erlendur Haraldsson, "Experiences of Encounters with the Dead: 337 Cases," *Journal of Parapsychology* 73 (2009): 91-118 (109). Also reported in Erlendur Haraldsson, *The Departed Among the Living: An Investigative Study of Afterlife Encounters* (Guildford: White Crow, 2012), 203.

father who was a clergyman. The husband of the deceased woman we saw had died. We had seen the woman around the time her husband had died.[29]

Haraldsson adds: "We interviewed the father of the respondent, who described the incidence [sic] to us and thus verified his daughter's account."[30]

Alternative Explanations

Cases such as the above certainly look impressive, and, as I said, prima facie, the case for the reality of apparitions seems strong. But whether the case remains strong after the prima facie stage has passed depends on whether we can rule out the various alternative explanations proposed by skeptics. Hence to these explanations we now turn.

A few of the potential explanations can be ruled out rather quickly. Folie à deux, a psychological disorder in which two people both share in the same delusion, has been proposed,[31] but this will be of no help. For a delusion, unlike a hallucination, is not a visual perception. It is, according to the DSM's definition, a false belief held in spite of clear evidence to the contrary.[32] Thus to argue that the witnesses of a collective apparition are suffering from folie à deux is clearly to beg the question of whether the apparition is real. For only if the apparition was not real can we argue that the witnesses' belief that they saw it is false, and hence that they are holding a false belief; but in order to show it was not real, we need some reasons for thinking it was not real.

(One might be inclined to suggest that if an individual is completely mad—for example, a fellow who thinks he is a poached egg—then we do not need to explain how the person's false belief came about, because such people will hold utterly insane beliefs for no reason at all. But we shall trust that the investigators of our cases have been capable of recognizing complete lunatics, and in many of the cases related here, the account contains some specific indication that the witness was not a complete lunatic. For example, we just examined an account written by a professional parapsychologist, and we shall examine another one written by a physician.)

The hypothesis of mass hysteria is also of no help for similar reasons. The problem with this hypothesis is the absence of a coherent definition of "mass hysteria." The term is not used in reference to a single phenomenon, but is used in any instance in which a group of people appear to be behaving irrationally, regardless of what the underlying cause of their irrational behavior is. Consider the following phenomena, all of which have been labeled "mass hysteria": the case of the mad gasser, in which people in the city of Mattoon, Illinois mistakenly believed they had been paralyzed from gas; the Hindu Milk Miracle, in which certain persons thought a statue of a

---

29. Haraldsson, "Experiences," 109.
30. Haraldsson, "Experiences," 109.
31. David Lester, *Is There Life After Death? An Examination of the Empirical Evidence* (Jefferson, NC: McFarland, 2005), 170.
32. *DSM-IV*, 297.

Hindu god was drinking milk (scientists discovered a natural explanation); and the time that listeners of the "War of the Worlds" program on the radio thought the events being read from the novel were actually happening (they misunderstood the nature of the radio program).[33] These are clearly diverse phenomena, with diverse causes, and hence to call a certain case of something mass hysteria is simply to say that a group of people were acting irrationally, but this does not explain why they were acting as they were.

The chance hypothesis, though it will have to be given careful consideration in the case of crisis apparitions, is also untenable in the case of collective apparitions. The chance hypothesis would avoid the problem of collective hallucinations by proposing that the two witnesses just happened to have individual hallucinations simultaneously. That is, the hypothesis would hold that if for example, Bob and Joe both see an apparition of Sally at the same time, this is because each of them just happened to have an individual hallucination of Sally at the same time, and the hallucinations were so similar that they came to believe they had seen the same thing. However, hallucinations occur so infrequently (approximately 90% of the population will never have one at all), that the odds of two people just happening to have a very similar hallucination at the same time would appear to be astronomical.

Lies

But some hypotheses deserve more careful consideration, and the first of these is the hypothesis that the witnesses lied, that they simply made up their story of the apparition. This was a hypothesis which Gurney and the other early researchers were well aware of, and which all subsequent parapsychologists, regardless of their subfields, have also had to consider, since the hypothesis can be proposed not just for apparitions, but for any type of paranormal phenomena.

---

33. See the Wikipedia entry for "mass hysteria" for an overview of these and other cases of mass hysteria. One might ask whether uncertainty over what constitutes mass hysteria is a problem we find only in popular sources such as Wikipedia, and whether more technical sources provide a more coherent definition. But technical sources reveal just as much confusion over the definition. Erich Goode and Nachman Ben-Yehuda provide a definition which involves three elements but then go on to say that few cases of mass hysteria demonstrate each of these elements (Erich Goode and Nachman Ben-Yehuda, *Moral Panics: The Social Construction of Deviance* (2nd; Chichester: Wiley-Blackwell, 2009), 136). James S. Brown gives a definition of mass hysteria which makes it synonymous with so-called mass psychogenic illness ("mass illness mimicking outbreaks of toxic chemical exposures or infectious diseases but later attributed to psychogenic origins"), but he then presents examples which clearly do not fall under this definition: the "War of the Worlds," and a case involving damage to an automobile (James S. Brown, *Environmental and Chemical Toxins and Psychiatric Illness* (Washington, DC: American Psychiatric Pub., 2002), 35). Diana Kendall provides a definition which is quite vague and could cover lots of different phenomena: "a form of dispersed collective behavior that occurs when a large number of people react with strong emotions and self-destructive behavior to a real or perceived threat" (Diana Elizabeth Kendall, *Sociology in Our Times: The Essentials* (Australia: Wadsworth, 2000), 549).

Gurney's primary response to this hypothesis was based on the fact that the apparition accounts which he and other researchers were receiving differed from fictional accounts of apparitions. He pointed out at least three significant differences. First, the Society received no cases of "blood-curdling" stories, that is, stories in which ghosts chased people around, tried to kill them, or otherwise terrorized them. Second, there were very few cases of apparitions leaving effects on the physical environment. Most apparitions did not affect the environment at all,[34] and if an apparition did, the evidence of the effect was almost always gone when the apparition left. For example, if an apparition opened a door, the door would not be found to still be open once the apparition had left. Third, the apparitions did not carry on long conversations with the percipients; they either said nothing or at least did not say very much. From these facts Gurney argued that the apparition accounts they had received were not likely to be lies, since people would be expected to base their lies on the ideas which popular imagination held about ghosts, and we would surely not see virtually all the witnesses deviating from popular stories about ghosts in the same way.[35]

Gurney's basic argument has only been made stronger in the 130 years since, for the apparition accounts which have been reported to parapsychologists have continued to be characterized by an absence of these characteristics.[36]

Other arguments which can be given against lies should also be noted: the fact that in the vast majority of the cases the witness would have no motivation to lie; the large number of cases received; the fact that few published cases were ever actually exposed as lies;[37] the fact that sometimes the witness could produce another witness who attested that he had heard the first witness report the story to them before it was published (in which case either this second witness was lying or the first witness must have made up the story well before he intended to publish it);[38] and the fact that in Gurney's survey and in the *Census*, as well as in the more recent survey of crisis apparitions by Erlendur Haraldsson, the witness's claim that so and so died on a given date was checked against actual records, and no evidence was found that the witnesses were inventing people or dates of death.[39]

---

34. Excepting haunting cases (haunting cases will be discussed below).

35. Gurney, *Phantasms*, (vol. 1) 164-66.

36. E.g., Charles F. Emmons noted the absence of these characteristics from his collection of 146 apparition accounts in Hong Kong (*Chinese Ghosts and ESP: A Study of Paranormal Beliefs and Experiences* (Metuchen, NJ: Scarecrow, 1982), 54, 62, 97, 115).

37. This has been noted by Ian Stevenson, "Changing Fashions in the Study of Spontaneous Cases," *Journal of the American Society for Psychical Research* 81 (1987): 1-10 (4).

38. The first case of a collective apparition which we will examine below provides an example of this.

39. Haraldsson's survey is cited below where we discuss collective apparition number four.

Hoaxing

Another hypothesis is that the witnesses were hoaxed, that is, that they did not deceive the investigator themselves, but that someone deceived them. If someone wanted to hoax witnesses into thinking they had seen an apparition, there are two general methods that could be employed. First, someone might dress up as a ghost. There is one recorded case in which a practical joker donned a white sheet in order to scare passersby, but threw off the white sheet upon being pursued by an aggressor.[40] Tony Cornell also performed two experiments in which he disguised himself as a ghost in order to study people's reactions to an ostensibly paranormal phenomenon.[41] The second method would be to use a device which can project an image that can be mistaken for a real apparition. One such device is the magic lantern, a device which, though not in common use today, was once quite popular. The device can produce life-sized images on a wall or other surface, and the images can be realistic enough to be mistaken for a real person.[42]

However, neither form of hoaxing can account for the collective apparitions we have examined. With regard to the first hypothesis, the apparitions could not have been hoaxed by someone in a costume, because in the four cases discussed above the apparitions were of people who were known to the witnesses—unlike the two cases mentioned in the last paragraph, the witnesses did not claim to see merely an unrecognized figure in white. (The one case among those above in which the apparition was not known to the witnesses was the Cornell case, but that it is even harder to explain as a hoax; clearly no hoaxer could arrange it so that only two of the three witnesses would see the apparition.) Barring a spectacular use of makeup and costume, it is not conceivable that someone dressed up as a deceased person would be able to fool witnesses who had known that deceased person in life. In fact, it would be rare that anyone would even have the motivation to attempt such a hoax, and further, no real person would be able to accomplish the sudden appearances and disappearances that are attested in many of the cases.[43]

---

40. Augustus K. Stephenson, "Ghost Stories of 100 Years Ago: A Warning to 'Ghosts' and Psychical Researchers of the Present Day," *Journal of the Society for Psychical Research* 11 (1904): 214-220.

41. A.D. [Tony] Cornell, "An Experiment in Apparitional Observations and Findings," *Journal of the Society for Psychical Research* 40 (1959-60): 120-24; A.D. [Tony] Cornell, "Further Experiments in Apparitional Observation," *Journal of the Society for Psychical Research* 40 (1959-60): 409-18.

42. A good case can be made that a magic lantern was responsible for the famous Marian apparition at Knock in 1879. See Kevin McClure, *The Evidence for Visions of the Virgin Mary* (Wellingborough: Aquarian Press, 1983), 67-70.

43. We should mention the case of the Cummings apparition, the alleged apparition of the deceased Lydia Blaisdell, who appeared in Sullivan, Maine in the year 1800. In this case, the apparition did appear and disappear suddenly, but for various reasons, the case is quite probably a fraud. However, in this case, there were two circumstances surrounding the appearances and disappearances which make them much easier to explain as fraudulent and which we will not find in the cases of collective apparitions to be examined below: In this case, appearances and disappearances always occurred in a darkened cellar and the witnesses were always required to vacate the cellar before the

The second form of the hypothesis also falters for the same reason. Although a magic lantern or similar showman device can be used to project images of ghosts, these ghosts were not images of actual deceased people (except in the case of famous individuals). They were images of figures which the witnesses would not recognize, since the figures were fictional creations. Images of average people would not be available to project, and thus without the right images available to project, no projection device could be used to fool the witnesses into thinking they had seen a known deceased person. In addition, a projected image would be quite limited as far as the actions it would be able to perform, and so it could not perform some of the actions which we find apparitions performing in some cases. For example, in the Whitman case the apparition touched Cosgrave, and in the Cornell case, the apparition was only visible to two of the three people present.

Misremembering

A suggestion which might seem particularly attractive to the skeptic, given certain developments in psychology over the course of the last forty years or so, is that the witnesses misremembered. Since around 1970, a large number of studies have appeared addressing the potential problems of eyewitness testimony. While some of the studies concern mistakes in perception, that is, illusions (which we will discuss below), the large majority have to do with mistakes in recollection. I will address this line of research in greater detail in chapter 6, but I will also address it briefly here. Consider, for example, the following experiment.[44] Two groups of subjects watched a video of a car accident, and were later asked to estimate how fast the cars were going at the time of the collision. However, the wording of the question was different for each group: one version of the question asked about the cars hitting each other, while the other version asked about the cars "smashing" each other. The group that was asked about the cars "smashing" into each other estimated a higher rate of speed and was more likely to report that the crash involved broken glass than the other group. Clearly, the way in which a witness is asked a question can affect the witness's memory of an event. Other experiments have identified a host of other factors which can influence their memory as well, and we will discuss the matter further in chapter 6.

---

apparition appeared. The case of the Cummings Apparition was published by Abraham Cummings, *Immortality Proved by the Testimony of Sense* (Bath, ME: J.G. Torrey, 1826). I analyze the case in Jake H. O'Connell, "The Cummings Apparition: Evidence for Life After Death?" currently unpublished. For other analyses, see Muriel Roll, "A Nineteenth-Century Matchmaking Apparition: Comments on Abraham Cummings' Immortality Proved by the Testimony of Sense," *Journal of the American Society for Psychical Research* 63 (1969): 396-409; Roger I. Anderson, "The Cummings Apparition," *Journal of Religion and Psychical Research* 6 (1983): 206-19.

44. See Elizabeth F. Loftus, *Eyewitness Testimony* (Cambridge, MA: Harvard University Press, 1996 [1979]), 96.

The reason this line of research cannot help the skeptic explain collective apparitions is that this research has only demonstrated the fact that witnesses will misremember minor details of an event; no experiments have shown that witnesses will misremember the major elements of the event.[45] In the example just discussed, no witness stated, for example, that there had not been any cars at all, or that the cars had been flying through the air, or that the cars were driven by green monsters. Thus, though these experiments show that we will have to be aware of the fact that the witnesses may have misremembered some of the details of the apparition experience, they provide no basis for thinking that the central element of the experience, the fact that the witnesses saw an apparition, was misremembered.

Collective Hallucinations

Hallucinations are the most popular explanation for apparitions, and it is precisely because collective hallucinations seem impossible that collective apparitions warrant so much attention, for collective apparitions seem to take away the skeptic's primary explanation. But it is now time to take up a suggestion I mentioned earlier, namely, that collective hallucinations are in fact possible. Although this idea has not received much attention in the literature of ordinary psychology or medicine,[46] it is sometimes found in the religious and parapsychological literature, and I have argued for it myself, though I intend to make some significant modifications to that argument below.[47]

However, before considering the evidence for collective hallucinations, we must first be clear on what we mean by the term. We do not mean an event in which two people share in the same hallucination. There is no evidence for that phenomenon, and if that phenomenon did happen it would have to be considered a paranormal phenomenon. For a hallucination is a perception which only exists in the mind of the one who perceives it, and if someone can pass to another person a perception which

---

45. An exception is fantasizing. Fantasizers sometimes confuse their fantasies with reality (see Jon G. Allen, *Coping With Trauma: Hope Through Understanding* (2nd ed.; Washington, DC: American Psychiatric Publishing, 2005), 199). However, fantasizing is highly unlikely to be a good explanation for any case involving at least two people (such as the two witnesses of a collective apparition, or the witness of a crisis apparition and the person who the witness mentioned it to) because it is not very likely two people would have the same fantasy and mix up the same fantasy. Also, even in cases involving only one person, highly unusual events are highly unlikely to be misremembered, as are events of considerable personal significance to the person.

46. The only exceptions I am aware of are E.W. Anderson, "Abnormal Mental States in Survivors, with Special Reference to Collective Hallucinations," *Journal of the Royal Naval Medical Service* 28 (1942): 361-77; N. Lukianowiczc, "Hallucinations a Troix," *Archives of General Psychiatry* 1 (1959): 322-31.

47. I made the argument in Jake H. O'Connell, "Jesus' Resurrection and Collective Hallucinations," *Tyndale Bulletin* 60 (2009): 69-105. For other sources arguing for collective hallucinations, see Leon Marillier, "Apparitions of the Virgin in Dordogne," *Proceedings of the Society for Psychical Research* 7 (1892): 100-110; D.H. Rawcliffe, *Illusions and Delusions of the Supernatural and the Occult* (New York: Dover, 1959), 111-15; Leonard Zusne and Warren H. Jones, *Anomalistic Psychology: A Study of Magical Thinking* (Hillsdale, NJ: Lawrence Erlbaum Associates, 1989), 117-19.

only exists in his mind, that is by definition telepathy. Now this idea of a telepathic transfer of apparitions is part of the super-ESP explanation for apparitions, which we will consider below when we consider paranormal theories of apparitions. But since it is not a normal explanation for apparitions, we will not consider it here, and it is not what we mean by "collective hallucinations."

The hypothesis which we mean to designate by the term "collective hallucinations" is instead the hypothesis that people may, while in each other's presence, have very similar individual hallucinations, and that these hallucinations may be so similar that the percipients may afterward believe they have seen the same thing. One can see that this is not a paranormal hypothesis: the hallucination is not transferred from one person's mind to another's; each has his own hallucination in his own mind. Of course, I said above that the odds of two people just happening to have very similar hallucinations at the same time are astronomical. But the suggestion which various authors have made is that random chance is not the only possible cause of simultaneous individual hallucinations, and so the hallucinations do not "just happen" to occur at the same time. Two other causes have been proposed which seem always to occur in conjunction with each other. These causes are expectation and emotional excitement. The hypothesis is that if a group of people gather together fervently expecting to see an apparition (there are a number of such cases involving religious apparitions), and if they have aroused themselves into a state of emotional excitement, these two factors might work together to bring about hallucinations.

However, in order to argue that these are causes of collective hallucinations, we first need reasons to think there are collective hallucinations. The presence of expectation and emotional excitement at such cases, besides being possible causes of the collective hallucinations, also constitute reasons to think the events are collective hallucinations; but there are also three other reasons, and to these five reasons I now turn. I have explained all of this in more detail in my article in *Tyndale Bulletin*.[48]

In that article, I looked at six cases of religion related group visions and identified five reasons to regard them as collective hallucinations rather than real visions.

As an example of one of the group visions I examined, consider the following case, which historian Patrick Walker experienced firsthand. He tells us that one day in 1686: "Many people gathered together for several afternoons" and saw "Showers of Bonnets, Hats, Guns, and Swords, which covered the Trees and Ground, Companies of Men in Arms marching in order, upon the Waterside, Companies meeting Companies, going all through other, through other, and then all falling to the ground and disappearing; and other Companies immediately appearing the same way."[49]

The five reasons I presented for regarding these cases as collective hallucinations were as follows. First, the visions were expected—the crowds always gathered together

---

48. O'Connell, "Jesus' Resurrection and Collective Hallucinations."

49. Patrick Walker, *Biographia Presbyteriana*, (vol. 1.; Edinburgh: D. Speare, West Register Street; and J. Stevenson, Prince Street, 1827), 32-33 (discussed on pp. 75-76 of my article).

expecting to see a vision; the vision never happened spontaneously. This supports the hallucination hypothesis, because if the visions were group hallucinations, they would have to be expected, since it would not be possible for a group of people to all coincidentally hallucinate at the same time for no reason. By contrast, an apparition sent by God does not have to appear only when people are expecting it to. Second, the appearances often involved extreme stress (emotional excitement). We know stress can cause individual hallucinations[50] and so it is plausible it may cause group hallucinations, but there is no reason to expect a real religious apparition to be preceded by stress. Third, not everyone present sees the vision. We should expect this if the apparitions are hallucinations, because since not everyone is equally prone to hallucinate, not everyone should hallucinate. But there is no reason a real religious apparition should fail to manifest to everyone present. Fourth, those who do see the vision see it differently. This is to be expected on the hallucination hypothesis: since the witnesses are having individual hallucinations, they must necessarily see the apparition somewhat differently. But if the apparition is real, there is no reason it should manifest itself differently to different people. Fifth, in no case does the apparition carry on a conversation with the group. This is to be expected if the apparition is a hallucination, because since individual hallucinations are involved, there can be no conversation between the apparition and the group. But an apparition which God has sent should be able to carry on a group conversation.

The preceding paragraph represents a summary of what I argued in my article, but I now need to modify that argument in several ways. First, I no longer think the fraud hypothesis, the hypothesis that the witnesses lied, is as improbable as I assumed it to be at the time I wrote the article. I assumed, based largely on the sheer number of people claiming to have witnessed something, that fraud was quite unlikely. Notice that the criteria above discriminate between collective hallucinations and real visions, but not between collective hallucinations and fraud. For all five features are expected on the fraud hypothesis. If we have a fraud, the visions must be expected, since a fraud must be planned in advance. The extreme stress (displayed, for example, by fainting) could be fake. Not everyone would see the apparition, for not everyone would be in on the fraud. Those who do see the apparition will see (or, rather, would claim to see) it differently, for with a large number of people involved, it will be difficult to coordinate the details of exactly what the apparition should look like. And there will be no group conversations, because it would be too difficult to agree on exactly what the apparition is supposed to have said.

Based on a case which I found subsequent to writing the article, I must now consider myself unsure as to whether the cases I examined are frauds or collective

---

50. See R. K. Siegel, "Hostage Hallucinations: Visual Imagery Induced by Isolation and Life-threatening Stress," *Journal of Nervous and Mental Disease* 172 (1984): 264-72; G. Asaad and B. Shapiro, "Hallucinations: Theoretical and Clinical Overview," *American Journal of Psychiatry* 143 (1986): 1088-1097.

hallucinations. That case is a case of visions, primarily of Mary, in Ezkioga, Spain and surrounding areas during the 1930s, investigated by William Christian Jr.[51] There is strong evidence that fraud was the cause in this case. Blood appeared on the hands of some of the visionaries, on crucifixes and images, and on a bus.[52] Though blood on the hands could possibly be explained naturalistically via the psychosomatic hypothesis,[53] blood on the crucifixes and images and a bus cannot, at least not in those cases where the blood was seen by all.[54] Bloody crucifixes or images have been at the center of some cases of pious fraud.[55] Also, when someone asked why an image which was known to bleed was not kept sealed off from passersby (so as to keep anyone from applying blood), one of the visionaries answered that the Virgin had forbidden it—a claim to be expected, I must say, on the fraud hypothesis.[56] Further, at least one visionary was examined by doctors and they concluded that she had inflicted the wounds on herself; a witness had claimed to have seen a razor blade on the ground near her.[57] Since the Ezkioga case is of the same type as the ones discussed in my article, if Ezkioga is a fraud, it seems likely that the ones in my article are as well. However, I remain unsure that Ezkioga is entirely a fraud. A couple points can be cited against the fraud hypothesis. First, Christian spoke to some of the visionaries when he investigated the case decades later, and none of the visionaries renounced their visions.[58] Second, there was some persecution of the visionaries.[59] In some cases, the persecution was mild (e.g., being denied communion),[60] but in at least one case, the persecution was more serious—the visionary either paid a large fine or was in jail for sixteen months.[61] Thus it is possible some of the seers were honest. (Since

51. William Christian Jr., *Visionaries: The Spanish Republic and the Reign of Christ* (Berkeley: University of California Press, 1996). There were over 250 seers in all (p.250).

52. Blood on seers' hands: 50, 182, 201, 273. Blood on images: 159, 200, 445 n49. Blood on crucifixes: 156, 159, 195, 434 n77, 155, 95, 208. Blood on a bus: 203.

53. For some cases of psychosomatic bleeding, see Edward F. Kelly et al., *Irreducible Mind: Toward a Psychology for the 21st Century* (Lanham, MD: Rowman and Littlefield, 2007), 199-209.

54. This appears to be the case for the cases related on pp. 159, 200, and 208. But in the case related on 95 it appears only the seers could see the blood. All could see the blood on the bus (203).

55. See Joe Nickell, *The Science of Miracles: Investigating the Incredible* (Amherst, NY: Prometheus, 2012), 57-78. See Nickell's whole book for the issue of pious fraud more generally. See also the case of pious fraud, partially related to Ezkioga but not involving the blood, related in Christian, *Visionaries*, 67-74.

56. Christian, *Visionaries*, 200.

57. Christian, *Visionaries*, 50-51.

58. This is mentioned at various points in his book, e.g., 381-83.

59. Christian, *Visionaries*, 195-211.

60. Christian, *Visionaries*, 198.

61. Christian, *Visionaries*, 199. It is not clear if the visionary was one of the ones who paid a large fine or one of the ones who remained in jail because of an inability to pay the fine. We must distinguish between persecution of the visionaries and persecution of the visionaries' followers. If the visionaries were liars, that does not necessarily mean their followers were being persecuted for something they knew was a lie; the followers may have honestly believed the message.

the bleeding crucifixes and images and bus mean fraud must have been at work, the hallucinations hypothesis in this case would be that though some of the phenomena were fraudulent, some were caused by hallucinations.)

Since I am unsure, let us now suppose the cases I examined are collective hallucinations. Let us see how the cases of collective apparitions related above fulfill the criteria I laid out. The apparitions are not expected. Extreme stress is not present. Everyone present sees the apparition—except in the Cornell case. And everyone who sees the apparition sees it in the same way—except, again, in the Cornell case. There are no group conversations, with the exception of the brief words "Willie, Willie" in case 3. We clearly have here imperfect fulfillment of the criteria, and I now need to modify the criteria I laid out.

My new opinion of the criteria is as follows. Criterion 1 is absolutely necessary and criterion 2 is likely absolutely necessary if a case of an apparition, either one of the dead or one sent by God, is to be regarded as a collective hallucination. As for criteria 3 and 4, though a hallucinatory apparition will necessarily be seen by only some present and be seen differently by those who see it, it appears likely that a real apparition will not necessarily be seen by all and be seen the same by all—and an apparition of the dead is more likely to be seen differently and not by all than an apparition sent by God. We have the same situation in regard to criterion 5: a hallucinatory apparition will not engage in group conversation, but a real apparition will not necessarily do so either—and this is more likely so with an apparition of the dead than one sent by God.

Expectation is absolutely necessary in the case of a collective hallucination, for only if there is expectation can we avoid the problem of the witnesses all happening to hallucinate at the same time for no reason. Stress also seems to be necessary given that there is experimental evidence which indicates expectation alone cannot cause hallucinations.[62] But now for the other three criteria. As for criteria 3 (not everyone seeing the apparition), this is surely necessary if the apparition is hallucinatory, for it is not likely that everyone in a large crowd will all be equally prone to hallucinate. But is it the case that a real apparition will necessarily be seen by all? I had assumed so, since I saw no reason to think apparitions are bound by any laws which might keep them from being able to manifest to all. But I must now change my opinion on that, and I must also distinguish between apparitions of the dead and apparitions sent by God

---

62. In one experiment, researchers attempted to test whether hallucinations can be induced by expectation by telling subjects that when they approached a certain area, they would not see anything, even though there was in fact something there. The intent was to see whether the subjects would experience a negative hallucination (failing to see something though something is actually there) because they expected not to see anything. However, all of the subjects did in fact see something (Graham F. Wagstaff, Steven Toner, and Jon Cole, "Is Response Expectancy Sufficient to Account for Hypnotic Negative Hallucinations?" *Contemporary Hypnosis* 19 (2002): 133-38). But we cannot be absolutely sure that expectation by itself cannot cause hallucinations. It may be that expectation (by itself) does have this power, but the experiment did not have a sufficient number of subjects to detect this. For example, suppose expectation produces this effect in 1 out of every 1000 people and there are 100 people in the experiment. The odds are 10:1 against the experiment detecting this phenomenon.

(as the apparitions examined in my article purportedly were, most of them Marian apparitions). In the Cornell case, the apparition was not seen by all present. Hence if we accept this case as real, we have a case of a real apparition not being seen by all present. Does it make sense that an apparition of the dead would have a difficult time manifesting to all present? Yes, because there is a good deal of evidence that apparitions have a hard time "getting through," and are thus bound by some kinds of laws:

1) Apparitions are more likely to be seen on some days rather than others depending upon the Earth's geomagnetic levels. This makes sense if apparitions have trouble getting through from the other side.[63] 2) There are some examples of "bystander apparitions," cases in which the apparition is seen not by the person who the apparition would seem to want to be seen by, but by someone else in their vicinity. For example, suppose Bob is in a room with Joe, and Bob's father appears to Joe. It would seem Bob's father should have appeared to Bob.[64] Such a fact also makes sense if apparitions have trouble getting through, as does: 3) there are examples of half formed apparitions.[65] Finally, 4) people who have experienced an electric shock are more likely to see apparitions.[66]

Hence, based on the Cornell case and these factors, we need not be surprised that apparitions of the dead may not be seen by all present (though they often are seen by all present—and if they are, they must be real, since, as we said, hallucinatory apparitions will not be seen by all). Now what about religious apparitions? Is there evidence they are affected by natural laws and thus could have trouble getting through? Yes: Some people who have reported cases of miraculous healings report that when being healed they experienced a feeling like lightning or a bolt of electricity.[67] If these healings are real, this would suggest miracles by God are facilitated by natural phenomena. The reality of these healings is of course disputed, but the evidence is at least suggestive.[68] Thus even a religious apparition might not be seen by all present, though given the uncertainty of our knowledge concerning this phenomenon of electricity in relation to miraculous healings, we cannot be as confident as we can in regard to apparitions of the dead.

---

63. Michael A. Persinger, "Spontaneous Telepathic Experiences from Phantasms of the Living and Low Global Geomagnetic Activity," *Journal of the American Society for Psychical Research* 81 (1987): 23-36.

64. See e.g., Erlendur Haraldsson, "The Iyengar-Kirti Case: An Apparitional Case of the Bystander Type," *Journal of the Society for Psychical Research* 54 (1987): 64-67. Recall that in the Whitman case, related above, one of the percipients felt an electric shock.

65. See e.g., Bill Guggenheim and Judy Guggenheim, *Hello From Heaven*, chapter 6.

66. See Michael Jawer, "Environmental Sensitivity: Inquiry into a Possible Link with Apparitional Experience," *Journal of the Society for Psychical Research* 70 (2006): 25-47.

67. See Craig S. Keener, *Miracles: The Credibility of the New Testament Accounts* (Grand Rapids, MI: Baker Academic, 2011), 471. Other cases are related at other points in Keener's book.

68. On this topic, see Keener's whole book.

Points 4 and 5 apply in the same way. As for point 4, different people seeing the apparition differently, I had assumed there was no reason to think an apparition would be bound by any physical laws making its manifestation difficult. But in the Cornell case, the apparition was seen differently by different people. And based on the possibility religious apparitions are bound by the same laws as apparitions of the dead, we must acknowledge this possibility in the case of religious apparitions as well. Yet, when we find cases which are the opposite, where the apparition is seen the same by all, as is so for all the cases of apparitions of the dead related in this chapter except the Cornell case, it cannot be hallucinatory. For, as we said, simultaneous individual hallucinations will necessarily be somewhat different. Finally, as for group conversations, if there is a group conversation (as there apparently was, a short one, in case 1) the apparition cannot be hallucinatory, since, as I explained, simultaneous individual hallucinations cannot involve one single conversation. But the opposite will not be the case. Notice that three of the four apparitions of the dead examined in this chapter do not speak; since we have evidence that apparitions are bound by natural laws, it is thus not a shock that they do not always speak.[69]

Our final conclusion then, is that the religious apparitions examined in my article, if they are not frauds, must be collective hallucinations, because they involved expectation and stress. The collective apparitions we have examined in this chapter cannot be collective hallucinations because expectation and stress are not present for any of them, and points 3 and 4 also apply as arguments against collective hallucinations for each case except the Cornell case, and point 5 also applies in Case 3.

Illusions

The final hypothesis to consider is that of illusions. Although the word illusion is frequently confused with the word hallucination, an illusion is not the same as a hallucination. A hallucination is a sensory perception in the absence of any visual stimuli, whereas an illusion is the misperception of actual visual stimuli.[70] In simpler terms,

69. One study (which I will address in greater detail in chapter 7), of both collective and individual purportedly real apparitions, found that only 27% of apparitions speak (Hornell Hart and Collaborators, "Six Theories About Apparitions," *Proceedings of the Society for Psychical Research* 50 (1956): 153-239 (159)).

70. See page 823 of the DSM-IV for this distinction between hallucinations and illusions. Some so-called "illusions" are however, better understood as hallucinations, because though they involved a misperception of an actual object, the malfunction of the senses must be rather extraordinary and on a par with the level of malfunction required by hallucinations. For example, in the case discussed in this section, in which the crew of a ship mistook a beam of wood which was off in the distance for their captain, no extraordinary malfunction of the senses seems required; a normal person might misperceive an object some distance away. But suppose the piece of wood had been right there on the ship with them, only a few feet away, and they had seen it transform into their captain right before their eyes. Although this is technically an illusion since it does involve an actual visual object, it seems like an entirely abnormal occurrence on a par with hallucinations. For more on this, see O'Connell, "Collective Hallucinations," 72 including n4.

a hallucination is the perception of something that is not there, whereas an illusion is the misperception of something that is there. For example, if I see a person in the next room when there is actually nobody there, that is a hallucination. However, if I think I see a person in the next room, but upon drawing closer, I find that what I thought was a person is actually a bookcase which was made to look like a person due to the reflection of the light, that is an illusion. Or consider a simpler type of illusion: mistaken identity. A witness could simply mistake an actual person for an apparition.

In the following case, the witnesses mistook a piece of wood for an apparition:

> All the crew of a vessel was frightened by the ghost of a cook, who had died some days previously. He was distinctly seen by all, walking on the water with a peculiar limp which had characterized him, one of his legs being shorter than the other. The cook, who had been recognized by so many, turned out to be a piece of wreck, rocked up and down by the waves.[71]

The possibility of illusion, whether of an object, or a person (mistaken identity), can be ruled out in a particular case if the following criteria are satisfied. First, the apparition must have been seen close up. If the apparition was seen from far away it would be difficult to perceive it accurately, but if an object is seen close up it is much more difficult to misperceive it. (Hence, Andrew MacKenzie relates one case in which two witnesses saw what they thought was an apparition, but being as the apparition was viewed from a distance of about 300 feet, we cannot be confident that the witnesses had a good enough view of it to be sure it was not a real person.)[72] Second, the apparition must have been seen for a fairly substantial period of time. If an object is seen only for a moment it is difficult to perceive it accurately even if one sees it close up,[73] but if it is seen for a period of, say, at least 10-15 seconds, a witness should be able to determine what the object is (as long as the object is not being manipulated by a conjuror, but that would reduce to the hoaxing hypothesis). Third, there must be nothing obstructing the witness's view of the figure. For even if something is seen close up and for an extended period of time, the witness may not perceive it accurately if his view of the object is obstructed. (I read of one case of a collective apparition, the citation for which I unfortunately cannot find, in which the witnesses' view of the figure was obscured by the falling snow of a snowstorm.) However, all four of the cases I related above fulfill these three criteria, as do many of the other collective apparitions

---

71. This is Edmund Parish's summary of the case (*Hallucinations and Illusions: A Study of the Fallacies of Perception* (London: W. Scott, 1897), 311). The case appears to have been first reported in John Brand, *Observations on Popular Antiquities* (vol. 2; London: Nichols, Son, and Bentley, 1813), 429.

72. Andrew MacKenzie, *The Seen and the Unseen* (London: Weidenfeld and Nicolson, 1987), 205-09.

73. In one apparition case, the witness looked up and saw an apparition standing near the fire place. He then attempted to return to his cleaning duties and when he looked up again, the figure had gone. Joe Nickell attempts to provide an explanation based on optical phenomena for apparitions, such as this one, which are seen only momentarily and then vanish: Joe Nickell, *Real Life X-Files: Investigating the Paranormal* (Lexington, KY: University of Kentucky Press, 2001), 291.

in the literature which I have not discussed. Thus the illusion hypothesis also fails to explain collective apparitions.

Crisis Apparitions

The fourth collective apparition related above was also a crisis apparition,[74] but it will be helpful to present a more detailed account as well:

> About 2 o'clock on the morning of October 21st, 1881, while I was perfectly wide awake, and looking at a lamp burning on my wash hand-stand, a person, as I thought, came into my room by mistake, and stopped, looking into the looking-glass on the table. It soon occurred to me it represented Robinson Kelsey, by his dress and wearing his hair long behind. When I raised myself up in bed and called out, it instantly disappeared. The next day I mentioned to some of my friends how strange it was. So thoroughly convinced was I, that I searched the local papers that day (Saturday) and the following Tuesday, believing his death would be in one of them. On the following Wednesday, a man, who formerly was my driver, came and told me Robinson Kelsey was dead. Anxious to know at what time he died, I wrote to Mr. Wood, the family undertaker at Lingfield; he learnt from the brother-in-law of the deceased that he died at 2 a.m. He was my first cousin, and was apprenticed formerly to me as a miller; afterwards he lived with me as journeyman; altogether, 8 years.[75]

Now to consider the alternative explanations. Delusion and mass hysteria will not work for the same reasons they would not work for collective apparitions: To call the apparition a delusion is only to say that the witness's belief is false, but saying this does not help explain why the witness's belief is false. Mass hysteria, as we saw, is an incoherent concept, and a crisis apparition is not a group apparition anyway. (And since the same can be said with regard to delusion and mass hysteria when they are applied to the other types of cases we are going to examine, we may as well stop considering these hypotheses.) As for lies, there is no more reason to think a witness will lie about a crisis apparition than there is to think they would lie about a collective apparition, and so all of the arguments against lies given above still apply. Hallucinations will not work because the mere fact of the crisis apparition is meant to rule out hallucination: if an apparition corresponds with a person's death and this is not a coincidence, then the apparition cannot be a hallucination because hallucinations should not be just happening to occur at the same time that the person whose hallucination it is dies.

---

74. For cases of crisis apparitions, in addition to the ones included in *Phantasms of the Living*, see: Sidgwick, "Census," 207-51; Ian Stevenson, "Six Modern Apparitional Experiences," *Journal of Scientific Exploration* 9 (1995): 351-66; Sylvia Hart Wright, "Paranormal Contact with the Dying: 14 Contemporary Death Coincidences," *Journal of the Society for Psychical Research* 63 (1999): 258-67; Haraldsson, *Departed Among the Living*, chapters 7 and 34.

75. Gurney, *Phantasms*, (vol. 1) 207.

Hoaxing and illusions are untenable for the same reason—hoaxes and illusions of an apparition should not correspond with the death of the person whose apparition it is any more often than a hallucination should, for a hoaxer would not plan to hoax the apparition right at the time the person whose apparition it is dies, and if the witness has an illusion of the person right at the time the person dies, this is just as strange a coincidence as a hallucination.

This leaves us with two alternative hypotheses which we examined in regard to collective apparitions, misremembering and chance, and some hypotheses which apply distinctively to crisis apparitions and not to other types of apparitions.

The possibility of misremembering is greater here than with collective apparitions because in the case of crisis apparitions the witness is not required to misremember the most basic element of the event (that there was an apparition), but only a fairly minor detail of the event: whether or not the apparition was seen on the same day that the person whose apparition it was died. While it is difficult to imagine a witness remembering they saw an apparition when in fact they did not see anything at all, it is not so difficult to imagine them seeing the apparition a day or two before or after the person's death and later remembering they had seen it on the same day. As mentioned above, Gurney was aware of this possibility and he presented the following criteria for ruling out misremembering: No case of a crisis apparition should be accepted unless: 1) the witness had written down an account of the apparition before learning that the person had died on that day, or 2) the witness had told someone else about the apparition prior to learning that the person had died on the same day (and the investigator must get a statement from this other person). The evidence of a written account is certainly stronger, but it would be unrealistic to expect this in very many cases. When we have the testimony of the person to whom the witness recounted the experience, that means not just one but two people must be mistaken as to when the apparition appeared. Thus the testimony of a second person is strong evidence, and it is the best type of evidence we could realistically hope for in such cases.

A word should here be said about a frequently cited case of alleged misremembering in relation to crisis apparitions, known as the Hornby case.[76] This was a case of a crisis apparition experienced by Sir Edmund Hornby, a prominent judge of the late nineteenth century. After the case was published by the SPR, a critic noted a problem with Hornby's story. The date on which the person whose apparition it was died was several months prior to Sir Edmund's marriage, yet Sir Edmund had claimed he was in bed with Lady Hornby on the night the apparition appeared, and Lady Hornby had supported the story. Hence there were two possibilities: Either Sir Edmund and his wife were in bed together before they were married, or Sir Edmund's memory of when the apparition occurred must have been off by several months. The story was retracted from the *Proceedings of the Society for Psychical Research* at Hornby's request,

---

76. On the Hornby case, see Alan Gauld, "Mr Hall and the SPR," *Journal of the Society for Psychical Research* 28 (1965): 53-62 (61-62).

which would imply Hornby admitted his memory was mistaken. However, given that premarital sex was entirely socially unacceptable in the world of upper class Victorian England (in the late 1800s and early 1900s, this was where almost all of the SPR cases came from), Hornby had a clear motivation to lie, and given that a lie in the face of a strong motivation is not improbable whereas an instance of misremembering of the magnitude that would be required in this case is, we should certainly regard the hypothesis of lying to be the better explanation.

Now for the chance hypothesis. In the case of collective apparitions, this hypothesis seemed completely implausible, for surely two people will not just happen to have essentially the same hallucination at the same time. But the hypothesis comes across as stronger in the case of crisis apparitions. Hallucinations are relatively common (approximately 10% of the population will experience them) and that a person might happen to have a hallucination of someone on the same day that person dies is not as startling a coincidence as two people in each other's presence both happening to have very similar hallucinations at the exact same time. In the case of a collective apparition, both events have to occur at the exact same time (and the events must be not just two simultaneous hallucinations, but two simultaneous hallucinations of the same person), but in the case of a crisis apparition the events only have to occur on the same day. Gurney developed a statistical argument to try to combat the chance hypothesis; this argument was based on the odds of a person dying on a given day and the odds of a person hallucinating on a given day, and he concluded that the odds of the thirty-one crisis apparitions in his collection happening by chance were over a trillion trillion to one.[77] However, for several reasons, Gurney's statistical argument has not persuaded most, nor has the modified version of this statistical argument presented in the *Census of Hallucinations*. (The primary criticism concerns the invalidity of the assumptions that all people are equally likely to die on a given day and that a person is equally likely to hallucinate on all days.)[78] There is, however, another type of statistical argument which can be made against the chance hypothesis. *Phantasms* as well as the *Census* found a vast number of cases of crisis apparitions, that is, apparitions which occurred on the exact day that the person whose apparition it was died. Now these studies also solicited all other type of cases of apparitions of the living and of the dead; there was no special emphasis on seeking crisis apparitions. If day of death apparitions truly are just a coincidence, apparitions are no more likely to occur on the day of the death than at any point during the days leading up to the death. But if that is the case, we should find just as many reports of day of death apparitions as we do apparitions which occurred two days before the death, three days before the death, four days before the death, and so on. However, we do not find this. We find lots of cases of day of death apparitions, and few reports of cases of apparitions in the days or weeks leading up to the death; this surely indicates day of death apparitions are occurring

77. Gurney, *Phantasms*, (vol. 2) 17.
78. For some comments on Gurney's statistical argument see Gauld, *Founders*, 183-85.

at a rate greater than what would be expected by chance. One could respond that this is because of misremembering: that the witnesses misremembered apparitions which occurred during the days leading up to the death as having occurred on the same day of the death, and that is why there are so many more reports of day of death apparitions. However, it is hard to imagine the amount of misremembering among witnesses being colossal enough to account for the great disparity in the number of day of death apparitions compared to the number of apparitions during the time leading up to death in *Phantasms* and the *Census*.

We shall now consider the hypotheses which apply distinctively to crisis apparitions.

1) An early critic of *Phantasms* objected that in some cases, the percipient may have been asleep.[79] Since statistical calculations endeavoring to rule out the possibility of chance have been based on the frequency with which hallucinations occur in the waking state, including cases in which the percipient was asleep could confound the statistical calculation. However, one ought to agree with Gurney's reply that in most cases, it is quite clear whether or not the percipient was asleep (for example, in the case quoted at the beginning of this section, the percipient explicitly stated that he was wide awake).

2) It might be objected that the witness may have known that the person who eventually died was sick and near death, and this may have caused the witness to hallucinate the person, and hence the hallucinations are not purely random, and the reason for the coincidence between the timing of the apparition and the death of the person whose apparition it was is thus clear. However, in most cases, the witness did not know the person was sick, and in some cases, they had not even seen the person recently. It might be objected that in those cases in which the witness had seen the person recently, though it may not have been obvious that the person was sick, the person might have given this away via subtle sensory cues. However, this explanation cannot account for the fact that day of death apparitions so disproportionately outnumber apparitions which occurred two days before death, three days before death, etc. For if the person was only somewhat more sick on the day of death than they were during the days leading up to this (if they were any more than somewhat more sick, then sensory cues would have been more obvious), then subtle sensory cues ought to have been only somewhat more obvious on the day of death than on the days leading

---

79. C.S. Peirce, "Criticisms on Phantasms of the Living," *Proceedings of the American Society for Psychical Research* 1 (1887): 150-57 (151). This article is a general critique of Gurney's argument for the reality of crisis apparitions. For other early critiques, see A.T. Innes, "Where are the Letters? A Cross-Examination of Certain Phantasms," *Nineteenth Century* 22 (1887): 174-94; and Parish, *Hallucinations and Illusions*, 272-320. The second and third criticisms which we are about to examine are also to be found in this early literature, as are a number of other criticisms which we do not have space to consider here. For Gurney's reply to Innes, see "Letters on Phantasms: A Reply," *Nineteenth Century* 22 (1887): 522-33. For his reply to Peirce, and for Peirce's reply back to Gurney, and another reply by Gurney, see pp. 157-214, 286-99 of the aforementioned volume of *PASPR* (see pp. 300-301 for Myers's comments).

up to that day, and thus there ought to be only somewhat more hallucinations on the day of death than on preceding days.

3) It may be objected that the figure perceived might have been an unclear looking figure which the witness did not recognize, and the witness, upon learning that someone they knew had died that day, and knowing of the belief that an apparition of a person is often a herald of that person's death,[80] then drew a connection between the unrecognized phantom they had seen and the person who died. The skeptic will then tell us to look at all the cases of unrecognized figures which did not correspond with a death,[81] and then tell us that out of all these (in the skeptic's opinion) subjective hallucinations, once in a while one of them will occur on a day when someone the witness knows dies.

In response to the skeptic, we should note: a) in some cases, the witness tells us that the apparition possessed some feature(s) which was distinctive to the person who died (e.g., in the case quoted above, the witness tells us that he recognized his cousin by his long hair and his manner of dress). And b), in all cases which Gurney accepted, the witness had either noted the occurrence of the apparition in writing or told another person about the apparition *before* receiving news of the person's death. And c), in some cases (such as the one quoted above), the witness tells us that seeing the apparition caused them to wonder whether the person whose apparition it was had died, a fact which surely requires that they were able to identify the apparition.

4) Some studies indicate that sudden deaths are more likely to occur on days when the geomagnetic level is low,[82] and Michael Persinger, in his examination of cases of crisis apparitions, found that crisis apparitions are more likely to occur on days when the geomagnetic level is low.[83] One might endeavor to argue that when these two facts are put together, we have our explanation for why crisis apparitions occur at a rate greater than expected by chance. However, these facts seem inadequate to explain why so many of the apparitions which are seen on a day when a person dies are *apparitions of the person who died*. Let us suppose Grandpa has died on a day when the geomagnetic level is low, and we now expect someone Grandpa knew to have a random hallucination. Will they necessarily have a hallucination of Grandpa? No, if the hallucination is random, that person may have a hallucination of their friend, or their boss at work, or a dog, or a cat, or of Grandma, or of Grandma and Grandpa's neighbor. Now though they may not draw a connection if the hallucination/apparition

---

80. This belief was fairly widespread during the late 1800s. In the case we examined above, the witness tells us that he thought the apparition of his cousin a possible indication that his cousin had died. Some of the other witnesses who provided cases for *Phantasms* also mentioned this.

81. See e.g., Sidgwick, "Census," 47 for cases of unrecognized apparitions.

82. E. Stoupel, et al., "Sudden Cardiac Death and Geomagnetic Activity: Links to Age, Gender and Agony Time," *Journal of Basic and Clinical Physiology and Pharmacology* 13 (2002): 11-21.

83. Michael A. Persinger, "Spontaneous Telepathic Experiences from Phantasms of the Living and Low Global Geomagnetic Activity," *Journal of the American Society for Psychical Research* 81 (1987): 23-36.

is of someone who did not have anything to do with Grandpa (such as their friend or their boss at work), they will draw a connection if the hallucination/apparition is of someone who had to do with Grandpa—such as Grandma, or Grandma and Grandpa's neighbor. Hence, we should find many cases of apparitions of people who have to do with the person who died occurring on the day of the person's death. We do not find this.

(Let me add in conclusion that the reality of crisis apparitions is also supported by the fact that it appears that paranormal events other than apparitions coincide with death at a rate greater than one would expect by chance. But though there is data suggesting that this is the case,[84] the matter has not been researched to the extent that crisis apparitions have.)

Informational Apparitions

The next type of apparition to consider is informational apparitions, that is, apparitions which provide the percipient with information which he did not already know.[85] In the case of this type of apparition,[86] it will be easier to consider most of the alternative explanations upfront. Delusion and mass hysteria we have already said we can cease considering. Hallucinations are out of the question because a hallucination, since it is a creation of the mind, cannot provide a person with any information not already in their mind. Likewise, illusion is ruled out because if the witness mistook an object for an apparition, the object would not be able to provide him with any information, and mistaken identity is ruled out because a person accidentally mistaken for the apparition would not be providing the witness with previously unknown facts concerning the apparition. Hoaxing faces the same problems it did in the case of collective apparitions; and it faces the further problem that the hoaxer would have to find information which he knew the witness did not know about, and have to find some way of causing the apparition (which must on this hypothesis either be a person dressed up or a projected image) to communicate the information orally without the witness realizing it is a trick. The only two hypotheses which deserve substantial

---

84. See e.g., James McClenon, "Content Analysis of an Anomalous Memorate Collection: Testing Hypotheses Regarding Universal Features," *Sociology of Religion* 61 (2000): 155-69 (162).

85. For other cases of informational apparitions besides those related here, see e.g., Frederick W.H. Myers, *Human Personality and its Survival of Bodily Death* (London: Longmans, 1903), pp. 37-40 of volume 1 and pp. 326-29 of volume 2; Anonymous [Society for Psychical Research], "Case of the Will of James L. Chaffin," *Proceedings of the Society for Psychical Research* 36 (1928): 517-24; Anonymous [Society for Psychical Research] "A Dream Suggesting Planned Evidence of Survival," *Journal of the Society for Psychical Research* 30 (1937-38): 182-86; Ian Stevenson, "The Case of the Teddy Bear Suit," *Journal of the Society for Psychical Research* 43 (1965): 92-93; Ian Stevenson, "A Series of Possibly Paranormal Recurrent Dreams," *Journal of Scientific Exploration* 6 (1992): 281-89.

86. There is some overlap between informational apparitions and crisis apparitions, because some cases of informational apparitions are simply cases of crisis apparition with the addition of the fact that the apparition conveys the information that he has died.

consideration are lies and a special form of misremembering called cryptomnesia (a concept I will explain below). Let us examine two cases of informational apparitions, and then consider how lies and cryptomnesia can be ruled out.

Case 1: A Blue Orchid (Stevenson 1964)[87]

This case centers on the apparition of Owen Howison. Owen picked a blue flower one day when he was on a mountain called Table Mountain. Sometime after this, when he saw his mother, he took the flower out of his shirt and showed it to her. After Owen died, Mrs. Feakes, a cousin of Owen, saw an apparition of him in which the apparition took a blue flower out of his shirt and told Mrs. Feakes to tell his mother he got it from Table Mountain. Mrs. Feakes did not know what this meant, but she wrote the mother about the matter, and was then told about the corresponding incident in Owen's life. Mrs. Feakes also had a vision of Owen in which he mentioned someone named Helen. Mrs. Feakes did not know who Helen was, but Mrs. Howison confirmed that Helen was a friend of Owen's. (Mrs. Feakes had other visions of Owen as well, but these did not provide her with any new information.)

The episode about the blue flower is summed up in the letter which Mrs. Feakes wrote to Ian Stevenson when she first informed him of the case (she mentioned Helen to him in other correspondence):

> In 1944 my cousin [Owen Howison] was killed in the East in action. He was 22 the day he died. I had not seen him or his family since 1939 when they moved to Capetown...
>
> I saw a ball of golden fog, it came along the floor, rose up in front of me, and in the ball of golden mist I saw the head and shoulders of my cousin Owen, and in that instant felt a blinding flash of heat and pain all down my left side and face. He said, "My tank was blown up. Tell Mum I'm not dead and remember me to Helen." I said, "Give me proof, please, Owen, so she'll believe us." He whispered "watch". He opened his shirt and took out one blue flower, (it had a sweet penetrating perfume) put it back in his shirt, then opened his shirt again, took it out again, showed me the flower and put it inside his shirt vest again. "Tell Mum, please, goodbye dear cousin."
>
> I could not understand the message but wrote to South Africa, and told Beatrice, [the mother of Owen]. She replied, "I thank God and you for this overwhelming proof and an incident of which you were so ignorant meant everything to us here. On Owen's last leave he climbed Table Mountain and stole the blue flower which is protected by law and may not be plucked. He tucked it inside the chest of his shirt to bring home and had just taken it out to show (as I can't climb and had never seen one) when there came a knock.

---

87. Ian Stevenson, "The Blue Orchid of Table Mountain," *Journal of the Society for Psychical Research* 42 (1964): 401-409.

He was nervous of discovery (a heavy fine for picking it) and put it back inside his shirt, but it was only sister Cynthia. He showed me again, when the front door banged and he popped it for a second time into his neck. This time it was brother Peter coming from work, so now I could really have a good look at this marvelous flower. It lasted a fortnight in water. He never mentioned this to anyone outside the family, and for Owen to re-enact this scene to you, proves to us he still lives.[88]

In addition to Owen's mother's oral confirmation, Mrs. Feakes was able to provide further confirmation by showing Stevenson two letters which Mrs. Feakes had written to the mother about the apparition when Mrs. Feakes first saw it. One of the letters is the one in which Mrs. Feakes mentioned that the apparition showed her a flower from Table Mountain; it is clear in the letter that Mrs. Feakes does not know what Owen's action meant and that Mrs. Feakes is asking Owen's mother about the matter for the first time.

Comment: To summarize, the paranormal aspects of the case are these: 1) Mrs. Feakes says she had a vision of Owen, who had a flower from Table Mountain, and he took it out of his shirt to show to her as proof that it was really him; Owen's mother confirmed that Owen had indeed once picked a flower from Table Mountain and taken it out of his shirt to show to her, though Mrs. Feakes knew nothing about the incident (and that Mrs. Feakes did not know what the apparition's action meant is confirmed from a letter written at the time). 2) Mrs. Feakes had also said that the apparition asked about Helen, though Mrs. Feakes did not know who Helen was. Owen's mother confirmed that Owen did have a friend named Helen, even though Mrs. Feakes did not know this (though this fact was not mentioned in the letter).

The evidential quality of this case is clearly strong. Mrs. Feakes learned three facts from the apparitions of Owen which she did not previously know: 1) that there was some significance to him presenting a blue flower; 2) that the flower had come from Table Mountain; 3) that Owen had a friend named Helen. The letter in 1949 proves that to the best of Mrs. Feakes knowledge she had never heard of the incident involving the blue flower. The information about Helen, though not confirmed by letter, is confirmed by Owen's mother's testimony.

It is evident that the apparition in this case appeared to be trying to give proof of survival. From Mrs. Feakes's testimony it is clear that the apparition presented the blue flower in order to provide proof that the event was real.

As for the hypotheses of lies and misremembering, lies must be considered unlikely based on the letter which Mrs. Feakes presented to the investigator. The letter is dated to long before Stevenson investigated the case; this would have to be a rather sophisticated fraud. And we must also note that informational apparitions as a class

---

88. Stevenson, "Blue Orchid," 403.

differ from fictional cases of apparitions in the same way collective apparitions and crisis apparitions do.[89]

The letter also rules out the hypothesis of misremembering in its more ordinary form: since in the letter Mrs. Feakes asks about the meaning of the blue flower and Table Mountain, it clearly could not be the case that she found out these details only after talking with Owen's mother and then misremembered the apparition as having mentioned the details when it did not. But at this point, the skeptic will want to suggest a form of the misremembering hypothesis which we have not previously encountered—the cryptomnesia hypothesis. Cryptomnesia is the phenomenon of thinking one has encountered some piece of information for the first time, when actually the information was encountered long ago and forgotten about.[90] This problem has proven particularly acute when it comes to evaluating reincarnation cases. There have been a number of cases where a person has reported memories of a "past life" which turned out simply to be forgotten memories of the person's own life. The most famous case is that of Bridey Murphy, who reported that in a previous life she had lived in Ireland. It was later found that the accurate details she had provided concerning Ireland stemmed from what she had learned about Ireland in her childhood.[91]

Is it possible that at some point prior to Owen's death, Mrs. Feakes actually had been told that Owen had picked a flower from Table Mountain and that he had a friend named Helen? Could Mrs. Feakes have then forgotten those facts and later subconsciously used them to build a hallucination of Owen? While this is the most likely of the skeptical hypotheses in this case, it would have to be a more complex case of cryptomnesia than we find in reincarnation cases, because not one, but two people would have to have misremembered. Thus, though the cryptomnesia explanation cannot be absolutely ruled out, it does not fit the data very smoothly.

Case 2: A Lover's Suicide (JSPR 1908)[92]

On May 29, 1907, a few days after proposing to a young lady and being rejected, Captain Oldham shot himself in London. Mrs. Wilson, a friend of his, learned of his suicide when it happened, and she knew the reason why he had killed himself. However, her daughter Miss Minnie Wilson, godchild of Captain Oldham, was living at a convent school in continental Europe (our source does not specify the country), and was not told about the captain's death or about his failed marriage proposal. On

---

89. This is not something which one can be sure of without having read through, as I have, a large number of cases of informational apparitions.

90. On cryptomnesia, see Ian Stevenson, "Cryptomnesia and Parapsychology," *Journal of the American Society for Psychical Research* 52 (1983): 1-30.

91. On the Bridey Murphy case, see the entry for "Bridey Murphy" in Robert T. Carroll, *The Skeptic's Dictionary*, http://www.skepdic.com/bridey.html.

92. Anonymous [Society for Psychical Research], "Cases," *Journal of the Society for Psychical Research* 13 (1908): 228-34.

August 6, Mrs. Wilson saw Minnie for the first time since Captain Oldham's death. Before Minnie was told anything by her mother, Minnie related that she had had an OBE in which she learned that the captain had committed suicide after being rejected by the lady he had proposed to. During the OBE, an apparition of a nun, who was a friend of hers, and who was still living, appeared to her and took her to another part of the convent, where she saw Captain Oldham, who told her what he had done. After this experience, Captain Oldham appeared to her on a number of other occasions, but in these later appearances he did not speak at all.

Minnie's account of the apparition is as follows:

> One Saturday morning I was in the church helping Mère Columba to dust. I was up a ladder dusting a statue when I was rather surprised to see a girl, who had left some time, dressed as a nun, come towards me, and beckon me to follow her; it gave me rather a shock to see myself on the ladder when I was in the act of following the nun. Passing through a door I reached the chapel by a way I had never been before. When I was kneeling in one of the pews, I was very surprised to see Uncle Oldham come up to me, as mother had not told me he was coming to Belgium. I thought something was wrong as he had such a pained expression; he took my hand and said he had done something very wrong and that it would help him a great deal to have me to pray for him; then he told me he had been refused by the woman he loved and that he had shot himself in his despair; after that he visited me every morning. When I found myself again on the ladder I must have looked rather pale, so Mère Columba made me lie down for some time; later on I told her I had seen my uncle and that he had shot himself, but she only said it was my imagination. I made her promise not to tell any one, as I knew no one would believe it and thought I should be laughed at; a few days after I heard from mother that Uncle Oldham had died suddenly. It gave me a shock, as I did not know who to believe and could not write, as all letters are read before leaving the convent. I only heard the truth from mother when I came home. MINNIE WILSON[93]

Minnie appeared before a group of SPR researchers and withstood "a somewhat rigorous cross examination."[94]

Comment: The paranormal fact is this: Minnie had an OBE in which the apparition of Captain Oldham told her he had committed suicide because his marriage proposal had been rejected, and unbeknownst to Minnie, this had in fact happened. Upon seeing her mother, Minnie related this experience without first hearing anything from her mother about it. It is unfortunate that the case is imperfectly corroborated: though Minnie and the mother attest to the facts narrated above, the young nun who appeared in the OBE could not be located for questioning; and Mère Columba, the old

---

93. Anonymous, "Cases," 232.
94. Anonymous, "Cases," 233.

nun who Minnie had related the experience to immediately after having it, could have offered confirmation, but she had died before the case was investigated.

Cryptomnesia seems out of the question in this case: It is hardly likely that between May (when Captain Oldham died) and August (when Minnie first saw her mother again) of the same year, Minnie would have heard about her godfather committing suicide and then have forgotten about it. Further, it is stated that no newspapers were allowed into the convent; the only materials allowed in were letters from friends and family, and the nuns read all these before the recipient was allowed to read them. Thus, there is no way Minnie could have known of the death of Captain Oldham before seeing her mother. The only realistic alternative hypothesis in this case is lies. Now Minnie could not have committed a fraud without her mother's help, because for her to do that, she would have to have known about the Captain's death before seeing her mother in August. As we explained, that was impossible. So if this was a lie, it would have to have involved both the mother and her daughter. Lies could be almost completely ruled out if the old nun to whom Minnie had related her experience before finding out about his death could have testified. But since she had died, we must trust the honesty of the mother and daughter. Nevertheless, the case is supported by the fact that it does not look like the fictional cases on record, and Minnie did subject herself to the cross examination of the SPR.

Recurring Apparitions

With our next two types of apparitions, recurring apparitions and apparitions recognized from a photograph, we enter clearly into the territory of ghosts and haunted houses, and it is now time to define those terms. One will notice that throughout the chapter I have used the term "apparition" rather than "ghost" except in regard to the Cornell case. In the parapsychological literature, "apparition" is used to refer to any appearance of a deceased person (and also, to non-bodily appearances of living persons),[95] whereas "ghost" is a more specific term which refers to only one type of apparition: an apparition which appears to someone who did not know the apparition in life, and in most cases, the appearance of such an apparition is connected with a specific locale. This locale is referred to as a "haunted house" (though the place need not technically be a house, but could be a hotel, a place of business, or any other type of place).[96] The reason for supposing that a locale often seems to be related when an

---

95. To be more precise, the term "apparition" is used in reference to any appearance of a *non-bodily* deceased person. An appearance of a bodily deceased person (such as Jesus, presuming he rose, or Lazarus) would not be referred to as an apparition. But one will find few if any cases of appearances of bodily deceased persons in the parapsychological literature. In regard to apparitions of the living, I mentioned these in n2.

96. The exact borderlines as far as what constitutes a ghost or haunted house are a bit difficult to determine. One problem is the fact that it is sometimes unclear whether a case should be classified as a case of haunting or a case of a poltergeist. Perhaps the primary distinction is that the phenomena

apparition appears to someone who did not know them in life, is that apparitions usually appear to a person who did not know them in life only if that person visits a locale which the apparition used to frequent during life (for example, the apparition's house). The fact that apparitions typically appear to a person who did not know them in life only if that person visits a particular locale which the apparition used to frequent has naturally led to the speculation that the locale in some way facilitates the apparition's appearance. And the fact that ghosts, in a much higher proportion than other apparitions, do not interact with the percipients at all, has also led to the speculation that ghosts as a class are somehow less aware of their surroundings, and are perhaps a different type of apparition. Though these are interesting issues, we cannot here address them at length, because theories of apparitions are not our main concern.[97]

Recurring apparitions, though they are not necessarily ghosts, are often ghosts, since recurring apparitions often appear to people who did not know them in life. Apparitions recognized from a photograph are necessarily ghosts since if an apparition is not recognized at the time, but is later recognized from a photograph, then it was necessarily an apparition which the percipient did not know in life (for if the percipient had known the apparition, he would have recognized the apparition upon first seeing it rather than needing a photograph to recognize it).

However, before adducing the evidence for ghosts, we need to clear up certain misconceptions about ghosts which have arisen via the popular media. There are now a number of shows on TV where groups of investigators attempt to find evidence for ghosts, and these sorts of shows have endorsed a variety of questionable criteria for the detection of ghosts, and this has brought into disrepute even the more well-informed investigations of hauntings.[98]

Contrary to what you will see on these programs, "ghost photographs" do not provide very good evidence for ghosts, for they turn out to be caused by various natural phenomena, such as dust, problems with the camera, or even outright fraud.[99] The evidence is weak that voices of ghosts can be captured on a tape recorder (EVP, that is,

---

in a haunting case is focused on the place, whereas the phenomena in a poltergeist case is centered on a particular person. Also, poltergeist cases typically involve much more forceful physical phenomena. On this issue, see Alan Gauld and Tony Cornell, *Poltergeists* (London: Routledge, 1979), 176-80, 207-10.

97. For sources discussing such ideas about ghosts, see the sources cited below under "Theories of Apparitions."

98. For more serious sources on hauntings, see "Second Report of the Committee On Haunted Houses," *Proceedings of the Psychical Research* 2 (1884): 137-51; Andrew MacKenzie, *Apparitions and Ghosts* (New York: Popular Library, 1971); Andrew MacKenzie, *Hauntings and Apparitions* (London: Heinemann, 1982); Ian Wilson, *In Search of Ghosts* (London: Headline, 1995); Joe Nickell, *The Science of Ghosts: Searching for Spirits of the Dead* (Amherst, NY: Prometheus, 2012); Houran and Lange, *Hauntings and Poltergeists*. And see the books listed under "Apparitions" and "Hauntings" in the SPR online library at http://www.lexscien.org/lexscien/index.jsp.

99. On ghost photos, see Joe Nickell, "Ghostly Photos," *Skeptical Inquirer* 20.4 (1996): 13-14; Nickell, *Science of Ghosts*, 297-306; Cornell, *Investigating*, 139-54; Ian Wilson, *In Search of Ghosts*, 35-56.

Electronic Voice Phenomena). EVP appears to simply be the result of witnesses mistaking indistinct sounds for actual words.[100] There is not yet any convincing evidence that sensitives can detect ghosts.[101] The evidence is also weak that ghosts can be exorcised.[102] The physical phenomena that occur in conjunction with hauntings (such as chills, footsteps, and other strange noises), though they are reported in the serious literature, and though they may well be a real part of a haunting, I would not use as part of the offensive case, because there are so many natural explanations for this type of phenomena, and it seems impossible to establish any criteria for ruling out these explanations.[103] The only way to successfully argue for the reality of apparitions is not by photographing them, tape recording them, or so forth, but by producing cases of apparitions of the five types explained in this chapter. But since the evidence for these cases comes entirely from witnesses' testimonies, and simply interviewing witnesses does not make for interesting TV, TV shows do not like to confine themselves to these types of cases.

Case 1: The Cheltenham Ghost (Morton [Despard] 1892)[104]

Turning now to the well-evidenced cases of hauntings, we should certainly consider the Cheltenham ghost, for it is surely the best-evidenced case of haunting on record. It is supported by the phenomenon of recurring apparitions, as well as a collective

---

100. On EVP, see David J. Ellis, *The Mediumship of the Tape Recorder* (Pulborough: D.J. Ellis, 1978); James Alcock, "Electronic Voice Phenomena: Voices of the Dead," *Skeptical Inquirer* (2004): http://www.csicop.org/specialarticles/show/electronic_voice_phenomena_voices_of_the_dead/; and the entry for "Electronic Voice Phenomena" in *The Skeptic's Dictionary* http://www.skepdic.com/evp.html.

101. On detection of ghosts by sensitives, see Joe Nickell, "The Case of the Psychic Detectives," *Skeptical Inquirer* 29.4 (2005): http://www.csicop.org/si/show/case_of_the_psychic_detectives; Cornell, *Investigating*, 365-76. However, though the evidence that sensitives can detect ghosts is as yet unconvincing, there is certainly evidence that sensitives can detect *something* peculiar. Michaeleen C. Maher performed a number of experiments of the following sort. First, the investigators interviewed the residents of a haunted house and established which rooms of the house the residents had experienced strange activity in. Then, the investigators got two groups: a group of sensitives, and a group of ordinary people. Members of each group walked through the house and were asked to guess which rooms were haunted. The results found that the sensitive group did significantly better at guessing which rooms were haunted than the non-sensitive group (Michaeleen C. Maher, "Riding the Waves in Search of the Particles: a Modern Study of Ghosts and Apparitions," *Journal of Parapsychology* 63 (1999): 47-80 (63-75)). So the sensitives could certainly detect something. However, they were not necessarily detecting ghosts. It may be that the sensitives were simply better than most people at detecting certain differences about the environment of the rooms. For example, perhaps the geomagnetic level or electromagnetic level in those rooms was different. The subject awaits further research.

102. On exorcisms, see Wilson, *In Search of Ghosts*, 271-86; Cornell, *Investigating*, 365-76.

103. For a thorough overview of the many different possible normal causes of the physical phenomena involved with hauntings, see Lynne Kelly, *The Skeptic's Guide to the Paranormal* (New York: 1st Thunder's Mouth Press, 2005), chapter 7.

104. Rose C. Morton [Despard], "Record of a Haunted House," *Proceedings of the Society for Psychical Research* 8 (1892): 311-32.

apparition and an evidential OBE. The events occurred to a family of about a dozen, living in Cheltenham, England during the 1880s. Many of these saw the apparition on at least one occasion, but the principal witness in the case was Rose Despard (called Rose Morton in the original account, to keep her identity anonymous), who saw the apparition on more occasions than anyone else, and who wrote the account of the case for the *Proceedings* of the SPR. She was an educated witness, who was at that time studying to be a physician, and when she obtained her medical degree in 1895 she was one of only 200 female doctors in England.[105] Our testimony as to the figure's appearances comes from Despard herself, who was as qualified an observer as anyone the SPR could have sent, as is clear from her medical achievements and her ability to write the journal article. And her testimony is supported by letters which she wrote during the time of the events, and by the testimony of a number of the witnesses, who also themselves wrote accounts for the SPR. She describes the apparition as follows:

> My father took the house in March, 1882, none of us having then heard of anything unusual about the house. We moved in towards the end of April, and it was not until the following June that I first saw the apparition.
>
> I had gone up to my room, but was not yet in bed, when I heard someone at the door, and went to it, thinking it might be my mother. On opening the door, I saw no one; but on going a few steps along the passage, I saw the figure of a tall lady, dressed in black, standing at the head of the stairs. After a few moments she descended the stairs, and I followed for a short distance, feeling curious what it could be. I had only a small piece of candle, and it suddenly burnt itself out; and being unable to see more, I went back to my room.
>
> The figure was that of a tall lady, dressed in black of a soft woollen material, judging from the slight sound in moving. The face was hidden in a handkerchief held in the right hand. This is all I noticed then; but on further occasions, when I was able to observe her more closely, I saw the upper part of the left side of the forehead, and a little of the hair above. Her left hand was nearly hidden by her sleeve and a fold of her dress. As she held it down a portion of a widow's cuff was visible on both wrists, so that the whole impression was that of a lady in widow's weeds. There was no cap on the head but a general effect of blackness suggests a bonnet, with long veil or a hood.[106]

On at least three occasions, the figure was seen by people who had not heard anything of its previous appearances.[107] In all, around a dozen people saw the figure;

---

105. Pamela M. Huby, "New Evidence About Rose Morton," *Journal of the Society for Psychical Research* 45 (1970): 391-92.

106. Morton, "Record of a Haunted House," 313-14.

107. On p. 314, three cases are related in which the witness saw it and did not think it was an apparition but thought it was a real person. Since they mistook it for a real person, they must not have known of the apparition's appearances. It is not clear from the account how many of the other witnesses who saw the apparition saw it without any previous knowledge that others had seen it.

not everyone in her family saw it, but people saw it who were not part of the family, such as the maid and the cook.

The apparition made so many appearances (the exact number of appearances is not given, but it appears to be in excess of twenty) that Despard took to performing experiments. Most of these were unsuccessful. She tried to touch the ghost on several occasions, but it always eluded her. She spoke to it and asked it to speak back, but it did not reply. She tried to photograph it: it did not appear in the photograph, but no conclusion can be drawn from this, because in those days (the 1880s) even a real figure would have to remain still for a fairly long period of time to be captured on photograph in the darkened conditions under which Despard attempted to photograph the apparition. One experiment, however, did reveal something: the ghost was in at least some respects immaterial. Despard tied very thin strings across the stairs which the ghost frequently walked up; these strings were so light that any person walking up the stairs would surely cause them to break. However, she on several occasions saw the apparition walk up the stairs and pass through the strings without disturbing them.[108]

As a mark against the hallucination theory, two facts should be noted. First, several times a group of family members gathered together hoping to see the ghost, but they saw nothing;[109] the ghost only appeared spontaneously. This is the opposite of the collective hallucinations we mentioned above. Second, all of those witnesses who could be questioned (which was the majority of them) stated that they had never seen any apparitions except this one, which certainly means they were not liable to hallucinations.[110]

The collective case was as follows:

> On the evening of August 11th we were sitting in the drawing-room, with the gas lit but the shutters not shut, the light outside getting dusk, my brothers and a friend having just given up tennis, finding it too dark; my eldest sister, Mrs. K., and myself both saw the figure on the balcony outside, looking in at the window. She stood there some minutes, then walked to the end and back again, after which she seemed to disappear.[111]

Finally, I mentioned that there was an evidential OBE. A friend of Despard's, on the night Despard first saw the apparition, had an OBE in which she traveled to Despard's house and saw the figure (which she had never heard about before) near Despard. The next day she wrote a letter to Despard about it, though she had not yet heard anything from Despard about the figure. (OBEs in which a person travels to a

---

108. Morton, "Record of a Haunted House," 321.
109. Morton, "Record of a Haunted House," 318, 322.
110. Morton, "Record of a Haunted House," 322.
111. Morton, "Record of a Haunted House," 317.

distant location and brings back accurate information about what was going on at that location are by no means uncommon.)[112] She tells us:

> I may add as a curious circumstance that on the night on which Miss Morton first spoke to the figure, as stated in her account, I myself saw her telepathically. I was in my room (I was then residing in the North of England, quite 100 miles away from Miss Morton's home), preparing for bed, between 12 and half-past, when I seemed suddenly to be standing close by the door of the housemaid's cupboard (see plan of second floor) at------, so facing the short flight of stairs leading to the top landing. Coming down these stairs, I saw the figure, exactly as described, and about two steps behind Miss Morton herself, with a dressing-gown thrown loosely round her, and carrying a candle in her hand. A loud noise in the room overhead recalled me to my surroundings, and although I tried for some time I could not resume the impression.[113]

Case 2: The Lady in Grey (MacKenzie 1967)[114]

The phenomena in the following case took place in a house in Cleve Court, England, over the course of the 1920s to the 1940s. Five people saw the same figure of a lady dressed in grey, and at least two of them saw it without any knowledge that any of the others had seen it. In addition, another person had a strange retrocognitive experience. The case also involved a variety of the physical phenomena (footsteps, unexplained noises, and animals behaving strangely) which we have said are unconvincing evidence by themselves. The five people who saw the apparition were Lady Carson (one of the owners of the house), a maid who had worked at the house prior to Lady Carson (the maid wrote Lady Carson about her experience after seeing Lady Carson report her own experience in the newspaper), and three children. The reason there is some question as to how many people saw it without any previous knowledge of it, is that first, we do not know if any of the children discussed it amongst themselves, and second, it is not clear if Lady Carson saw the apparition before or after she knew of the experiences of the children. But at the very least, the maid and either Lady Carson or the first child to see it, saw it without knowledge of any previous experiences.

Andrew MacKenzie, who published the case, explains what Lady Carson told him of her experience:

---

112. See Hornell Hart, "ESP Projection: Spontaneous Cases and the Experimental Method," *Journal of the American Society for Psychical Research* 48 (1954): 121–146; Carlos S. Alvarado, "ESP During Out-of-Body Experiences: A Review of Experimental Studies," *Journal of Parapsychology* 46 (1982): 209-230; Carlos S. Alvarado, "ESP and Out of Body Experiences: A Review of Spontaneous Studies," *Parapsychology Review* 14 (1983): 11-13.

113. Morton, "Record of a Haunted House," 324.

114. Andrew MacKenzie, "A Case of Haunting in Kent," *Journal of the Society for Psychical Research* 44 (1967): 131-49.

In December, 1949, she was awakened by her Spaniel, Susan, at 1.30 in the morning. The animal obviously wanted to be let out of the house. Lady Carson put on her dressing-gown and, leaving one light burning on the landing by her bedroom, went down the stairs accompanied by the dog. As she walked down the stairs she accidentally switched off the light as she brushed past a switch. When she was at the foot of the stairs the dog did not go to the door but ran whimpering back up the stairs. Lady Carson switched on all the lights and saw, to her astonishment, a woman coming down the stairs from the direction of her room. The woman was wearing a dress with a very full grey skirt, she had a piece of white lace on her hair, and seemed to be wearing a fichu of very pale grey. Lady Carson's first reaction was that she was seeing an intruder. She told me that she was about to shout 'What are you doing here?' when she realised that the woman was moving noiselessly and that she was seeing an apparition. The figure walked and did not float. Lady Carson could not see the features clearly as they were averted from her. She stood at the foot of the stairs and watched the figure turn at the landing above and walk into the Elizabethan part of the house.[115]

The maid's testimony is as follows:

Many years ago, forty-five to be exact, I was fifteen years of age, and had decided to go into domestic service, and my first job was as under-housemaid at Cleve Court. A Mrs Garrard and a companion lived there with about five maids and butler. Guests were expected and I was given a room to prepare as a day nursery.

It was in the old part of the house, at the end of a passage. I was very busy about 7 o'clock one morning when I heard footsteps coming along the passage. I looked up expecting to see one of the maids, but to my surprise it was a lady in an old-fashioned dress. As I got up to leave the room she just waved one hand and went away. When the maid came in to inspect my work and I told her of the lady she was most indignant.

I knew it was neither of the two old ladies who lived there, and as there were no guests at the time, as she pointed out to me, I must be telling an untruth. However, I still stuck to my story, and I am wondering now if it was the Gay *(sic)* Lady I saw. I have often wondered who she really was, and never for one moment did this solution come to me.[116]

The retrocognitive experience was experienced by Dr. Moon, the family physician. A retrocognitive experience is an experience in which one seems to be transported from the present back to a previous time.[117] If this experience occurred by

---

115. MacKenzie, "Haunting in Kent," 135-36.
116. MacKenzie, "Haunting in Kent," 136.
117. On retrocognition, see Andrew MacKenzie, *Adventures in Time: Encounters with the Past* (London: Athlone, 1997).

itself we could dismiss it as an ordinary hallucination, but since it occurred as part of a case in which there is other evidence for paranormal phenomena, it deserves note as supplementary evidence.

> After attending him [Lord Carson] he [the physician] paused at the front door, looking down while he considered whether he should have prescribed a stronger tonic. When he looked up he was astonished to see that his car which he had left in the small drive in front of the house had disappeared, as had the thick hedge which is between two sets of gate posts. Instead of the lane down which he had driven that day there was a muddy cart track, and coming towards him was a man who was wearing a coat with many capes, a short top hat, and gaiters at which he flicked noiselessly with a hunting crop. The man stared at Dr Moon who, not believing the evidence of his eyes, went back into the house. He then decided to have another look and when he did so the scenery of the present day, which included his car, had reappeared.[118]

Alternative Explanations

Before we address alternative explanations for recurring apparitions, we should note that cases involving recurring apparitions may also involve other evidential types of apparitions. The Lady in Grey case involved a retrocognitive experience, though we noted the experience could only be used as supplementary evidence. The Cheltenham case involved a collective apparition and an evidential OBE. We have already discussed collective apparitions; as for the OBE, while we cannot here discuss OBEs in detail, the only skeptical hypothesis that presents itself, other than an outright lie, is that the witnesses misremembered. However, the Cheltenham case would have to be a rather spectacular case of misremembering because Despard and her friend would have to not only misremember what occurred during the OBE, but would also have to misremember sending and receiving letters about it.

But what explanations can be offered for recurring apparitions themselves? Illusions are hypothetically possible; it is possible that various people could mistake the same object for an apparition. But it is clear from the witnesses' testimony that the two cases above fulfill the criteria I set out for ruling out illusion. Hoaxing is hypothetically possible, but can be ruled out for a variety of reasons in the two cases above. In the Cheltenham case, the apparition was seen for several years. Would a hoaxer continue that long? And how could a hoaxer arrange for the apparition to walk through the strings without disturbing them, or for Rose Despard's friend to have an evidential OBE? In the Lady in Grey case the maid saw the apparition forty-five years prior to the time Lady Carson's family saw it. Would a hoaxer stage the apparitions forty-five years apart? And how could a hoaxer cause the physician to have a retrocognitive

---

118. MacKenzie, "Haunting in Kent," 134-35.

experience? As for misremembering, it will not work for the same reason it did not work with collective apparitions: the witness only has to remember the basic fact: that they saw an apparition. Lying does not seem at all likely either. If the Cheltenham case was a lie, it would have to have involved not just Rose Despard, but the numerous other witnesses who also spoke with the SPR, as well as forged letters. And the account differs from fictional cases of hauntings; such cases are typically of the frightening type.[119] The Lady in Grey is also not like the fictitious cases, and in order for the case to be a fraud, that would require that the old maid who had worked at the house years before conspired in the fraud, even going so far as to forge a letter. This only leaves hallucinations. Now as we said above, it is not unlikely that multiple people will be in grief over the same loved one, and so recurring apparitions can sometimes be hallucinations. But in these two cases, none of the witnesses were in grief over the person whose apparition it was. Further, in the Cheltenham case, no witness had ever previously had a hallucination, and there were so many appearances over such a long time, that it would be incredible if they were all prone to hallucinations of just this one figure. (And the fact that the figure never appeared when they were expecting it to appear, though they did on some occasions gather together hoping it would appear, rules out the possibility that the hallucinations could have resulted from expectation as they did in the cases of the group religious visions referred to above.) In the Lady in Grey case, we have an even more ideal type of recurring apparition: witnesses saw the same apparition without knowing that previous witnesses had seen it. This type of case is exceedingly difficult to explain as a hallucination, because we would not expect that two or more people would coincidentally hallucinate the same figure without knowing that this figure was supposed to haunt the house.

Ghosts Recognized From a Photograph

We have said that you cannot take pictures of ghosts, but photographic evidence of another sort does come into play in the case for the reality of apparitions.[120] I have reference to cases in which the witness did not recognize the apparition at the time he saw it, but later recognized it after seeing a photograph. For example, suppose Bob is in a house and he sees an apparition which he has never seen before, and he wonders who it is; and suppose he is later shown a photograph of the previous owner of the house, and he finds that the apparition he has seen looks just like the previous owner (or even better yet, Bob might be presented with a set of photographs, and successfully pick out the owner's photograph from the set). Since Bob is not likely to have a hallucination which coincidently happens to look like the previous owner of the house, this suggests the apparition is real.

---

119. For unreliable tales of hauntings, see Ian Wilson, *In Search of Ghosts*, 13-33.

120. For other cases of apparitions recognized from a photograph, see Ernst Bennett, *Apparitions and Haunted Houses* (London: Faber & Faber, 1939) cases 5, 8, 18, 23, 25, 29, 31, 36.

Consider one particularly impressive case of this kind, in which the witness recognized the apparition from a set of twenty photographs.[121] A navy officer and his wife had moved into a house with another family, the family of Mr. G. One night, the officer was sitting at a table in the den, when he heard the dogs, who had been sleeping, growl and then run quickly up the stairs. The witness then looked up, and saw someone standing there. He explains:

> I sat in my chair for about ten or fifteen seconds, looking at him, as he seemed about to speak. Then I rose from my chair and took about two steps towards him, when all of a sudden, he was not there. He didn't go up, nor down nor sideways; neither did he slowly disintegrate. He simply vanished instantly. It seemed strange that I was not frightened; but I was not.[122]

About a week later, the witness saw the apparition again and told Mrs. G., the wife from the other family, about it. Mrs. G then:

> Got about twenty photographs of cabinet size and asked me to look through them. I shuffled them through carelessly and at about the seventh or eighth picture I came across the portrait of the man I had seen a few minutes before. There is no doubt in my mind as to its being the same man. I would know him among a thousand.[123]

After seeing the photograph, the witness saw the apparition again two more times.

The behavior of the dogs in this case should be noted. It is not unusual for animals to react when an apparition appears (e.g., by growling or running), and the fact that the animals seem to notice the apparition has been taken as evidence that the apparition is real. The response to this argument has been that if the human is visibly distressed upon seeing the apparition, then the animals might act as they do simply because they notice the distress of the human being rather than because they see the apparition.[124] However, in this particular case, the witness is quite clear that the animals growled and ran up the stairs *before* he saw the apparition. Hence their actions could not be in response to any action on his part.

As for alternative explanations, lies are not a good explanation, since ghosts recognized from a photograph differ from fictional ghosts in the ways we have explained above,[125] and hoaxing can be dismissed for the same reasons we dismissed it when we

---

121. Anonymous [American Society for Psychical Research], "An Apparition Identified from a Photograph," *Journal of the American Society for Psychical Research* 25 (1931): 53-57.

122. Anonymous, "An Apparition," 55.

123. Anonymous, "An Apparition," 55.

124. Cases in which animals appear to perceive the apparition and the difficulty in establishing whether or not the animal actually sees it are discussed in Sidgwick, "Census," 326-30.

125. As with informational apparitions, one must read through a large number of cases of apparitions recognized from a photograph to be convinced of this.

first considered that hypothesis. Hallucinations and illusions will not work because a person should not have a hallucination or illusion which just happens to look like a deceased person who has reason to be in the house. However, there are four skeptical hypotheses which need more detailed consideration.

First, it has been suggested that in cases of this kind the witness may be anxious to find an identity for the figure he has seen, and thus if he is shown any photograph which bears a vague resemblance to the ghost, he may subconsciously think the resemblance is closer than it is, and identify that figure as the ghost.[126] But though this scenario is plausible in a case in which the witness identified the apparition from a single photograph, it cannot explain a case such as the above in which the witness identified the apparition from a set of photographs. (And we may also be able to rule this out in other cases, depending on the particulars of the case. For example, if the apparition was very distinctive looking, misidentification is not likely, because there would not be many other people to whom the apparition would bear a close resemblance.) Second, it may be objected that there could be subconscious cueing on the part of the person who presents the witness with the photographs: the person presenting the photographs might subconsciously do something to indicate which photograph is the correct one, and the witness might subconsciously pick up on this cue. Now this has to be acknowledged as a possibility in some cases, but in other cases, this hypothesis is problematic. In the case above, the witness was handed the photographs and looked through them himself, so it is hard to see how the other person could have cued him. Third, cryptomnesia might be suggested: perhaps the witness actually did know the person whose apparition it was before that person died, but the witness had forgotten about it. But in some cases, including the one above, we can establish with certainty that the witness did not know the apparition. In the case above, the two families had never met before they lived together, thus the witness could not have known the woman's father. Fourth, one could resort to the chance hypothesis. One could argue that there might be many cases in which a witness is presented with a set of photographs and identifies the wrong one, but these cases are never published, since failures are not very exciting to read about, and the successes which are published could therefore be explained by chance. In this case, the witness recognized the apparition from a set of twenty photographs. But now suppose there have been nineteen other cases in which a witness attempted to identify an apparition, but was incorrect, and these cases were never published. If 20 people make an attempt at something for which the odds are 20:1, we should expect that 1 of those 20 people will succeed just by chance (e.g., if the odds of getting a certain poker hand are 20:1, and I deal out 20 hands, chances are someone will get that hand). Thus the argument is that the published cases simply represent the successes to be expected by chance,

---

126. For criticism of cases of apparitions recognized from a photograph, see Frank Podmore, "Phantasms of the Dead From Another Point of View," *Proceedings of the Society for Psychical Research* 6 (1889): 229-313 (232-33).

and that there have also been just as many failures as is expected by chance, but the failures are not published, and so we do not know about them. In response, we should say that many a witness will not regard a non-match between the apparition and the photograph as a "failure," but only as a fact establishing that the apparition is not that of a known deceased person. There are many reports of unrecognized apparitions in the literature, thus witnesses are not uninterested in reporting these; and so they should not be uninterested in reporting cases involving the supposed failed attempts to recognize the apparition from a photograph.

Theories of Apparitions

Now that the case has been made for the reality of apparitions, it is time to move on to the next question, which is: If apparitions are real, what type of paranormal phenomena are they? As we have said, the answer will not have much effect on the question of whether the resurrection appearances were apparitions, thus we will not examine it in great depth, but our discussion would certainly be incomplete if we did not address the question to some extent.[127]

The traditional view of an apparition is that if it is real it is a disembodied spirit, a conscious being without a body. The alternative to this view is that an apparition is a mere image, a thing which looks like a conscious being but isn't, rather like the images on a TV screen. There are various versions of this image theory. For example, one is that buildings possess some kind of psychical energy by which events can be "captured" and then seen again by someone who is sufficiently psychically sensitive. This theory, which is usually only applied to haunting cases since the building is an essential entity, would explain a ghost such as the Cheltenham one in the following way. The person whom the Cheltenham apparition represents somehow left their mental imprint on the environment before they died. This mental imprint can be accessed by other people who possess a sufficient amount of psychic sensitivity. (Different people probably possess different amounts of psychic sensitivity. Hence in one instance Despard could see the apparition even though others in her presence could not,[128] and in the Cornell case, P.D. and the woman could see the apparition even though Cornell could not.) When someone who is sufficiently psychically sensitive comes into contact with this mental imprint, they will see an apparition of the person, just as they will see an image of someone on TV if they turn on the TV. Another version of this theory holds that apparitions are telepathic images. Gurney invented this theory as part of

---

127. For an overview of theories of apparitions, see e.g., Hart, "Six Theories"; Alan Gauld, *Mediumship and Survival: A Century of Investigations* (London: Paladin Books, 1982), 215-60; Harvey J. Irwin and Caroline Watt, *An Introduction to Parapsychology* (5th ed.; Jefferson, NC: McFarland, 2007), 201-06; Bryan Williams, Annalisa Ventola, and Mike Wilson, "Apparitional Experiences: A Primer on Parapsychological Research and Perspectives," http://www.publicparapsychology.org/Public%20Parapsych/Apparitional%20Experiences%20Primer%20Final.pdf.

128. Morton, "Record of a Haunted House," 315.

his treatment of crisis apparitions.[129] He held that crisis apparitions result as follows. When one person is near death, and they are thinking about another person, the dying person subconsciously sends an image of himself to that other person, and the other person sees the image—an image sent by the dying person, but not truly the dying person himself. For the dying person's consciousness is not in that image but in the dying person's body. Post-mortem apparitions Gurney hypothesized to be the result of "delayed telepathy." That is, the dying person's mind intended to send an image of himself to the other person at the time of death, but this message was for some reason delayed, and so was not seen until after his death. However, at the time Gurney wrote (he died in 1888), it was disputed as to whether there were any well-evidenced cases of apparitions of the dead other than those which appeared within a few days after the person's death. Gurney realized that if evidential cases of apparitions of those who had been dead for months or years could be found, his theory would be in rougher shape. Hence these days it is more common to explain non-haunting apparitions of the dead by a third type of image hypothesis: the hypothesis that the apparition is entirely a hallucination of the percipient (albeit a paranormal hallucination which can incorporate ESP; this idea will become clear below. We can call this the hallucination/ESP form of the image hypothesis).

The image hypothesis does strike me as a plausible explanation for some haunting cases, namely those in which the apparition does not seem to interact with the witnesses. One would expect a conscious being to want to interact with those around it, and if the apparition does not do this, it seems at least plausible that the apparition is not a conscious being. (However, we must also consider the possibility that the apparition is a conscious being which wishes to interact with the witnesses but cannot do so because it is having trouble "getting through" from the other side. This hypothesis is also plausible since there is evidence that apparitions have trouble getting through.) But while I find the image hypothesis plausible for some haunting cases, the hypothesis has a harder time explaining those cases in which the apparition does interact with the percipients. If the apparition interacts with the percipients, it is behaving as a conscious being would and one therefore loses the reason to think it is an image. If we suppose that things which look and act like conscious beings are actually consciousless images, how do we know some of the human beings we see every day are not actually consciousless images? But this argument against the image hypothesis becomes even stronger when we encounter one particular type of case.

The type of case I have reference to is that in which the apparition reveals to the percipient information he did not already know. The large majority of these cases are not haunting cases and so we can exclude the haunting form of the image hypothesis. Consider how the hallucination/ESP form of the image hypothesis would have to explain this type of case. It would postulate that the percipient creates a hallucination of the apparition and that the percipient incorporates into this hallucination

---

129. Gurney, *Phantasms*, (vol. 1), lxiv-lxv.

information which he acquired by ESP. For example, suppose a witness sees an apparition, the apparition tells him that later that day he will be given a check for $50, and this prediction does in fact come true. The ESP/hallucination theory would propose that the percipient subconsciously acquired by ESP the knowledge that he would receive a check later in the day, and that his subconscious mind then built up a hallucination of an apparition telling him that he would receive a check—his subconscious mind tricked him into thinking the apparition was real. On Gurney's hypothesis, the explanation must be even more complex. One would have to propose that the dying person's subconscious mind not only sends a delayed image of the dying person to the percipient, but that incorporated in this telepathic message is not only an image of the dying person, but also information designed to fool the percipient into thinking the dying person still exists as a spirit. The dying person's mind must somehow look into the future, see that the percipient will one day come across some information (such as that he is going to receive a check for $50), and decide that at some point well after the dying person's death, the percipient will have a hallucination of the dying person in which the dying person, acting just as if he were really there, tells the percipient about the check. Whereas according to the ESP/hallucination theory your own subconscious mind tries to trick you, according to this theory someone else's does!

But let us explain more exactly why these theories appear convoluted. To propose that our mind (or someone else's mind) is tricking us into thinking a person is there when he really is not would require us to call into question many of the things we take for granted about our day to day existence. If our mind tricks us into thinking non-bodily people appear to us, how can we be sure it does not trick us into thinking bodily people appear to us? If our mind can go to the lengths which these theories proposes it goes to trick us into thinking apparitions are real, could it not be tricking us into anything else? How can you know it is not tricking you into thinking that this book is real, or that your own body is real, or that the whole external world is real? Once we admit our mind, or someone else's mind, tricks us into thinking other people (even non-bodily ones) are real we open up an epistemological Pandora's box. Our minds could be tricking us into anything. Thus the image hypothesis cannot be endorsed without seriously reexamining our whole understanding of the nature of reality. (It could be argued that our mind clearly does trick us into thinking other people are real because our mind causes hallucinations. But in the case of hallucinations (of the ordinary variety) our mind provides us with some means to see when it is tricking us, since it allows us to identify criteria to distinguish a hallucination from a real sensory perception. But if either of these two image theories is right, our mind tricks us into thinking apparitions are real, and it provides us with no way of finding out that it is tricking us.)

(Now that I have addressed theories of apparitions, I wish to mention one terminological issue which it is easier to address after theories of apparition have been discussed. One will often come across in the parapsychological literature the term "objective hallucination." This term refers to one of two ideas. Either the idea that the apparition is a consciousless ESP projection, or the idea that the apparition is indeed the deceased person, but that the deceased person is appearing with a non-material body. (This is because the hypothesis that the deceased person is appearing may take one of two forms: either the hypothesis that the body is entirely immaterial, or the hypothesis that the body is made of some sort of very light matter, matter which is much different from the matter constituting our ordinary physical bodies, but which is nevertheless some type of matter.) The word "hallucination" is used in this regard because if the apparition does not have a material body, then the apparition does not correspond to any physical stimuli. The term "objective" is used because though the apparition does not correspond to any physical stimuli, it does not correspond to something other than the subjective mind of the witness: If it is an ESP projection, then it incorporates objective information which the witness has gotten by ESP, and if it is caused by the mind of a deceased person, it corresponds to the mind of the deceased person. However, I think it quite confusing to use the word hallucination in this manner, and hence I have not used that word except in reference to ordinary hallucinations. But I include this explanation so that readers who decide to delve into the parapsychological literature will not find themselves confused.)

Conclusion

The evidence for the reality of apparitions is, I think, strong enough to lead us to the conclusion that it is more probable than not that some apparitions are real. If I have not convinced the reader of this, I hope the reader is at least convinced it is plausible they are real, in which case the hypothesis that the resurrection appearances are examples of apparitions is worth seriously examining. But what I want to reflect on now is the question of what needs to happen to convince the scientific community at large that apparitions are real.

I think three essential things need to be done in order for a wider consensus on the reality of apparitions to be reached. The first and most essential is for proponents of the reality of apparitions to be as persuasive as possible in ruling out alternative explanations for apparitions. Though the sorts of cases I have examined here will seem impressive prima facie, they will not continue to seem impressive if some alternative explanation appears capable of explaining the data. Although I have addressed the matter of alternative explanations as much as I can here, more space is required to be as exacting as I would like to be in addressing all of the alternative explanations, and I hope to address the subject more fully at some point.

Second, new cases of apparitions need to be collected. One will notice that many of the cases discussed here are from the late 1800s or the early part of the 1900s, and this will raise the question of why we are not seeing such cases as often today. (In fact, already in 1942 G.N.M. Tyrell had to contend with this question.)[130] I do not think the reason we are seeing them less often is because they are less common; it is more likely simply the fact that researchers do not look for them as much. And I think the primary reason why this is so is because of the uncertainty in regard to how to rule out alternative explanations. Hence the previous point is related to this one. If researchers can be surer of how to rule out alternative explanations, they will spend more time collecting cases.

Third, a thorough review of all the evidential cases which have been published is necessary, so that there will be a greater sense of the amount of evidence that has been collected. A large number of evidential cases have been published over the course of the last 130 years, but there is no thorough overview of all these cases available, and thus it is difficult to appreciate just how much evidence has been collected.

These three suggestions, and especially the first, are easier said than done, and I have given only a very brief outline of the work which needs to be done to arrive at a greater consensus on the reality of apparitions.

---

130. G.N.M. Tyrell, *Apparitions* (New York: Collier, 1963 [1953]), 30. Tyrell's book, though published in 1953, is based on a lecture he gave in 1942.

4

1 Corinthians 15 and the Gospels

IT IS NOW TIME for us to see what data we can garner concerning Jesus' resurrection if we do not assume the general reliability of the Gospels. This objective entails two tasks. First, we must examine Paul's statements concerning the resurrection appearances in 1 Corinthians 15. Second, we must determine what data from the resurrection narratives can be accepted as historical if we do not assume the general reliability of the Gospels.

1 Corinthians 15

In 1 Corinthians 15:3-8, Paul relates six resurrection appearances: an appearance to Peter, an appearance to the Twelve, an appearance to a group of over 500, an appearance to James, an appearance to "all the apostles," and an appearance to Paul himself:

> For I delivered to you as of first importance what I also received, that Christ died for our sins according to the Scriptures, and that He was buried, and that He was raised on the third day according to the Scriptures, and that He appeared to Cephas, then to the twelve. After that He appeared to more than five hundred brethren at one time, most of whom remain until now, but some have fallen asleep; then He appeared to James, then to all the apostles; and last of all, as to one untimely born, He appeared to me also.

The large majority of scholars who have examined this list have expressed a very favorable opinion concerning its historical reliability.[1] For example, Pinchas Lapide states that this list "may be considered as a statement of eyewitnesses."[2] Ulrich Wilckens tells us that it "indubitably goes back to the oldest phase of all in the

---

1. For a general overview of this passage, including the state of scholarly opinion about it, see William Lane Craig, *Assessing the New Testament Evidence for the Historicity of the Resurrection of Jesus* (rev. ed.; Lewiston: Edwin Mellen, 2002 [1989]), 3-62; Gary R. Habermas and J.P. Moreland, *Beyond Death: Exploring the Evidence for Immortality* (Eugene, OR: Wipf & Stock, 1998), 128-33,141-47; Michael R. Licona, *The Resurrection of Jesus: A New Historiographical Approach* (Downers Grove, IL: IVP Academic, 2010), 223-35.

2. Pinchas Lapide, *The Resurrection of Jesus: A Jewish Perspective* (Minneapolis: Augsburg, 1983), 99.

history of primitive Christianity."[3] And Gary Habermas, after a survey of over 2,200 publications on Jesus' resurrection, reports that the data Paul relates in these verses is "frequently taken almost at face value" by scholars.[4]

The reason why there is so much more agreement as to the reliability of this material than there is in the case of the reliability of the Gospel narratives is that there is much more agreement as to the source of the information. In contrast to the Gospels, the authorship of 1 Corinthians is not disputed (virtually everyone agrees Paul wrote it) and, again in contrast to the Gospels, it is unanimously agreed that the author, Paul, was very close to the events in question. For it is clear from various places in Paul's epistles that he knew a number of the people who participated in these appearances. For example, in Galatians 1:18, Paul tells us that after his conversion he spent two weeks in Jerusalem with Peter, during which time he also saw Jesus' brother James, and in Galatians 2:1-10 he tells us that he later went up to Jerusalem again to consult with Peter, James, and John. In regard to the two weeks he spent with Peter and John, since Paul had at this time just joined a movement based on Jesus' resurrection, since he had had a resurrection appearance himself, and since he tells us this list of appearances was "of first importance"[5] to him, it is safe to assume that the resurrection appearances were a frequent topic of conversation during those two weeks. As Dodd says, "we may presume they did not spend all the time talking about the weather."[6] And if they somehow did not discuss the resurrection appearances on this occasion, it is still very probable they discussed the appearances with him on one of the numerous other occasions they saw him (such as the occasion related in Galatians 2:1-10, in which he saw Peter, John, and James).[7] Since Peter and/or James were involved in every one of the appearances listed in 1 Corinthians 15:3-8, except the appearance to the 500 (Peter was one of the Twelve, and Peter and James were both part of "all the apostles"),[8] we can assume Paul has spoken to at least one of the participants for every appearance except the appearance to the 500. In regard to that appearance, since Paul makes the comment "most of whom remain until now, but some have fallen asleep," he must have made some inquiries about this appearance, otherwise he could not know who the witnesses were and hence could not know that most of them were still living when

---

3. Ulrich Wilckens, *Resurrection: Biblical Testimony to the Resurrection: An Historical Examination and Explanation* (Atlanta: John Knox, 1978), 2.

4. Gary R. Habermas, "Resurrection Research from 1975 to the Present: What Are Critical Scholars Saying?" *Journal for the Study of the Historical Jesus* 3 (2005): 135-53 (136).

5. We will discuss the meaning of the term translated "as of first importance" (*en prōtos*) in the next chapter.

6. C.H. Dodd, *The Apostolic Preaching and Its Development* (London: Hodder & Stoughton, 1944), 16.

7. The occasions on which Paul saw the apostles are detailed by Paul in Gal 1-2, and in various places in the Acts of the Apostles.

8. "All the apostles" referred to a group of Christian leaders. See the entries for "apostolos" in *TDNT* and *ABD*; and Kevin Giles, "Apostles Before and After Paul," *Churchman* 99 (1985): 241-56.

he wrote 1 Corinthians. We will consider the matter of the appearance to the 500 in more detail below, but our basic picture is already clear: Paul relates one appearance firsthand (the appearance to himself), four appearances secondhand (the appearances to Peter, James, the Twelve, and all the apostles), and one appearance (the 500) for which it is not immediately clear where Paul's information comes from. We can see that we are certainly in a better position with 1 Corinthians 15 than the position most scholars think we are in in the case of the Gospels. Most scholars think the Gospels were written by authors who did not know anyone who was close to the events, and who simply recorded Christian beliefs as they were forty to seventy years after Jesus' death, by which time a substantial amount of legendary accrual may have infiltrated the tradition. But in the case of 1 Corinthians 15, we know who the author was, and we also know he was close to the events. However, we can also see that the testimony he provides us is mainly secondhand, and thus our judgment of the reliability of this material will largely depend on how much weight we accord secondhand testimony.

Secondhand Testimony

Certainly secondhand testimony cannot be any more accurate than firsthand testimony, and some will recall that I alluded earlier to the psychological findings which seem to call into question the reliability of firsthand testimony (eyewitness testimony). I will deal with those arguments in a subsequent chapter, but for now, since the prima facie viewpoint is certainly that firsthand testimony is reliable, we will accept that view, and only ask how trustworthy secondhand testimony is relative to firsthand testimony.

Our common sense tells us that secondhand testimony is indeed usually trustworthy. We trust it all the time when reading works of ancient history, as well as when reading contemporary articles in scholarly journals. Consider for example, the works of Josephus. Though Josephus relied at many points on firsthand testimony, the testimony was only firsthand to him—it is not firsthand to us, since Josephus did not reproduce any of the witnesses' statements. We have to trust Josephus' testimony as to what those witnesses told him, and our knowledge of the facts is thus secondhand. And Josephus is an entirely typical case; it is almost always this way when we rely on ancient historians. And it is also very frequently this way when we read a modern journal article in which the researcher's interview with a witness, or patient, or subject, serves as the basis of the article (for example, a psychologist giving us a case study of a schizophrenic, or a historian presenting the results of interviews with Holocaust victims). Though in some cases the researcher may reproduce the witness's testimony word for word (as with many of the apparition accounts we examined in chapter 3), it is very often the case that for some or all of the witness's testimony, we have to rely on the researcher's summary of what the witness said. This evidence, though firsthand to the author, is secondhand to us. Yet our general knowledge of the world (our knowledge of psychological disorders, the Holocaust, medicine, etc) largely depends on the findings published in scholarly journals and hence depends at least in part upon secondhand testimony.

Beyond this common sense observation, we should also consider the empirical evidence *Phantasms of the Living* brought to bear on this issue. On the one hand, Gurney relates a rather humorous case which shows just how unreliable non-firsthand testimony can be. (The case is technically thirdhand rather than secondhand, but we can easily imagine the same thing happening with secondhand testimony, and one of our appearances, the appearance to the 500, may be beyond secondhand anyway.)

> Miss A. described to me a remarkable incident, as related to her by the Rev. B., who had heard of it from the lady to whom it occurred. The Rev. B., on being applied to, said that he had heard of it, not from the lady to whom it occurred, but from the Rev. C. The Rev. C. was applied to, but had only heard the story from the Rev. D.; with whose appearance on the scene hope revived. The Rev. D. reported that he had not heard the story from the heroine of it, but from a friend of hers, Mrs. E., who would procure it from the heroine. Mrs. E., in turn, reported that her authority, Miss F., was not herself the heroine, but had been informed by Miss G., who was. Miss F., on being applied to, had only heard Miss G.'s story third-hand, but referred me to Miss H., a nearer friend of Miss G.'s. Miss H. kindly applied to Miss G., but reported, as the result, that Miss G.'s own information was only third or fourthhand. Such is the last state (as far as I am concerned at any rate) of a story which began by being third-hand, and has been traced back through seven mouths.[9]

However, in plenty of other cases, secondhand testimony did stand up. We have a number of cases in which the researchers initially received a report secondhand and then found the eyewitness, and the eyewitness was shown the secondhand report and he or she confirmed that the report was either entirely accurate or contained only minor errors.[10]

Thus sometimes secondhand evidence is accurate and sometimes it is not, and so we need to ask the question of when it is accurate and when it is not. From common sense, we can deduce two major factors which will affect the accuracy of secondhand testimony.[11]

---

9. Edmund Gurney, Frederic William Henry Myers, and Frank Podmore, *Phantasms of the Living* (vol. 1.; London: Trubner & Co., 1886), 155.

10. E.g., *Phantasms* (vol. 1), 212-13, 236-37, 246-47.

11. Some studies have been done on the accuracy of secondhand testimony. These studies have concerned cases of child abuse, because in cases of child abuse, the testimony is often secondhand (that is, the testimony comes from an adult whom the child spoke to rather than the child themself), so that the child does not have to testify in court. While these studies have identified various causes of inaccuracy in secondhand testimony, these causes either only show that the witness may make minor errors (e.g., misperception, faulty memory), or when causes of major errors have been identified, the causes are causes which would be confined to testimony involving children (e.g., peer pressure, being interviewed by adults in authority, or misinterpreting the meaning of terms such as "touch" or "rubbing"). For an overview of this research, see Judith K. Adams, "Interviewing Methods and Hearsay

First, the more significant the data is to the secondhand witness, the more likely he is to remember it accurately. If the person regards the fact as extremely significant, he is very likely to remember it correctly. Suppose, for example, that your sister tells you what she bought at the mall. You will not likely have much interest in this, and so you may forget it. But suppose she sees your father murdered and tells you about this. Certainly you are much more likely to remember a description of that event. Thus if the resurrection appearances were regarded as very significant, it is very likely that Paul would remember them accurately. I will argue in the next chapter that the early Christians did indeed regard the resurrection appearances as very significant, and so this factor does come into play in this case.

Second, as with firsthand testimony, the more major the detail is, the more likely the witness is to remember it, whereas the more minor the detail, the less likely the witness is to remember it. Now in the case of 1 Corinthians 15, Paul is only being asked to recall the most basic elements of the events: that Jesus appeared and who he appeared to. Hence the information he relates in 1 Corinthians 15 is information he is very likely to have remembered correctly.

Thus for these reasons, the secondhand testimony Paul provides us with in 1 Corinthians 15 is not very much less reliable than firsthand testimony. Hence, we are justified in accepting the appearances he relates in this passage as historical.

The Appearance to the 500

But the appearance to the 500 is the one appearance for which we may not have secondhand testimony and so we need to analyze that appearance. Although Paul does not tell us the names of the witnesses of this appearance, I think we can demonstrate that Paul's testimony may have been secondhand, was possibly thirdhand, and is at the very least fourthhand. But even if it was fourthhand, the testimony is still reliable.

We know Paul made frequent trips to Jerusalem (see Gal 1:17-24 and various passages in Acts), and since many of the resurrection appearances took place in Jerusalem, the appearance to the 500 may have taken place there, and so Paul may have had an ideal opportunity to question the witnesses. And even if the appearance took place in Galilee, it is not especially unlikely that Paul might have made a trip to Galilee in order to talk to the witnesses. This was the largest of Jesus' appearances, and Paul's statement that most of the witnesses were still alive though some had fallen asleep implies that the appearance served an apologetic function for the early Christians. As C.H. Dodd says "There can hardly be any purpose in mentioning the fact that most of the 500 are still alive, unless Paul is saying, in effect, 'The witnesses are there to be

---

Testimony in Suspected Child Sexual Abuse Cases: Questions of Accuracy," *Institute for Psychological Therapies* 9 (1997): http://www.ipt-forensics.com/journal/volume9/j9_1_4.htm.

questioned.'"[12] Thus Paul may very well have been curious enough to investigate the appearance himself, and if he did, our testimony is secondhand.

But we cannot be sure that Paul talked to the witnesses. Another possibility is that he got the information from the people who got it from the witnesses, and in that case his testimony is thirdhand. Paul knew Peter, James, and John (Gal 1:18-19; 2:9), and it is likely Peter, James, and John may have talked to the witnesses. They were three of the main leaders of the early Christian movement, and we know the early Christian movement put considerable effort into maintaining the accuracy of its teachings.[13] Peter, James, and John lived in Jerusalem and ran the church there, and all three had grown up in Galilee, living there until the time of Jesus' ministry. These three thus had a greater opportunity to question the witnesses than Paul did, since they lived in Jerusalem and had previously lived in Galilee, whereas Paul only visited Jerusalem on occasion and had no connection with Galilee. And they also had more reason to do so than Paul, since for them investigating the appearances was not merely a matter of personal interest, but of guaranteeing the accuracy of the church's teachings, something which was their responsibility, for the Jerusalem church served as the head church. Ancient people, like modern ones, understood the importance of talking to the eyewitnesses, so the three of them would have been aware of this.[14] Further, Peter, James, and John, unlike Paul, were involved in the resurrection appearances when those appearances, including the appearance to the 500, were first happening, and the excitement of the new movement would have given them another reason to inquire of the witnesses. The Gospels portray Peter and the Beloved Disciple running to the tomb as soon as they hear it is empty (Lk 24:12; Jn 20:4), and the disciples who were traveling to Emmaus return to Jerusalem as soon as they realize Jesus is raised (Lk 24:33). One would think the disciples would also be anxious to investigate an appearance to 500 people. If this is what Peter, or James, or John did, then our testimony to the appearance is thirdhand.

But at the very least, our testimony must be fourthhand, for given the role Peter, James, and John played as the guardians of the church's tradition, we ought to expect that if they did not talk to any of the witnesses themselves, they must have at least sent someone whom they trusted to do so. For without a report on the matter from someone whom they trusted, it is not at all likely they would have made the appearance to the 500 part of the material which they regarded "as of first importance" and which was to be passed along to new converts such as Paul. (We will discuss the fact that Paul and the other apostles regarded the appearances as a matter of primary

---

12. C.H. Dodd, *More New Testament Studies* (Grand Rapids, MI: Eerdmans, 1968), 128.

13. This point has been demonstrated at considerable length by Birger Gerhardsson, *The Reliability of the Gospel Tradition* (Peabody, MA: Hendrickson, 2001).

14. On the value ancient historians placed on eyewitness testimony, see Samuel Byrskog, *Story as History—History as Story: The Gospel Tradition in the Context of Ancient Oral History* (Tubingen: Mohr Siebeck, 2000).

importance in more detail in chapter 5.) Thus I think the worst case scenario as far as the chain of transmission of the testimony to this appearance is: witnesses>someone sent by the leaders of the Jerusalem church>the leaders of the Jerusalem church>Paul. Although one may worry that fourthhand testimony is getting us too far away from the original source, I do not think that is so in a case like this where all of the parties understood the importance of the material (it was a matter "of first importance") and so would be careful to pass it along accurately. The case we have here is analogous to a case in which a crime is a committed, a police officer interviews the witness to the crime, the officer reports the interview to the chief of police, and the chief of police is interviewed by a reporter, who then publishes a summary of the interview. Here we have fourthhand testimony, for the chain of transmission is: witness>police officer who conducted the interview>chief of police>reporter. Now if the four individuals had been playing telephone, whispering to each other information which they did not care about (the early church's handling of its teachings is sometimes supposed to have been analogous to this), we would not trust such testimony. But given that the individuals involved in transmitting the information consider the information important and made an effort to pass it on accurately, we will believe the accuracy of the report we read in the newspaper. We have the same situation in the case of the appearance to the 500, and hence I think the evidence is sufficient to accept the appearance to the 500 as historical.

Finally, we should make the important point that it is likely some of the Corinthians would have checked on the claim of the appearance to the 500, as well as the other claims of resurrection appearances, at some point in between the time Paul first presented them with these claims (ca. 51 CE), and Paul's epistle to them in 55 CE. Given the significance of changing one's religion, it is difficult to believe that no one in the Corinthian community bothered to check into Paul's claims when he first preached the Gospel there. If the Corinthians had found Paul's claims to be unreliable, he surely would not have been repeating the same claims in his epistle to them.

However, we do need to consider two objections to the historicity of the appearance to the 500. First, we need to ask why the appearance is not mentioned in the Gospels. Since the appearance was to such a large group, should not the Gospel writers have included it because of its apologetic value? In response, while the appearance to the 500 certainly has apologetic value, I do not think its apologetic value was so superior to that of the other appearances that the Gospel writers would have felt compelled to relate it. The Gospels already give us an appearance in which Jesus denies that he is a ghost, an appearance in which he can be touched and eats, an appearance in which Jesus appears to an obstinate unbeliever (Thomas), and Matthew's story of the guards at Jesus' tomb. These stories all have strong apologetic value, and so there was no pressing need to mention the appearance to the 500.

Second, some scholars have suggested the appearance to the 500 may actually be a reference to Pentecost.[15] If this is correct, the appearance to the 500 would not really be an appearance, since Pentecost did not involve a visual appearance of Jesus, but rather the phenomenon of mass tongues speaking. However, the evidence linking the appearance to the 500 with Pentecost is very slight. The only reason for thinking there is any connection between the two is that the Greek words for Pentecost and 500 both involve the *pente* prefix. This is clearly very scant evidence. Further, if there was legendary development, it would more likely be the other way around—what was originally an appearance to the 500 became the event of the Pentecost tongues speaking. The reason why this is a likelier scenario is because the appearance to the 500 is found in Paul, who was close to the eyewitnesses, whereas Pentecost is found only in a later source, Luke, whom skeptical scholars do not think was very close to the eyewitnesses. If there is a conflict, we should surely prefer the source which is closer to the eyewitnesses.

Other Issues

Three other issues related to 1 Corinthians 15:3-8 need to be addressed, because each of these issues has been thought to be relevant to the historical reliability of this material,[16] though in fact none of these issues actually are. The first is the question of whether Paul was the first to put this list of appearances together, or whether this list existed prior to Paul.[17] It has been thought that if the list existed prior to Paul, then the list is earlier than Paul, and since an earlier source is more reliable, this fact strengthens the historical reliability of the list. But this question is actually irrelevant, because even if the list itself is not pre-Pauline, the information certainly is. That is, even if Paul was the first to put the appearances into the form of a list (or to combine originally separate lists), he was not the first person to create the appearances. As we have seen, he learned of the appearances from Peter and James, who were firsthand witnesses for all of the appearances except the appearance to the 500. The only important question is who Paul got the information from; whether the information ever existed as a list prior to Paul, or whether Paul combined two originally separate lists, is irrelevant to the data's historical accuracy—unless it is the case, as Adolf Von Harnack postulated, that the list is a combination of two originally separate lists which

---

15. E.g., Kirsopp Lake, *The Beginnings of Christianity: Part 1: The Acts of the Apostles* (London: Macmillan, 1933), 421; Reginald H. Fuller, *The Formation of the Resurrection Narratives* (Philadelphia: Fortress, 1980), 36.

16. One will find all these issues discussed in the sources I referred to in n1 which provide an overview of 1 Cor 15:3-8.

17. For the argument that the list originally ended with 1 Cor 15:5, see Jerome Murphy-O'Connor, "Tradition and Redaction in 1 Cor 15:3-7," *Catholic Biblical Quarterly* 43 (1981): 582-89. For the argument that the list always existed in its full form, see Kirk R. MacGregor, "1 Corinthians 15:3b-6a,7 and the Bodily Resurrection of Jesus," *Journal of the Evangelical Theological Society* 49 (2006): 225-34.

were used by rival Christian groups to serve as evidence that their leaders were the true leaders.[18] This hypothesis holds that there were originally two lists: one list mentioned Peter and the Twelve, the other list mentioned James and all the apostles. Paul, according to this hypothesis, put these lists together, adding the appearance to the 500 and the appearance to himself. However, there is nothing in the passage itself to support this hypothesis. The idea would make sense only if we had some evidence that there was a rivalry between Peter and James, but there is no such evidence.[19] And the hypothesis has further problems even if there was a rivalry between Peter and James. First, it would be strange to have "lists" of only two appearances (Peter and the Twelve; James and all the apostles). Second, since Paul tells us Peter was an apostle (Gal 1:19), how can Peter be excluded from James' supposed group of "all the apostles"?

The second issue is the question of whether the creed was originally in Aramaic or Greek. The thinking here seems to be that if the list was originally in Aramaic it is earlier, since the Aramaic speaking Christian community existed before the Greek speaking Christian community; and since an earlier source is more reliable, if the list was originally in Aramaic this would strengthen its historical reliability. But it actually makes no difference how early the list was formulated. This argument again confuses when information was put together with when it originated. The information originates with the witnesses to the appearances, and Paul got the information from these witnesses. When the information was put together as a list is not important, whether it was two years later, or thirty years later makes no difference, just as long as it came from the witnesses. (It is true that witnesses' memories may fade over time, but in this case the witness only has to remember the bare fact: that Jesus appeared. The witness would not forget this bare fact no matter how many years had passed. (And the psychological data is not even very consistent in regard to what extent a witness's memory will be affected as time passes.).)[20] Whether the list was originally in Aramaic or Greek, or even if the material never existed as a list before Paul, this does not affect the historical reliability of the material.

The third issue is the question of when Paul received this information. Did he receive it immediately after his conversion, or during the two weeks he spent with Peter and James, or at some other point? However, when Paul received this information is also irrelevant because, again, his source for the information is the same (Peter and James) regardless of when he got the information, for even if he got it prior to his first meeting with them, we can assume he verified it with them at some point. And it does not matter when he verified it with them. Peter and James are not more or less reliable

---

18. Adolf von Harnack, *Die Verklärungsgeschichte Jesu: Der Bericht des Paulus (I. Kor. 15, 3FF.) und die beiden Christusvisionen des Petrus* (Berlin: Walter de Gruyter, 1922), 67.

19. On the general harmony among the apostles, see David Wenham, *Paul: Follower of Jesus or Founder of Christianity?* (Grand Rapids, MI: Eerdmans, 1995).

20. See Ebbe Ebbesen and Vladimir J. Konecni, "Eyewitness Memory Research: Probative V. Prejudicial Value," *Expert Evidence* 5 (1996): 2-28 (7-8).

depending on when they gave Paul the information, or depending on whether others had given it to Paul before them.

It is clear that all three of these issues illustrate the same error: thinking that the earlier the information is, the more reliable it is. Now it is generally true that when dealing with history, the earlier a source is, the more reliable it is. But the reason why this is generally true is that, generally, the earlier a source is, the closer the source is to being an eyewitness source. For example, a source from five years after the event it is more likely to be based on eyewitness testimony than a source from fifty years after the event, because after fifty years, it will be harder to find eyewitnesses. But this is not always the case. If a source from fifty years after the event is based on the testimony of an eyewitness, and a source from five years after the event is tenthhand, we will prefer the source from fifty years afterwards. Though the date of a source is a general guide to how close it is to being an eyewitness source, the reliability of the source is ultimately based on its proximity to the eyewitnesses, not its date. The material of 1 Corinthians 15:3-8 does not differ in its proximity to the eyewitnesses based on when Paul got the information, or when the information was put into a list, or what language the list was originally in, thus these questions do not affect the historical reliability of this material. Analogously, suppose I hear today a story from an eighty year old person of an event from when he was twenty. I am hearing the information sixty years after the events, yet I can be confident the story is correct (providing the fellow has no memory disorder). And if I tell the story if and when I am eighty, some fifty years after I write this, the person hearing my testimony will be hearing testimony from 110 years after the event, yet that testimony is still sound (provided I have not, in my old age, acquired a memory disorder), and is to be preferred over tenthhand testimony from one week after the event.

The Gospels

The Empty Tomb

A substantial amount of literature has been devoted to the question of the historicity of the empty tomb.[21] The chief arguments for its historicity are as follows.[22]

---

21. For in depth analyses of the historicity of the empty tomb, see Craig, *Assessing*, 255-74; James D.G. Dunn, *Jesus Remembered* (Grand Rapids, MI: Eerdmans, 2003), 828-40; Dale C. Allison Jr., *Resurrecting Jesus: The Earliest Christian Tradition and its Interpreters* (New York: T&T Clark, 2005), 299-331; Peter Kirby, "The Case Against the Empty Tomb," in Robert M. Price and Jeffrey Jay Lowder eds., *The Empty Tomb: Jesus Beyond the Grave* (Amherst, NY: Prometheus, 2005), 233-60; Jeffrey Jay Lowder, "Historical Evidence and the Empty Tomb Story: A Reply to William Lane Craig," in *The Empty Tomb*, 261-306.

22. I should briefly explain why I reject two of the other popular arguments for the empty tomb. First, there is the argument that the earliest Jewish-Christian polemic assumes the empty tomb, for in Mt 28:11-15, we are told that to the Christian claim that the tomb was empty, the Jews replied that this is because the disciples had stolen the body; thus it is argued that the Jews admitted the historicity of

First, the fact that women discovered the empty tomb is argued to be embarrassing, and it is argued that the historicity of the empty tomb is therefore confirmed by the criterion of embarrassment. Various texts indicate that women's testimony was looked down upon in ancient Judaism, and thus if the story of the empty tomb was legendary, we should not expect the legend to involve women as the primary witnesses, since female witnesses would be unfavorable to Christianity. Hence since women are the primary witnesses, the story must be historical. Texts from ancient Judaism which reflect a low view of women include the following: "Sooner let the words of the law be burnt than delivered to women,"[23] and "Happy is he whose children are male, but woe to him whose children are female."[24] And Josephus tells us women's testimony was not allowed in court:

> But let not the testimony of women be admitted, on account of the levity and boldness of their sex, nor let servants be admitted to give testimony on account of the ignobility of their soul; since it is probable that they may not speak truth, either out of hope of gain, or fear of punishment.[25]

It has been objected against this argument that other texts can be cited which reflect a more favorable view of women, for example, "God has endowed women with a special sense of wisdom which man lacks."[26] And in other sources, women's testimony is accepted.[27]

In response to this, we should say that though these other texts do show that not all ancient Jews looked down on women and their testimony, the fact that some texts do express bias tells us that bias against women was at least common. If bias against women was common even if not universal, it is still unlikely the early Christians would invent a story with women as witnesses, since that fact would make the story less credible in the minds of some of the people in their audience, even if not all

---

the empty tomb, for if they denied it, they would not have proposed that the body was stolen. But the problem with this line of reasoning is that the Jews' proposal that the disciples stole the body could have been an assuming for the sake of argument argument. That is, their argument could have been that, assuming for the sake of argument that the tomb was empty, the stolen body hypothesis was still better than the resurrection hypothesis. Since we cannot question the Jews Matthew has in mind, we cannot know. Second, there is the argument that the empty tomb is necessary to account for the disciples' belief in Jesus' resurrection, which is a chief argument of N.T. Wright's book *The Resurrection of the Son of God*. I critique that argument in chapter 7.

23. Babylonian Talmud, Sotah 19a.
24. Babylonian Talmud, Mas. Sanhedrin 100b.
25. Josephus, *Antiquities of the Jews*, 4.8.15.
26. Babylonian Talmud, Nidah, 45.
27. For an overview of the ancient sources reflecting a more positive view of women's testimony, see Richard C. Carrier, *Not the Impossible Faith: Why Christianity Didn't Need a Miracle to Succeed* (Lulu, 2009), 297-322. But for an overview of the texts reflecting a negative view, see Richard Bauckham, *Gospel Women: Studies of the Named Women in the Gospels* (Grand Rapids, MI: Eerdmans, 2002), 268-77.

of them. Hence the women's presence in the story is indeed a good argument for its historicity.

A second argument is that of multiple attestation. The empty tomb is attested by all four Gospels, which means we have four sources attesting to the event. It might be objected that the four sources are not independent of each other, since Matthew and Luke used Mark as a source, and it is possible John used Mark as well, and thus we really only have two sources, or perhaps even one source. However, Matthew, Luke, and John all have information concerning the empty tomb which is not found in Mark, and thus they must have had other sources for the empty tomb besides Mark, hence we do have four different sources. Matthew includes the information about the guards at the tomb (Mt 28:11-15) and an appearance to the women on the way back to the tomb (28:8-10). Luke changes the list of women at the tomb even though he would have no conceivable reason to do this (and even if he had a reason, it would constitute inventing an event, which we have said is unlikely) and he also includes the fact that Peter ran to the tomb (24:12), another event not found in Mark. And John has Peter and the Beloved Disciple running to the tomb (20:4) and an appearance to Mary Magdalene by the tomb (Jn 20:11-18), both events which are not found in Mark. Thus, since each Gospel writer had independent information about the empty tomb, they do not all derive their account from Mark, and so we do have four independent sources.

We should however, add an important qualifier to the criterion of multiple attestation, and that qualifier is that the criterion is only helpful if we accept the view that the Gospels are at least fairly reliable. For an event is not more likely to be historical if it is attested by multiple unreliable sources, and hence if one does not think the Gospels are at least fairly reliable, the criterion of multiple attestation will not work (but as I explained in chapter 1, most scholars do think the Gospels are fairly reliable). And we should also add that even for those who think the Gospels are fairly reliable, the details of multiple attestation are rather hazy. How many documents need to attest to a fact before we should accept it as historical? Are two Gospels enough to render it probable that an event occurred, or do we need three or four? If two render it probable, how much is the probability raised if three or four Gospels attest to it? Given the haziness of the exact workings of multiple attestation, I would not accept a fact as historical simply because it is multiply attested. Multiple attestation should only be used as a supplementary criterion for a claim for which there are also other good arguments.

The third argument, and in my opinion the strongest, is that if the tomb was not empty, the Christians could not have believed Jesus was raised from the dead, and that even if they somehow did manage to believe this, the Jews could have stopped the Christian movement by producing Jesus' body. The reason why the Christians would not have been able to believe Jesus was raised from the dead if the tomb was occupied is because, as I explained in the introduction, resurrection for ancient Jews and the early Christians meant only bodily resurrection. If someone was resurrected, their body was raised, and thus it was not possible for the person's body to be in their tomb. Hence if Jesus' body was in his tomb, the Christians could not believe he was raised from the dead. But supposing the disciples somehow overcame this intellectual hurdle and believed Jesus was raised despite his body being in the tomb, the other half of this argument is that the Jewish leaders would certainly have produced Jesus' body and stopped the Christian movement.

The objections that can be made against either or both halves of this argument are as follows:

1. It is objected that Jesus may never have been buried, but that he may merely have been thrown into a ditch, or that if he was buried, his burial place may have been unknown. If either scenario is true, then neither the Jews nor the Christians would know where Jesus was buried, and if they did not know where he was buried, they could not check to see if his body was still in the tomb. The reason for supposing Jesus may not have been buried is that the Romans typically did not bury crucifixion victims; the denial of burial was part of the shame of crucifixion. However, Craig Evans, in a thorough review of the relevant ancient sources, has demonstrated that it is very clear from the writings of Josephus that the Romans made an exception for the Jews because of the importance with which the Jews regarded burial.[28] For example, Josephus tells us "Jews are so careful about funeral rites that even malefactors who have been sentenced to crucifixion are taken down and buried before sunset."[29] Thus even if we have no specific evidence to indicate Jesus was buried, we should assume that he was, since virtually all Jews were buried. But further, there is also more specific evidence that Jesus was buried: Paul, who we have seen is a reliable source, tells us Jesus was buried in 1 Corinthians 15:3 ("...and that he was buried...").

As for the suggestion that the location of Jesus' tomb may not have been known, this is very unlikely. Crucifixions were public events designed to attract a crowd, and so anyone who wanted to know where Jesus was buried would likely have only had to ask around.[30] Further, if Jesus' burial place was not common knowledge, one could simply ask Joseph of Arimathea to identify the location.

2. A second objection is that the Jewish leadership could not have produced Jesus' body because it was illegal to remove a corpse from a tomb. However, it would not be necessary for the Jews to actually remove the body. If neutral people whom the townspeople trusted inspected the tomb and verified that the body was there, it is difficult to see why that would not have been enough to convince everyone that the body was indeed there. (But we will have to address the question of whether it was legal to move a corpse when we consider the possibility that Jesus was buried in the ground, a question we will consider below.)

---

28. Craig A. Evans, "Jewish Burial Traditions and the Resurrection of Jesus," *Journal for the Study of the Historical Jesus* 3 (2005): 233-48.

29. Josephus, *Jewish Wars*, 4.5.2.

30. This point is made by Allison, *Resurrecting*, 362.

3. A third objection is that since the disciples did not begin to proclaim the resurrection until forty days after Jesus' death, by that time, Jesus' corpse may have decayed to the point where it could not be recognized as Jesus'. Hence even if there was a body in Jesus' tomb, there would be no way to be sure it was Jesus' body. But the problems with this argument are first, we should expect the disciples to have checked the tomb much sooner than forty days; they certainly would have checked it as the appearances were going on. So this objection could work in theory only against the Jewish leadership's attempt to inspect the tomb. However, the expert opinion is that a corpse would indeed still be recognizable after forty days.[31] Further, the nail wounds from crucifixion would be visible even if an exceptional amount of time had passed, and if a corpse with nail wounds in it was found in Jesus' tomb, it would certainly have to be admitted that it was Jesus' body, for surely the Christians would have a difficult time arguing that some other crucifixion victim had been placed in the tomb after Jesus rose.

4. A fourth objection is that the disciples may have been so excited about Jesus' appearances that they never bothered to look in the tomb, and that though we have been assuming the Jewish leadership desired to stop the Christian movement, perhaps they did not really care about it, and so never bothered to check the tomb. But it seems incredible to believe that not one of the hundreds of people who saw the resurrection appearances was interested in examining the tomb. Luke and John both portray the disciples as running to the tomb (Lk 24:12; Jn 20:4), and certainly that is the natural reaction to the situation the disciples were in. As for the Jewish leadership not being interested, this idea is very implausible given that the Jewish leadership was involved in putting Jesus to death (even if we do not accept the Gospels' reliability, this is attested by Paul in 1 Thess 2:14-15),[32] and given that by Paul's time, in the early or mid 30s, the Jewish leadership was persecuting Christians (for Paul was persecuting them), and that they continued to do so (for Paul tells us he was later persecuted himself (2 Cor 11:24)). Thus at the time of Jesus' death, the Jewish leaders were interested in stopping the Christian movement, and they were also interested in stopping it during the 30s and into the 40s or 50s. Why would they not have been interested shortly after Jesus' death?

5. A fifth objection is that even if the Jews had produced Jesus' body this may not have stopped the Christian movement, because the disciples might have believed so firmly in Jesus' resurrection on the grounds of the appearances, that they might have invented a convoluted explanation to dismiss any facts to the contrary. For example, maybe they would argue that Jesus' body being in the tomb was a trick caused by the

---

31. Stephen T. Davis tells us he checked with a pathologist regarding how long a corpse would still be identifiable, and was told that a corpse would still be identifiable well after seven weeks ("The Counterattack of the Resurrection Skeptics: A Review Article," *Philosophia Christi* 8 (2006): 39-64 (55)).

32. This verse is sometimes argued to be an interpolation, but the arguments are weak. See Carol J. Schlueter, *Filling Up the Measure: Polemical Hyperbole in 1 Thessalonians* 2:14-16 (Sheffield: JSOT Press, 1994).

Devil. One can find other examples of members of a religious movement being presented with seemingly incontrovertible evidence that its beliefs are wrong but refusing to cease believing in spite of obvious evidence. Take the case of Sabbatai Sevi, a Jew of the seventeenth century who claimed to be the Messiah, but who later renounced his claim to messiahship, and Judaism as well, when he was captured by Muslims and forced to either convert to Islam or die. Sevi's apostasy would seem to prove quite definitely that he was not the Messiah, but some of his followers, rather than give up this belief, postulated that the real Sevi had been taken to heaven and replaced by an impostor, or that Sevi's apostasy was a temporary ruse to test the faith of his followers.[33]

Now we should admit that based on cases like these, it is not implausible that some of the Christians would have continued to believe in the resurrection even after Jesus' body was produced. However, the problem for the skeptic is that in this case Christianity would have remained only a small movement. For though a few diehard followers may have continued to believe despite Jesus' corpse being produced, surely Christianity would have had a very difficult time making converts if it was faced with such obvious evidence against its central claim. For potential converts would not have had the emotional investment of the original disciples, and thus no motive to deny obvious facts. But Christianity had no difficulty attracting converts. In fact, it spread across the Mediterranean at an extremely quick pace. And it thrived in Jerusalem, right where the Jewish leaders who desired to stop the movement were headquartered.

Was Jesus Buried in the Ground?

Some recent work by Jodi Magness potentially throws a monkey wrench into the debate on the empty tomb.[34] To my knowledge, nearly every scholar who has examined the historicity of the burial of Jesus has assumed that if Jesus was buried, he was buried in a *tomb*. However, Magness has drawn attention to the fact that the vast majority of people in ancient Israel (just like the vast majority of people today) were buried in the ground, not in a tomb. (Perhaps the most well-known example of burial in the ground is the cemetery excavated at Qumran.)[35] The archeological evidence reveals that it was only the wealthy who owned tombs, for all of the tombs that have been uncovered from this period have belonged to wealthy individuals. This is clear from a number of facts. First, the number of tombs in Jerusalem from the late first century BCE to

---

33. On Sabbatai Sevi, see Gershom Gerhard Scholem, *Sabbatai Sevi: The Mystical Messiah: 1626-1676* (Princeton: Princeton University Press, 1973).

34. Jodi Magness, "Ossuaries and the Burials of Jesus and James," *Journal of Biblical Literature* 124 (2005): 121-154 (145-47); Jodi Magness, *Stone and Dung, Oil and Spit: Jewish Daily Life in the Time of Jesus* (Grand Rapids, MI: Eerdmans, 2011), 155-64. Magness herself thinks Jesus was buried in a tomb. I address her argument below.

35. On the Qumran cemetery, see Roland de Vaux, *Archeology and the Dead Sea Scrolls* (London: Oxford University Press, 1973). For references to burials in the ground in rabbinic literature, see Magness, *Stone and Dung*, 158-60.

the first century CE is not great enough to accommodate more than about 18,000 people; but Jerusalem's population at this time was always in the area of 60,000. Thus many more people died than there were tombs available for, so clearly, not everyone was buried in a tomb. Second, the tombs are primarily found in or around Jerusalem. This is what we would expect if the tombs were only used by the wealthy, because the wealthy lived primarily in Jerusalem. But if the tombs were used by the common people, the tombs should be found throughout Israel. Third, those inscriptions on the ossuaries in these tombs which mention the occupation of the deceased always refer to upper class occupations.[36] Thus tomb burial was clearly only a privilege of the upper class. (The reason why discussion of burial in Jesus' time has focused entirely on tomb burial, even though it was not the most common form of burial, is probably because of the fact that it is much easier for tombs to survive in the archeological record—for tombs are not easily destroyed, but burials in the ground are marked only by a gravestone and such gravestones are easily destroyed. Since a disproportionately high number of tombs survive in the archeological record, this creates the false impression that tomb burial was more common than it actually was.[37])

Now, as Kris Komarnitsky has realized,[38] this finding has a very significant implication for our topic: It means merely demonstrating that Jesus was buried does not demonstrate he was buried in a tomb. And two of the most significant pieces of evidence for Jesus' burial (the general evidence showing that all Jews in Jesus' time were buried, and Paul's statement in 1 Corinthians 15:3) only attest to the fact that Jesus was buried. Thus we must contend with the possibility that if the Gospels are not generally reliable, Jesus may have been buried in the ground, and we must then ask how burial in the ground would affect the argument that if Jesus' burial place was occupied, the Christians would not have been able to believe in the resurrection and the Jewish leaders would have produced the body.

Our rebuttals to the third, fourth and fifth objections to this argument are not affected at all. Jesus' corpse would have been recognizable whether he was buried in a tomb or in the ground, provided that the burial place could be identified as his. And whether buried in a tomb or the ground, the Christians and Jews would have been interested in seeing the burial place. And if Jesus' body was produced, whether it came from a tomb or from the ground, this would have stopped the Christian movement. However, our responses to the first and second objections are potentially affected.

Our response to the second objection is potentially affected, because if Jesus was buried in the ground, it would not be possible to see whether or not his body was gone simply by looking into the tomb; one would need to dig up the body. Thus checking Jesus' burial place would be a more complicated process. Our response to the first

36. On all three of these points, see Magness, *Stone and Dung*, 156-57.
37. Magness, *Stone and Dung*, 157.
38. Kris Komarnitsky, *Doubting Jesus' Resurrection: What Happened in the Black Box?* (Draper, Utah: Stone Arrow, 2009), 29.

objection is affected in that if Jesus was buried in the ground, it raises the possibility that his burial place could not be identified. For it is the case that many of the ground burials that have been uncovered by archeology have gravestones which do not bear an inscription or any other marker which would differentiate one grave from another; and in some cases, there is not even a gravestone at all.[39] Further, Luke 11:44 indicates that graves with no gravestones were common. In this passage, Jesus refers to accidentally stepping on a grave as if it is a common occurrence ("Woe to you, because you are like unmarked graves, which people walk over without knowing"), and the only way one can accidently step on a grave is if the grave does not have a gravestone. If no gravestone was put up to mark Jesus' grave, or if there was a gravestone but it was indistinguishable from other gravestones, this would suggest that it would not have been possible for anyone to identify Jesus' grave.

Before we consider whether having to dig up the body would pose a problem for our argument, let us consider the more fundamental problem of whether burial in the ground would have meant Jesus' burial place could not be identified.

In order to show Jesus' burial place would have been identifiable even if he was buried in the ground, I will make two arguments. First, I will argue that rabbinic sources, as well as a few other pieces of data, indicate that Jews did always mark graves by using a gravestone and that each grave was marked in a distinctive way so that one grave would not get mixed up with another one. However, since the historical reliability of the rabbinic sources is questionable,[40] and since the other pieces of data may not prove persuasive by themselves, I will also argue that even if Jesus' grave was not marked, it would still have been possible to identify the grave.

Despite the fact that archeology has turned up some graves that are unmarked, and despite Jesus' saying in Luke 11:44, the evidence suggests that Jews did always mark graves. Consequently, any unmarked graves must be graves which were originally marked, but for which the gravestone was destroyed.

The reasons for thinking all graves in Jesus' time were marked with a gravestone are: 1) Numbers 19:11-22 tells us that a person will contract ritual uncleanness if they make contact with a corpse or grave.[41] Hence gravestones must have been used to mark graves, for otherwise there would be no way to know a body was buried and thus no way to avoid contracting ritual uncleanness. 2) There are references in the rabbinic literature to gravestones being destroyed by a plow, or destroyed during the rainy

---

39. Magness, "Ossuaries," 146.

40. For an overview of different views of the historical reliability of the rabbinic literature, see Ben Tsiyon Rozenfield, *Torah Centers and Rabbinic Activity in Palestine, 70-400 CE : History and Geographic Distribution* (Leiden: Brill, 2010), 1-2. In regard to burial in particular, Glenn Miller cites a number of instances of what he argues are contradictions between the rabbinic literature and archeology or Josephus ("Good Question: Was the Burial of Jesus a Temporary One, Because of Time Constraints?" http://christianthinktank.com/shellgame.html).

41. For a discussion of corpse impurity in ancient Judaism, see Hannah Harrington, *The Purity Texts* (London: T&T Clark, 2004), 71-83.

season, and having to be put back up. Thus we know graves could easily be destroyed, and this is likely the explanation for the unmarked graves uncovered by archeology and for Jesus' statement in Luke 11:44.[42] 3) The rabbinic literature also tells us that at Passover time, it was routine practice for Jews to whitewash graves (that is, paint the gravestones white) so the graves would stand out so that pilgrims coming to Jerusalem would not accidentally step on them.[43] (Graves were not necessarily only in cemeteries but could be set up any place,[44] thus there was the danger of someone accidentally making contact with a grave which they failed to notice. And we may note in passing that from the fact that the concern is with stepping on the graves, we can deduce that many if not all of these gravestones laid flat on the ground rather than being vertical like most gravestones today.)

Thus graves were marked with some kind of a stone. But the question then becomes whether they were marked in a distinctive way, so that one could tell one grave from another. Although the graves of one excavated Jewish cemetery from ca. 100-600 CE have inscriptions on them,[45] other grave sites have been excavated where the gravestones do not have any inscriptions on them (such as the cemetery at Qumran). Since not all graves had inscriptions, this raises the possibility that the graves were not marked in a distinctive way. However, we can conclude that graves were indeed marked in a distinctive way, because passages from various sources indicate one grave could be clearly distinguished from another.

First, Hegesippus tells us James' gravestone was still visible during his day, so he must have thought it possible to tell one grave from another.[46] Second, a passage in the Babylonian Talmud prohibits two corpses from being buried in one grave unless the two individuals were married.[47] The passage cannot have tomb burial in mind, since multiple people were obviously buried in the same tomb; thus it must mean burial in the ground. (Whether a given passage about burial refers to burial in a tomb or burial in the ground must be determined from the context; it is not possible to tell from the words used, since the same words were used to refer to both tomb burial and burial in the ground.) Now since the passage allows for the possibility that husband and wife could be buried together in the ground, the ground burials must have been marked in a distinctive way, since once the second person died, those doing the burying would have to be able to find the original grave in order to bury the other person in it. (And the passage cannot have in mind a situation in which both husband and wife had died at the same time, for it refers to one corpse being a skeleton and the

---

42. On gravestones being destroyed by rain, see Jerusalem Talmud, Moed Qatan, 5b. On graves accidentally being destroyed by plows see Mishnah, Oholot, 18.4.

43. Mishnah, Moed Qatan, 1.2; Babylonian Talmud, Moed Qatan, 5b.

44. For graves in places other than graveyards, see Babylonia Talmud, Ebel Rabbathi, EE.

45. See Rozenfeld, *Torah Centers*, 77-79.

46. Hegesippus, quoted by Eusebius *Ecclesiastical History* 2.23.15-18.

47. Babylonia Talmud, Ebel Rabbathi, 13d.

other not being a skeleton.) Third, in the Qumran cemetery, in some of the graves, there are two bodies, and archeologists are agreed based on the way in which the soil was affected that the two bodies were buried at separate times.[48] The fact that the two people were buried together would suggest the two people had some sort of a relationship with each other. The only other conceivable motivation for burying two people in one grave would seem to be to save space, but the graveyard possessed plenty of space in which to bury people, so this is not likely the reason. If the two people had a relationship with each other, this means the grave must have been marked in a distinctive way, because, again, when the second person died, the buriers would have to be able to locate the first person's grave in order to bury the second person. Fourth, the Mishnah may attest to secondary burial for those buried in the ground, and this would require that it was possible to identify the graves of those buried in the ground. Mishnah, Sanhedrin, 6.5-6 reads:

> They did not bury the condemned in the burial grounds of his ancestors, but there were two graveyards made ready for the use of the court, one for those who were beheaded or strangled, and one for those who were stoned or burned. When the flesh had wasted away they gathered together the bones and buried them in their own place [the family burial place].

The passage is describing secondary burial for condemned criminals. Since, as we have explained above, tombs were used only by the wealthy, the Jerusalem leaders would certainly not have buried criminals in tombs; they would have been buried in the ground. Hence if the bones of criminals were sometimes gathered by their families for secondary burial, they must have been gathered from graves, and thus we have here evidence that one grave was distinguishable from another, for if the graves were indistinguishable, it would not be possible for a family to tell which grave held their family member. However, given that secondary burial for those buried in the ground is not, to my knowledge, attested anywhere else, and given the questions concerning the historical reliability of the rabbinic literature, it is possible that the Mishnah is simply mistaken here; it may have in mind tomb burial, but it may have forgotten that criminals were not buried in tombs.

Thus it appears that graves were marked in a distinctive way. With regard to how graves were marked, they must have been marked in a way that is not clear from the archeological record. Perhaps they were inscribed with a material that did not survive for a very long time, such as chalk.

It may be objected that however gravestones were marked, they may have been marked so subtly that only those who were at the burial would be able to recognize the grave. If so, then only the disciples would have been able to recognize Jesus' grave, not the Jewish leaders. However, if the Jewish leaders wanted to find Jesus' grave, they

---

48. See Rachel Hachlili, *Jewish Funerary Customs* (Leiden: Brill, 2005), 16-17, 469.

could simply have asked Joseph of Arimathea, who of course had buried Jesus, and who was a member of the Sanhedrin.

However, the most significant point for our argument is that even if Jesus' grave was not marked in a distinctive way, in fact, even if it was not marked at all, it would still be possible to identify Jesus' grave. For when a grave is dug, the soil covering the grave is necessarily destroyed, and after the soil is placed back, it has a different color and texture than the soil of the surrounding graves.[49] Hence as long as Joseph of Arimathea (or any other witnesses of the burial) remembered the general area of the cemetery where Jesus was buried, it would be quite easy to find Jesus' grave. Further, I consulted with a representative of the National Funeral Directors Association, who informed me that a newly dug grave would be distinguishable for months if not years based on the difference in grass growth and the outline of the grave being visible. The only potential problem our argument runs into is the fact that if there were other newly dug graves very close to Jesus', then though the new graves would all stand out from the older graves, none of the newly dug graves would stand out from each other, and hence Jesus' grave could potentially be mixed up with another newly dug grave. However, the only sort of people who conceivably would have been buried alongside Jesus would have been other people who had died at around the same time Jesus did; and the only potential candidates for this would be other crucifixion victims besides Jesus. If other crucifixion victims had been buried next to Jesus, Jesus' grave could still have been distinguished provided someone who had observed the burial remembered which spot Jesus was buried in (and they certainly would have remembered this after only three days had passed; 1 Corinthians 15:4 tells us Jesus was raised on the third day). There could not have been very many crucifixion victims (the Gospels tell us there were two others, but even without the Gospels' testimony, we can assume there were not a massive number of people being executed that day), and thus it would not have been difficult to remember which grave Jesus had been buried in. Further, if all of the witnesses to the burial had somehow forgotten which grave was Jesus' (which seems quite unlikely after three day, but conceivable after forty days), given that there were a number of exceptions to the rule that a corpse was not to be exhumed (which I am about to discuss in the following paragraph), it is likely that the Jewish leaders would exhume all the corpses, if that was what was necessary to identify Jesus' body and stop the spread of Christianity.

Thus it seems that if Jesus was buried in the ground, his burial place would still be identifiable. But we must now consider how the possibility of burial in the ground affects the argument that it was illegal to remove a corpse, for if Jesus was buried in the ground, removal of the corpse would be required, since identifying the body would not just be a matter of looking into the tomb; Jesus would have to be dug up. However, though it was generally illegal to disturb a corpse, there were a number of exceptions

49. See Tosha L. Dupras et al, *Forensic Recovery of Human Remains: Archeological Approaches* (2nd ed.; Boca Raton, FL: CRC Press, 2016), 99.

to this rule. We have already seen that two people were sometimes buried in the same grave, and this practice required that when the second person was buried, the first person's grave was disturbed. And from the fact that secondary burial is a well attested practice, we can deduce that a corpse could also be removed for secondary burial in a tomb.[50] Further, the rabbinic sources indicate that there were debates on various other possible exceptions, such as whether a corpse could be exhumed in a situation where it would affect whether a sale of a house was legal, in a situation where it would potentially help to decide a murder trial, in a situation where life was at stake, and in a situation in which the corpse was about to be consumed by fire.[51] Given the desire of the Jewish leaders to stop the Christian movement, if there was any ambiguity, it is likely the Jewish leaders would err on the side of doing what was necessary to stop the Christian movement, rather than on the side of not desecrating the corpse of someone whom they had thought it right to put to death. Further, concerns about not desecrating the corpse would not have affected the Christians' willingness to dig up the grave, for since they were convinced, based on the resurrection appearances, that Jesus had risen, they would have been sure that his body would not actually be in the grave and thus be sure that digging up the grave would not desecrate Jesus' corpse. And even if the Christians were unsure which grave was Jesus', and so they needed to dig up multiple bodies, in a situation such as this, where it would be ambiguous as to whether it would be justified to exhume the corpses, it is difficult to believe the Christians would be so scrupulous that they would think the possibility of desecrating a corpse outweighed the importance of establishing whether or not Jesus had actually risen from the dead. And remember that since there were hundreds of witnesses to the resurrection appearances (if the appearance to the 500 is historical; if not, there were still well over a dozen), even if most would err on the side of not desecrating a corpse, it would only take one deviant thinker to dig up the bodies.

The Burial by Joseph of Arimathea

We have contended that our argument is not affected even if Jesus was buried in the ground, but now the question will surely become: What about the arguments for the historicity of the story of tomb burial by Joseph of Arimathea? William Lane Craig tells us "the vast majority of New Testament critics concur that Jesus was buried by Joseph of Arimathea in his own tomb."[52] However, it must be admitted that for a number

---

50. On secondary burial, see Craig A. Evans, *Jesus and the Ossuaries* (Waco, TX: Baylor University Press, 2003); Magness, "Ossuaries."

51. For the first three texts, see Avraham Steinberg, *Encyclopedia of Jewish Medical Ethics* (New York: Feldheim, 2003), 78. For the fourth, see Babylonian Talmud, Sabbath, Gemara on Mishnah 7.

52. William Lane Craig, "Opening Address," in Paul Copan ed., *Will the Real Jesus Please Stand Up? A Debate Between William Lane Craig and John Dominic Crossan* (Grand Rapids, MI: Baker, 1998), 25-32 (27).

of reasons the fact that most Jews were buried in the ground significantly weakens the case for tomb burial by Joseph of Arimathea.[53]

First, Paul's statement in 1 Corinthians 15:3 is often cited as confirmation for tomb burial by Joseph of Arimathea, as is the fact that all Jews in Jesus' time were buried. But now that we have seen that "burial" does not necessarily mean burial in a tomb, these facts cannot be taken as evidence for tomb burial, for they are equally compatible with burial in the ground.

Second, the fact that Jews were typically buried in the ground eliminates the reason why many scholars find the burial by Joseph of Arimathea initially probable. Many, perhaps most, of those scholars who think the tomb burial is historical do not think that Joseph of Arimathea buried Jesus because he was a disciple of Jesus'. They think this claim of the Gospels is an embellishment, and that Joseph was actually just a member of the Sanhedrin burying Jesus because the Jews considered it an obligation to provide burial for all.[54] Hence they think the story of the tomb burial fits in with typical Jewish practice, and therefore has a high initial probability. But now that we know most Jews were buried in the ground, and that tombs were only for personal use by the wealthy, the initial probability of Jesus being buried in a tomb by Joseph of Arimathea becomes much lower. For if Joseph of Arimathea was simply a member of the Sanhedrin burying an executed criminal whom he had no personal interest in, he would have buried Jesus in the ground. If he buried Jesus in a tomb, he must indeed have been a friend of Jesus' who was doing something unusual in order to give Jesus a more honorable burial.

(Jodi Magness argues that given the Jewish command to bury a dead person the day of their death, and given that there was not enough time between Jesus' death and the start of the Sabbath to dig a grave, Joseph would have buried Jesus in his personal tomb to ensure the burial took place in time.[55] However, Semahot 16.1 states that burial need not take place the same day if more time is needed to dig a grave. Moreover, a number of rabbinic texts indicate burial could take place on the Sabbath.[56] Even if these texts are untrustworthy, we should remember that Jesus was not the only person to die on a Friday afternoon. With millions of Jews in Israel, practically every week, some Jew would be dying on a Friday afternoon. If death on a Friday afternoon

---

53. For the case for the historicity of tomb burial by Joseph of Arimathea see Craig, *Assessing*, 117-41; Allison, *Resurrecting*, 352-63.

54. E.g., Raymond E. Brown, *The Virginal Conception and Bodily Resurrection of Jesus* (New York: Paulist, 1973), 114-15; James F. McGrath, *The Burial of Jesus: History and Faith* (Charleston, SC: BookSurge, 2008), 78; Allison, *Resurrecting*, 362.

55. Magness, *Stone and Dung*, 170-71. Josephus attests to the Jewish practice of burying executed criminals before sunset in *Jewish Wars*, 4.5.2.

56. See the references in Glenn Miller, "Good Question: Was the Burial of Jesus a Temporary One, Because of Time Constraints?" http://christianthinktank.com/shellgame.html. The references are under the subheading: "2.The restrictions to performing funerary procedures on the Sabbath is generally grossly overstated--many of the standard Sabbath restrictions were relaxed for weddings and funerals."

actually did create a scenario where ground burial was impossible due to lack of time, then tomb burial would have been necessary for many other Jews besides the rich ones (for it was not merely rich Jews who died on a Friday afternoon!). But, as Magness herself has shown, tomb burial was only for the rich. Hence, a non-rich Jew dying close to Friday evening would either be buried in the ground on the Sabbath, or the burial would be put off till after the Sabbath. Chances are, Joseph would be satisfied with the typical practice. Moreover, Magness's hypothesis would require that Jesus was subsequently removed from the tomb and buried in the ground. The reason why Magness's hypothesis would require this is because if random people who died on Fridays were buried in tombs and remained in tombs, then the tombs which have been excavated ought to be overloaded with non-rich individuals. But they are not. Hence Magness's hypothesis becomes a newer version of the classic hypothesis that Joseph of Arimathea moved the body. But the essential problem with this hypothesis has always been that if Joseph moved the body, he ought to have spoken up when the disciples began to proclaim Jesus' resurrection and stopped the spread of Christianity. Further, it seems unlikely that an extremely temporary burial such as the one envisaged by Magness would even count for burial, for all of our literary references that discuss the timing of burial or the possibility of burial on the Sabbath seem to envisage complete burial.[57] If a practice such as the one proposed by Magness was at all common, it should have left some mark upon the literary record.)

Third, the argument that the tomb story is confirmed by the criterion of embarrassment because it would be embarrassing for Joseph of Arimathea, a member of the Sanhedrin, the group that had condemned Jesus to death, to bury Jesus, loses its force once we realize Jews were typically buried in the ground. For though it would indeed be embarrassing for Joseph of Arimathea to bury Jesus, it would not be embarrassing for him to bury Jesus in a tomb. One can imagine that the story was originally of Joseph of Arimathea burying Jesus in the ground, and that this was then changed to a story of tomb burial to make Jesus' burial more honorable.

The criterion of multiple attestation still supports the tomb burial, since the burial is attested by all four Gospels. But we have discussed the limitations of that criterion.

Thus for these reasons, unless we allow the general reliability of the Gospels, I do not think we can affirm that it is historical Joseph of Arimathea buried Jesus in a tomb. Thus I think the only argument for an empty tomb (as opposed to an empty burial place), other than multiple attestation, is the fact that women are said to have discovered the tomb. While I think this argument is sufficient to make it more probable than not that the empty tomb is historical, I do not think it makes the probability of the empty tomb exceedingly high. One may thus prefer to speak of Jesus' empty

---

57. This is a key point made by Glenn Miller (in the source cited in the immediately preceding footnote), who, in responding to Richard Carrier's hypothesis of reburial (which is similar to Magness's hypothesis), addresses many references which might appear at first glance to attest to such a practice.

burial place (which allows for the possibility that he was buried in the ground) rather than his empty tomb.

Buried in a Mass Grave?

Before we conclude, one other possibility needs to be considered: the possibility that Jesus was buried in a mass grave—a grave for multiple people instead of just one person. If Jesus was buried with multiple other corpses, it would make the question of whether he had vacated his burial place more complex, since one would have to search through a collection of various corpses. Mass graves are well attested in the Roman world (called puticoli)—though the word "grave" in this case does not have its normal sense, because the graves were in fact open pits. They were large holes in the ground into which people were thrown, and they were not closed after a person was thrown inside, they were left open so that many more people could eventually be thrown into them. Such graves were used for executed criminals, slaves, and the poor.

However, the evidence indicates that mass graves were a Roman phenomenon; Jews did not bury their dead in this way. There is no archeological evidence for such graves in Israel, and no one has found any literary references to them. It is not surprising that this form of burial was not practiced in Israel given the importance which Jews ascribed to burial, for since the pits were not covered over when a body was placed in it, it is difficult to consider such burials true burial. As Donald Kyle says, "dumping in such pits, open to the elements until covered over when full, would not constitute the provision of even minimal burial."[58] That the Jews would use such a form of "burial" is hardly likely given that one of the curses for breaching Israel's covenant is that bodies will be left in the open air (Deut 28:26). Further, the evidence indicates that puticoli were not even used by the Romans during Jesus' time. The Roman writer Varro, writing in the first century BCE, refers to this form of burial as something which only took place in the past.[59] Thus mass burial does not appear to have been in use anywhere at the time of Jesus' death.

However, Jodi Magness has cited two passages in the Mishnah which Magness interprets to mean that throwing dead bodies into pits was common in Israel.[60] Thus we should examine these passages.

> He who plows in a pit filled with bones, in a pile of bones, in a field in which a grave was lost, or in which a grave was [afterwards] found. . . he does not make a grave area.[61]

---

58. Donald G. Kyle, *Spectacles of Death in Ancient Rome* (London: Routledge, 2001), 165.
59. Varro, Lat. Lang, 5.25
60. Magness, *Stone and Dung*, 163-64.
61. Mishnah, Ohalot, 17:2.

The "pit filled with bones" is what could conceivable be a puticoli type structure, but on this interpretation, the passage would not make sense. For if the scenario here is that of a pit in which bodies lay in the open air, how could someone plow in the pit? One could not plow over bodies. In order to understand what the passage actually does have in mind, let us consider its context.

The larger passage in which this passage is found, we are told by Simcha Fishbane,[62] concerns situations in which a grave area is not created though it might appear that one is created. The general concern of the larger passage is with someone accidentally plowing over a grave (an isolated grave in a field, rather than a graveyard); the concern is that such an action will accidentally cause pieces of the corpse to get caught by the plow and then, because the plow keeps moving, the pieces of the corpse will be spread. Since corpses caused ritual impurity, it was important to avoid any pieces of a corpse that might have been spread by the plow. Thus the rabbis created the concept of a "grave area," which was the farthest distance which they estimated pieces of the corpse could reasonably be thought to have spread. They decided that a "grave area" would be the twenty feet past the grave. But as for our specific passage, it is concerned with situations in which a grave area is *not* created, but where one could mistakenly think that a grave area has been created.

In light of Simcha Fishbane's observation that Mishnah 7:1-2 says that a grave area can only be created if someone intentionally plows a grave,[63] we can deduce that the reason the scenarios in this passage do not create a grave area is because in these scenarios the grave was unintentionally plowed. Let us consider each scenario. "In a field in which a grave was lost" likely refers to a situation in which someone plows in a field in which someone has been buried, but the gravestone for their grave is no longer visible. A person plowing over the grave would thus be acting unintentionally. "In which a grave was [afterwards] found" likely refers to a situation in which a grave in the field is noticed after the person had plowed, thus making it conceivable he could have contacted the corpse without realizing it. Again, any contact with it was clearly unintentional. "In a pile of bones" likely refers to a situation in which the person plowing accidentally dislodges pieces of a corpse which have been buried shallowly. This brings us, finally, to the meaning of "a pit filled with bones." As we said, since the pit is being plowed, it cannot refer to a puticoli type structure, for if the bodies were above the earth, one could not plow the area. Hence the bodies must be buried under the ground of the pit. Why would bodies be buried under the ground of a pit? The most likely hypothesis would be that since burials were typically in a burial field, if there was a pit within such a field, there is no reason why the pit should not be used for burial in the same way as the rest of the field. Hence someone plowing the field would plow in the pit and might accidentally dislodge pieces of the corpses.

---

62. Simcha Fishbane, *Deviancy in Early Rabbinic Literature: A Collection of Socio-Anthropological Essays* (Leiden: Brill, 2007), 132.

63. Fishbane, *Deviancy*, 132.

> A cistern into which they throw abortions or slain people—one gathers bone by bone and all is clean.[64]

This passage does appear to describe burials in which the bodies are left exposed to the open air, for the bodies are thrown into a well, but the situations are very atypical (a mother trying to dispose of her aborted fetus as quickly as possible, and the burial of a group slain in battle)[65] and could not conceivably apply to Jesus' burial.

Magness also cites rabbinic sources which mention dogs carrying parts of corpses and she argues that this indicates the situation in Palestine was similar to Rome, where dogs gnawed on corpses lying in the open air in the streets.[66] However, from the fact that dogs sometimes found corpses, it does not follow that the corpses were left in the open air. We already saw from one of the passages examined above that corpses could be dug up by a plow, and from this it is evident that corpses were not buried very deep in the ground. If the corpses were buried shallow enough that a plow could dig them up, they were also shallow enough for a dog to do this.

Magness also claims that potters' fields included pits for mass burial.[67] But there is no evidence for this, and thus we ought to presume that those buried in potters' fields were buried in individual graves just as in any other burial field.

The Rest

Outside of the empty tomb (or empty burial place), I do not think we can extract any historical information from the resurrection narratives unless we first demonstrate that they are generally reliable. But arguments have been presented for the historicity of many of the appearances, and so these arguments need to be considered.

The Emmaus Appearance (Lk 24:13-35). The obscurity of Cleopas and Emmaus may be cited as evidence of historicity on the grounds that they are nowhere else attested in the Gospels, and so why should legend invent a story about a person or place which was not otherwise significant?[68] However, legends do sometimes invent otherwise unattested things. The Infancy Gospel of Thomas tells us Jesus had a schoolteacher named Zacchaeus (20:21), and though Edessa played no role in the Gospel

---

64. Mishnah, Ohalot, 16:5.

65. See Hachlili, *Funerary Customs*, 26, 477, for examples of those slain in battle being buried above ground.

66. Magness, *Stone and Dung*, 164.

67. Magness, *Stone and Dung*, 163.

68. Allison, *Resurrecting*, 253-54. In citing arguments given by scholars in support of the historicity of individual appearances, I should say that it is not always the case that the scholar has thought the argument definitely renders the appearance historical. In the case of some of the arguments cited here, the scholar has only noted that the argument supports the historicity of the appearance (i.e., increases the probability of the appearance's historicity at least somewhat), without saying that it supports it so much that we can conclude the appearance actually happened.

stories, later tradition invented letters between Jesus and the king of Edessa (*The Epistles of Jesus Christ and Abgarus, King of Edessa*).

The Appearance to Thomas (Jn 20:24-28). It has been argued that the appearance to Thomas is confirmed by the criterion of embarrassment.[69] The argument is that for an apostle to be obstinate to the extent that Thomas was would surely be embarrassing to the early church. However, the Gospels are filled with stories of the disciples being foolish or stupid, and though we can be assured by the criterion of embarrassment that at least some of these stories are historical, we cannot know which ones these are, because once some stories of this nature entered the tradition, and thus it became known that the disciples did embarrassing things, it does not further the embarrassment very much to invent more stories of the disciples doing embarrassing things. Hence any given story of the disciples doing something embarrassing in the Gospels could be a legend which arose after it was known that the disciples had done embarrassing things.

The Appearance to the Twelve in Jerusalem (Lk 24:36-43; Jn 20:19-23). It is argued that the agreement on certain details of this appearance between Luke and John indicates that the appearance is based on earlier tradition (e.g., in both accounts Jesus presents his wounds, and in both he says "Peace be with you").[70] However, though the agreement shows the tradition is earlier than the Gospel writers, we do not know how much earlier it is, and therefore we do not know how close it is to the eyewitnesses.

The Appearance to the Twelve in Galilee (Mt 28:16-20). It could be argued that the doubting of the disciples is embarrassing and thus historical.[71] But in addition to the point made above concerning embarrassment, it is not clear what the nature of the doubting was (we will address this passage in chapter 7), and thus it is not clear whether the doubting is even embarrassing.

The Guards at the Tomb (Mt 27:62-66; 28:11-15). The chief argument in favor of the historicity of the guards is the argument that the Jewish-Christian polemic which lies behind the story indicates that the Jews accepted the story of the guard as fact.[72] To the Christian claim that the disciples could not have stolen the body because the tomb was guarded, the Jewish response is that the guards fell asleep. If the guards were not historical, we would expect the Jews' response would not be that the guards fell asleep, but rather that there were no guards. However, we do not know when this polemic originated. It may date as late as the 90s or so, by which time the Jews could not disprove the assertion that there was a guard, and the argument that the guards fell asleep may have simply been a for the sake of argument argument: That is, the Jews

---

69. Craig L. Blomberg, *The Historical Reliability of John's Gospel: Issues and Commentary* (Downers Grove: InterVarsity, 2002), 269-70.
70. Craig, *Assessing*, 194.
71. Craig, *Assessing*, 199.
72. Craig, *Assessing*, 150-61.

may have been saying that, granting for the sake of argument that the guards were there, the guards may have fallen asleep.

The Account of the Empty Tomb (Mk 16:1-8; Mt 28:1-10; Lk 24:1-12; Jn 20:1-10). The question here is whether any of the details of the empty tomb narrative, other than the fact of the empty tomb itself, can be shown to be historical. One argument for the historicity of the story as a whole is that the empty tomb story is part of a pre-Markan passion narrative and thus predates Mark.[73] However, quite apart from the question of whether there was a written pre-Markan passion narrative, it is not clear how much earlier than Mark such a passion narrative would be. Simply because it is earlier, that does not mean it is early enough for us to be confident it is close to the eyewitnesses. A second argument is that the account is simple and unadorned, which is what we would expect from accurate tradition.[74] However, Mark's whole Gospel is simple and unadorned; he usually has fewer details than Matthew or Luke. So this may just be a characteristic of Mark's Gospel rather than of early tradition.

The Ascension (Lk 24:50-53; Acts 1:9-11). One could argue that the ascension is supported by the criterion of multiple attestation because it is referred to in Ephesians 4:8-10, 1 Timothy 3:16, and 1 Peter 3:22, as well as in Acts and Luke.[75] However, though these other three passages refer to Jesus' ascension, they refer only to the fact that he ascended; they do not tell us the ascension occurred as part of a resurrection appearance. That is, if we have only these texts to go by, there is no way to know whether there were any witnesses to the ascension; in fact, there is no way to know whether Jesus even literally ascended, that is, went up towards the sky. Since the texts only suggest he was in the sky, he could have dematerialized his way up to the sky instead of ascending. Hence, we cannot be sure these texts attest to the ascension in the sense in which that event has normally been understood.

The Appearance to Mary Magdalene (Jn 20:11-18). The following arguments have been given on behalf of the historicity of the appearance to Mary Magdalene:

The first argument is the fact that in all of the Gospels, Mary is named first in the list of the women who go to the tomb. Something must explain her prominence, and if she was really the first to see the risen Jesus, this fact would explain it.[76]

However, this argument can be turned around: If Mary was already prominent for some other reason (for example, because she was Jesus' favorite female disciple, or because she provided Jesus with the most financial support),[77] this would explain why

---

73. Craig, *Assessing*, 262-64.

74. Craig, *Assessing*, 264-65.

75. That these passages probably refer to the ascension is noted by Hans Kung, *Eternal Life? Life After Death as a Medical, Philosophical, and Theological Problem* (Garden City, NY: Doubleday, 1984), 126-27.

76. Allison, *Resurrecting*, 249.

77. Luke 8:3 tells us Mary Magdalene was one of the women who provided Jesus with financial support.

she appears first in the lists, and it also gives us a good reason as to why legend would invent an appearance for her.

A second argument is that the presence of Aramaic words (*Miriam*; *rabbouni*) (Jn 20:16) indicates historicity because the earliest traditions of Jesus would have been passed on in Aramaic.[78] But just because the earliest traditions of Jesus would have been passed on in Aramaic, that does not mean every Aramaic saying is early. Legends could have arisen among Aramaic speaking Christians just as they could have arisen among Greek speaking ones.

A third argument is that the appearance is multiply attested (Jn 20:11-18; Mt 28:8-10).[79] However, if the harmonization concerning Matthew and John's account of the appearance to Mary Magdalene which I will propose in chapter 6 is correct, Mary Magdalene was actually not with Mary and the other women at the time Jesus appeared to them in Matthew 28:8-10. He appeared to Mary Magdalene at the tomb, whereas he appeared to the other women on the way back from the tomb. Thus these are two different appearances, and each is only singly attested.

A fourth argument is that the apocryphal Gospels, though they invent appearances for those who were already known to have had appearances (such as Peter and James), do not invent appearances for people who had never had any appearance in the first place.[80] If this principle extends back to the time of the Gospels, then there must have been an appearance to Mary Magdalene.

But this argument is factually incorrect, for in some cases the apocryphal Gospels do invent appearances for those not previously known to have had them. The Gospel of Peter 38 tells us of an appearance to the soldiers and the Jewish religious leaders, and the Gospel of the Hebrews mentions an appearance to the servant of the priest.[81]

No arguments of any substance can be given for the historicity of the appearance to the disciples by the Sea of Galilee (Jn 21:1-11), or the appearance to Peter (Lk 24:34) (other than the fact that the appearance to Peter happened, but we already know this from 1 Cor 15:5).

Material from Outside the Resurrection Narratives

In addition to the resurrection narratives themselves, we also need to consider the arguments for the historicity of three other things in the Gospels and Acts relevant to

---

78. J.D.M. Derrett, "Miriam and the Resurrection (John 20,16)," *Downside Review* 111 (1993): 174-86.

79. Allison, *Resurrecting*, 249; Craig, *Assessing*, 181.

80. Allison, *Resurrecting*, 252.

81. The passage in question from the Gospel of the Hebrews is the passage quoted by Jerome, *On Illustrious Men*, 2 (the entire Gospel of the Hebrews is not extant; we have only quotations of it from other sources).

Jesus' resurrection: the Acts sermons, the appearance to Paul, and Jesus' predictions of his resurrection.

The Acts Sermons. It is often argued that the sermons of Peter and Paul which are recorded in Acts, in which the resurrection appearances are sometimes referred to, preserve early tradition (Acts 2:14-36; 3:11-26; 10:34-43; 13:16-41). The chief arguments for this are that the speeches reflect an Aramaic origin, and that they evince a low Christology (Jesus' divinity is not referred to, but only the fact that he is the Messiah).[82] But we have already seen the problems with arguing that a source is historical simply because it contains traces of Aramaic. As for the low Christology, this is not an indication of an early date, because a very high Christology is already found in Paul's epistles (see especially Phil 2:6-11; Col 1:15-20), which are the earliest documents of the New Testament.[83] In fact, it is not possible to establish that any New Testament document has a low Christology—for simply because a document does not indicate a belief in Jesus' divinity, this does not mean the author did not believe it; an author does not necessarily tell us everything he believes. And all of the things that would potentially evince a low Christology are still compatible with a high Christology. For a "low" Christology means a Christology focused on Jesus as the Messiah rather than Jesus as divine, but it is not as if the early Christians thought Jesus being the Messiah was incompatible with him being divine. Thus any Christological statements expressing the idea that Jesus is the Messiah are also compatible with the idea that he is divine.

The Appearance to Paul. We know of course from 1 Corinthians that the appearance to Paul is historical, but the question here is whether we can accept the Acts account of his appearance as historical. The chief arguments for its historicity are: 1) Paul often agrees with Acts on a number of matters.[84] 2) There are differences between the three versions of the Acts account and these differences indicate Luke had different sources, and thus the event depends on earlier tradition.[85] In response to 1), simply because Paul agrees with Acts on some things, that does not mean he agrees with it on everything. In response to 2), unless the variance among the accounts reaches the level of contradiction, the variance does not indicate Luke had sources, but only that Luke was capable of telling the story in more than one way, and I do not think any of

---

82. On the Acts sermons as early material, see Craig, *Assessing*, 28-29 (with many further references); Licona, *Resurrection*, 216-20.

83. On the fact that many of the New Testament documents display a higher Christology than appears to be the case at face value, see Larry W. Hurtado, *Lord Jesus Christ: Devotion to Jesus in Earliest Christianity* (Grand Rapids, MI: Eerdmans, 2003); Larry W. Hurtado, *How on Earth Did Jesus Become a God? Historical Questions About Earliest Devotion to Jesus* (Grand Rapids, MI: Eerdmans, 2005).

84. Allison, *Resurrecting*, 264. Some may in fact wish to appeal to the alleged contradictions between Paul and Acts. But for a response to that, see F.F. Bruce, "Is The Paul of Acts the Real Paul?" *Bulletin of the John Rylands Society* 58 (1975-76): 282-305; Stanley E. Porter, *Paul in Acts* (Peabody, MA: Hendrickson, 2001). Porter's whole book is useful for this question, but see especially 187-205.

85. E.g., C.K. Barrett, *A Critical and Exegetical Commentary on the Acts of the Apostles* (vol.1; Edinburgh: T&T Clark, 1994), 445.

1 Corinthians 15 and the Gospels

the differences constitute contradictions.[86] Further, even if Luke is reliant on earlier sources, that does not mean these earlier sources were reliable, for just because they were earlier than Luke, that does not mean they are close to the eyewitnesses.

Jesus' Predictions of His Resurrection. In a number of passages in the Gospels, Jesus predicts that he will rise from the dead (Mk 8:31-33; Mk 9:30-32; Mk 10:32-34; and parallels). Michael Licona has presented the most thorough case for the historicity of these predictions, so we will consider his six arguments.[87]

The first argument is that the predictions are based on early tradition: Paul attests to Jesus' predictions in 1 Corinthians 11:23-25, and the predictions contain Aramaisms. But we have already explained why Aramaisms do not necessarily indicate early tradition, and as for Paul's statement, he does not tell us Jesus predicted his resurrection, but only that he predicted his death. The second argument is that the predictions are multiply attested. But we have already seen the problem with this criterion. The third argument is that the predictions fulfill the criterion of embarrassment, because the disciples do not believe Jesus' words and because Peter rebukes him. But as we said, once it was established historically that the disciples did some embarrassing things, it does not further the embarrassment very much to invent more embarrassing things. The fourth argument is that the predictions lack signs of theologizing by the church. But this fact only takes away a possible argument against the historicity of the predictions; it is not an argument for them. The fifth argument is that Jesus refers to himself as "the Son of Man" in these predictions, and the fact that Jesus actually did refer to himself as the Son of Man has been established by various criteria, such as dissimilarity and multiple attestation. However, simply because Jesus' use of the phrase "the Son of Man" is historical, that does not mean every saying in the Gospels in which such a phrase appears is historical. Once it was known that Jesus referred to himself in this way, legends could arise involving this saying. Sixth, the predictions are plausible because they fit in with the Jewish context: Jewish prophets often suffered martyrdom, and so had John the Baptist, thus it makes sense Jesus would hold such an idea. But the early church was just as fond of Jewish prophets and John the Baptist as Jesus was, and so if it would make sense for Jesus to come up with this idea, it would also make sense for the early church to come up with it.

Finally, the point needs to be made that even if Jesus predicted a post-mortem vindication, this does not necessarily mean he predicted his resurrection. Jesus may have made some sort of generic prediction of post-mortem vindication. That is, he may have simply stated that after his death he would be vindicated, but without specifying the details of how he would be vindicated, and after the disciples came to believe he was raised from the dead, these predictions may have been described as being more

---

86. The difference which would seem to come closest to a contradiction concerns whether or not Paul's companions heard the voice of Jesus. On this, see Gleason L. Archer, *New International Encyclopedia of Bible Difficulties* (Grand Rapid, MI: Zondervan, 1982), 382.

87. Licona, *Resurrection*, 284-302.

specific than they actually were. They may have been described as being predictions specifically of resurrection rather than of a generic vindication. Consider the way in which Jesus' prediction of his death is recorded in Luke 9:44, "the Son of Man is going to be delivered into the hands of men." This is much more general than what we find in other passages, which give the impression Jesus predicted his death in less obscure terms (e.g., Mk 8:31, "And He began to teach them that the Son of Man must suffer many things and be rejected by the elders and the chief priests and the scribes, and be killed, and after three days rise again"). Likewise, Jesus' predictions of his resurrection may actually have been generic predictions of a post-mortem vindication of some unspecified type, and these predictions may have been interpreted as being predictions of his resurrection after he rose. Now if Jesus really did rise, the church was correct to interpret the generic predictions in this way. But if Jesus did not rise, then it is not clear whether the church read in a more specific meaning than Jesus had intended. Thus we cannot use these predictions to establish the historicity of the resurrection, since if they were generic predictions of a post-mortem vindication, we cannot know they were predictions of resurrection unless we first know Jesus did rise from the dead (thus if we use the predictions to establish that he rose from the dead, we will be arguing in a circle).

Conclusion

Our investigation has found that the appearances of 1 Corinthians 15:3-8 can be accepted as historical, but we have also found that the only claim of the Gospels which can be accepted as historical (if the general reliability of the Gospels is not accepted) is that the tomb was discovered empty (and to nuance this further, I think it only somewhat probable, but certainly more probable than not, that Jesus' *tomb* was discovered empty, but highly probable that his *burial place* was discovered empty).

5

The Reliability of the Resurrection Narratives

THE ARGUMENT WHICH I am going to present for the historical reliability of the resurrection narratives in this chapter is based upon the significance with which the early church regarded the resurrection appearances.[1] My argument is that the early church regarded the resurrection appearances as very significant, and that since they regarded them as very significant it is likely that stories of the resurrection appearances were passed down accurately from the time they were first told until the time the Gospels were written. I assume for the sake of argument in this chapter that the Gospels were written during the period 70-100 CE and that we do not know who the authors were. I concede this for the sake of argument, even though I doubt it myself (for I think the Gospels are generally reliable),[2] because it has been the majority opinion among Biblical scholars since at least 1850 or so,[3] and I wish to present an argument which is based on premises accepted by the large majority of scholars, in order to show that the resurrection narratives can be accepted as reliable even by those who only accept such premises. If the Gospels were written by eyewitnesses, or near eyewitnesses (in the case of Mark and Luke), or were written prior to 70, then we do not need to appeal to the present argument, since the general reliability of the Gospels, and hence the general reliability of the resurrection narratives, would be assured by the fact that the Gospel writers were eyewitnesses or almost so, or by the fact that they were written at a time when most of the eyewitnesses were still alive, and when some of those eyewitnesses, such as James, Peter, and John, were guarding the church's teachings

---

1. This chapter is a significantly revised version of the following article: Jake H. O'Connell, "The Reliability of the Resurrection Narratives," *European Journal of Theology* 19 (2010): 141-52.

2. I think a strong case can be made for the traditional authorship of Luke and John, though I am less sure about Matthew and Mark. On the authorship of Luke, see Colin J. Hemer, *The Book of Acts in the Setting of Hellenistic History* (Winona Lake: Eisenbrauns, 1990), 308-64. On the authorship of John, see Richard Bauckham, *Jesus and the Eyewitnesses: The Gospels as Eyewitness Testimony* (Grand Rapids, MI: Eerdmans, 2006), 384-411.

3. But perhaps the Gospel of Luke is an exception. Craig Keener, after doing a thorough survey of the relevant literature as part of the research for his five thousand page commentary on Acts, comes to the conclusion that a majority of modern scholars accept the traditional authorship of Luke and Acts (Personal conversation between Craig Keener and Michael R. Licona, cited in Michael R. Licona, "Review of Bart Ehrman's Book Forged: Writing in the Name of God," http://www.risenjesus.com/articles/52-review-of-forged).

and preventing them from corruption.[4] It is debatable whether legendary corruption could even have infiltrated the tradition by the period 70-100 CE (some have argued it is not possible for legendary corruption to set in within such a short time),[5] but I am going to concede the majority position that legends could have arisen in this amount of time. But the majority position also holds that there is a good amount of historically reliable material in the Gospels, and this fact will serve as the basis for my argument.

The Argument

As I explained in chapter 1, it seems to be widely accepted among scholars that the Gospels are at least fairly reliable sources. As I explained, by "fairly reliable," I mean that even though the Gospels are not as reliable as a good eyewitness—not reliable enough for us to trust whatever they say until there is evidence to the contrary (if they were that reliable, they would be "generally reliable")—it is still the case that the Gospels contain quite a lot of accurate information. In contrast to the apocryphal Gospels, such as the Infancy Gospel of Thomas, or the Protoevangelium of James, the canonical Gospels are not so overridden with legend that they constitute merely a collection of fables. Craig Evans, a prominent historical Jesus scholar, tells us that there is a "remarkable amount of consensus in recent scholarship" that the Gospels yield "significant historical data."[6] Likewise, Evans states that "the Gospels are now viewed as useful, if not essentially reliable, historical sources."[7] (I believe by "essentially reliable" Evans means what I have called fairly reliable, rather than generally reliable, since it is not the consensus view of scholars that the Gospels are generally reliable.)

I propose that during the period in between Jesus' ministry and the writing of the Gospels (ca. 30-70 CE), the stories of the resurrection appearances were regarded as at least equally significant as, if not more significant than, any other Jesus tradition ("Jesus traditions" being stories about or sayings of Jesus). This fact helps to form an argument for the reliability of the resurrection narratives when it is combined with the fact that the Gospels are fairly reliable. For if the Gospels are fairly reliable, this means

---

4. On the fact that the early church was concerned with preserving their traditions from corruption, see Birger Gerhardsson, *The Reliability of the Gospel Tradition* (Peabody, MA: Hendrickson, 2001); James D.G. Dunn, *Jesus Remembered* (Grand Rapids, MI: Eerdmans, 2003), 173-254.

5. For the argument that 40-70 years is too short of a time for legendary corruption to have set in, see William Lane Craig, *Assessing the New Testament Evidence for the Historicity of the Resurrection of Jesus* (rev. ed.; Lewiston: Edwin Mellen, 2002 [1989]), 276-80; Norman L. Geisler and Patrick Zukeran, *The Apologetics of Jesus: A Caring Approach to Dealing with Doubters* (Grand Rapids, MI: Baker, 2009,), 37-38. For the contrary argument see Robert M. Price, "Is There a Place for Historical Criticism?" *Religious Studies* 27 (1999): 371-88; Richard C. Carrier, "The Spiritual Body of Christ and the Legend of the Empty Tomb," in Robert M. Price and Jeffrey Jay Lowder, eds., *The Empty Tomb: Jesus Beyond the Grave* (Amherst, NY: Prometheus, 2005), 105-231 (168-77).

6. Craig A. Evans, "Life-Of-Jesus Research and the Eclipse of Mythology," *Theological Studies* 54 (1993): 3-37 (34).

7. Evans, "Life-Of-Jesus Research," 14.

that many traditions about Jesus were reliably transmitted up to the time of the writing of the Gospels. Now, if the early church regarded the stories of Jesus' resurrection as among its most important Jesus traditions, and the early church was able to accurately preserve many Jesus traditions (which it did, if the Gospels are fairly reliable), then it is likely that the resurrection traditions were accurately preserved. This is because it would make little sense for the church to transmit its most significant traditions less accurately than it transmitted its less significant traditions. My argument may be outlined in syllogistic form as follows:

1. The Gospels are fairly reliable.
2. Therefore, the early church was able to accurately transmit many Jesus traditions.
3. The early church would likely transmit the Jesus traditions it valued the most at least as accurately as the ones it valued less.
4. The early church valued traditions of the resurrection appearances the most.
5. Therefore, the traditions of the resurrection appearances were transmitted accurately.

Therefore the resurrection narratives of the Gospels are accurate.

For this argument to be successful, we of course need reasons for thinking the resurrection narratives were regarded as very significant. In what follows, I will present three such reasons.

(Also, in addition to the primary argument of this chapter, I will add in an appendix one other argument, and that argument is that there are two overlooked passages in Irenaeus which constitute evidence for the reliability of the resurrection narratives. Although this argument is not related to my main argument, it is prudent to add it, since it has not been made in the literature before, and it can be presented quickly.)

Reasons to Think the Early Church Considered the Resurrection Appearances Significant

The Resurrection as the Climax of a Narrative History

Ancient Jews understood their history as a narrative history, that is, they did not just enumerate facts about their nation's history; they related their nation's history in story form.[8] The Old Testament gives us stories of all of the major events in ancient Israel from earliest times onward, stories of how God created human beings, destroyed the world with a flood, freed the Hebrews from Egypt by performing miracles, punished Israel by allowing the Babylonians to destroy them, and so on.

---

8. This point is brought out in considerable detail by R. Rendtorff, "The Concept of Revelation in Ancient Israel," in Wolfhart Pannenberg ed., *Revelation as History* (New York: Macmillan, 1968), 25-53.

Jesus' Resurrection and Apparitions

The early Christians clearly regarded Jesus' life as the climax of Israel's history. This is clear from passages such as Mark 1:15 ("The time is fulfilled, and the kingdom of God is at hand"), Acts 3:24 ("all the prophets who have spoken, from Samuel and his successors onward, also announced these days"), and Hebrews 1:1-2 ("God, after He spoke long ago to the fathers in the prophets in many portions and in many ways, in these last days has spoken to us in His Son"). Since Jesus' life was the climax of Israel's history, and Israel's history was told in the form of narratives, we should expect that not just during the period when the Gospels were written, but from the very beginning of Christianity, narratives of Jesus' life were told, and were considered significant, just as the Old Testament narratives were considered significant.

Now in regard to the resurrection, we know that the early church held Jesus' resurrection to be of central importance. This is clear from passages such as Romans 4:25, which tells us Jesus' resurrection makes possible our justification, Romans 10:9, which tells us Jesus' resurrection serves as the grounds for our salvation, and most significantly, 1 Corinthians 15:12-19, which tells us that "if Christ has not been raised, then our preaching is vain, your faith also is vain" (1 Cor 15:14) and "if Christ has not been raised, your faith is worthless; you are still in your sins." Contemporary scholarship does not dispute this clear fact. Reginald Fuller states: "The resurrection of Jesus from the dead was the central claim of the church's proclamation. There was no period when this was not so."[9] Likewise Karl Barth tells us:

> It is impossible to read any text of the New Testament in the sense intended by its authors, by the apostles who stand behind them, or by the first communities, without an awareness that they either explicitly assert or at least tacitly assume that the Jesus of whom they speak and to whom they refer in some way is the One who appeared to his disciples at this particular time as the Resurrected from the dead. All the other things they know of him, his words and acts, are regarded in the light of this particular event, and are as it were irradiated by its light.[10]

Now let us put these two facts together. We know that ancient Israel looked at its history as a narrative history, and we know that the early Christians saw Jesus' life as the climax of Israel's history. Thus the early Christians would very likely tell stories about Jesus' life. Now which of these stories would they regard as the most significant? Certainly the stories of the most significant events of Jesus' life. Since we know that they considered Jesus' resurrection to be the most important event of his life, stories of the resurrection appearances would thus have been considered very significant.

---

9. Reginald H. Fuller, *The Formation of the Resurrection Narratives* (New York: MacMillan, 1971), 48.

10. Karl Barth, *Church Dogmatics* (vol. 2; New York: T&T Clark, 1957), 442.

The Necessity of Apologetics

When the Christian movement first arose, Christianity would have had a serious need for apologetics (apologetics not in the sense of a systematic academic discipline, but in the sense of a defense of a position). Consequently, any key apologetic argument for Christianity would have been considered significant by the Christians, and the evidence is clear that the resurrection appearances served as one of their key apologetic arguments.

There are at least two reasons why apologetics would have been important to the early Christians. First, we know that Jewish Christians were persecuted by the Jewish leaders during the first century. For example, Peter and John are imprisoned (Acts 5:18), Paul persecutes the Christians (Acts 9:1-3; Gal 1:1-13), James the brother of John was killed by Herod (Acts 12:2), and Josephus tells us James the brother of Jesus was killed during the early 60s.[11] The Gospels also attest to persecutions (e.g., Mt 5:11-12; Mt 10:17-18), and Paul attests that he was later persecuted by Jews himself (2 Cor 11:25). Since Jewish Christians were being persecuted, it was clearly difficult to be a Christian, and thus in order for Christians to attract new followers and keep members from departing, they would need to focus on the reasons why someone ought to be a Christian.

As for the Gentile Christians, they were not persecuted till the end of the period with which we are concerned (the Neronian persecution took place in about 64 CE), but there would have been another reason why Gentile Christians would need to be prepared to give a defense of Christianity: the fact that Jesus was crucified. Paul speaks of the "foolishness" of the message of the cross in 1 Corinthians 1:23. This remark occurs in the context of Paul's discussion of Jewish and Gentile rejection of Christianity: Jesus' crucifixion is a "stumbling-block" to Jews and "foolishness" to Gentiles. Because of the Christian heritage of contemporary society, the proclamation that the savior of the world was crucified does not strike most modern ears as particularly strange. But this was not so in the ancient world, where crucifixion was regarded as a gruesome, shameful punishment to be inflicted on the worst members of society. The ancient sources on crucifixion have been thoroughly examined by Martin Hengel, whose observations include the following.[12]

Hebrews 12:2 speaks of Jesus suffering the shame of the cross, and this is echoed by Celsus who writes that Jesus was "bound in the most ignominious fashion" and "executed in a shameful way" (Hengel, p. 7). In response to Maecenas' comparison of the sufferings of old age with the slow death of crucifixion, Seneca responds that such a life is not worth living and that one should commit suicide before suffering a death that can be compared to being fastened to "the accursed tree" (p. 30-31). Isidore of

---

11. Josephus, *Antiquities of the Jews*, 20.9.1.

12. Martin Hengel, *Crucifixion in the Ancient World and the Folly of the Message of the Cross* (Philadelphia: Fortress, 1977).

Seville calls hanging better than the cross (p. 29). Crucifixion was a punishment given to those who had committed awful crimes such as treason, murder, and sorcery (p. 34), and it was especially applied to slaves (pp. 51-63). Juvenal thought it an abomination that an actor from the upper class had portrayed a crucified victim in a play, and thereby lowered himself to the level of the lower classes (p. 35). The Gospels provide the most thorough descriptions of crucifixion in ancient literature, as Greco-Roman writers avoided the subject (p. 25). "Crux" was used as a vulgar insult (p. 9). Hengel writes that "the Roman world was largely unanimous that crucifixion was a horrific, disgusting business" (p. 37). In Greek romances, heroes who were bound up to be crucified were always rescued from the cross before actually dying (p. 81).

Since Jesus' death by crucifixion was considered such a shameful, degrading affair, it is likely that potential converts would have been quite reluctant to adopt the new faith, and Paul tells us as much in 1 Corinthians 1:18-31. The notion that someone who was sinless (2 Cor 5:21) and divine (Philippians 2:6-11) had suffered this sort of punishment would draw great suspicion. People would be reluctant to embrace Christianity, and thus Gentile Christians would also need to engage in apologetics.

It may be objected that there are other examples of a religion being adopted even though the god had suffered some extreme humiliation, and even though the religion's apologetic arguments, if Christianity is true, must not have been correct. The Sumerian goddess Inanna was killed by being stripped naked and impaled on a pole, and Attis, a Greek god, was castrated. But I am not arguing that Christianity would have needed good arguments to convert people; whether Christianity's arguments were good or bad, it will be possible to find some followers for anything. My argument at this point is only that anyone who did become Christian would need to be prepared to present their arguments for Christianity, and so these arguments would be considered significant. I expect that the followers of Inanna and Attis also faced criticism and that their apologetic arguments were also significant to them.

Hence Christians would face opposition from society and would have to give a defense of why they were Christian. Thus any important argument in favor of Christianity would be considered significant by the Christians. It is clear from three of the resurrection narratives, as well as from 1 Corinthians 15, that the resurrection appearances were used as an apologetic argument. In 1 Corinthians 15:6, Paul comments "most of whom [the 500] remain until now, but some have fallen asleep." As C.H. Dodd says, "There can hardly be any purpose in mentioning the fact that most of the 500 are still alive, unless Paul is saying, in effect, 'The witnesses are there to be questioned.'"[13] In Matthew's Gospel, we are told that there was a guard at the tomb and that the Jews and Christians debated how the tomb became empty (Mt 28:11-15). Matthew tells us that the Jews argued the guards had fallen asleep, and that the Christians argued that the guards were bribed to say that. In Luke, an appearance is related in which Jesus goes out of his way to prove he is not a ghost: the disciples

---

13. C.H. Dodd, *More New Testament Studies* (Grand Rapids, MI: Eerdmans, 1968), 128.

mistake Jesus for a ghost, but he tells them he is not, and that he has flesh and bones; and he then eats fish. There must have been some concern among critics that Jesus was only a ghost rather than physically resurrected (Lk 24:36-43). In John, we have the appearance to Thomas, which occurs after Thomas refuses to believe the testimony of the other disciples and insists on seeing Jesus for himself (Jn 20:24-19). John must have included this story because critics of Christianity said they would not become Christian without seeing Jesus for themselves.[14]

Thus the resurrection appearances were clearly used as an apologetic argument, and hence the only question is whether they were considered one of Christianity's *significant* apologetic arguments (for chances are that, as is the case of any position, they had many apologetic arguments, but some were considered more significant than others). The reason why we should think their arguments based on the resurrection were among their most significant apologetic arguments is that, as we have seen, the resurrection was the central event of Christianity. If the event was so central, one would expect that the apologetic arguments for that event would also be considered central.

Paul

For the third argument that the resurrection appearances were considered significant, we must return to 1 Corinthians 15.

> Now I make known to you, brethren, the gospel which I preached to you, which also you received, in which also you stand, by which also you are saved, if you hold fast the word which I preached to you, unless you believed in vain. For I delivered to you as of first importance what I also received, that Christ died for our sins according to the Scriptures, and that He was buried, and that He was raised on the third day according to the Scriptures, and that He appeared to Cephas, then to the twelve. After that He appeared to more than five hundred brethren at one time, most of whom remain until now, but some have fallen asleep; then He appeared to James, then to all the apostles; and last of all, as to one untimely born, He appeared to me also. For I am the least of the apostles, and not fit to be called an apostle, because I persecuted the church of God. But by the grace of God I am what I am, and His grace toward me did not prove vain; but I labored even more than all of them, yet not I, but the grace of God with me. Whether then it was I or they, so we preach and so you believed. (1 Cor 15:1-11)

---

14. Incidentally, Jesus' saying, "blessed are those who have not seen and have believed" does not endorse blind faith, but only faith based on adequate evidence, for Thomas was not asked to believe on the basis of no evidence, but on the evidence of the testimony of the other disciples, which is the same evidence we are asked to believe on today, if the New Testimony is reliable and therefore gives us the disciples' testimony.

Before explaining how Paul indicates that the resurrection appearances were considered very significant, let us first explain Paul's general aim in this passage, since it will be harder to understand how he indicates they are significant if we do not understand the general context. Paul here looks to set straight those in Corinth who are denying the future resurrection. To make his argument, Paul first appeals to that which he says is of "first importance" (15:3), and what constitutes the essence of the Gospel (15:1-2). Then he enumerates the resurrection appearances (15:3-8). In 15:12-19, (which we have not quoted above because of its length) Paul argues from the fact of Jesus' resurrection to the absurdity of the Corinthians' denial of the general resurrection. He goes into detail concerning a point he makes elsewhere (Rom 8:11; Phil 3:20; 2 Cor 4:12; 1 Thess 4:14): Jesus has been raised as the first fruits of the general resurrection; he has been raised so that the rest of humanity will eventually be raised as well. Paul argues that if there is no general resurrection, then the purpose of Jesus' resurrection would be defeated, and so a denial of the former is essentially a denial of the latter. But Jesus' resurrection is the very foundation of the faith, and since the Corinthians affirm Jesus' resurrection, it is absurd for them to deny the general resurrection.

Paul's argument makes it clear that he considers the resurrection of Jesus to be tremendously important. Paul states that if Jesus' resurrection did not occur, then the Christian's faith is in vain (15:14), and he assumes that the Corinthians agree with him on this (it is the general resurrection which they deny). This reinforces the point we made above: Paul's epistles evince the fact that Jesus' resurrection was of central concern to the earliest Christians.

But it is in this passage that we find tremendous importance ascribed not only to Jesus' resurrection itself (i.e., the fact that Jesus was raised from the dead), but also to the resurrection appearances (i.e., the fact that after Jesus was raised he appeared to various people). That tremendous importance was ascribed to the resurrection appearances is clear from the fact that

Paul declares in 15:3 that the information which he is reminding the Corinthians of is *en prōtos*. This is often translated as "as of first importance" (i.e., of primary importance), but it can also be translated "from the first" (i.e., from when Paul first met the Corinthians). Since we are arguing that the resurrection appearances were considered significant, we would certainly prefer the translation "as of first importance." For this to be the right translation, it must be clear from the context that Paul is saying the resurrection appearances are of first importance. That this is what Paul is saying is clear from the fact that he says the information he is relating is the essence of the Gospel, the message that constitutes the Corinthians' salvation (15:1-2). Since the list of resurrection appearances is part of this information, it constitutes part of the essence of the Gospel. Since the Gospel was considered very significant (consider

Paul's words in Galatians 1:6-9),[15] if the resurrection appearances constituted part of the Gospel, they must have been considered very significant.

Hence, it is clear Paul considered the resurrection appearances very significant. And from this passage, we can deduce, based on three points, that many others in the early church also considered them very significant:

1. Paul writes that he had "passed on" this information to the Corinthians when he had first founded the church in Corinth. Thus, the resurrection appearances were part of the foundational material which Paul delivered to the churches he established. Therefore, all churches which Paul founded, not just the Corinthian church, would have been instructed that the resurrection appearances were part of the foundation of the faith. In addition, since Paul considered the appearances to be a matter of primary importance, we can assume that Paul not only presented the appearances to the churches which he founded, but that he also presented them to the many other churches which he visited. Since Paul's missionary travels were quite extensive, that means a very large number of the first century churches must have shared Paul's high regard for the resurrection appearances.

2. Paul indicates that this list of appearances did not originate with him, nor did the practice of passing it along to new converts. For Paul plainly states that he received this information.[16] We explained in chapter 4 that Paul would have discussed these appearances at some point with the Jerusalem church. Thus from the fact Paul says he received it, it is clear others also considered this information important. But just how many others does not become clear until we consider what Paul says in 1 Corinthians 15:9-11, which leads into the third point:

3. In 15:11, Paul explicitly states that the other apostles agree with the summary of the Gospel which he gives in verses 3-8. Paul declares that: "Whether then it was I or they [the other apostles], so we preach and so you believed" (15:11). The referent of "they" here is the apostles, the group mentioned in verses 7 and 9. When Paul refers to what he and the other apostles preached, he surely means the information summarized in 15:3-8: the death, burial, and resurrection of Jesus, the fact that these events fulfilled the Scriptures, and the resurrection appearances. Thus the other apostles agreed with Paul on the primary importance

---

15. "I am amazed that you are so quickly deserting Him who called you by the grace of Christ, for a different gospel; which is really not another; only there are some who are disturbing you and want to distort the gospel of Christ. But even if we, or an angel from heaven, should preach to you a gospel contrary to what we have preached to you, he is to be accursed! As we have said before, so I say again now, if any man is preaching to you a gospel contrary to what you received, he is to be accursed!"

16. It is often noted that the terms "received" and "passed on" can be used as technical terms for passing on sacred tradition. E.g., Gary R. Habermas and J.P. Moreland, *Beyond Death: Exploring the Evidence for Immortality* (Eugene, OR: Wipf & Stock, 2004), 129; Christopher Bryan, *The Resurrection of the Messiah* (Oxford: Oxford University Press, 2011), 261-62.

of this information. With regard to the identity of the apostles, there is some uncertainty as to precisely what Paul means by this term.[17] However, it is clear from 1 Corinthians 12:28 that the apostles functioned as prominent leaders in the Christian movement. In this verse, Paul affirms that the apostles are of first rank, ranking ahead of prophets, teachers, and other prominent individuals in the early church. This is also confirmed by Galatians 1:19 where Peter and James, each prominent Christian leaders and heads of the Jerusalem Church, are identified as apostles.[18] Thus when Paul states in 1 Corinthians 15:11 that all of the apostles agree with his preaching, this is a statement that numerous Christian leaders, including the leaders of the Jerusalem church (the "mother church" of the Christian movement),[19] agree with him on the importance of the resurrection appearances.

Once it is realized that the apostles regarded the resurrection appearances as very significant, it becomes difficult to disagree with Walter Kunneth's judgment that:

> It is extremely difficult to see how the gospel accounts of resurrection could have arisen in opposition to the original apostolic preaching and that of Paul... The authority of the apostolic eyewitnesses was extraordinarily strong. It would be inconceivable how there should have arisen in opposition to the authoritative witness of the original apostles a harmonious tradition telling of an event that has no basis in the message of the eyewitnesses.[20]

1 Corinthians 15:3-11 is thus a very important passage for the present argument. From this passage we learn that Paul considered the resurrection appearances to be part of the foundation of the faith, and that all of the other apostles (including Peter and James) agreed with Paul on this. Therefore the conclusion follows that during the period 30-70 CE, the leaders of the Christian church were agreed in ascribing tremendous significance to the resurrection appearances.

Objections

There are three objections that may be given against my argument.

---

17. On the identity of the apostles, see the entries for "apostolos" in *TDNT* and *ABD*; Kevin Giles, "Apostles Before and After Paul," *Churchman* 99 (1985): 241-56.

18. On the fact that Gal 1:19 indicates James was reckoned as an apostle (which is sometimes disputed) see John Painter, *Just James: The Brother of Jesus in History and Tradition* (Columbia, SC: University of South Carolina Press, 2004), 60; Frank J. Matera and Daniel J. Harrington, *Galatians* (Collegeville, MN: Liturgical 2007), 66.

19. The centrality of the Jerusalem church is evident from the fact that this is where the early Christians gathered together to resolve the Gentile controversy (Acts 15). And see Richard Bauckham, "James and the Jerusalem Church," in Richard Bauckham, ed., *The Book of Acts in its Palestinian Setting* (Grand Rapids, MI: Eerdmans, 1995), 415-80.

20. Walter Kunneth, *The Theology of the Resurrection* (London: SCM, 1965), 92-93.

The Reliability of the Resurrection Narratives

1. The question may be raised as to how far the list of appearances originally extended. It will be recalled that in the last chapter we admitted that there is disagreement as to whether the list existed in full form prior to Paul. If Paul has added some appearances to the list, then can we be sure those appearances he added are still part of what the other apostles "preached"? But, just as in the last chapter, it is unimportant to what extent the appearances in vv. 3-8 were in list form prior to Paul. Paul says that these appearances are part of what was passed on as of first importance, so if Paul did add other appearances to an earlier list, he was still only adding appearances which he (and the other apostles, per Paul's words in 15:9) considered to be of first importance. The only way this is not the case is if Paul meant to designate by "first importance" only some of the appearances, and then added the rest of the appearances as parenthetical information. But that would not make sense, for two reasons. First, Paul's stated aim is to remind the Corinthians of what is of first importance. Why would he remind them of what is of first importance for only part of this list, and then add in things that are not of first importance? (It could be argued that he does make parenthetical remarks in vv.9-10,[21] but these remarks are obviously parenthetical, since such personal information could obviously not be part of "the Gospel." However, it would be very confusing for Paul to make some of the appearances parenthetical, and thus not of first importance, without giving any indication that those appearances are not part of what he meant to designate by "first importance.") Second, when Paul says in v. 11 "so we preached and so you believed" this is clearly a reference to all of what he has just said (excluding the obviously parenthetical information in 9-10), so clearly he and the apostles preached all this information, including all the appearances, and he tells us that what they preached (15:2) is the Gospel and is of first importance.

   Now the question will be asked: What about the resurrection appearances which are not mentioned in this passage? Did Paul mean to say that all the resurrection appearances are of first importance, or only that the resurrection appearances enumerated in this list are of first importance? For three reasons, I think Paul meant all the resurrection appearances were of first importance, not just the ones in this list. First, on the assumption that the Gospels are fairly reliable, it is difficult to see why the appearances to the 500, James, and all the apostles would be omitted from the Gospels if these appearances were considered more important than the various resurrection appearances which the Gospels do relate. (It is not difficult to explain how this would happen if the Gospels are unreliable and so very far removed from the beliefs of the Christians in Paul's time. But I am operating on the assumption that they were fairly reliable, which means there was

---

21. "For I am the least of the apostles, and not fit to be called an apostle, because I persecuted the church of God. But by the grace of God I am what I am, and His grace toward me did not prove vain; but I labored even more than all of them, yet not I, but the grace of God with me."

a good amount of continuity between the Christians of Paul's time and the time of the Gospels.) Second, the other events in the passage which are designated as being of first importance, are clearly summaries of larger things which are also of first importance. When Paul identifies Jesus' death as of first importance, he surely does not mean only the fact that Jesus died; he means the whole story of Jesus' passion (that this is so is clear from the fact that Paul says Jesus' Eucharistic words are part of the tradition he received (1 Cor 11:23-25)). When he says Jesus' death and resurrection being in fulfillment of the Scripture is of first importance, he surely has some specific Scriptures in mind (such as those quoted in the Acts sermons). Thus when he enumerates some of the resurrection appearances, this is probably just a shorthand way of saying the resurrection appearances in general are of first importance, just as saying Jesus' death is of first importance is a short hand way of saying the story of his passion is of first importance. Third, if only the appearances in this list were considered of first importance, it does not make sense that Paul would have added his own appearance to the list, for why would he think his own appearance was more significant than the various other resurrection appearances which had occurred and had not made the list?

2. A second argument is that Mark, generally regarded as the first Gospel, and usually dated to ca. 65-70 CE, ends his Gospel without relating any resurrection appearances. The last eleven verses of Mark's Gospel, which do narrate appearances, are regarded by virtually all scholars as a later addition to the Gospel. This means Mark's Gospel originally ended with the discovery of the empty tomb in 16:8. Would Mark end his Gospel in this way if he considered the resurrection appearances significant?

In response, first of all, Mark did not actually end his Gospel this way if, as some scholars maintain, the original ending of Mark has been lost.[22] But even on the assumption that Mark did originally end at 16:8, the absence of a narration of resurrection appearances in his Gospel should not be taken to imply that Mark did not consider the appearances significant. Five times in his Gospel Mark anticipates the resurrection of Jesus (8:31; 9:9, 31; 10:32-34; 14:28) (and he mentions in particular an appearance in Galilee in 14:28 and again at the end of his Gospel in 16:7), and we know that other ancient authors had predictions in their narratives of events which they did not go on to narrate but which they clearly still considered significant. The *Iliad* predicts but does not narrate the fall of Troy, and the *Odyssey* predicts but does not narrate Odysseus' final trial.[23] Yet clearly these authors considered those events significant, for the fall of Troy is the

---

22. On this possibility, see N. Clayton Croy, *The Mutilation of Mark's Gospel* (Nashville, TN: Abingdon, 2003); Robert H. Stein, "The Ending of Mark," *Bulletin for Biblical Research* 18 (2008): 79-98.

23. Craig S. Keener, *The Gospel of John: A Commentary* (vol. 2; Peabody, MA: Hendrickson, 2003), 1194-95.

climax of the Trojan War and Odysseus' final trial is the climax of his adventures in the *Odyssey*.

3. A third argument is that the Gospels do not devote much space to the resurrection narratives. It might be asked, why, if the Gospel writers thought the resurrection appearances so significant, do they devote only one chapter out of their entire Gospel to them? The answer to this question is that the Gospels follow the conventions of Greco-Roman biography,[24] and in the case of Greco-Roman biography it was typical to devote a disproportionately large amount of space to narrating the person's death, and to spend only a short amount of space on the aftereffects of the person's life.[25] With the Gospels we have the same setup: A lot of space is devoted to Jesus' death, and then a short amount of space is devoted to Jesus' resurrection appearances, these appearances being the aftereffects of Jesus' life.

Conclusion

I have given what I think are three strong reasons to think the early church considered the resurrection appearances significant. If these reasons are correct, then it seems to me that if we accept the premise that the Gospels are fairly reliable, then we should believe that the resurrection narratives are generally reliable. There are quite a number of claims which the Gospels make about Jesus' life which are accepted as historical by the sizable majority of scholars, but which we have no reason to think were considered as significant as the resurrection appearances were. For example, most scholars agree that Jesus worked miracles (that is, events believed to be miracles), spoke in parables, was concerned with eschatology, was concerned with women, and came from Nazareth. If the early church accurately preserved all these things, does it make sense that they would fail to accurately preserve the resurrection appearances, when they held the appearances to be more significant than these other things? Thus if I am right that the resurrection appearances were considered very significant, scholars are in a situation where they must go one way or the other, and either agree the resurrection narratives are accurate, or else stop believing in the accuracy of many other claims in the Gospels which they currently believe are accurate.

---

24. We addressed this issue in chapter 1. See Richard Burridge, *What Are the Gospels? A Comparison with Greco-Roman Biography* (2nd ed.; Grand Rapids, MI: Eerdmans, 2004); Craig S. Keener, *The Historical Jesus of the Gospels* (Grand Rapids, MI: Eerdmans, 2009), 73-83.

25. See Burridge, *Gospels*, 225.

Appendix: Irenaeus

A couple passages in Irenaeus which are not related to the specific argument given above but which are relevant to the general question (whether the resurrection narratives are reliable) ought to be noted. In *Against Heresies* 3.3.4 Irenaeus recalls how, during his youth, he met Polycarp:

> But Polycarp also was not only instructed by apostles, and conversed with many who had seen Christ, but was also, by apostles in Asia, appointed bishop of the Church in Smyrna, whom I also saw in my early youth, for he tarried [on Earth] a very long time, and, when a very old man, gloriously and most nobly suffering martyrdom, departed this life, having always taught the things which he had learned from the apostles, and which the Church has handed down, and which alone are true.

Further, in Irenaeus' *Letter to Florinus* (quoted in Eusebius' *Church History*, 5.20.5-7) he writes:

> For when I was a boy, I saw you in lower Asia with Polycarp, moving in splendor in the royal court, and endeavoring to gain his approbation.
>
> I remember the events of that time more clearly than those of recent years. For what boys learn, growing with their mind, becomes joined with it; so that I am able to describe the very place in which the blessed Polycarp sat as he discoursed, and his goings out and his comings in, and the manner of his life, and his physical appearance, and his discourses to the people, and the accounts which he gave of his intercourse with John and with the others who had seen the Lord. And as he remembered their words, and what he heard from them concerning the Lord, and concerning his miracles and his teaching, having received them from eyewitnesses of the Word of life, Polycarp related all things in harmony with the Scriptures.

Note that in these passages Irenaeus refers to John and the others who had "seen Christ" and had "seen the Lord." These are the witnesses to the resurrection appearances (Jn 20:18, 24: "we have seen the Lord"; 1 Cor 9:1: "have I not seen the Lord?"). The fact that Irenaeus emphasizes Polycarp's personal familiarity with the witnesses of the appearances implies that Irenaeus had heard Polycarp relate accounts of the resurrection appearances. Otherwise, it is difficult to understand how, in the first place, Irenaeus would know that Polycarp had conversed with those who had seen the Lord, and, in the second place why Irenaeus would make mention of it. Further, at the end of the second passage, Irenaeus explicitly states that Polycarp heard stories of Jesus' miracles and teaching from those who had seen the Lord, and that Irenaeus heard the same stories from Polycarp. But if these witnesses to the appearances related stories of Jesus' miracles and teachings, surely they also related stories of his appearances. If this is so, then Irenaeus has heard stories of the resurrection appearances as recounted by someone who spoke with the eyewitnesses. Now, it is well-known that elsewhere in his writings Irenaeus affirms the fact that he regards the four Gospels as authoritative.[26] Since Irenaeus also regards Polycarp as a reliable source, it is highly likely that the descriptions of the resurrection appearances which Irenaeus read in the four Gospels are substantially the same as the accounts of those appearances which Irenaeus had heard from Polycarp.[27]

---

26. See especially *Against Heresies* 3.11.

27. It might be wondered how Irenaeus can be so close to the events given that he wrote in ca. 180 and the resurrection appearances occurred in ca. 30. However, the time gap is not as significant as it first appears. According to Martyrdom of Polycarp 9.3, Polycarp was eighty-six when he died in 155, and thus was born in the year 69. If the witnesses to the appearances were about the same age as Jesus, they would have been about eighty to ninety years old in ca. 85 CE when Polycarp was sixteen. If Irenaeus was sixty years old when he wrote (Josephus wrote three of his four works while he was between the ages of fifty-seven and sixty-two) he would have been about twenty when Polycarp was seventy-one. Thus there is nothing implausible about Irenaeus being only one link removed from the witnesses to the appearances. Incidentally, it would be profitable to search Irenaeus' writings to see if he relates any information on the resurrection appearances which is not found in the New Testament; any such information may well derive from his conversations with Polycarp.

6

Objections

NOW THAT WE HAVE presented the case for the reliability of the resurrection narratives, we must consider objections to their reliability. There is of course not enough space to address every conceivable objection, but I have chosen for this chapter four of the most significant.

First, the argument that the resurrection narratives contradict each other. The issue of contradictions in the narratives is such a well-known topic that a discussion of the reliability of the resurrection narratives would be incomplete without it. Second, the argument that Matthew relates an obviously unhistorical tale in 27:53-54 when he claims that when Jesus died, many people were raised from the dead, and that these people later appeared in Jerusalem. This is an event the historicity of which even some of the most well-known advocates of the historicity of Jesus' resurrection have had trouble defending.[1] Third, the historicity of the Emmaus appearance will be considered, for a number of arguments have been cited against the historicity of this appearance. Fourth, we must consider in more detail an argument which we dealt with briefly in chapter 3, the argument that eyewitness testimony is not reliable. For if it is not, our entire case has surely been doomed from the outset.

Contradictions

The first problem to address is that of apparent contradictions in the resurrection narratives. Consider the following statements, which express the viewpoint of many scholars. Bart D. Ehrman tells us "there are numerous differences in our accounts that cannot be reconciled with each other."[2] According to Reginald H. Fuller, "the stories

---

1. William Lane Craig and Michael Licona interpret the passage figuratively, an approach we will consider and reject below (William Lane Craig, "Resurrection and the Real Jesus," in Paul Copan ed., *Will the Real Jesus Please Stand Up? A Debate Between William Lane Craig and John Dominic Crossan* (Grand Rapids, MI: Baker, 1998), 156-79 (165); Michael R. Licona, *The Resurrection of Jesus: A New Historiographical Approach* (Downers Grove, IL: IVP Academic, 2010), 548-53); N.T. Wright simply comments, "some stories are so odd that they just may have happened. This may be one of them" (N.T. Wright, *The Resurrection of the Son of God* (Minneapolis: Fortress, 2003), 636).

2. Bart D. Ehrman in "Is There Historical Evidence for the Resurrection of Jesus? A Debate between William Lane Craig and Bart D. Ehrman," College of the Holy Cross, Worcester, MA, March 28, 2006; online at: http://www.holycross.edu/departments/crec/website/resurrdebate.htm.

themselves appear incredible on the grounds of their palpable inconsistencies."[3] And C.F. Evans is emphatic that "it is not simply difficult to harmonize these traditions, but quite impossible."[4]

This problem is an old problem—the issue was raised by Porphyry as long ago as the fourth century, and before him by Celsus in the third century. Eusebius responded to Celsus, and Augustine to Porphyry,[5] and ever since then, critics have not ceased to point to alleged contradictions in the narratives, and defenders of the reliability of the narratives have not ceased to propose harmonizations. However, for my present purpose, which is only to defend the general reliability of the accounts rather than their inerrancy, it is not necessary to harmonize all alleged contradictions, but only the major ones. This is because if a witness has made a minor error, that error does not invalidate the rest of his testimony, and thus if an account is wrong on minor details, that does not lead to the conclusion that it is wrong about major details. For example, consider former NBA basketball player Wilt Chamberlain's 100 point game. This game was not caught on videotape and there are thus a number of discrepancies surrounding the details. Chamberlain claims he had ten assists that game,[6] while the official box score reveals he had only two.[7] Some accounts have Chamberlain scoring his 100th point on a lay up,[8] while others say it was a dunk.[9] When Chamberlain scored his 100th point, the crowd rushed onto the court, but some accounts say the game was called at this point,[10] while others claim that the crowd was cleared and the game resumed.[11] But clearly, minor contradictions such as these do not cast doubt on the essential accuracy of the story.

Further, Norman Anderson, the lawyer whom we quoted in chapter 1, tells us that "it is common experience for a lawyer to note how a number of witnesses will almost invariably give accounts which differ widely from each other, initially at least, about any incident at which they have all been present."[12] And Timothy and Lydia McGrew give a number of examples of events whose historicity no one doubts even though the surviving accounts contradict each other.

---

3. Reginald H. Fuller, *The Formation of the Resurrection Narratives* (Philadelphia: Fortress, 1980), 2.

4. C. F. Evans, *Resurrection and the New Testament* (Naperville, IL: Alec R. Allenson, 1970), 28.

5. See David Laird Dungan, *A History of the Synoptic Problem: The Canon, the Text, the Composition, and the Interpretation of the Gospels* (New York: Doubleday, 1999), 98-141.

6. Wilt Chamberlain, *A View From Above* (New York: Villard, 1991), 190-91.

7. See a copy of the box score in Bryan Burwell, *At The Buzzer! Havlicek Steals, Erving Soars, Magic Deals, Michael Scores: The Greatest Moments in NBA History* (New York: Doubleday, 2001), 127.

8. Burwell, *Buzzer*, 126.

9. Burwell, *Buzzer*, 126.

10. Burwell, *Buzzer*, 126.

11. Burwell, *Buzzer*, 126.

12. Norman Anderson, *A Lawyer Among the Theologians* (London: Hodder and Stoughton, 1973), 109.

Even a passing acquaintance with the documents that form the basis of secular history reveals that the reports of reliable historians, even of eyewitnesses, always display selection and emphasis and not infrequently contradict each other outright. Yet this fact does not destroy or even significantly undermine their credibility regarding the main events they report. Almost no two authors agree regarding how many troops Xerxes marshaled for his invasion of Greece; but the invasion and its disastrous outcome are not in doubt. Florus' account of the number of troops at the battle of Pharsalia differs from Caesar's own account by 150,000 men; but no one doubts that there was such a battle, or that Caesar won it. According to Josephus, the embassy of the Jews to the Emperor Claudius took place in seed time, while Philo places it in harvest time; but that there was such an embassy is uncontroversial. Examples of this kind can be multiplied almost endlessly.[13]

Thus minor errors in the resurrection narratives are no reason for us to doubt the general reliability of those narratives. But the question then becomes whether there are any major errors in the accounts. I would contend that there are only four errors which, if they are actually errors, should be considered major errors (though it is necessarily a subjective judgment as to which errors are major and which minor).

But before we address these apparent errors, something needs to be said about methodology. When addressing apparent errors in the narratives, we should only be expected to provide plausible explanations, not explanations which are probable in and of themselves. This is because a hypothesis which is only plausible if considered by itself becomes probable if the alternative hypothesis is to suppose that a generally reliable witness made a mistake (and any witness can be assumed to be generally reliable until there is evidence to the contrary, since the large majority if witnesses are generally reliable, by which I mean they make few errors and any errors they make will be minor ones). For a generally reliable witness does not make very many mistakes, and thus a high burden of proof is required of the one who charges the witness with error. We will, as I said, consider below the argument that eyewitness testimony is not very reliable, but I am operating for now on the common sense view which says that eyewitness testimony is generally reliable. I contend that the average person, if asked to serve as a juror and presented with a witness on the witness stand, would believe whatever that witness said until there was evidence to the contrary. For example, if the witness says they saw car A crash into car B, the jury will believe this until there is evidence presented to the contrary; the burden of proof will be on the one who accuses the witness of error. And for the jury to believe that the witness has committed an error, the witness will have to be unable to provide a plausible explanation for the apparent error. If the other side argued the witness could not be trusted because the witness

---

13. Timothy and Lydia McGrew, "The Argument From Miracles: A Cumulative Case for the Resurrection of Jesus of Nazareth," in William Lane Craig and J.P. Moreland eds., *The Blackwell Companion to Natural Theology* (Oxford: Wiley-Blackwell, 2009), 593-662 (598).

was just waking up from sleep, the other side would have to produce strong evidence that the witness was asleep; and if the witness responded with a claim which would only seem plausible if considered by itself, this claim would be accepted as probable if the alternative was to suppose the witness erred. For example, if the evidence that the witness was just waking up is the fact that someone else saw the witness getting out of bed immediately before the crash, and the witness provides us with a plausible reason as to why they were getting out of bed other than that they were asleep (e.g., they say they were eating in bed), we will believe the witness. The idea that someone was eating in bed would only seem plausible if taken by itself (people do not eat in bed that much, so if you asked me the odds a given person was eating in bed today, I would say the odds are low), but we would accept it as probable if the alternative was to believe the witness erred. In the same way, if the Gospel writers are charged with making an error, we need only present a plausible explanation to show they have not committed an error. Thus, to take one example up front, Mark says a young man was at the tomb when the women discovered it, whereas the other Gospel writers say it was an angel. The proposed harmonization is that the young man was an angel. Now if I was asked to bet in advance on whether Mark would refer to an angel as a young man, I would say the idea was plausible rather than probable, because writers of that time sometimes refer to angels as young men, but the majority of the time they do not. But once I see that this hypothesis is necessary to avoid believing a seemingly reliable witness erred, I will come to believe this hypothesis is probable rather than only plausible.

To put this in Bayesian terms, the reason we proceed in this way is because though the probability that a witness will correctly tell us that an event which is improbable in and of itself occurred is low, the probability that a witness will incorrectly tell us that an event which is improbable in and of itself occurred is immensely lower. This is because our experience is that the number of times a witness correctly tells us such an event occurred is immensely greater than the number of times a witness incorrectly tells us such an event occurred. To illustrate, suppose someone tells us that today is his birthday. This is an event which is improbable in and of itself; that is, it is improbable prior to our having received the testimony of the witness. For prior to this individual's testimony, the odds it is his birthday were only 365:1. But once he has told us it is his birthday, the probability it is his birthday becomes very high, because the number of times that people correctly tell us it is their birthday vastly outnumbers the number of times people incorrectly tell us it is their birthday. Thus, though the odds a given person will correctly tell us today is their birthday may be only 1 in 365, the odds a given person will incorrectly tell us today is their birthday are immensely lower, and so if we are presented with a person who tells us today is their birthday, we should conclude that it is very probable it is indeed their birthday.

Jesus' Resurrection and Apparitions

Major Contradictions

1. The first apparent major contradiction is the fact that Mark says there was a young man at the tomb (Mk 16:5), whereas the other Gospels say there was an angel(s). If Mark does not think the young man was an angel we have a rather serious contradiction, since an author ought to know whether it was an angel or a human being who was at the tomb. But that it is plausible Mark thinks the young man was an angel is clear from the fact that ancient Jewish sources often conceived of angels as young men (e.g., Tobit 5:5-10; 2 Macc 3:26), and from the fact that the young man wore a white robe, which is the traditional garb of angels (e.g., Dan 10:6; 2 Macc 11:8).[14]

2. The second potentially major contradiction concerns whether the women said nothing to anyone after they left the tomb (Mk 16:8 "they said nothing to anyone, for they were afraid") or whether, as the other Gospels claim, they told the disciples about the empty tomb. However, it is certainly plausible that when Mark says the women said nothing to anyone, he means they said nothing to anyone as they were on their way back from the tomb; but they did say something to the disciples once they reached them. This is suggested by two facts. First, it is not likely the women would disobey a command of an angel, and the angel had commanded them to tell the disciples. Second, earlier in Mark, there is a very similar verse (1:44) in which Jesus tells the leper he has just healed: "say nothing to anyone," but then says "go show yourself to the priest." Clearly the leper was only to say nothing to anyone on his way back, but once he reached the priest, he would have to say something.[15]

3. The third contradiction to consider concerns where the appearances took place. Matthew and Mark mention only appearances in Galilee, Luke mentions only appearances in Jerusalem, and John mentions appearances in both Galilee and Jerusalem. C.F. Moule and William Lane Craig have pointed out that appearances in Galilee, then Jerusalem, and then again in Galilee are exactly what we should expect if the disciples did what pilgrims to Jerusalem often did: go up to Jerusalem for Passover, then return to their home towns (in the case of the disciples, Galilee) for about forty days, and then return to Jerusalem for Pentecost.[16] We would thus have no trouble postulating that there were appearances in both Galilee and Jerusalem, and that Matthew and Mark chose to relate only the appearances in Galilee, while Luke chose to relate only the appearances in Jerusalem, were it not for the following fact: Luke seems to exclude the possibility that there were any appearances in Galilee. In Luke 24:49, in an appearance which seems to take place on the day Jesus rose from the dead, Jesus tells the disciples: "but you are to stay in the city [Jerusalem] until you are clothed with power from on high." If on the day of the resurrection Jesus told the disciples not to

---

14. For more texts on each of these facts, see Dale Allison, *Resurrecting Jesus: The Earliest Christian Tradition and its Interpreters* (New York: T&T Clark, 2005), 335 n540.

15. This point is made by Allison, *Resurrecting*, 304.

16. C. F. Moule, "The Post-Resurrection Appearances in Light of Festival Pilgrimages," *New Testament Studies* 4 (1957-1958): 58-61; Craig, *Assessing*, 223-225.

leave Jerusalem until Pentecost, it is not possible that the disciples returned to Galilee before Pentecost.

However, it is not clear that the words of Jesus recounted in 24:49 were said on Easter day, for it is plausible these words were actually said forty days after Easter and thus after the Galilean appearances had already taken place. It becomes clear that this is a possibility once we realize that there is a time gap somewhere in Luke 24:36-53. Luke seems to say in his Gospel that the ascension took place on Easter: Jesus ascends in 24:50-53, and this event appears to happen right after Jesus' words in 24:44-49, and those words appear to have been said at the time of Jesus' appearance to the Twelve on Easter day (Lk 24:36-43). But though all this seems to take place on one day, this cannot actually be the case. For in Acts 1 Luke tells us the ascension took place forty days after Jesus' resurrection. Thus unless Luke blatantly contradicted himself, the events of 24:36-53 could not all have taken place on Easter day, since that would require that the ascension took place on Easter day instead of forty days later. Therefore there must be a time gap somewhere in these verses. And if there must be a time gap, there are two options as to where it could be. Either the words of Jesus in 24:44-49 were said by Jesus on the day of the resurrection, and so there is a gap between 24:49-50 (that is, the appearance to the Twelve (36-43), and the words of 24:44-49 happened on Easter day, and the ascension happened forty days later (50-53)). Or the words of Jesus in vv. 44-49 were said forty days after the resurrection, at the ascension, and so there is a time gap between vv. 43-44 (that is, the appearance to the Twelve happened on Easter day, and the words of Jesus (v. 44-49) and the ascension (vv. 50-53) took place forty days later). If the latter is the case, the words of Jesus instructing the disciples not to depart from Jerusalem were said forty days *after* the resurrection and thus after the Galilean appearances had already happened, and so Jesus' words to stay in Jerusalem do not rule out appearances in Galilee. If we did not have the testimony of the other Gospels that there were appearances in Galilee, either of these suggestions would appear equally likely, but given what we have said above about a plausible explanation becoming probable if the alternative is to suppose that the witness erred, we should accept the second hypothesis, since this is what is necessary to avoid supposing the witness erred.

A question remains, however. Why does Luke change the words of the angel so as to keep the angel from mentioning a Galilean appearance? Mark's "he is going ahead of you to Galilee; there you will see him, just as he told you" (Mk 16:7) is changed to "Remember how He spoke to you while He was still in Galilee, saying that the Son of Man must be delivered into the hands of sinful men, and be crucified, and the third day rise again" (Lk 24:6-7). This change may make it appear as if Luke is trying to deliberately stifle Galilean appearances. However, another hypothesis is that the change is not made because Luke has a vendetta against Galilee appearances, but only because Luke would think it out of place for the angel to have a prediction of a Galilean appearance if Luke did not intend to go on to narrate such an appearance. But the question then of course becomes why Luke chose not to relate any Galilean appearances. The answer to this is that it is clear his intent was to relate only appearances which took place on Easter day, and then also to relate the ascension. For he chose to omit not just Galilean appearances, but all appearances in between Easter and the ascension. This is apparent from the fact that he goes straight from Jesus' appearance to the Twelve on Easter to the ascension, though it is clear from Acts that he knows the ascension took place forty days later. Thus he clearly has no hostility towards these other Jerusalem appearances even though his Gospel is written without giving any indication that he knows of them, just as he gives no indication he knows of the Galilean appearances. Since he does not have any problem with the other Jerusalem appearances which took place during the forty days, there is no reason to think he had a problem with the Galilean appearances which took place during this same time period. (And if Luke truly did have a problem with Galilean appearances, it is not likely he would have used Mark as his primary source if Mark disagreed with him on this.)

It may be argued that this solution only backs the problem up one step, for the question simply changes from why Luke did not relate Galilean appearances to why he did not relate any of the appearances which occurred in between Easter and the ascension. But the answer to this question is probably the fact that Luke's Gospel is close to the maximum length for a scroll,[17] so if he had wanted to include more material, he would have had to omit something else from his Gospel. Since there is no reason to think the appearances between Easter and the ascension were more important than anything else in Luke's Gospel, there is no reason why Luke's omission of other appearances poses a problem.

4. Finally, John seems to blatantly contradict the Synoptics as to whether the women at the tomb knew Jesus was resurrected before they met the disciples.[18] In the Synoptics, the women arrive at the tomb and meet an angel who tells them that Jesus is risen and that they are to go and tell this to the disciples. However, John has Mary Magdalene return from the tomb alone, and when she returns, she is not only unaware of Jesus' resurrection, but she tells Peter and the Beloved Disciple that she thinks someone has taken Jesus' body. Peter and the Beloved Disciple then run to the tomb and see it is empty, but also see no angel. Hence, in John, Mary Magdalene has not encountered an angel at the tomb announcing Jesus' resurrection, while the Synoptics appear to indicate she has.

This apparent contradiction can be resolved by taking into account three facts.

First, although John's account mentions only Mary Magdalene, it implies that Mary had gone to the tomb with at least one other person. Mary states "They have

---

17. Craig S. Keener, *The IVP Bible Background Commentary: New Testament* (Downers Grove, IL: InterVarsity, 1994), 323.

18. The following discussion of Mary Magdalene's visit to the tomb is taken from Jake H. O'Connell, "John Versus the Synoptic Gospels on Mary Magdalene's Visit to the Tomb," *Conspectus* 14 (2012): 123-31.

taken away the Lord out of the tomb, and we do not know where they have laid Him" (20:2). The clear implication of Mary's use of the word "we" is that Mary Magdalene went to the tomb with others, but left them at some point in order to tell Peter and the Beloved Disciple.[19]

Second, the disciples were not all staying in the same place on Sunday morning. The term "disciples" is never in the Gospels equated with "The Twelve." "Disciples" is a broad term used to refer to more than just the Twelve. Thus, however many disciples there were, there were certainly more than twelve of them, and they were sufficiently large in number that we should not expect them all to be staying in one place. In addition, we have testimony from at least two sources that the Twelve themselves were not all gathered in one place on Sunday morning. This is obvious in John's account: only Peter and the Beloved Disciple are present when Mary arrives, and only they go to the tomb. Hence, John thinks the other disciples are someplace else. The same situation is implied in the Synoptics, which have Jesus saying "strike the shepherd and the sheep will be dispersed" (Mk 14:27), implying that the disciples would scatter after his arrest. Likewise, Mark 16:7, since it presents the job of telling Peter and telling the disciples as two different commands, may imply that Peter was staying separately from the main group of disciples. Thus there is ample reason for believing that different disciples, even different members of the Twelve, were staying in different locations on Sunday morning.[20]

Third, Luke indicates that the angels were not at the tomb immediately upon the women's arrival. Luke says it was "while they were puzzling over" (24:4) the missing body that the angels appeared and told them Jesus was raised. Thus the women did not know Jesus was raised immediately upon seeing the empty tomb. Rather, for an indefinite amount of time, they remained at the tomb "puzzling over" why the body was missing, and only after the appearance of the angels did they realize Jesus

---

19. Some (e.g., Francis J. Moloney, *The Gospel of John* (Collegeville, MN: Liturgical, 1998), 518-19) think Mary includes Peter and the Beloved Disciple in the "we" (i.e., "They have taken the Lord from the tomb, and we (herself, Peter, and the Beloved Disciple) don't know where they put him."). But Mary clearly seems to be speaking to Peter and the Beloved Disciple in this passage, not exclaiming into the air, which means that on this interpretation she is telling Peter and the Beloved Disciple that Peter and the Beloved Disciple don't know where Jesus' body is. This does not make a great deal of sense. Another suggestion is that Mary uses "we" as a substitute for "I" (e.g., Rudolf Bultmann, *The Gospel of John: A Commentary* (Philadelphia: Westminster, 1971), 684 n1). While this is not impossible, it appears highly unlikely because John's normal procedure is to have characters in his Gospel refer to themselves in the first person (e.g., Martha in 11:24: "I know he will rise again in the resurrection at the last day").

20. Even apart from the specific evidence presented by the resurrection narratives, it would still be reasonable to suppose that the Twelve may have been staying in different places Easter morning. There is no reason why all twelve men would always have stayed together in one place. The Gospels are in any event filled with traditions assuming the Twelve did not always gather en masse: Only Peter, James, and John accompany Jesus at the transfiguration (Mk 9:2 and parallels), only James and John come to Jesus in Mk 10:35, Judas travels apart from the Twelve in Mk 14:43, Peter and the Beloved Disciple travel apart from the others in Jn 18:15, Peter is apparently unaccompanied when he sees Jesus (Lk 24:24; 1 Cor 15:5), and Thomas is not with the rest of the Twelve in Jn 20:19-22.

was resurrected. Thus, there was a time gap of unspecified length from the time the women arrived at the tomb until the time when the angels appeared.

Taking these three facts into account, a plausible reconstruction can be posited: John indicates that Mary went to the tomb with others and then left. Luke relates that the angels were not at the tomb immediately upon the women's arrival; rather the women stood at the tomb puzzling over the missing body for an unspecified length of time prior to the arrival of the angels. If we hypothesize that Mary Magdalene left the tomb while the other women were still puzzling over the missing body, the solution becomes apparent: *Mary Magdalene did not know Jesus was raised, because she left the tomb before the angels arrived.* Since the angels were the ones who announced that Jesus had been raised, if Mary left the tomb before the angels arrived, she would not know that Jesus was resurrected. Rather, as she ran to tell Peter and the Beloved Disciple, she would still be "puzzling over" what had happened to Jesus' body, just as the other women still at the tomb were doing. Hence when she sees Peter and the Beloved Disciple, her best guess is that someone has stolen the body. As Mary Magdalene was in the process of telling Peter and the Beloved Disciple, the rest of the women saw the angels, heard that Jesus was resurrected, and then left the tomb. Since different disciples were staying in different places Sunday morning, and since Mary Magdalene, in her panic, may not have told anybody where she was going, the women went to tell a different group of disciples besides Peter and the Beloved Disciple. As Peter and the Beloved Disciple were heading to the tomb, the other women were leaving. By the time Peter and the Beloved Disciple arrived at the tomb, the women had left.

The Minor Contradictions

Concerning the minor contradictions in the narratives, though I have said that it is not necessary to harmonize them to defend the general reliability of the resurrection narratives, I may as well explain why I do not think there is any difficulty in doing so. Though one often hears that there are a multitude of apparent contradictions in the narratives, in addition to the four we examined above, I see only the following:

1. To what extent the sun had risen when the women came to the tomb (Matthew 28:1, "as it began to dawn." Mark 16:2, "when the sun had risen." Luke 24:1, "at early dawn." John 20:1, "while it was still dark").

2. How many women accompanied Mary Magdalene to the tomb? Matthew 28:1 mentions Mary Magdalene and the other Mary. Mark 16:1 mentions Mary Magdalene, Mary the mother of James, and Salome. Luke 24:9-10 mentions Mary Magdalene, Mary the mother of James, Salome, and unspecified other women. John mentions only Mary Magdalene, but she implies that she went to the tomb with others when she says, "They have taken away the Lord out of the tomb, and we do not know where they have laid Him" (Jn 20:2).

3. How many angels were at the tomb. Matthew mentions one (28:5), Mark mentions one (16:5), Luke mentions two (24:4), and John mentions two (20:12).

4. The precise words which the angels said to the women (this varies in each of the Gospels).

5. Whether the angel(s) were inside the tomb (so Mark, Luke, and John) or outside (Matthew has him sitting on the stone, 28:2).

6. Whether Jesus showed the disciples his hands and feet (Lk 24:39) or his hands and side (Jn 20:20).

7. Whether Jesus gave the disciples the Holy Spirit at his appearance Easter day (Jn 20:22-23) or at Pentecost (Lk 24:49).

Other alleged contradictions have been proposed, but I think these seven are the only ones which can be considered reasonable. I mean that quite a number of alleged contradictions have been proposed which must be considered entirely unreasonable, and it would not be practicable to respond to all of these. For example, Theodore Drange argues that the four Gospels contradict 1 Corinthians 15 because they do not mention an appearance to James, and that the other Gospels contradict Luke because they do not mention the Emmaus appearance.[21] But why should the Gospels mention the appearance to James, or why should the other Gospels besides Luke mention the Emmaus appearance? If we are going to harmonize the accounts we will have to confine ourselves to those objections which we consider reasonable; we cannot consider every objection like Drange's, otherwise we will never be able to stop. If my judgment is right, we only have to deal with the four major contradictions we have already dealt with above, and the seven minor ones.

The seven minor contradictions can be resolved as follows. 1) There is no contradiction between saying it was "dawn," "when the sun had risen," and so forth. These are all simply different ways of saying the sun was coming up. 2) No Gospel writer claims to give a complete list of the women who accompanied Mary Magdalene to the tomb. When, for example, Matthew says the other Mary accompanied her, that does not mean the other Mary was the only other person who accompanied her, and so he does not exclude Salome or the unspecified other women mentioned by Luke. And the same is true for the other Gospel writers—though each only mentions certain women, none claims to be giving a comprehensive list. 3) Mark and Matthew do not say there was *only* one angel; the fact that they only mention one angel does not mean there were not two. 4) We have admitted the Gospel writers do not give us the exact words of their characters. 5) The angel was outside the tomb at the time he first appeared, but by the time the women reached the tomb he was inside. When Matthew refers to him sitting on the stone, this is at the time he rolled back the stone and the

---

21. Theodore M. Drange, "The Argument from the Bible," http://www.infidels.org/library/modern/theodore_drange/bible.html.

guards saw him, but the guards had left by the time the women arrived, which is the time he is supposed to have been inside the tomb. 6) When Luke says Jesus showed the disciples his hands and feet, this does not exclude his also showing them his side, and when John says he showed them his hands and side, this does not exclude him also showing them his feet. 7) There is nothing implausible about Jesus giving the disciples the Holy Spirit twice, especially since each case seems to be for a different purpose. In John, the disciples receive the Holy Spirit in order to forgive sins, whereas in Acts they receive the gift of tongues.

(One of the most essential points to remember in dealing with alleged contradictions is that an omission is not a contradiction. If Mark does not mention a second angel, that is not the same as saying there was no second angel. If Matthew does not mention Salome, that is not the same as saying Salome was not there.)

Harmonizing the resurrection narratives thus turns out to be a not very difficult task. In fact, it is only in the case of the Galilee-Jerusalem issue and the matter of whether Mary Magdalene knew Jesus was raised at the time she left the tomb that we have had to do anything even mildly complex. Thus the problem of contradictions in the narratives, though it is a frequently cited problem, seems to me to be quite exaggerated. It is pertinent to note here Craig Blomberg's comment that "it is remarkable to observe how often the alleged contradictions in the Gospels are cited without a discussion of the many proposed solutions that can fit them together in a very plausible and natural manner."[22] Indeed, though it is very common to hear statements from scholars, such as those quoted in the opening paragraph of this chapter, asserting that the resurrection narratives contradict each other, it is very uncommon to see any of these scholars respond to specific harmonizations and explain why they are inadequate.[23] This is despite the fact that Gleason Archer, a Biblical scholar who also has a law degree, tells us that harmonization is the procedure routinely used by lawyers when dealing with reliable witnesses: "Bible critics who have never had any training in the laws of evidence may decry the 'harmonistic method' all they wish; but, like it or not, it is essentially the harmonistic method that is followed every day

---

22. Craig L. Blomberg, *The Historical Reliability of the Gospels* (2nd ed.; Downers Grove, IL: InterVarsity, 2007,) 140.

23. In regard to apparent contradictions in the resurrection narratives, many of the apparent contradictions are dealt with at various points in Craig, *Assessing*. See also John Wenham, *Easter Enigma* (Exeter: Paternoster, 1984). For harmonizations of the many alleged contradictions in the rest of the Bible see Gleason L. Archer, *New International Encyclopedia of Bible Difficulties* (Grand Rapid, MI: Zondervan, 1982); Norman L. Geisler and Thomas A. Howe, *When Critics Ask: A Popular Handbook of Bible Difficulties* (Wheaton, IL: Victor Books, 1992). For discussions of harmonization from a methodological point of view, see Craig L. Blomberg, "The Legitimacy and Limits of Harmonization," in D.A. Carson and John D. Woodbridge ed., *Hermeneutics, Authority, and Canon* (Grand Rapids, MI: Zondervan, 1986), 139-74; Gregory A. Boyd and Paul Rhodes Eddy, *The Jesus Legend: A Case for the Historical Reliability of the Synoptic Jesus Tradition* (Grand Rapids, MI: Baker Academic, 2007), 419-29.

that court is in session throughout the civilized world."²⁴ Further, consider one case related by Paul Rhodes Eddy and Gregory Boyd which shows how cautious one must be before acknowledging that a contradiction exists:

> In their book on methodology for conducting local historical research, [Barbara] Allen and [William] Montell investigated two different accounts of the 1881 lynching of two young men—Frank and Jack McDonald ("the McDonald boys")—in Menominee, Michigan. One account claimed they were hung from a railroad crossing, while the other claimed they were strung up on a pine tree. The accounts seemed hopelessly contradictory until Allen and Montell discovered old photographs that showed the bodies hanging *at different times from both places*. As macabre as it is, the McDonald boys apparently had first been hung from a railroad crossing, then taken down, dragged to a pine tree, and *hoisted up again*.²⁵

The Resurrection of the Saints

According to Matthew 27:53-54, when Jesus died, "the tombs broke open and the bodies of many holy people who had died were raised to life. They came out of the tombs, and after Jesus' resurrection they went into the holy city and appeared to many people."²⁶

Many scholars are quite skeptical of the historicity of this event, known as the resurrection of the saints (or resurrection of the holy ones). (The word "saint" here simply means holy person, and does not bear the technical meaning it came to bear in later theology.)

Dale Allison comments:

> That an earthquake opened the tombs of some long-dead saints, who then awoke from their collective slumber, entered Jerusalem, and appeared to many—all of which is attested solely by a document coming from perhaps sixty years after the alleged events—does not clearly commend itself as solemn fact to the sober-minded historian. . . . Mt. 27:51-53 is a religious yarn spawned by the same source that gave us the legend of the seven sleepers of Ephesus and other transparent fictions—the human imagination.²⁷

Robert Miller expresses similar sentiments:

---

24. Archer, *Encyclopedia*, 315.
25. Eddy and Boyd, *Jesus Legend*, 424.
26. As we will see, the exact translation of this passage is unclear. This follows the translation of Glenn Miller, "Good Question—Surely That Thing About All Those Resurrected People Walking Around in Jerusalem After Jesus' Death is Bogus, Right," http://christianthinktank.com/oddrise.html.
27. Allison, *Resurrecting Jesus*, 217.

> To put it bluntly, there is no good reason to think that this event really happened. For it is mentioned nowhere else—not in another Gospel, not in any other Christian writing, not in the writings of Josephus. . . . In most cases it is invalid to conclude that an event did not happen simply because it is mentioned in only one source. . . . But this story is a very special exception to the rule because it narrates what by any measure has to be the most amazing event of all time. . . It is inconceivable that an event so sensational and of such magnitude would not be noticed by the historians of the day.[28]

This event is not technically part of the resurrection narratives, since it occurs one chapter prior to Matthew's resurrection narrative. But a serious error concerning a resurrection related event which is supposed to have happened shortly before Jesus' resurrection would certainly call into question the reliability of the resurrection narratives as well, and thus the historicity of this event ought to be considered.

One possible defense which we should quickly dismiss is the idea that the passage is to be taken figuratively. It has been suggested that these words are not intended as an account of actual events, but rather are an example of the kind of figurative speech found in apocalyptic writings.[29] That is, they are on a par with Joel's statements that the sun will be darkened and the moon turned to blood (Joel 2:31), which are quoted by Peter on the day of Pentecost (Acts 2:20). Joel did not mean this literally, or at least Peter does not think he did, since Peter quoted the passage as applying to Pentecost even though nothing literally happened to the sun and moon that day. However, the problem with this interpretation is that there is no indication in the text that Matthew is suddenly switching to figurative language (we have agreed that the Gospels are historical accounts and thus any given statement in them is to be assumed to be meant historically unless there is evidence to the contrary). The only basis for thinking he is switching to figurative language is the fact that the event appears to be unhistorical, since no other source mentions it. But if the event appears to be unhistorical, and there is no evidence the author meant it figuratively, we should simply conclude that the event is unhistorical and that Matthew has made an error.

And there is also a further problem for the figurative language hypothesis: apocalyptic language is never known to occur in the midst of an ordinary historical account; it always appears as part of an apocalyptic book or apocalyptic oracle. But in this case, the events are part of a historical narrative, and moreover, we are told that the centurion, upon seeing these events, commented "truly this was the Son of God" (Mt 27:54). While references to earthquakes, torn veils, and resurrections might seem comparable to figurative apocalyptic language like the sun turning dark and the moon turning to blood, stating that a centurion made a comment is obviously not something

---

28. Robert J. Miller, "What Do Stories About Resurrections(s) Prove?" in Copan ed., *Real Jesus*, 77-98 (90).

29. This is the justification given by the proponents of the figurative language hypothesis mentioned in n1.

that would be found in apocalyptic speech, but only in a historical account. Yet since the centurion's comment does not make sense unless Matthew believes the events the centurion is commenting on are historical, Matthew must have believed these events were historical.[30] Thus the figurative interpretation will clearly not get us out of the dilemma. If the events are unhistorical, Matthew has made an error.

As Robert Miller makes especially clear, the central reason for doubting this event's historicity is the fact that Matthew is the only source to mention it even though it seems to be the type of event which should be attested by more than one source. Thus I want to argue two points. First, the event is multiply attested to a partial extent by at least one other Christian source, the Odes of Solomon, and possibly by another Christian source, 1 Peter. Second, contrary to what seems prima facie to be the case, the event is not the sort of event which we would necessarily expect to find attested in secular sources.

The Odes of Solomon strongly implies that when Jesus descended into Hades (this event is referred to in Odes 42 and 22:1), dead people left Hades in their physical bodies, rather than as spirits. Odes 22:1 refers to Jesus' return from Hades ("He who caused me to descend from on high, and to ascend from the regions below") and seven verses later (22:8-10) refers to resurrections which are not to take place in the future (so the passage is clearly not concerned with the general resurrection), but which have already taken place at some point in the past. Given that the Ode has just referred to Jesus' descent into Hades (22:1) and to his defeat of the devil (22:5-7), it is quite likely the Odes believe these resurrections took place around the time of Jesus' death. Odes 22:8-10 reads

> And it [God's right hand] chose them from the graves, and separated them from the dead ones. It took dead bones and covered them with flesh. But they were motionless, so it gave them energy for life. (22:8-10)

Hence, although the Odes do not actually mention appearances of the resurrected saints, they do at least attest to the fact that people were raised from the dead around the time of Jesus' death.

However, in order for the Odes to provide independent confirmation of this event, we must be confident of two facts. First, that the Odes are not dependent on

---

30. Licona, *Resurrection*, 548-50, in support of the contention that the event is not meant historically cites cases in which an ancient historian (e.g., Dio Cassius, Josephus) claims that spectacular events happened around the time of the death of a prominent person, and Licona argues that since many of the events they refer to probably did not actually happen, the historians may have meant the events were figurative. But from the fact that the events are unhistorical, it does not follow that the author intended for them to be understood figuratively. To prove that the events were meant to be understood figuratively, one must prove not just that the events are unhistorical, but also that the author knew the events were unhistorical. For if the author thought they were historical though they were not, he has not spoken figuratively, but simply written mistaken history. In the cases Licona cites, I do not see any reason to think the authors knew the events were unhistorical.

Matthew, and second, that they date close enough to the event that there is a strong chance they preserve authentic tradition rather than only legendary embellishment.

With regard to the first issue, there is no reason to think the Odes are dependent on Matthew. There are no clear cases of dependence on the Synoptics in the Odes,[31] and if the Odes are dependent on Matthew in this passage, one would expect them to refer to some of the other events Matthew mentions in this passage: the tearing of the veil, the earthquake, the rending of the rocks, and the appearances of the saints. But none of these things appear in the Odes, and hence, dependence on Matthew is unlikely.

With regard to the date of the Odes, most scholars date them to the late first to early second century, and if this date is correct, they are indeed early enough to preserve authentic tradition about Jesus' life. Reasons for dating the Odes to this period include their affinities with the Dead Sea Scrolls and the possible influence of Jewish apocalypticism on the Odes, but I believe the strongest argument for this date is the nature of the relationship between John's Gospel and the Odes. It is widely recognized that there are many parallels between John and the Odes, but it does not seem likely that the Odes are dependent on John. The language and concepts that appear in John's Gospel also appear in the Odes, but they are not found in only a few passages; they permeate the Odes. We would not expect dependence on John to be such thorough dependence. And the Odes do not refer to specific passages of John, as we would expect them to do if they were dependent on John. Rather, as I said, the Odes invoke the language and concepts of John.[32]

The nature of the parallels between John and the Odes suggests an author who did not know the Gospel of John but who was thoroughly acquainted with Johannine thought. This indicates that the Odes were produced by someone(s) associated with the community that produced John's Gospel. (It has been postulated that the Odes come from the separatists mentioned in 1 John.)[33] If the Odes do indeed come from members (or former members) of the Johannine community, then a date before ca. 100 CE is certainly likely.

The fact that the Odes have physical resurrection in mind when they describe Jesus' descent into Hades leads us into the reason for thinking 1 Peter may attest to the

---

31. Arthur J. Bellinzoni tells us the Odes "contain traditional Christian features or express ideas common to several New Testament writings, without leading to a conclusion that asserts a literary dependence on a specific text" (*The Influence of the Gospel of Saint Matthew on Christian Literature Before Saint Irenaeus* (Macon, GA: Mercer University Press, 1993), 77).

32. On the fact that the nature of the parallels between John and the Odes argues against literary dependence, James Charlesworth states, "The numerous and pervasive parallels between the Odes and John cannot be explained by literary dependence of the Odist upon John or vice versa" (James H. Charlesworth, *John and Qumran* (London: Geoffrey, 1972), 135). For an overview of the question of the date of the Odes more generally, see the entry for the Odes in James H. Charlesworth ed., *The Old Testament Pseudepigrapha* (Garden City, NY: Doubleday, 1983-85).

33. See R.A. Culpepper, "The Odes of Solomon and the Gospel of John," *Catholic Biblical Quarterly* 35 (1973): 298-322.

Objections

resurrection of the saints as well. If the Odes of Solomon understood Jesus' descent into Hades as involving physical resurrection (and in fact, various Patristic authors also understood the event in this way[34]), this raises the possibility that 1 Peter 4:6, the one New Testament text which may refer to Jesus' salvation of the dead in Hades (whether this is actually what the text refers to is notoriously disputed),[35] might, like the Odes, have in mind physical resurrections. In this case, 1 Peter would provide a third source attesting to the resurrection of the saints. This possibility is admittedly uncertain, but given that the Odes of Solomon, as well as Patristic sources, do associate physical resurrection with Jesus' descent into Hades, it is not implausible that this is the belief reflected in 1 Peter.

Secular Sources?

But the skeptic's response will of course be that if there really were a bunch of resurrected people walking around in Jerusalem, we should find this fact attested not just in Christian sources, but in secular sources as well, in fact in many secular sources, for the event would have been one of the most spectacular in the history of the human race. However, this objection loses its force once we realize that the event was not as spectacular as it initially seems. This is clear for three reasons.

First, there is no evidence the appearances were public appearances. The assumption of scholars such as Allison and Miller seems to be that the resurrected saints appeared to huge crowds which included neutral and hostile witnesses such as Pilate and Caiaphas. If this was the case, one would certainly expect the event to be widely attested, but in fact there is nothing in the text which indicates the appearances were like this. We are told only that the resurrected saints appeared to "many," and it may be that these appearances, like the resurrection appearances, occurred primarily to those who were already followers of Jesus. In this case, the appearances would have no more apologetic value than the resurrection appearances themselves, and thus they could be explained via whatever hypothesis critics used to explain the resurrection appearances (e.g., lies or hallucinations). Claims of appearances of the dead were not particularly uncommon in the ancient world (as we mentioned at the end of the first chapter) and although the appearances of Matthew 27 were supposed to be physical appearances rather than apparitions, with no video camera available the evidence for these appearances would not be any stronger than the evidence for Jesus' appearances.

Second, even if the resurrected saints did appear to huge crowds and prominent skeptics, the appearances still may have been unconvincing. We are not told whether

---

34. See Richard Bauckham, *The Fate of the Dead: Studies on the Jewish and Christian Apocalypses* (Leiden: Brill, 1998), 244.

35. On whether this is the correct interpretation of the text, see the commentaries on 1 Pt. The seemingly related text, 1 Pt 3:18-19, definitely does not have reference to Jesus' descent into Hades. I discuss 1 Pt 3:18-19 in chapter 7.

these saints were long dead, recently dead, or some combination of both. If the resurrected saints were long dead individuals (such as Adam and Moses), then even if they really did appear, there would be no way to positively identify them because no one in Jesus' time would know what these people were supposed to look like. Since none of, for example, Moses' contemporaries, were alive to positively identify him, how could one be sure that the person knocking on the door claiming to be Moses was really Moses rather than an impostor sent by Jesus' followers? With no way of identifying the individuals, the appearances could have been dismissed as a hoax just as the empty tomb was dismissed by claiming the disciples stole the body (Mt 28:11-15).

In fact, there are people today who claim to be the returned Elijah—but of course nobody believes them.[36] If most people in our time have dismissed appearances of Old Testament characters as hoaxes, then similar appearances in ancient times could have been dismissed in the same way.

Third, let us suppose that the saints not only appeared to skeptics, but attempted to provide miraculous proof that they were not impostors. It is still not necessarily the case that the event would have convinced most skeptics. We have numerous eyewitness accounts of appearances of the ghost of Lydia Blaisdell who supposedly appeared to large crowds of people on numerous occasions in the year 1800, ostensibly shape-shifting into a ball of light and dematerializing before them and also displaying ESP.[37] Yet many of the witnesses (quite rightly in this case) suspected a hoax, and far from being an event which could not fail to escape notice, an obscure book by the minister Abraham Cummings is the only source which records it. Thus even if the resurrected saints performed apparently miraculous feats, they may not have been believed, just as Jesus and the disciples performed apparently miraculous healings but not everyone became a Christian (regardless of whether we think these healings were really miraculous, the majority of scholars do agree that Jesus and the early Christians performed what appeared to be miraculous healings).[38]

Hence if the resurrection of the saints did occur, it is not an event which would necessarily be attested by a large number of sources.

The Unsurprisingness of the Event

Before considering objections to my argument, I want to make the point that if the event is historical, then rather than seeming like a shock, it should not come as a surprise to us, because the event fits in with contemporary Jewish expectation about

---

36. For a couple such claimants, see Gari-Anne Patzwald, *Waiting for Elijah: A History of the Megiddo Mission* (Knoxville: University of Tennessee Press, 2002), 75.

37. See n43 in chapter 3.

38. On this point, see especially Graham H. Twelftree, *Jesus the Miracle Worker: A Historical and Theological Study* (Downers Grove, IL: InterVarsity, 1999); Andrew Daunton-Fear, *Healing in the Early Church: The Church's Ministry of Healing and Exorcism From the First to the Fifth Century* (Colorado Springs: Wipf & Stock, 2009).

what would happen at the Messiah's coming. The whole series of events described by Matthew—an earthquake, rending of rocks, and resurrections—are portrayed in a wall panting from the Dura Europos synagogue, and the expectation is that these events will be brought about by the Messiah. Raymond Brown tells us:

> The connection of the tomb openings with the preceding rending of the rocks is splendidly visible in the Dura Europos synagogue wall-paintings that portray the raising of the dead as part of the enlivening of the dry bones in Ezek 37--a 3d-cent. CE tableau that is very helpful in understanding how Matt and/or his readers might imagine the scene he is narrating. There in the splitting of a mountain covered by trees (almost surely the Mount of Olives rent by an earthquake), rocks are rent, thus opening up tombs burrowed into the sides of the mountain and exposing bodies of the dead and their parts. A figure is depicted who may be the Davidic Messiah (see Ezek 37:24-25) bringing about this raising of the dead. [In my opinion, the figure is very likely the Messiah, given the expectation that the resurrection of the dead would occur at the Messiah's coming, and given that there is no other belief that anyone else would raise the dead.] [39]

This painting probably has in mind the general resurrection, not a preliminary to the general resurrection, so it does not portray exactly what Matthew describes. But once we see that what Matthew describes is a variation on a belief already common within Judaism, the resurrection of the saints begins to seem like the sort of thing which we should not be surprised to find if Jesus rose from the dead.

Objections

There are three objections which might be given against my defense of the historicity of this event. These are as follows.

1. It may be objected that the description of the saints' resurrection in Matthew 27 does not make any sense, for it seems to say the saints were raised at Jesus' death, but then remained in their tombs until after Jesus' resurrection. So, the NASB: "The tombs were opened, and many bodies of the saints who had fallen asleep were raised; and coming out of the tombs after His resurrection they entered the holy city and appeared to many."

Thus we have the strange picture of the saints being raised on Friday, but remaining in their tombs till after Jesus' resurrection on Sunday. Now the skeptic thinks he knows what is going on here: Matthew has the saints being raised at Jesus death, but then he or a later scribe realized that nobody is supposed to have risen from the dead before Jesus (Jesus is the first fruits of those raised from the dead (1 Cor 15:20), and the firstborn of the dead (Col 1:18; Rev 1:5)), and thus a rather implausible solution was

---

39. Raymond E. Brown, *The Death of the Messiah* (vol. 2; New York: Doubleday, 1994), 1123-24.

thought of: The saints were raised on Friday, but stayed in their tombs until Sunday, and only left their tombs after Jesus rose. This idea of the saints staying in their tombs for at least two days after being raised is indeed implausible, but once we realize that the verse can be translated differently the problem is resolved. There are two translation options in this regard. The first option is to translate the verse so that the saints, rather than leaving their tombs after Jesus' resurrection, leave their tombs at the time of Jesus' death, and so it is only the appearances in Jerusalem which occur after his resurrection. Robert Gundry tells us that based on the Greek, "it is unclear whether they came out of their tombs only after Jesus' resurrection, or came out earlier but stayed in the countryside till Jesus had risen."[40]

Thus the verse can also be translated, as it was translated in the quotation at the beginning of this section, as "the tombs broke open and the bodies of many holy people who had died were raised to life. They came out of the tombs, and after Jesus' resurrection they went into the holy city and appeared to many people."

If the verse is translated this way, then the passage is saying that the saints were raised and left their tombs on Friday, but did not actually appear in Jerusalem until after Jesus' resurrection. The appearances took place after Jesus' resurrection, but the resurrections and exits from the tombs took place on Friday. When the saints were raised, rather than walking out of their tombs like Lazarus did, they presumably went to heaven. Then, later, they made appearances, just as Jesus did.

There is also another translation option. John Wenham has proposed that the passage be translated in a way which would resolve the problem even more smoothly.[41] As he translates it, not just the appearances of the saints but also the raising of them occurred after Jesus' resurrection. The translation is something along the lines of: "The tombs broke open. And after Jesus' resurrection, the bodies of many holy people who had died were raised to life, and came out of the tombs." While no one seems to have disputed the fact that this translation is grammatically possible,[42] the potential problem with it is that if the saints were not raised till after the time of the other events (the earthquake, tearing of the veil, and rending of the rocks), the resurrection of the saints seems unconnected to the other events, and if that is the case, it would not make sense for Matthew to note it. However, it can be argued that the event is connected in that the opening of the tombs (caused by the earthquake) occurred at Jesus' death, and since the resurrected saints subsequently left these tombs which

---

40. Robert H. Gundry, *Matthew: A Commentary on His Literary and Theological Art* (Grand Rapids, MI: Eerdmans, 1982), 576.

41. John W. Wenham, "When Were the Saints Raised?" *Journal of Theological Studies* 32 (1981): 150-52.

42. Wenham's proposal is endorsed by Leon Morris, *The Gospel According to Matthew* (Grand Rapids, MI: Eerdmans, 1992), 725; Mark E. Moore, *The Chronological Life of Christ* (Joplin, MO: College Press, 1996); 649; Craig L. Blomberg, *Making Sense of the New Testament: Three Crucial Questions* (Grand Rapids, MI: Baker Academic, 2004), 169; Grant R. Osborne, *Matthew* (Grand Rapids, MI: Zondervan, 2010), 990.

were opened when Jesus died, their resurrections are connected with the events of Jesus' death.

This translation as well as the previous one are both plausible. Thus if this event is historical, it does not require us to believe that the saints stayed in their tombs till three days after they rose.

2. The skeptic may ask: if many people really did rise at the time of Jesus' death, what of all the empty tombs? Even if the appearances could be explained as trickery, surely the empty tombs would convince everyone and thus this event should be mentioned by secular sources. But the problem with this argument is that these empty tombs would have been difficult to find. There were at least 900 rock hewn tombs in Jerusalem during Jesus' time.[43] If Matthew's "many" means, say, ten people, that means only one out of every ninety tombs were opened. Skeptics seeking to investigate would have to search through ninety tombs simply to find one empty one. And even if skeptics were willing to search through all of the tombs, being as not very many tombs were empty relative to the total number of tombs, they could still postulate that the disciples had stolen the bodies, just as they did in the case of Jesus' empty tomb.

It is relevant to note here that there is nothing implausible about the idea of an earthquake opening tombs. Walter Kaiser explains:

> The tombs of the wealthier people were generally natural caves suitably enlarged or else artificial caves carved into softer rock. Several hillsides around Jerusalem had many of them. The tombs were closed with a rock door which was like a cork worked into the small opening of the cave. An earthquake which moved the rock around it could pop such a door open.[44]

3. A final objection is a theological one: If this event is historical, then these saints were raised before Jesus, but does not this, as some think Matthew or a later scribe concluded, contradict Paul's statements that Jesus is the first fruits of those raised from the dead, and that Jesus is the firstborn of the dead?

First of all, if we adopt Wenham's translation, according to which the saints do not leave their tombs until after Jesus' resurrection, we can dismiss this entire problem a priori. But even if we allow that the saints were raised before Jesus, there is still not any contradiction between Matthew and Paul and Revelation. The term "first fruits" means only the first batch of crops for a year, not the literal first crop (see Lev 23:9-14). For example, the first fruits of carrots would refer to the first batch of carrots for the year, not the very first carrot to sprout. Thus, even if other people rose from the dead before Jesus, he is still among the first people to be resurrected and so is still part of the first fruits, and since it was only because of Jesus' power that these other people

---

43. Jodi Magness, *Stone and Dung, Oil and Spit: Jewish Daily Life in the Time of Jesus* (Grand Rapids, MI: Eerdmans, 2011), 156.

44. Walter Kaiser Jr. et al., *Hard Sayings of the Bible* (Downers Grove, IL: IVP Academic, 1996), 400-401.

were raised, I do not think the fact that they were raised before him detracts from the significance of his resurrection at all. (We may note that Enoch and Elijah conquered death before Jesus, since neither of them died at all.) As for the term firstborn, though it can denote a literal firstborn, it can also mean simply first in rank, first in prominence.[45] This is how the term is used in Colossians 1:15, where Jesus is called the firstborn of all creation; he was not literally the firstborn, Adam was. Hence it is plausible that when Paul and Revelation call Jesus the firstborn from the dead, they simply mean he has preeminence among those who rose from the dead.

(Another potential way of avoiding the problem in question is to suppose that the resurrected saints were recently dead people like Lazarus and that, like Lazarus, they died again, and thus they were not resurrected permanently as Jesus was (scholars generally refer to such temporary raisings as resuscitations rather than resurrections).[46] But if we suppose that that is the case, it becomes more difficult to explain why the event is not more widely attested, for one would expect that if these dead people were actually living in Judea for many years afterwards, this could not fail to convince everyone of the truth of Christianity. It is true that the Gospels do tell us Jesus raised a number of people from the dead during his lifetime and this did not convince everyone. But outside of Lazarus, we are not told that any of the dead people he raised rose from their tombs; they were always people who had died very recently. A large number of raisings from out of the tombs would be more impressive, and hence should convince more people. Yet given what I have written elsewhere concerning how people may not believe even in the face of obvious miracles,[47] I would not regard it as impossible that even this event would fail to convince everyone. However, there are two other reasons to prefer the idea that these saints were raised permanently. First, Ezekiel's vision of the dry bones was understood to refer to eschatological resurrection in subsequent Jewish thought.[48] Thus, if the resurrection of the saints has its basis in this idea, one would expect that permanent resurrections are meant, not temporary resuscitations. Second, the Odes of Solomon clearly has in mind resurrection, for it refers to people's bones being covered with flesh, and this means the people in question must have been dead for some time, not recently dead (it takes a long time for the flesh to decay), and it is only recently dead people who are resuscitated in the Bible.)

Emmaus

The one resurrection appearance whose historicity has been questioned perhaps more than any other is the Emmaus appearance (Lk 24:13-33). In this appearance, Jesus

---

45. See the entry for firstborn (*prototokos*) in the *Theological Dictionary of the New Testament*.

46. This is suggested by Miller, "Good Question."

47. Jake H. O'Connell, "Divine Hiddenness: Would More Miracles Solve the Problem?" *Heythrop Journal* 54 (2013): 261-67.

48. See Osborne, *Exegetical Commentary*, 990

accompanies two disciples as they walk from Jerusalem to Emmaus, downcast because of his death, and he explains the Scriptures to them, but they do not know the person with them is Jesus until the end of their journey when they begin to share a meal with him. Three main arguments have been deployed against the historicity of this appearance.

First, the dialogue contains Lukan themes (Jesus as a prophet who is handed over and crucified, but is the redeemer of Israel, and fulfills the Messianic prophecies); this suggests Luke has composed the narrative himself rather than relating an actual event.[49]

Second, the disciples' recognition of Jesus during the breaking of the bread (24:30-32) is reminiscent of the Christian celebration of the Eucharist, the meal in which Christians experience the presence of Jesus. Thus the argument is that the Emmaus story may be an invention based on the Eucharist. John Alsup tells us, "It is widely accepted in NT research that we have here, in fact, the Eucharistic setting of the early church with all of the ramifications of the institution of the Lord's Supper."[50]

Third, the Emmaus story parallels many Jewish and pagan stories about angels or gods which appear on Earth disguised in human form and are not recognized as spiritual beings until the end of their appearance. These parallels include, from the Jewish world, the story of Sodom and Gomorrah, Tobit, and T. Abe; and from the Gentile world, the stories of Asclepius, Apollonius, and Romulus.[51]

In response to the first argument, the fact that the dialogue contains Lukan interests is entirely compatible with the notion that Luke has paraphrased the actual words of the individuals. Thus the fact that the speech of the characters in the Emmaus appearance displays Lukan interests does not argue against the historicity of the appearance itself.

In response to the second argument, it is not at all anachronistic for the resurrected Jesus to engage in a Eucharist type celebration with the Emmaus disciples. For the celebration of the Eucharist did not begin after Jesus' resurrection. It began, we are told, with Jesus on the night before his death, when he took the bread and wine, and said, "this is my body" and "this is my blood," and said to the disciples, "do this in remembrance of me."[52] The historicity of this event should be accepted even by those who do not accept the historicity of the Gospels because the words are attested by Paul in 1 Corinthians 11:23-25, and as we have seen, Paul is a reliable source. Now

---

49. This point is made by Allison, *Resurrecting*, 253.

50. John E. Alsup, *The Post-Resurrection Appearance Stories of the Gospel Tradition* (London: SPCK, 1975), 197.

51. For the argument that the Emmaus narrative is based on pagan stories, see C.H. Dodd, "The Appearances of the Risen Christ," in D.E. Nineham ed., *Studies in the Gospels* (Oxford: Blackwell, 1955), 9-36; Arnold Ehrhardt, "The Disciples of Emmaus," *New Testament Studies* 10 (1964): 187-201.

52. On Jesus' Eucharistic words, see Joachim Jeremias, *The Eucharistic Words of Jesus* (New York: Scribner, 1966); I. Howard Marshall, *Last Supper and Lord's Supper* (Grand Rapids, MI: Eerdmans, 1981).

if Jesus did institute the practice of the Eucharist on the night of his death, it is not at all surprising that he would engage in a Eucharist style event after he rose from the dead. Thus though the event is the sort of event the early Christians might invent, it is also the sort of event the resurrected Jesus is likely to engage in. (In Bayesian terms, the probability of getting the datum is just as high given h as it is given ~h. Thus the question simply becomes which hypothesis has a higher prior probability: the hypothesis that Jesus actually rose from the dead, or the hypothesis that the early Christians invented things. If we think the evidence is strong that Jesus rose from the dead and weak that the early Christians invented stories, we will regard h as the likelier explanation, but if we think the evidence is weak that Jesus rose from the dead and strong that the early Christians invented stories, we will regard ~h as the likelier explanation.)

With regard to the parallels between the Emmaus story and other ancient stories of spiritual beings in disguise, this takes us into a question familiar to Biblical scholars, namely, whether the fact that some event in the Bible is paralleled in some other source should lead us to believe that the Biblical event is an invention based on that other source. In other words, does parallel equal invention? This question was very often answered in the affirmative in the heyday of what was known as the history of religions school—a school of thought among German scholars of the nineteenth century who were fond of citing parallels to this or that story in the Bible and arguing that the later story must have been invented based on the earlier one. This approach has, however, largely fallen out of favor with scholars, who have recognized that the parallels are not so striking that they need be explained by anything more than coincidence. One scholar, Samuel Sandmel, dubbed the overzealousness on the part of some scholars to find parallels, "parallelomania."[53]

I want to contribute to this issue by drawing an analogy between parallelomania and fake psychics. I think parallelomania results from the human inclination to see design where there is none, which is the same penchant that causes us to see things in the clouds, and also the same penchant which accounts for the success of fake psychics. Whether there are any real psychics in this world is of course disputed, but we do know there are people who admit to being fake psychics and who can duplicate the feats of "real" psychics, and they have told us that success as a fake psychic (as well as success as a real one, if we presume the "real" ones are also fake) comes from being able to prey upon this human penchant to see design where none exists. I think this same fault is what leads scholars to see design when there is none in the case of the Bible, which causes them to think that parallels which are only coincidental were actually designed by the author. Let me cite four of the principles which lead to the success of fake psychics and explain why these same four principles are also at work in the case of parallelomania.[54]

---

53. Samuel Sandmel, "Parallelomania," *Journal of Biblical Literature* 81 (1962): 1-13.

54. For an explanation of the tricks fake psychics use, including the principles discussed here, see Ray Hyman, *The Elusive Quarry: A Scientific Appraisal of Psychical Research* (Amherst, NY:

Remembering the hits and forgetting the misses. One of the reasons fake psychics succeed is because people will remember the things the psychic got right much more often than they will remember the things the psychic got wrong. If the psychic's statements are, say, 20% correct and 80% incorrect, and the subjects are asked afterwards to estimate how successful the psychic was, subjects will overestimate the psychic's percentage of accuracy. We see this same phenomenon with parallelomania as well. Scholars will note the parallels between two stories (for example, in the case of Romulus and Jesus, the fact that the body was not found), but not note the many things in the two stories that are not paralleled (for example, Romulus appears to a farmer, Jesus does not). By focusing only on the hits, the impression is conveyed that there are far fewer misses than there are.

The shotgun method. A fake psychic can improve their odds of getting a hit if they direct their statement to more than one subject. For example, suppose a psychic is doing a reading for one person, and says "your father's name is James." Approximately 3% of the male population is named James,[55] thus there is a 3% chance (odds of approximately 33:1) the psychic will be right just by chance. But now suppose the psychic directs this statement to a group of 33 people. The odds become almost certain that someone in that group has a father whose name is James. This phenomenon also occurs with parallelomania, for scholars often draw from a very large pool when trying to find parallels. In the case, for example, of Jesus' burial, a scholar will probably not look at only one burial story and try to find a parallel. He will search the dozens of burials stories in Jewish and/or pagan literature in an attempt to find a parallel. By doing this, the scholar greatly increases his odds of getting an impressive looking hit just by chance, just as the psychic does when he directs his statement to 33 people instead of 1 person.

Interpreting the hits as more specific than they are. People who visit psychics often misremember a vague statement by a psychic as being more specific, and thus a more impressive hit, than it actually was. For example, "your son was sick recently" may be remembered as "your son had a cold last week," or "you have had marital problems" may be remembered as "you have gotten divorced." This same phenomenon occurs with Biblical scholars when parallels are thought to be more specific than they actually are. For example, many parallels to Jesus' resurrection are cited which are not actually cases of resurrection, but which are cases of revivifications, ascensions, or appearances of a disembodied spirit. When scholars fail to note that these are not actually

---

Prometheus, 1989), 399-441; Lynne Kelly, *The Skeptic's Guide to the Paranormal* (New York: 1st Thunder's Mouth Press, 2005), 34-48. But even more impressive than reading about such tricks, is seeing them in action. To see such videos search YouTube for "cold reading."

55. For a list of what percentage of the population has which names see http://names.mongabay.com/male_names.htm.

resurrections, the parallels between these phenomena and Jesus' resurrection seem more specific and thus more impressive than they actually are.[56]

Thinking things which apply to everyone only apply to a select few. Suppose I told you I know that unlike most people, you do not have mostly good thoughts in your dreams—your dreams are filled with a lot of negative imagery. This might shock you. But the trick here is that it is not in fact the case that most people have mostly good thoughts. Most people do have mostly bad thoughts in their dreams.[57] But most people do not know that. Psychics exploit this fact that people often think things which apply to many people only apply to themselves. The same phenomenon occurs when Biblical scholars cite parallels between two stories though the parallels are present in many stories, not just those two. For example, Michael Goulder cites the fact that a stone was sealed as a parallel between Matthew's resurrection narrative and Daniel 6:17.[58] But many tombs in many stories were sealed, not just Jesus' tomb and the tomb in Daniel. If sealed tombs were found only in these two stories, that would suggest one borrowed the idea from the other, but since sealed tombs show up in many stories, the parallel is not very impressive.

Hence the same principles that lead to the success of fake psychics certainly seem to be at work in the case of parallelomania.

Finally, in regard to the Emmaus story, it should be noted that there are, in fact, many real life accounts of hidden angel appearances. Whether these accounts describe real angels or whether the witnesses just mistook a real person for an angel is disputed, but many people today have experienced events in which they encountered what they believed was a disguised angel. Hence, since the phenomenon occurs today, it would not be surprising if it occurred in the ancient world as well, and thus the similarity of the Emmaus story to stories of hidden angels does not necessarily mean the Emmaus story is similar to legendary stories, for many of those stories may be based on actual events.[59]

Eyewitness Testimony

I argued in the last chapter that the resurrection accounts were passed down accurately. However, to pass an account down accurately is only to accurately reproduce

---

56. On the spuriousness of the alleged parallels to Jesus' resurrection, see Glenn Miller, "Good Question: Was Jesus Christ Just a Copycat Savior Myth?" http://christianthinktank.com/copycatwho1.html.

57. Katja Valli et al., "Dreams Are More Negative Than Real Life: Implications for the Function of Dreaming," *Cognition and Emotion* 22 (2008): 833–61.

58. Michael Goulder, "The Empty Tomb," *Theology* 79 (1976): 206–14.

59. For contemporary accounts of hidden angels, see Rense Lange and James Houran, "Role of Contextual Mediation in Direct Versus Reconstructed Angelic Encounters," *Perceptual and Motor Skills* 83 (1996): 1259–70; Emma Heathcote-James, *Seeing Angels: True Contemporary Accounts of Hundreds of Angelic Experiences* (London: John Blake, 2002).

an account, and if the original account was not itself accurate, then the final product will not be accurate even if there were no errors in transmission. The skeptic is sure to appeal to the alleged inaccuracy of eyewitness testimony as a reason why the accounts may not have been accurate in the first place. (This question of the accuracy of eyewitness testimony is an issue which has in fact recently made its way into the field of Biblical studies.)[60]

As I mentioned in the chapter on apparitions, over the course of the last forty years or so, a substantial amount of literature within the field of psychology has been devoted to examining the accuracy of eyewitness testimony, and when one comes across an overview of this literature it is easy to get the impression that eyewitness testimony is not very accurate. I will begin by presenting the sort of overview of this research one often encounters when reading a psychology source.[61] But then I will explain why this overview can easily give the wrong impression.

We are told that modern psychology has discovered a number of factors which negatively affect the accuracy of eyewitness testimony. Some of the chief factors in question are the following.

Length of exposure: The accuracy of eyewitness testimony is affected by how long the witness was exposed to the stimulus. For example, in one study, subjects viewed four slides, each showing a different position of the same human face. Some subjects looked at the slides for 10 seconds, while others looked at them for 32 seconds. Afterwards, the subjects were shown 150 slides with various human faces and were asked to indicate which of these slides had been the target. 58% of those who had viewed the face for 32 seconds correctly identified the face, whereas only 47% of the subjects who viewed the face for 10 seconds correctly identified it.[62]

Weapon focus: The presence of one particularly captivating stimulus can capture the witness's focus to such an extent that it negatively affects his recollection of other aspects of the event. For example, if a person is threatened with a weapon, they may

---

60. See Bauckham, *Eyewitnesses*, 319-57; Eddy and Boyd, *Jesus Legend*, 275-85; Judith Redman, "How Accurate are the Eyewitnesses? Bauckham and the Eyewitnesses in the Light of Psychological Research," *Journal of Biblical Literature* 129 (2010): 177-97; Dale C. Allison Jr., *Constructing Jesus: Memory, Imagination, and History* (Grand Rapids, MI: Baker Academic, 2010), 1-30. Bauckham and Eddy and Boyd come away with a more optimistic view of the accuracy of eyewitness testimony than does Redman or Allison. Bauckham and Eddy and Boyd make a number of minor points regarding the accuracy of eyewitness testimony which could be added to the points I make here. They mention the most significant point, that the major elements of an event are not likely to be forgotten, but I think that I emphasize the importance of this point more. Redman and Allison note a number of factors which can cause eyewitness testimony to be inaccurate, just as I do here, but what I say in response to the factors discussed here applies to the other factors they cite as well.

61. For such overviews, see e.g., Elizabeth Loftus, *Eyewitness Testimony* (Cambridge, MA: Harvard University Press, 1996 [1979]); David G. Myers, *Social Psychology* (8th ed.; New York: McGraw-Hill, 2005), 605-18; Laura Engelhardt, "The Problem with Eyewitness Testimony: A Talk by Barbara Tversky, Professor of Psychology and George Fisher, Professor of Law," *Stanford Journal of Legal Studies*, http://agora.stanford.edu/sjls/Issue%20One/problem.htm.

62. Loftus, *Eyewitness Testimony*, 23.

focus so much on the weapon that their recollection of other details is not very accurate. In one experiment, one group of subjects overheard a conversation between two people, after which one of the two people entered the room the subject was in with a pen in his hand and then left. The other group of subjects overheard an angrier conversation between the two people, after which one of the two entered the room the subject was in with a bloodied letter opener. The subjects were later asked to identify the culprit out of a series of 50 photographs. 49% of those in the non-weapon group correctly identified the subject, whereas only 33% in the weapon group did.[63]

The misinformation effect: Information presented to the witness in between the time of the event and the time of the recall of the event can distort the witness's recollection of the event. In one experiment, 8 demonstrators entered a professor's classroom and disrupted the class. Later, the subjects were given a questionnaire, and one of the questions gave the subjects false information about how many demonstrators there were. For one group of subjects, the question referred to 12 demonstrators, whereas for the other group of subjects, the question referred to 4 demonstrators. One week later, the subjects were presented with a new set of questions, and one of the questions asked them how many demonstrators there had been. The test was to see whether the subjects would recall the actual number of demonstrators (8), or whether they would be thrown off by the questionnaire, which had referred to either 4 or 12 demonstrators. The group that had been told there were 4 demonstrators guessed on average that there were 6.4 demonstrators, whereas the group that was told there were 12 demonstrators guessed on average that there were 8.9 demonstrators.[64]

Cross race identification: Witnesses are more likely to accurately recall a person who is of the same race as them. In one experiment, there were two groups of subjects, one group white and the other black. Each subject saw photographs of 10 black and 10 white faces, and they were later asked to pick the faces they had seen out of a group of 40 black and 40 white faces. On the whole, the whites were more accurate at identifying white faces, and the blacks were more accurate at identifying black faces. For example, at one of the universities where the study was conducted, the exact result was that blacks correctly identified 7.4 black faces, and 6.8 white faces, whereas whites correctly identified 6.1 black faces and 7.9 white faces.[65]

Other factors which have been argued to influence the accuracy of eyewitness testimony include stress, length of time in between the time of the event and the time of recall, and the confidence of the witness.

---

63. Loftus, *Eyewitness Testimony*, 35.
64. Loftus, *Eyewitness Testimony*, 56-7.
65. Loftus, *Eyewitness Testimony*, 137.

OBJECTIONS

The Problems with this Line of Research

Though this research seems at first to cast considerable doubt on the reliability of eyewitness testimony, once it is examined more closely, it becomes clear that it does not do so.

1. The first point to note—and it is the most essential—is that even if things are exactly as they seem to be in the above summary (and, as I will explain, things are not quite as they seem), this research has only shown that witnesses are more prone than we thought to making minor mistakes. All of the types of mistakes enumerated above are concerned not with major facets of the event, but with minor details. For example, consider the misinformation effect. In the experiment I described, the subjects misremembered anywhere from 4 to 12 people being present when in fact the true number was 8. But the subjects did not remember 1 person instead of 8, or 100 people instead of 8. The mistake in judgment was of a minor kind. And consider an example we saw in the apparition chapter. Two groups of subjects watched a video of a car accident and were later asked to estimate how fast the cars were going at the time of the collision. However, the wording of the question was different for each group: one version of the question asked about the cars hitting each other, while the other version asked about the cars "smashing" each other. The group that was asked about the cars "smashing" each other estimated a higher rate of speed than the other group and was more likely to report that the crash involved broken glass. But again, these are minor errors. No witness stated for example, that there had not been any cars at all, or that the cars had been flying through the air, or that the cars were driven by green monsters.

I should say that there is one exception to this rule that a witness will not misremember major facets of the event. There are cases in which a witness has misremembered an entire event; they have come to think a whole event happened which actually did not. We have seen this happen in real life with alleged cases of alien abductions and of childhood sexual abuse, where a person comes to "remember" having experienced these events, long after they allegedly occurred; and researchers have also performed experiments in which they have induced false memories in the subjects.[66] But these

---

66. On the phenomenon of false memories, see Elizabeth F. Loftus and Katherine Ketcham, *The Myth of Repressed Memory: False Memories and Allegations of Sexual Abuse* (New York: St. Martin's, 1994); D.S. Lindsay and J.D. Read, "Psychotherapy and Memories of Childhood Sexual Abuse: A Cognitive Perspective," *Applied Cognitive Psychology* 8 (1994): 281-338; Susan A. Clancy et al., "Memory Distortion in People Reporting Abduction by Aliens," *Journal of Abnormal Psychology* 111 (2002): 455-61.

Another exception is fantasizing. Fantasizers sometimes confuse their fantasies with reality (see Jon G. Allen, *Coping With Trauma: Hope Through Understanding* (2nd ed.; Washington, DC: American Psychiatric Publishing, 2005), 199). However, fantasizing is highly unlikely to be a good explanation for any case involving at least two people (as is clearly the case for the resurrection appearances) because it is not very likely two people would have the same fantasy and mix up the same fantasy. Also, even in cases involving only one person, highly unusual events are highly unlikely to be misremembered, and so are events of considerable personal significance to the person. The resurrection appearances were both highly unusual and highly significant to the disciples.

examples of false memories will not help the skeptic explain either the resurrection appearances or accounts of apparitions. For in these instances of false memory, what has been required in order for the person to come to believe that some event which they do not recall had indeed happened long ago, is some plausible reason for why the event had been forgotten. In the case of alien abductions, we have encountered the reason that aliens gave the subjects amnesia. In regard to Satanic ritual abuse, or even child abuse generally, the reason proposed is that the events were repressed because they were so traumatic. In experimental research, researchers have succeeded in showing that subjects can come to believe they have forgotten memories from their childhood (the plausible reason here is that people know they forget many things from their childhood), that they can come to believe they have forgotten something if the researchers falsely tell them that some test has been done indicating they have likely forgotten it (the plausible reason here is that the subject is under the impression that the test is real and he has confidence in the researchers' authority), and that they can come to believe they have forgotten an event which is similar to actual events they have experienced (for example, a conversation which is similar to conversations they have actually had. The reason why it is plausible they may have forgotten this is that if the event is similar to actual events it is not something which stands out and is therefore not something a person would have a difficult time forgetting.). Thus in order to propose that the witnesses of the resurrection appearances or of apparitions misremembered the entire event, we would have to explain what sort of reason the witnesses came up with which convinced them it was plausible they had forgotten the event. But not only does no such reason come to mind, there are facts in each case which make it highly unlikely there could have been any such reason. In the case of the resurrection appearances, there were over 500 witnesses (1 Cor 15:6), but research has found that it is difficult to induce false memories in subjects. One study found that only about 20% of subjects came to accept a false memory even of a seemingly ordinary, plausible event.[67] If the 500 witnesses represent a 20% success rate, we would have to suppose that the disciples went about trying to convince 2500 people they had seen Jesus and forgotten about it. And quite apart from that particular appearance, the number of witnesses to the resurrection appearances rules out the possibility that the witnesses all misremembered: For there is no case on record in which dozens of people all came to misremember the same event. And as for apparition accounts, we have the witness's testimony, and in no case does the witness ever tell us they had originally forgotten the event and only later come to remember it. If this is what actually happened, it would be incredible that no witness should ever mention it, for those who have come to remember alien abductions and other spectacular phenomena have been quite explicit in their testimony about the fact that the memory had been forgotten.

---

67. Kathy Pezdek et al., "Planting False Childhood Memories: The Role of Event Plausibility," *Psychological Science* 8 (1997): 437-41.

(A point which should be born in mind in a discussion of false memory is that there is a distinction between someone coming to believe that they have experienced an event and coming to actually remember an event. A person could come to believe they have been abducted by aliens without actually having a memory of this occurring (analogously, I believe I was born, but I do not have a memory of this event). The literature on false memories furnishes us with examples of both sorts of misremembering, but in citing any particular case, it should be kept in mind which sort of case is being cited.)

Thus this research gives us no reason to think the resurrection narratives err on major details such as that the tomb was empty, that the disciples saw Jesus, whether the appearance was to a group or an individual, or the general gist of the words spoken by Jesus. Errors could conceivably be present in regard to minor details, such as Jesus' exact words, exactly which women went to the tomb, or what time of the morning the empty tomb was discovered. But even in the case of minor details, though the studies have shown that mistakes can be made, this is something we already knew from common sense prior to the studies. And there are, to my knowledge, no studies which have attempted to determine what percentage of the time witnesses are mistaken on minor details. Therefore, this research gives us no reason to question the common sense observation that a reliable witness will be right much more often than they will be wrong. And so even in the case of a minor detail, we should assume a witness right until we have evidence to the contrary. Thus the studies really do not tell us anything we did not already know. They tell us that an apparently reliable witness is usually right, but sometimes they are wrong; and they tell us that witnesses are much more likely to be wrong on a minor detail than a major detail.

(It is worth noting that while errors in minor details do not matter in regard to the historicity of the resurrection, or in regard to apparitions, they might matter in other cases.[68] Details which are minor in terms of their centrality to the event can be major in terms of significance. For example, suppose the culprit in some crime had a small, unusual scar on his hand. This is a minor detail if our goal is simply to reconstruct an essentially accurate narrative of the event (we can construct such a narrative with or without the knowledge that the culprit had such a scar), but that detail may prove major in an attempt to identify the culprit from a group of suspects who all look similar. But in regard to the resurrection narratives or apparitions, I do not see any instances in which we find ourselves in a position where a minor error makes a major difference.)

2. The second point is that the argument we made in chapter 4 in regard to secondhand testimony, the argument that the more significant the data is to the witness, the more likely they are to remember it, surely applies to firsthand testimony as well. We have all probably heard someone express this sentiment by saying something like, "I wouldn't forget a thing like that!" It would be difficult to imagine, for example, Peter

---

68. Richard Bauckham makes this point in *Jesus and the Eyewitnesses*, 356.

forgetting that Jesus had asked three times if he loved him, or the disciples forgetting that Jesus had commissioned them to preach the Gospel, or the disciples forgetting the promise of Jesus' return. On the other hand, it would not be surprising if the disciples, as well as witnesses to apparitions, forgot aspects of the event which were not of significance to them.

3. The third point to make is that the influence of these various factors (length of exposure, weapon focus, stress, and so on) is not very great. With regard to the experiment on length of exposure which we cited above, the difference between the two groups was only 58%- 47%. In the experiment on weapon focus, the difference was only 49%-33%. In the experiment on cross race identification, the number of accurate hits varied from 6.1-7.9. While experiments with these sorts of results do show that the factors in question have an influence on eyewitness testimony, the influence is so small that the experiments have little practical value. It does not do us much good in an actual court case, or an actual event of history, to know that the chances of a witness being wrong are 58% instead of 47%, or 49% instead of 33%. In either case, all we really know is that the witness might have made a mistake. It might come as a surprise to some that researchers would make so much of the influence of these factors if their influence is so small that the practical value is slight. But this mistake is, for whatever reason, common in scientific research. In the case of medical research, for example, one often hears that eating some food or doing some activity raises or lowers your odds of getting this or that disease. But what many people do not realize is that the factor often raises or lowers your odds so slightly, that most people would see no point in worrying about it at all. For example, most people have heard that taking aspirin reduces your risk of a heart attack, but in fact, the most thorough study on this subject found aspirin only lowers your risk of a heart attack from 1.7% to 0.9%.[69] Most would not consider this to be a significant difference.[70]

4. From the way I have spoken so far, it may seem as if the various factors in question always have an influence on the accuracy of eyewitness testimony, even though they have a minor influence on minor details. But the research actually indicates that many, if not all, of these factors do not even always have an influence; sometimes they do and sometimes they do not. For example, with regard to stress, a review of 21 studies found inconsistent results: 11 suggested memory was worse with higher arousal and 10 suggested memory was better. With regard to weapon focus, studies have found that when the person could observe the person with a weapon for a long time, there was little to no effect in regard to weapon focus. Similar problems have

---

69. See Jessica M. Utts, *Seeing Through Statistics* (2nd ed.; Pacific Grove, CA: Brooks, 1999), 196-97.

70. I use the term "significance" here in its ordinary sense (i.e., "practical significance"). I do not mean the technical sense the term possess in the sciences (i.e., "statistical significance"). On the fact that statistical significance does not necessarily equate to practical significance, see Roger E. Kirk, "Practical Significance: A Concept Whose Time Has Come," *Educational and Psychological Measurement* 56 (1996): 746-59.

been cited for many other factors.[71] Thus not only do these factors have a minor influence, but they do not even always have an influence.

So for these four reasons, the findings of modern psychology do not overthrow the common sense view that eyewitness testimony is generally reliable. (Per our definition of "generally reliable" in chapter 1, which is that major mistakes are very unlikely to be present, and that even though it is not exceedingly unlikely the witness will make mistakes on minor details, the number of minor details the witness got wrong will be largely outnumbered by the number of details the witness got right, so even on minor details the witness should be assumed right until there is evidence to the contrary.) We have seen that the research has only found that the factors in question raise the probability the witness may make minor mistakes, not the probability that he will make major ones. And we have seen that not only do the factors merely raise the odds of a minor mistake, but that they do not even raise the odds very much. And not only do they do nothing more than raise the odds slightly, they sometimes do not even raise the odds at all.

Thus I think this research does nothing to undermine the reliability of eyewitness testimony. It has only taught us what we already knew, namely that witnesses sometimes make minor errors. Since one may be under the impression that the more skeptical interpretation of this research is the one which is standard in psychology,[72] I should note that the experts themselves are divided over this question. Though some see the research as disproving our common sense view of eyewitness testimony, other psychologists agree with the sort of analysis I have given. Those in the latter category have argued that eyewitness experts should not be allowed to testify about the limitations of eyewitness testimony in court, since such testimony is more likely to prejudice the jurors than to enlighten them. Judges likewise have disagreed as to whether experts should testify about this in court, or whether the research adds nothing to the common knowledge of the jurors. Hence the experts are not agreed as to whether this research indicates that eyewitness testimony is any different from what we already thought it was.[73]

---

71. With regard to the points about stress and weapon focus, as well as all these other factors, see Ebbe Ebbesen and Vladimir J. Konecni, "Eyewitness Memory Research: Probative V. Prejudicial Value," *Expert Evidence* 5 (1996): 2-28. And see also Rogers Elliott, "Expert Testimony About Eyewitness Identification: A Critique," *Law and Human Behavior* 17 (1993): 423-37.

72. I think this is the impression one would get from the works of Allison and Redman referred to in n60.

73. See Ebbesen, "Eyewitness Memory"; Elliott, "Expert Testimony,"; Robin Preussel, "The Experts Aren't Reliable Either: Why Expert Testimony on the Reliability of Eyewitness Testimony is Unwarranted in Alabama State Courts," Yale Digital Commons, http://digitalcommons.law.yale.edu/.

7

Analyzing the Data with Bayes' Theorem

NOW THAT WE HAVE analyzed the New Testament to determine how much data we have, it is time to analyze that data using BT. To do so, we will proceed as follows. First, we will address the issue of initial probability and explain why it is both possible and prudent to analyze the resurrection hypothesis and the apparition hypothesis without reaching a judgment on the initial probability of those hypotheses. Then we will examine the specific evidence.

With regard to our examination of the specific evidence, I explained at the end of chapter 2 that the key to analyzing the apparition hypothesis vs. the resurrection hypothesis is to consider consequent probability—to look for data which is more probable given that the apparition hypothesis is true, and for data which is more probable given that the resurrection hypothesis is true. Thus the first thing we will do is examine the data which is alleged to be more probable given h (the resurrection hypothesis), but is actually not. (That is, these are the arguments which have been given on behalf of the resurrection hypothesis, but which are actually not good arguments.) Then, we will examine the data which actually is more probable given the resurrection hypothesis. (That is, these are the good arguments for the resurrection hypothesis.) And in presenting the arguments which are more probable given the resurrection hypothesis, I will divide the arguments up into arguments which come from the data of 1 Corinthians 15, arguments which come from the data we can get from the Gospels if their general reliability is not accepted, and arguments which come from the data we can get from the Gospels if their general reliability is accepted. Thus the reader will be able to see how the probability of the hypotheses change depending on how much data we have to work with. Then, after examining the data which is more probable given the resurrection hypothesis, we will examine the data which could be argued to be more probable given the apparition hypothesis. But we will conclude that there is actually no data which is more probable given the apparition hypothesis. (That is, these are the arguments in favor of the apparition hypothesis, but we are going to conclude that none of these arguments is persuasive.)

But before we begin, I must first say something in regard to how I am going to phrase arguments which have previously appeared in the literature, and I must also remind the reader of three points concerning BT, since these points will be important to keep in mind as we proceed.

With regard to how previous arguments will be phrased, we have said that though many arguments have been given both for and against the apparition hypothesis, the arguments have not been phrased in terms of consequent probability; they have most often been phrased by simply noting that a similarity or a difference is present. But any argument can be phrased in terms of consequent probability, because consequent probability is part of BT, and since we have shown BT underlies all logical thought, that means we use consequent probability subconsciously any time we evaluate a hypothesis. Thus what I am going to do, in addition to phrasing the arguments which are original to me in terms of consequent probability, is rephrase any argument which has already appeared in the literature in terms of consequent probability. Thus readers should know that in the case of any argument for which I cite a source below, I am not phrasing the argument in the manner in which the author phrased it, but rephrasing it as it must be phrased if the argument is to be evaluated in terms of consequent probability. Readers who want to see how the author themself phrased the argument can consult the source cited.

1. Concerning BT, the first point to keep in mind is that the disparity between the probability of a datum given h and the probability of that datum given ~h is more important than the actual values of the probability of the datum given h and the probability of the datum given ~h. And thus for a datum to support h, the datum does not need to be probable given h; it can support h (in fact, it can even support h a lot) if it is improbable given h, so long as it is even more improbable given ~h.

For example, suppose the odds of getting the datum given h are 100:1, and the odds of getting the datum given ~h are 1000:1. The datum still supports h by odds of 10:1. So even though it is improbable we would find the datum in the first place if h is true, once we do find it, the datum makes h very probable. We encounter this situation in real life quite frequently. For example, suppose the odds of passing out given that you have malaria are 100:1, but the odds of passing out given that you have the flu are 1000:1. If you pass out, this means it is 10 times more likely you have malaria, and thus the datum supports the malaria hypothesis by odds of 10:1 even though the datum is improbable given that hypothesis. (Of course there are many other reasons why you might pass out besides having malaria or the flu. But suppose that based on your other symptoms, the doctor has narrowed down the possible diagnoses to flu or malaria.) Or suppose Bob is accused of committing murder and we find his fingerprints on the murder weapon. Now given that h is true (given that Bob committed the murder) we must admit that it is in fact improbable we would find Bob's fingerprints on the murder weapon. For if we look at all of the cases of murder ever committed, we will find that in only a fairly small minority of cases are the murderer's fingerprints on the murder weapon. In most cases, the murderer is not so clumsy; he wears gloves, or in some other way avoids leaving his fingerprints. Suppose we find a representative sample of murders to examine and we find that the murderer left his fingerprints on the murder weapon in only 10% of cases. If that is so, the probability of Bob's fingerprints being on the murder weapon given that he committed the murder is 10:1 against. However, we are certainly inclined to say that Bob's fingerprints being on the murder weapon supports h. And this is because though the odds of Bob's fingerprints being on the murder weapon given that he committed murder are low, the odds his fingerprints would be on the murder weapon given that he did not commit murder (~h) are immensely lower. For to determine the probability Bob's fingerprints would be on the murder weapon given that he did not commit murder, we must go through our cases of murder and determine what percentage of the time the murderer's fingerprints were on the murder weapon even though he did not actually commit the murder. Suppose we find that this happens in only 0.001% (1000:1) of cases. If that is so, then though the odds of Bob's fingerprints being on the murder weapon given that he committed the murder are low (10:1), the odds of his fingerprints being on the murder weapon given that he did not commit the murder are immensely lower (1000:1), and thus the datum favors h by odds of 100:1. (I should note that in this analogy we are assuming we have a case in which Bob has presented us with an implausible reason as to why his fingerprints were on the gun. For example, suppose he claims he was framed, or claims he just happened to be dusting the gun on the day of the murder even though he never did so before and had no reason to do so. If Bob can actually present us with a good reason as to why his fingerprints were on the gun (for example, if he can prove the owner of the gun expected Bob to dust the gun every day, say because Bob was his butler) then Bob's fingerprints being on the gun will not be less probable given ~h and thus the datum will not support h.)

Now one may wish to object that in situations such as these it is deceptive to say the datum is not probable given h, for our common sense tells us that it seems strange to say a datum which raises the probability of a hypothesis is improbable given that hypothesis. This brings us to the distinction between absolute probability and relative probability. A datum may have a low *absolute probability* given h, but a high *relative probability* given h. While the absolute probability of passing out given that you have malaria is low (100:1), its relative probability is high; that is, relative to the hypothesis you have the flu, the probability of the datum given the malaria hypothesis is indeed high. For given the flu hypothesis, the probability is only 1000:1, and 100:1 is probable relative to 1000:1. Thus in the scenarios above, we could say that the probability of getting the datum given h is high, if we mean its probability relative to some alternative hypothesis. But if we say this without first indicating what we think the absolute probability of getting the datum given h is, and what we think the absolute probability of getting the datum given ~h is, we will have skipped a step in our thinking, for we cannot determine relative probability without first determining absolute probability. (I cannot determine that 100:1 is high relative to 1000:1, unless I first know that the odds are 100:1 and 1000:1.) Thus to avoid skipping an important step, when I use the term "probable" below, I will mean absolute probability, unless the context makes it clear that I mean relative probability. This has the disadvantage of requiring the reader to do more thinking as he considers each argument (for when we hear a datum has a low probability given h, our natural inclination is to conclude it does not support h, and we must stop and pause to overcome this natural inclination), but it has the advantage of helping the reader to understand BT more deeply.

Before we proceed, it would perhaps be a good idea to give an example of a datum which has a low absolute probability given the resurrection hypothesis, but which still supports the resurrection hypothesis. Consider the fact that the resurrected Jesus ate fish. Now this is something which has a low or at least no more than neutral probability given h. For if we heard that someone was resurrected and we had to bet in advance on whether they had eaten fish, we would not lay high odds, for though this is the sort of thing a resurrected person *may* do, it is not something we can confidently say a resurrected person would be very likely to do. This is in contrast to a datum such as Jesus' empty burial place. For if we heard a person was resurrected, we would lay very high odds that his burial place is empty, for a resurrected person must necessarily leave behind an empty burial place. But as for eating fish, though we would not lay high odds that a resurrected person would eat fish, we would lay immensely lower odds that an apparition would eat fish (for though a resurrected person does not seem especially likely to eat fish, an apparition seems much more unlikely to do so, since a non-physical being ought not to be able to eat fish at all). Hence, if Jesus ate fish this would support h very much despite the datum having a low absolute probability given h.

(Now that this distinction between absolute and relative probability is understood, I must say something more concerning to how arguments which have previously appeared in the literature will be phrased. As I said, I must rephrase the arguments in terms of BT, but since a datum does not necessarily have to be probable (in terms of absolute probability) given a hypothesis to support a hypothesis, it is often not clear whether an author would think the datum he cites probable given h, or whether he would simply think it improbable given h but more improbable given ~h. Thus in a case where it appears unclear to me whether the author would think the datum probable given h, I will phrase the argument in both possible ways, phrasing the argument as it would be phrased if the datum is probable given h, and phrasing it as it would be phrased if the datum is improbable given h but more improbable given ~h.)

2. The second point to keep in mind regarding BT is that the exact numbers I use are not essential. The reader does not have to agree with the exact numbers I assign in order to agree that a given datum supports h or does not support h to the approximate extent I argue it does. In order to agree that the datum strengthens the hypothesis or weakens the hypothesis to the extent that I argue it does, the reader only needs to agree with me on the qualitative terms which the numbers may reasonably be thought to correspond to. For example, if the reader does not agree that the probability of a

datum given h is 10:1 against, but agrees the probability is low, or does not agree that the probability is 100:1 against but agrees the probability is very low (or does not agree that the probability is 10:1 in favor but agrees it is high, or does not agree the probability is 100:1 in favor but agrees it is very high), then he will agree that the datum has the approximate evidential force which I argue it does. And if he agrees the data have the approximate evidential force which I argue they do, he will agree with my conclusions.

3. The third point concerns dependence. We will be considering various data, and as we said in chapter 2, the probability of a datum can be dependent on the presence of another datum. For example, if Bob commits murder once a month, the probability he will commit murder on any given day is 30:1, and if Joe commits murder once a month, the probability he will commit murder on any given day is also 30:1. Thus the odds Bob and Joe will both commit murder on a given day are 30:1 x 30:1 = 900:1. But that calculation assumes the data are independent. Suppose they are not. Suppose 50% of the time Joe commits a murder, Bob also commits murder. In that case, the probability they will both commit murder on the same day is 1/30 (Joe's odds of committing murder) x 1/2 (Bob's odds of committing murder if we have already established Joe committed murder) = 1/60.

Thus a Bayesian analysis of any set of data must be aware of the possibility of dependence, and so the question becomes how we can tell whether two factors are dependent. The answer is that the only prudent method is to assume that any two factors are independent, until we have evidence to the contrary. For our experience of the world is that the vast majority of factors are independent of each other, and thus in the case of any two factors, the initial probability they are independent is very high and so we assume they are independent until we get evidence to the contrary. For example, if I was asked to determine the odds that a bomb will go off in Paris tomorrow and the odds that my house will burn down tomorrow, I would assume the factors are independent and determine the odds they would both happen by determining independently the odds that a bomb will go off in Paris and the odds my house will burn down, for the factors certainly appear unrelated to each other, and thus I assume that they are. Now if I get evidence that they are related (for example, if I find out that a person in Paris has conspired to have someone start a fire in my yard on the same day he sets off a bomb in Paris), I will realize the factors are dependent and change my calculations accordingly. But barring any evidence to the contrary, the default position is that the factors are independent of each other. And this will be the methodology we will use below. We will assume any two factors are independent unless there is evidence to the contrary, but we will take into account any evidence which does appear to be to the contrary.

I have just explained how we will analyze the resurrection hypothesis in relation to the apparition hypothesis. But we also need to consider the objective vision theory and combination apparition/objective vision theory. I have said that we can analyze these briefly, and that is what we will do after we have analyzed the apparition hypothesis. In the case of the other two hypotheses, the key aspect of BT will not be consequent probability, but initial probability.

Throughout this chapter, h means the resurrection hypothesis, and ~h means the apparition hypothesis (until the end of the chapter when ~h comes to mean the objective vision theory or apparition/objective vision theory). ~H does not include all of the other non-resurrection hypotheses (the hallucination hypothesis, stolen body hypothesis, etc), because we are only considering the resurrection hypothesis and the apparition hypothesis.

Initial Probability

We have said that initial probability plays a crucial role in determining the probability that a hypothesis is true—the lower the initial probability, the more strongly the specific evidence must support the hypothesis, and the higher the initial probability, the less strongly the specific evidence needs to support the hypothesis. And since the epistemic probability of a hypothesis cannot be determined without knowing the initial probability, it is always necessary to evaluate the initial probability in order to determine the epistemic probability that a hypothesis is true. As for how we determine the initial probability, the initial probability is derived from a consideration of all of the other data other than the specific data which we are currently concerned with (the data which we are currently concerned with is the New Testament data). The arguments in chapter 3 should serve to show that the probability some apparitions are real is not very low, and thus the probability which we should assign, in advance of our examination of the specific evidence (the New Testament data), to the hypothesis that the post-mortem appearances of a given person were real apparitions should not be especially low. This means the initial probability Jesus' appearances were appearances of an apparition is significantly higher than the initial probability they were appearances of a resurrected person *if* the resurrection is as initially improbable as skeptics generally think it is. What I mean is, when skeptics speak of the resurrection of Jesus as being in the same category as, for example, alien abductions or the existence of Atlantis, they are saying that the resurrection is an event which has an extraordinarily low initial probability (because skeptics think there is virtually no evidence for alien abductions or Atlantis). Now if you have been at all persuaded by the case for apparitions I presented in chapter 3, you will agree that the initial probability of the apparition hypothesis is not extraordinarily low, and thus if the initial probability of the resurrection really is on a par with alien abductions or Atlantis, the initial probability is very much in favor of the apparition hypothesis. (Presuming, of course, that alien abductions and the existence of Atlantis do have an extraordinarily low initial probability. Some may wish to dispute that.)

Now one's initial inclination is probably to accept the skeptic's view that the initial probability of the resurrection is extraordinarily low. After all, if I told you my friend Bob rose from the dead, you would regard this claim as having an extremely low initial probability. However, it can be countered that not all claims of raisings of the dead necessarily have the same initial probability. Just because claims of raisings of the dead do generally have a very low initial probability, that does not mean all such claims do; the claim my friend rose from the dead may not have the same initial probability as the claim Jesus rose from the dead. As an analogy, the claim that a certain person committed a murder generally has a very low initial probability, but not always. In the case of my friend Bob, for example, there is no reason to think he would go around killing people, and so the initial probability he murdered anyone is very low. But in other cases, the initial probability someone committed murder is not very low. For example, suppose we know that Joe is a gangster and he has murdered quite a lot of people. In that case, the initial probability Joe committed a murder is not especially low. Thus it can be argued that though claims of resurrections do generally have a very low initial probability, the claim Jesus rose from the dead does not have a very low initial probability.

How would one argue for a high (or simply not exceedingly low) initial probability for Jesus' resurrection? One would have to argue that there is reason to think the initial probability of the resurrection is not especially low. In the case of the resurrection, the evidence relevant to establishing the prior probability would be all of the evidence for or against the truth of Christianity, since the resurrection is tied to the Christian belief system and its probability is affected by the probability of all of the other beliefs which constitute that system. If we think the evidence is strong that God exists, that Messianic prophecy is true, that the other miracles Jesus performed are real, that miracles happen today, and so on; and if we are unpersuaded by the arguments against Christianity, such as the problem of evil, divine hiddenness, the incoherence of the Incarnation, and so on, we will require less evidence to be convinced of the reality of the resurrection than we would if we regarded all of the other arguments in favor of Christianity as weak and all the arguments against it as strong.

Hence most previous Bayesian analyses of the resurrection have involved a discussion of the initial probability of the resurrection, and we reviewed these in chapter 2. Richard Swinburne, for example, argues that even without the New Testament, we can deduce from reason alone that it is likely God would want to become incarnate in order to atone for sins, to identify with our suffering, and to provide us with an example of how to live a good life; and that if God became incarnate, we should expect him to lead a perfect moral life, to tell us he is God incarnate, and to perform an astounding miracle such as a resurrection.[1] Since these reasons give us cause to expect that God will become incarnate, lead the sort of life Jesus is supposed to have led, and rise from the dead, when we come across the New Testament's alleged account of these events, we should not think the initial probability of the story it tells us is extremely

---

1. Richard Swinburne, *The Resurrection of God Incarnate* (Oxford: Oxford University Press, 2003).

low. The recourse by skeptics is of course to argue against whatever arguments seem to raise the initial probability of the resurrection, and to produce arguments which make the initial probability of the resurrection low (for example, by arguing that there is a low probability God exists).

However, though the initial probability is essential to determining the epistemic probability of a hypothesis, it is in fact possible to use BT to analyze a hypothesis without addressing the question of initial probability. This of course means that we will have to end the analysis without arriving at an epistemic probability. But though it may sound counterintuitive, there is actually nothing the matter with doing this. The odds form of BT allows us to clearly separate the initial probability from the specific evidence. (Although the initial probability and specific evidence are just as conceptually distinct from each other with any other form of BT, it is more difficult to observe their distinctness if we use another form.) For example, if we use the odds form of BT:

$$\frac{p(h|e)}{p(\sim h|e)} = \frac{p(h)}{p(\sim h)} \times \frac{p(e|h)}{p(e|\sim h)}$$

And we have:

$$\frac{500}{1} = \frac{10}{1} \times \frac{50}{1}$$

We can see the initial probability is 10:1 in favor of h, and the specific evidence is 50:1 in favor of h, and our final result is 500:1 in favor of h. But the initial probability and the specific evidence are clearly distinct, and we can tell which is which. It is because they are kept distinct that it is possible to discuss only the specific evidence and still arrive at an intelligible conclusion. For example, suppose there are three pieces of specific evidence for the resurrection: one has odds of 2:1 in favor of h, one has odds of 5:1 in favor of h, and one also has odds of 5:1 in favor of h. Multiplying these together (2:1 x 5:1 x 5:1), I arrive at odds of 50:1 in favor of h. I can place these numbers into the odds form of BT and simply leave the initial probability and epistemic probability blank:

$$\frac{?}{?} = \frac{?}{?} \times \frac{50}{1}$$

If I leave the equation like this, I cannot determine an epistemic probability, but I have given the reader all the information he needs in order to determine one for himself. If for example, you think the initial probability is 10:1 in favor of the resurrection, you now have 10:1 as the first number, thus: 500:1 = 10:1 x 2:1 x 5:1 x 5:1. If you think the initial probability is 10:1 against, you now have 5:1 = 1:10 x 2:1 x 5:1 x 5:1. Since in the case of the resurrection, the knowledge relevant to establishing the prior is so vast, I find it preferable to do the Bayesian analysis in this manner, and leave it to the reader to fill in an initial probability for themself and hence determine his own epistemic probability. (When likelihood ratios are presented by themselves rather than being presented along with an initial probability, they are called Bayes' factors. For example, in the example I just gave, 2:1, 5:1, and 5:1 are all Bayes' factors, and they result in a final Bayes' factor of 50:1.)

But though we will do our analysis in this way in the case of the apparition theory, for reasons I will explain, we will not be able to do it this way in the case of the objective vision theory or the objective vision/apparition theory. In evaluating those hypotheses, we will have to address the initial probability. But for reasons that I will also explain, it is much simpler to address the initial probability in those cases. (And there is also one particular version of the apparition theory itself which will require us to invoke initial probability. But in that case as well, the issue of initial probability can be addressed very simply.)

The Concept of Physical Resurrection

Although I do wish to omit the prior probability in this analysis, I said in chapter 2 that there are no absolute boundaries between the specific evidence and the evidence relevant to establishing the prior, but that these boundaries are only prudential ones. And I think it would be prudent to consider as specific evidence one piece of evidence which seems to be on the borderline between the specific evidence and the evidence relevant to establishing the prior. Several proponents of the apparition theory have presented objections to the concept of physical resurrection.[2] If the concept of physical resurrection is incoherent, then clearly Jesus could not have risen from the dead. So let us consider three objections to the rationality of the concept of physical resurrection.[3]

The first two objections are so closely related to each other that we may consider them two halves of one objection. The first is that the idea God will raise the same bodies we had when we died does not make sense because the atoms which comprise our bodies are constantly changing; the atoms which constitute your body now are completely different from the atoms which constituted your body seven years ago (or ten years ago, or however much time it takes to replace all our atoms).[4] If God resur-

---

2. E.g., Michael C. Perry, *The Easter Enigma: An Essay on the Resurrection with Special Reference to the Data of Psychical Research* (London: Faber & Faber, 1959), 103-19; Paul Badham, *Christian Beliefs About Life After Death* (New York: Barnes and Noble, 1976), 47-64; Dale C. Allison Jr., *Resurrecting Jesus: The Earliest Christian Tradition and its Interpreters* (New York: T&T Clark, 2005), 219-28.

3. For a general defense of the concept of physical resurrection, see Stephen T. Davis, *Risen Indeed* (London: SPCK, 1993), 43-61.

4. E.g., "As the body of the aged man is the same as that which he had in his infancy, while all its particles have been repeatedly changed, so with the resurrection body" (Conrad Emil Lindberg, and Conrad Emanuel Hoffsten, *Christian Dogmatics and Notes on the History of Dogma* (Rock Island, IL: Augusta Book Concern, 1922), 551). "As we now know, we change our entire physical kit, every atom and molecule, over a period of seven years or so. I am physically a totally different person now from

rects our bodies, which atoms will he raise? The second is the idea that even if God did want to resurrect the atoms which constituted our bodies at the time we died, such a resurrection would be impossible because atoms are interchangeable: The atoms which make up my body when I die will eventually leave my body and become a part of other people's bodies.[5] Thus an attempt to resurrect our bodies faces the problem that the same atoms would have to be resurrected into different bodies, but this is of course impossible.

These two ideas are, as the quotations in n4 and n5 show, ideas which have been repeated again and again without any actual documentation, their truth being taken for granted. But sometimes the things you think you know just ain't so. For as a matter of fact, these ideas are false. Concerning the first idea, the current consensus of the scientific community[6] is that there are two areas of the body where our atoms remain the same from birth until death: the enamel of the teeth and the lens of the eye (some of the atoms in the lens of the eye are replaced, but not very many). Thus, unless you lose your teeth and eyes, you never lose all of your atoms. However, this does not fully answer the objection, for we do want to be raised with more than just some of our teeth and some of our eyes. But the following fact provides an answer. Although our atoms are constantly changing while we are alive, this process stops at death, and thus the atoms which comprise our body when we die remain a part of our body until the

---

the person I was ten years ago. And yet I am still me. Thus it really doesn't matter whether we get the identical molecules back or not, though some continuity is perfectly possible" (N.T. Wright, *Surprised by Hope: Rethinking Heaven, the Resurrection, and the Mission of the Church* (New York: HarperOne, 2008), 157). "We constantly replace out atoms over time and there is no reason to think that an eighty year old person has even a single atom in common with the newborn babe" (Frank B. Dilley, "Resurrection and the Replica Objection," *Religious Studies* 19 (1983): 459-74 (462)).

5. E.g., "Reason and Revelation reject the idea of the resurrection of the material body. The exact particles, the same ultimate atoms of matter have been in many different human bodies at the time those bodies died. Used by one and returned to the elements, they have again and again been taken up and rebuilt into vegetable and animal forms . . . the same particles of matter have belonged to many different human bodies. . . A bodily resurrection would find a hundred claimants for the constituents of the same body, each with a clear title" (John Wesley Hanson, *A Pocket Cyclopaedia : Brief Explanations of Religious Terms as Understood by Universalists* (Boston: Universalist, 1892), 18-19). "You can see how the bodies of the dead cannot be brought back atom by atom as they were originally. Certain individual atoms may belong to a thousand different bodies, and since no body can occupy two places at once, this makes it impossible for the actual body which was buried to arise with its original component atoms and molecules" (M.R. De Haan, *The Second Coming of Jesus* (Grand Rapids, MI: Kregel, 1996 [1944]), 55). "Thus it might prove an extremely difficult business to resurrect 'this' flesh at the end of time, for the atoms that will constitute me at the moment of death will return to the environment and will doubtless become part of innumerable other individuals" (Linda Badham, "Problems about the Resurrection of the Body," in Stuart C. Brown ed., *Philosophy of Religion: An Introduction with Readings* (London: Routledge, 2000) 133-36 (134)).

6. My source for information on this subject is Jonas Frisen, a biologist at the Karolinska Institute, who has conducted experiments on the rate at which cells are replaced. For a summary of Frisen's research, along with a list of his journal articles on the subject, see: http://askanaturalist.com/do-we-replace-our-cells-every-7-or-10-years/. I also consulted with two physicists, but both said that the issues were more a biologist's area of expertise.

body disintegrates. Hence, if God simply raises those atoms which constituted our body at the time of death, he will not have any dilemma in regard to which atoms to raise.

But this leads us into the second idea, the idea that all atoms are interchangeable and hence the atoms which make up our bodies at the time of death will necessarily become a part of other people's bodies. However, despite the prevalence of this idea, there is no scientific evidence that this actually happens; science only affirms that this is hypothetically possible. Atoms are indistinguishable; it is not possible to tell the difference between one atom and another atom. (The reason different physical objects look different is not because the atoms themselves are different, but only because the atoms are arranged in a different shape.) Thus since all atoms are the same, it is hypothetically possible that the atoms which make up my body at death could enter into another person's body. But there is no evidence that this actually happens. Although this is hypothetically possible, it is also possible that those atoms simply dematerialize, or go into outer space, or go into other physical objects besides people's bodies. Hence, if God wants to resurrect the atoms which made up my body at the time of death, he could simply guide the path of those atoms in such a way that those atoms never become part of another person's body. (In the case of cannibalism, some of a person's atoms do indeed become part of another person. But provided God makes sure that not all of the person's atoms are absorbed into the body of the cannibal, God will still have some atoms from which to raise the person. And in fact, it seems highly unlikely that all of a person's atoms can be absorbed into another person's body. For current research indicates that if a human eats bone, not all of the bone is absorbed into that human's body.[7] Further, God can even get the atoms which went into the cannibal back, as long as he makes sure that by the time the cannibal dies, the atoms eaten by the cannibal do not constitute a major part of the cannibal's own body.)

But finally, I should say that I am not at all sure that any passage in the Bible affirms that those whose bodies have completely decayed must be resurrected in the same body, as opposed to God simply creating a new body. Although many passages affirm that the body which died will be raised, those passages always seem to have in mind a situation in which the body, or at least some of the body, *is still in existence at the time of the raising*. Although we are told that Jesus rose in the same body, and that the bones of those in Ezekiel 37 came back to life, and that the dead who are in their tombs will come out (Jn 5:28-29), we are never told that anyone's atoms were, or are going to be, reassembled. Thus although the Bible affirms that anyone whose body still exists at the time they are raised from the dead will be raised in that same body, the Bible appears silent on the question of whether those whose bodies no longer exist are raised in the same body or in a different body.

---

7. See Rachel Nuwer, "Shrew-Eating Scientists Show Humans Can Digest Bone," http://www.smithsonianmag.com/smart-news/shrew-eating-scientists-show-humans-can-digest-bone-66337580/.

A second objection is that if Jesus rose from the dead, there is no place where his body could have gone while he was not on Earth. For modern thought has rejected the notion that heaven is a physical place above our heads; but this notion seems necessary to make sense of where Jesus' body was in between each appearance, and the idea seems clearly advocated in the story of Jesus' ascension.

In response, we should distinguish the two notions: the notion heaven is a physical place and the notion heaven is a physical place above our heads. Heaven would be a physical place without being a place above our heads, if, rather than being a planet off in the far distances of our own universe, it is a parallel dimension. This idea should not strike us as implausible, for quite apart from any questions of religion, scientists have suggested that parallel dimensions might exist (with black holes perhaps being their entry point). Thus the notion that heaven is a parallel dimension where physical beings reside is harmonious with the ideas of modern science.

Further, even the idea of heaven as some far distant planet within our own universe ought not to be thought absurd. Though it is true that this idea is widely believed to have been disproved by modern science, why this is so widely believed is not clear. Although astronomers have not detected heaven with their instruments, vast areas of space cannot be detected with present technology, and so it remains possible heaven might actually be "out there," a physical place somewhere far, far off in our own universe. But before we suppose this, we should ask the question of whether the Bible actually advocates the idea that heaven is above our heads. It may very well be that that is not the case. We know the Bible uses figurative language in regard to a number of other aspects of the cosmology it presents. For example, the Bible speaks of the "windows of heaven," but since "trouble" (Isa 24:18) and "blessing" (Mal 3:10) come through these windows, the windows must be figurative. Likewise, it speaks of "the waters under the Earth," but since fishermen cast their nets into these waters (Deut 4:18), the waters cannot be literally underneath the Earth. Thus given that the Bible frequently uses figurative language in regard to cosmology, it may be that its references to heaven as being above our heads are also figurative.[8]

But if heaven is not really a place above our heads, then we must ask why Jesus ascended up to heaven. The answer may be that this was a symbolic gesture: since the sky was figuratively spoken of as the place of the presence of God, Jesus ascended into the sky to symbolize the fact that he was going into God's presence. In fact, that it was merely a symbolic gesture is suggested by the fact that Jesus did not ascend all the way up, but only ascended a certain distance before a cloud took him from the disciples' sight (Acts 1:9). If heaven is literally above our heads, why did Jesus not keep going all the way up?

---

8. On the windows of heaven, waters under the Earth, and various other uses of figurative language in reference to Biblical cosmology, see Walker C. Kaiser, *The Old Testament Documents: Are They Reliable and Relevant?* (Downers Grove, IL: InterVarsity, 2001), 76-77. But for the argument that heaven is a physical place, see Randy C. Alcorn, *Heaven* (Wheaton, IL: Tyndale House, 2004), 51-64.

A third objection to physical resurrection is the so-called age regression argument, which is as follows.[9] Human beings change throughout the course of their lives. If you are forty you are quite a bit different now than you were when you were ten, and you will be different again at eighty. Now if God is to resurrect you, which version of you will he resurrect? For there are multiple yous to choose from. But this objection confuses essential properties with inessential properties. Though there are many things about you that are different now than when you were ten, there are also many things that are still the same, and since you are still the same person, your essential properties (whatever things are necessary for you to still be you) are still present. As long as God resurrects you with all of your essential properties, *you* are still being resurrected, regardless of which inessential properties God chooses to raise you with. Thus regardless of what age God chooses to raise us at, we will still be ourselves at the resurrection.

Data Alleged to be More Probable on the Resurrection Hypothesis But Which Actually Are Not

1. The Disciples Came to Believe Jesus Rose from the Dead[10]

The Argument: It is argued that only a real resurrection can explain why the disciples came to believe Jesus rose from the dead.[11] First century Jews, according to this argument, conceived of resurrection purely as a communal event which would take place at the end of the age; there was no expectation that an individual would rise from the dead prior to the general resurrection. Hence if the disciples saw non-physical appearances of Jesus after his death, they would not have concluded he had risen from the dead; they would have concluded he was appearing as a non-bodily apparition (just as some other Jewish heroes were believed to have done, such as Jeremiah in 2 Maccabees 15:13-16). The prevalence of apparition experiences throughout the ancient and modern world has been cited as support for this argument: for people in both

---

9. Paul Edwards, "Introduction," in Paul Edwards ed., *Immortality* (New York: MacMillan, 1992), 1-70 (60); Keith Augustine, "The Case Against Immortality," http://www.infidels.org/library/modern/keith_augustine/immortality.html.

10. Gary R. Habermas, "Dale Allison's Resurrection Skepticism: A Critique," *Philosophia Christi* 10 (2008): 303-13 (309); Michael R. Licona, *The Resurrection of Jesus: A New Historiographical Approach* (Downers Grove, IL: IVP Academic, 2010), 635. In citing those who have proposed arguments which have previously appeared in the literature, whether for or against the apparition theory, I will not attempt to cite every person to have proposed the argument, so it may be that other proponents or critics of the apparition theory besides those whom I cite have also favored the argument.

11. The fact that the disciples came to believe Jesus rose from the dead even though it seems they ought not to have by normal means has been cited as an argument for the truth of the resurrection even apart from its use against the apparition theory. N.T. Wright makes it the central argument of his book *The Resurrection of the Son of God* (Minneapolis: Fortress, 2003). And see also, e.g., Craig, *Assessing*, 290; Gary R. Habermas, "Explaining Away Jesus' Resurrection: The Recent Revival of Hallucination Theories," *Christian Research Journal* 23.4 (2001): 26-31, 47-49 (49).

the ancient and modern world see apparitions of the dead, but these appearances are always interpreted as non-bodily appearances; they are never interpreted as appearances of someone physically raised from the dead. Since the disciples interpreted the appearances as resurrection appearances, something must have been different about these appearances—Jesus must have actually been raised.

Bayesian Formulation: If Jesus rose from the dead (h) it is probable the disciples would come to believe Jesus rose from the dead. But if Jesus did not rise from the dead (~h), it is improbable the disciples would come to believe he rose from the dead.

Response: Though something must have been different, it was not necessarily that Jesus was actually raised. There were certain factors involved in the appearances of Jesus which are not to be found in a typical apparition case, and these factors could have brought the disciples to belief in Jesus' resurrection even if the appearances were actually non-bodily.

The first factor is the fact that the resurrection appearances happened in the context of a failed (if ~h is true, and Jesus was not really raised) apocalyptic movement. Jesus' followers believed they were part of a movement that was to inaugurate the end times, and with the death of the movement's leader, the movement seemed to have failed.[12] Now this same scenario has played itself out on a number of other occasions throughout history, and what has often happened is that some members of the movement, rather than simply admit their error and renounce their movement, have invented a convoluted explanation to explain why the apparent failure was not really a failure. When William Miller's prediction that Jesus would return in 1844 proved false, some of his followers concluded that though Miller had been wrong to interpret Daniel 8:14, a passage concerning the cleansing of the sanctuary, to mean that Jesus would return to Earth, Jesus had still fulfilled the prophecy, because the passage did not really mean that Jesus would return to Earth; it he meant he would cleanse the sanctuary in heaven, something which they convinced themselves he had indeed done on the day in question. The Jehovah's Witnesses expected Jesus to return in 1914, and when he did not, they did not admit they were wrong, instead, they concluded he had returned to Earth spiritually.[13] When Sabbatai Sevi, a Jewish messianic claimant of the seventeenth century, renounced his claim to messiahship, and Judaism as well,

---

12. The fact that eschatology was a central concern of Jesus' mission is supported by a variety of arguments, for example: Jesus' mentor John the Baptist was an eschatological prophet, and the early church was an eschatological movement, so it is likely, Jesus, the step in between, was concerned with eschatology; Jesus formed a group of twelve disciples, this is clearly reminiscent of the twelve tribes of Israel, thus signifying a new Israel, and it may also reflect the belief that the twelve tribes were to be regathered during the last days; eschatological material permeates the Gospel narratives. See Dale C. Allison Jr., *Jesus of Nazareth: Millenarian Prophet* (Minneapolis: Fortress, 1998); Bart D. Ehrman, *Jesus: Apocalyptic Prophet of the New Millennium* (Oxford: Oxford University Press, 1999). However, the fact that Jesus' mission was concerned with eschatology does not necessarily entail the view, held by Allison and Ehrman, that Jesus mistakenly believed the end of the age was soon at hand.

13. One will find the origin of the Seventh Day Adventists and Jehovah's Witnesses chronicled in any encyclopedia entry for either group.

by converting to Islam, some of his followers concluded that the real Sevi had actually been assumed into heaven and that the supposed Sevi who had apostatized was actually an impostor.[14] A group of flying saucer enthusiasts during the 1950s expected that on one particular day, a worldwide flood would sweep away the inhabitants of the Earth, but that they themselves would be rescued by being taken aboard a flying saucer. When the flying saucer did not come, some members of the group, rather than admit they were mistaken, concluded based on a message one of their members received from the aliens, that because of the devotion shown by this group, God had decided not to destroy the world.[15] And these are not the only four examples; other cases can be cited.[16]

Thus it would not be a surprise if the disciples reinterpreted their belief that resurrection would not occur before the end of the age if this reinterpretation was what was needed to keep the movement going. In fact, one can see how such an interpretation would make sense to the disciples. If the appearances were interpreted as apparitions, it would not seem as if Jesus had had much of a vindication, since post-mortem apparitions are common, and so there would be nothing special about an apparition of Jesus. But if Jesus was raised bodily from the dead, that would be an impressive vindication, for no one had ever risen from the dead before. (I only propose that the disciples could have reasoned this way subconsciously and thus honestly misinterpreted a hallucination or a real apparition as a bodily resurrection. I do not propose that the disciples lied about this.)

It has been objected that the suggestion that the Christian movement would have reacted to apparent failure by reinterpreting its beliefs and continuing the movement in the way modern movements have done does not take into account the fact that ancient messianic movements did not react in this way.[17] A number of messianic

---

14. On Sabbatai Sevi, see Gershom Gerhard Scholem, *Sabbatai Sevi: The Mystical Messiah: 1626-1676* (Princeton: Princeton University Press, 1973).

15. See Leon Festinger, Henry Riecken, and Stanley Schachter, *When Prophecy Fails* (Minneapolis: University of Minnesota Press, 1956). For the argument that the resurrection appearances were of the same nature as these other responses to failed movements see Kris D. Komarnistky, *Doubting Jesus' Resurrection: What Happened in the Black Box?* (Drapper, Utah: Stone Arrow, 2009), 48-76.

16. For other cases, see Dale C. Allison Jr., *The End of the Ages has Come: An Early Interpretation of the Passion and Resurrection of Jesus* (Philadelphia: Fortress, 1985), 163-68; Dale C. Allison Jr., *Constructing Jesus: Memory, Imagination, and History* (Grand Rapids, MI: Baker Academic, 2010), 148-53 and the sources cited there.

17. So Wright, *Resurrection*, 700. Wright also presents three other arguments (697-701) against the analogy between the resurrection appearances and the flying saucer group studied by Festinger et al., (Wright does not consider other cases), but they are not persuasive. 1) Wright argues that since the three sociologists themselves constituted a sizable percentage of the group, they could have subconsciously affected the behavior of the members of the group. But the sociologists' subconscious influence would have to have been rather grand if the members were in fact not naturally inclined towards this. Besides, this argument would at most only work against that particular case, not the Jehovah's Witnesses, Seventh Day Adventists, etc. 2) He argues there is no evidence that the group studied by Festinger continued longer than one month, whereas Christianity continued for a long time. But first of all, the group may have continued; we do not know, since the sociologists did not continue to study

movements arose in the first century,[18] and when they failed, proponents of this argument say, that was the end of the movement. There were no radical reinterpretations of the failure in order to keep the movement going. Thus, since Jesus' movement was an ancient Jewish movement rather than a modern one, we would expect the disciples to react in the way ancient Jewish messianic movements did and simply cease the movement.

But is this really the way ancient Messianic movements reacted? Proponents of this argument tell us that the death of the leader brought an end to the movement, but all we really know is that it brought an end to the record of the movement in the history books. That is, we know that once a movement failed, it no longer appears in any historical records. But does that necessarily mean the movement came to an end? Perhaps in some cases some of the followers did reformulate their movement and continued to believe, but the movement did not pick up any momentum and thus the fact that it continued to exist is unknown to us. This is almost what happened to the flying saucer cult: If a small group of sociologists had not decided to study this movement, we would never have known the movement had tried to continue after its apparent failure. In fact, there is at least one ancient movement which is very nearly an ancient Jewish movement, and which did continue in the face of apparent failure: A Samaritan group called the Dositheans denied the death of their leader, and continued their activities.[19] And we should also note that the movement of Sabbatai Sevi was a Middle Age Jewish movement, not a modern movement.

Thus, there is no reason to doubt that ancient Jewish messianic movements would sometimes react in the same way as the modern movements we have mentioned.

But in fact, there is strong reason to think that the disciples would not even have needed to reinterpret their beliefs in order to believe that an individual would rise from the dead before all others. That Jesus in particular had risen in this way was indeed a new idea, but the idea that a person could rise from the dead prior to the end times was quite possibly one which the disciples already held. If this is so, the interpretation of the appearances as resurrection appearances would be even less surprising. The evidence for my claim comes from two passages in the Gospels: Mark 6:14 where Herod thinks that Jesus is John the Baptist risen from the dead, and Matthew 16:14 where it is suggested Jesus is Jeremiah or one of the prophets risen from the dead. If

---

it. Second, this argument also applies at most only to this particular group; the Jehovah's Witnesses and Seventh Day Adventists have been with us for a long time. 3) He argues that the reinterpretation which Festinger's group adopted was more in line with their original expectations than the belief in Jesus' resurrection was in line with the expectations of the early Christians. But how is the belief that the flying saucer had not come because of the group's devotion at all in line with their previous beliefs? Or how is the belief that the real Sevi was taken to heaven and replaced by an impostor in line with the previous beliefs of Sevi's followers?

18. For a review, see Craig A. Evans, "Messianic Hopes and Messianic Figures in Late Antiquity," *Journal of Greco-Roman Christianity and Judaism* 3 (2006): 9-40.

19. On the Dositheans, see Stanley Jerome Isser, *The Dositheans: A Samaritan Sect in Late Antiquity* (Leiden: Brill, 1976).

some thought Jesus was John the Baptist or Jeremiah risen from the dead, then some thought it possible that an individual could be raised from the dead prior to all others. In fact, N.T. Wright, whose case for the historicity of Jesus' resurrection is based largely on the present argument, admits this is so (saying of Herod's thought "it seems to be an exception to the general rule, that 'the resurrection of the dead' would happen to all the righteous simultaneously, not to one or two here and there,"), though he says the opinion was a non-mainstream one (saying we should not "regard Herod and his court as the most accurate indicators of mainstream second-Temple Jewish belief").[20] But if there really were non-mainstream Jews who believed in the resurrection of an individual before the end times, then there is nothing surprising about the disciples coming to this belief in the case of Jesus. All we have to suppose is that the disciples were among the minority of Jews who thought individual resurrection was possible.[21]

It might be objected that the idea expressed in these passages is not that someone could be resurrected before the end times, but only that someone could be raised back to an ordinary human life (resuscitated), in the same way that people such as Lazarus and Jairus' daughter were. However, this interpretation is not likely. Herod suspects that Jesus' being raised from the dead is the reason mighty powers are at work in him—this is not likely if Jesus was only resuscitated, for resuscitated people never display mighty powers. But it makes sense that a person who had experienced eschatological resurrection may have such powers. And the people in Matthew 16:14 suspect Jesus may be Jeremiah: Jeremiah had been dead for a very long time, and people dead for that long are never resuscitated anywhere in the Bible.

(Some mention should here be made of Gabriel's Revelation. Gabriel's Revelation is a stone tablet from the late first century BCE which contains 87 lines of text in Hebrew. The tablet was discovered by Israel Knohl in 2008. Knohl contends that one line of the tablet contains a statement that the Messiah will rise from the dead after three days.[22] If Knohl's interpretation is correct, the tablet would seem to show that the idea of the Messiah rising from the dead before the end times was a pre-Christian idea (and pre-John the Baptist idea).

However, Knohl's interpretation of the tablet is highly questionable. The idea that it refers to the death and resurrection of the Messiah comes primarily from the words of two lines. One line Knohl contends reads "Ephraim," which he takes to be a reference to Messiah ben Joseph, a suffering Messiah who would die. But, as Adela Yarbro Collins, has pointed out, there are two problems with this suggestion.[23] First,

20. Wright, *Resurrection*, 413.

21. This point has been made specifically in response to Wright by Robert M. Price, "N.T. Wright's The Resurrection of the Son of God," http://www.robertmprice.mindvendor.com/rev_ntwrong.htm.

22. Israel Knohl, "'By Three Days Live': Messiahs, Resurrection, and Ascent to Heaven in Hazon Gabriel," *Journal of Religion* 88 (2008): 147-58.

23. Adela Yarbro Collins, "Response to Israel Knohl, Messiahs and Resurrection in "The Gabriel Revelation," in Matthias Henze ed., *Hazon Gabriel: New Readings of the Gabriel Revelation* (Atlanta: Society of Biblical Literature, 2011), 93-98 (95-96).

paleographers do not agree on whether "Ephraim" is the correct reading (the text is fragmentary, and thus many readings are uncertain). And even if this is the correct reading, there is no solid basis for taking Ephraim to mean Messiah ben Joseph: The concept of a Messiah son of Joseph is not attested until the Middle Ages, and when it is attested, the Messiah ben Joseph is not called Ephraim. (Knohl supposes he is called Ephraim here simply because Ephraim was the son of Joseph.) The second line Knohl thinks reads "after three days," but whether this is the correct reconstruction is also disputed. Given these uncertainties, Gabriel's Revelation cannot help us very much in determining whether the idea of resurrection before the end times existed prior to Jesus.)

At this point, the question arises as to how easy it would be to mistake an apparition for a physical appearance. In order for the disciples to interpret the appearances as resurrection appearances, they must have thought Jesus was appearing with a physical body—for even if the disciples were inclined to interpret post-mortem appearances of Jesus as resurrection appearances, they could not have done so if the appearances were clearly non-physical. It is possible that the odds of this vary somewhat depending on the culture. In Hornell Hart's study of 165 apparitions from the US and the UK, characteristics which would make an apparition look clearly different from an ordinary person were uncommon: 2% were transparent, 7% were partially formed, and 4% glided instead of walked.[24] On the other hand, in Charles Emmons's study of apparitions in China, 24% were transparent or insubstantial, 24% were partially formed, 13% displayed abnormal walking, and 7% were sickly or horrible looking.[25] This would seem to indicate cultural variance in regard to these characteristics. However, a number of confounding variables prevent us from being able to say that the differences in Emmons's study are definitely due to cultural variance. First, Hart's is a sample of only ostensibly real apparitions, whereas Emmons's sample consists of all the apparition accounts which he collected. Second, most of the apparitions in Emmons's study were of unrecognized figures, whereas Hart's study consisted mostly of apparitions of the dead. Third, there were a disproportionately high number of accounts from teenagers in Hart's study. Thus it seems unclear whether the differences between the studies resulted from the different cultures or from one or more of the other variables. However, even if Emmons's study reflects real differences in culture, it is still the case that his study supports the notion that many, even if not most, apparitions look like real people (since Emmons still found plenty of cases of these); in which case, it would be difficult for the disciples to distinguish an apparition from a physical appearance.

Finally, even if it is granted for the sake of argument that non-physical appearances alone would not convince the disciples Jesus rose from the dead, non-physical

---

24. Hornell Hart and Collaborators, "Six Theories About Apparitions," *Proceedings of the Society for Psychical Research* 50 (1956): 153-239 (168, 171).

25. Charles Emmons, *Chinese Ghosts and ESP* (Jefferson, NC: McFarland, 1982), 78, 84, 87, 83.

appearances plus the empty tomb could certainly bring them to this belief. An empty tomb would clearly suggest resurrection, and if the tomb became empty for some natural reason (such as grave robbery or reburial), this could have caused the disciples to misinterpret the appearances as physical appearances. William Lane Craig recognizes this problem and argues that an empty tomb plus non-physical appearances would only have resulted in the belief that Jesus had been assumed into heaven, not the belief he was resurrected. Craig cites T. Job 40 where Job's children's bodies are found missing and people conclude that they have been assumed into heaven.[26] We can also add Chariton's *Chaereas and Callirhoe* 3.3.1-7, where a woman's tomb is found empty and people conclude she has been assumed into heaven.

However, we cannot draw such a broad conclusion from two texts. The fact that the characters in T. Job and Chariton's work infer an assumption rather than a resurrection only tells us that if the authors of these documents had discovered Jesus' empty tomb, they would likely have inferred Jesus had been assumed into heaven (at least, if they knew nothing of the belief that John the Baptist was raised from the dead). But without a larger sample size, it is illegitimate to conclude that all Jews, or even most Jews, would draw the same conclusion as these authors.[27]

Bayesian Conclusion: It is probable that if Jesus rose from the dead (h), the disciples would come to believe he rose from the dead (since the appearances of a resurrected person should cause people to believe he rose from the dead). But it is also probable that if Jesus did not rise from the dead, the disciples would come to believe he rose from the dead, because it is probable that an apocalyptic group whose mission seemed to have failed would adopt a convoluted reinterpretation of their beliefs in order to keep the movement going.

Now one might be inclined to respond that it is only possible, not probable, that the disciples would have reacted like this, for even if there are some movements that have reinterpreted their beliefs in the face of apparent failure, surely there are others which have not. Thus even if the datum is not exceedingly improbable on ~h, the datum still supports h, because it has a much higher probability on h (its probability on h being virtually 100%, for how could the disciples fail to believe Jesus rose from the dead if he actually did so?). But if we accepted this argument, we should also have to agree that, for example, the fact that the Jehovah's Witnesses came to believe Jesus

---

26. William Lane Craig, *Reasonable Faith: Christian Truth and Apologetics* (3rd ed.; Wheaton, IL: Crossway, 2008), 394.

27. With regard to the idea of assumption in ancient Jewish literature, though there were a number of cases of people believed to have been assumed into heaven before they died (e.g., Enoch and Elijah), it seems to me that the only unambiguous case of an assumption of a dead person is the case of Job's children in T. Job 40. Other possibilities include Moses and the righteous person in Wisdom of Solomon 5. But it is not clear to me whether they were believed to have been bodily assumed to heaven or simply taken to heaven as a spirit. For a review of assumptions in ancient Jewish literature, see Jonathan Kendall, "The Vindication of the Messiah: Why Resurrection?" in James Patrick Holding ed., *Defending the Resurrection: Did Jesus Rise From the Dead?* (Maitland, FL: Xulon: 2010), 134-81 (146-53).

returned to Earth spiritually is evidence that he really did. For if he actually did do so, the probability of the Jehovah's Witnesses coming to this belief is obviously near 100%, but if he did not actually do so, we must suppose the Jehovah's Witnesses adopted a novel reinterpretation of their beliefs to arrive at this conclusion. And since this happens less than 100% of the time, the probability that it happened here is necessarily less than 100%; and consequently the datum supports h, since on h the probability is 100%, whereas on ~h the probability is less than 100%.

The problem here is failure to consider multiple trials. The Christians were not the only apocalyptic group in the first century; there were plenty of others.[28] And though the odds that any particular apocalyptic group would adopt a novel reinterpretation of its beliefs are low, when we consider the large number of groups, the odds that one of those groups would do this is very high. Analogously, if the odds are 20:1 (5%) of getting a certain poker hand, and I deal out 20 hands, the odds are not 5% but close to 100% someone will get that hand. Thus ~h does not ask the question "what is the probability the Christians would come to believe Jesus rose from the dead?" but rather, "what is the probability that some apocalyptic group from that time would adopt a novel reinterpretation of its beliefs in order to keep the movement going in the face of apparent failure?" The answer to this second question is that the probability is indeed very high.

2. Jesus Predicted His Death and Resurrection[29]

The Argument: Jesus predicted his resurrection, and this makes sense if Jesus was actually resurrected, for it would not be a surprise if a resurrected person possessed supernatural powers. But if he was an apparition, we should expect him to have been a normal person with no supernatural ability, and thus no ability to predict the future.

(Note, by the way, that this argument and the previous argument conflict: For if Jesus predicted his resurrection in advance, it is hardly surprising that the disciples interpreted his appearances as resurrection appearances.)

Bayesian Formulation: If Jesus rose from the dead (h), it is probable he would have made predictions of a resurrection. But if Jesus did not rise from the dead (~h), it is improbable he would have made predictions of a resurrection. (Or even if it is improbable that if Jesus rose from the dead he would have predicted his resurrection, it is much more improbable that a person who appeared as an apparition would do so.)

Response: As I argued in chapter 4, there is insufficient evidence to conclude that Jesus did prophesy he would rise from the dead. As I explained there, although Jesus may have spoken in general terms about some type of post-mortem vindication, the predictions may have been so general that they could have been interpreted *either* as

---

28. See the article previously referred to by Craig Evans, "Messianic Hopes and Messianic Figures in Late Antiquity."

29. Habermas, "Resurrection Skepticism," 308.

predictions of resurrection *or* as predictions of a non-bodily post-mortem vindication. Since the disciples understood Jesus' post-mortem appearances as resurrection appearances, his predictions were naturally interpreted as predictions of a resurrection (which is the correct interpretation *if* Jesus really rose from the dead). But his predictions may very well have been so vague that they could also have been interpreted as predictions of any type of vindication after death, including a non-bodily one.

Moreover, even if Jesus did specifically predict that he would rise from the dead, this is not any better explained on h than on ~h, for a failed religious leader might also predict he would be resurrected. In fact, at least one has. Ching Chi Vui aka Ivan, the leader of a Malaysian cult, predicted he would rise from the dead.[30] His followers did not bury his corpse when he died, they instead prayed over it, hoping he would rise, but he did not.

Further, if Jesus did predict his resurrection, this actually increases the probability apparitions of Jesus would be mistaken for physical appearances, since the disciples would be primed to expect a resurrection, and apparitions can mimic the appearance of physical human beings.

Bayesian Conclusion: If Jesus rose from the dead (h) it is not exceedingly improbable he would have predicted his resurrection, because it is not surprising that a person who rose from the dead would also have other supernatural powers such as the power of predicting the future. But the predictions are also not exceedingly improbable on ~h, because a mistaken apocalyptic prophet might also predict that he would rise from the dead. Thus the datum is not any more probable on h than ~h.

3. Jesus' Claims[31]

The Argument: Jesus, unlike typical apparitions, made great claims to personal authority. For example, Jesus claimed to be the Son of Man. He entered Jerusalem on a donkey in fulfillment of Zechariah's prophecy, implicitly claiming to be the Messiah. He claimed to have an especially close relationship with God, saying no one comes to the Father except through him. And he saw himself as the agent through whom the kingdom of God was being inaugurated.[32] By contrast, people who appear as apparitions do not do any of this.

Bayesian Formulation: If Jesus rose from the dead (h), it is probable he would also have made great claims to personal authority. But if he did not rise from the dead, it

---

30. See "Malaysian Cult Keeps Leader's Decomposed Body for 13 Months," http://www.religionnewsblog.com/23708/malaysian-cult-keeps-leader%E2%80%99s-decomposed-body-for-13-months. I recall having seen other examples of cult leaders who unsuccessfully predicted their resurrection, but I cannot locate any other examples.

31. Gerald O'Collins, *Christology: A Biblical, Historical, and Systematic Study of Jesus* (2nd ed.; Oxford: Oxford University Press, 2009), 98.

32. On Jesus' personal claims, see Ben Witherington, *The Christology of Jesus* (Minneapolis: Fortress, 1990).

is improbable he would have made great claims to personal authority. (Or even if it is not probable he would make great claims to personal authority if h is true, it is even more improbable if ~h is true.)

Response: Although the premise of the argument is correct (Jesus made great claims to personal authority), the conclusion does not follow from the premise. Why would someone be less likely to appear as an apparition, or more likely to rise from the dead, simply because they made great claims to personal authority? One might argue that the fact Jesus made such claims raises the odds Jesus is the Messiah and hence raises the initial probability of the resurrection. But while claiming to be the Messiah lends a slight increase to the odds that you actually are the Messiah (if there is one Messiah, and we picked a person at random, the odds he would be the Messiah would be 1 out of however many people have ever lived on Earth. But if we selected a person who claimed to be the Messiah, our odds would be 1 out of however many messianic claimants there have been over the course of history),[33] it does not increase the odds very much (there have been so many messianic claimants that the odds are still very low that a given messianic claimant is the Messiah, especially since we cannot assume there even is a real Messiah). Now if there is evidence to support Jesus' Messianic claims (e.g., Messianic prophecy, other miracles besides the resurrection), that evidence certainly increases the initial probability of h. But merely making a Messianic claim does not raise the probability very much. Milton Rokeach, a psychiatrist, tells us a story of three patients in a mental institution who each believed they were the Messiah.[34] But is anyone very confident that any of them was the Messiah simply because they claimed to be? Hence, though an actual Messiah would be expected to make great claims to personal authority, so would a pretend Messiah, and so the fact that Jesus made such claims only negligibly increases the probability he is the Messiah.

Bayesian Conclusion: It is probable that if Jesus rose from the dead (h), he would have made great claims to personal authority in life (since the Messiah ought to possess such authority and ought to tell us so). But it is also probable that if Jesus was a mistaken apocalyptic prophet he would have made the same types of claims (since false messiahs make these same claims).

4. Jesus' Death[35]

The Argument: Jesus died a violent death, whereas most people who are seen as apparitions died a normal death. Thus it is not likely Jesus was an apparition.

---

33. For a list of Messianic claimants throughout history, see James Smith, *The Promised Messiah* (Nashville: Thomas Nelson, 1993), 470-74.

34. Milton Rokeach, *The Three Christs of Ypsilanti: A Psychological Study* (New York: Knopf, 1964).

35. O'Collins, *Christology*, 98.

Jesus' Resurrection and Apparitions

Bayesian Formulation: If Jesus rose from the dead (h) it is probable he would have died a violent death. But if he did not rise from the dead (~h), it is improbable he would have died a violent death. (Or even if it is improbable that if Jesus rose from the dead he would have died a violent death, it is even more improbable that if he was an apparition he would have died a violent death.)

Response: This argument is based on faulty statistical reasoning. Just because most people who are seen as apparitions die a non-violent death, it does not follow that if someone dies a violent death they are unlikely to be seen as an apparition. For just because most members of a group (such as people who are seen as apparitions) are unaffected by a certain factor (such as dying a violent death), it does not follow that if someone is affected by that factor they are not likely to a member of that group. In fact, someone who is affected by the factor in question might be more likely to be a member of the group—despite the fact that most members of the group are not affected by the factor.

In order to clarify this confusing sounding assertion, let us consider the analogy of cigarettes and lung cancer. One always hears that cigarettes "cause" lung cancer, a statement which many people interpret to mean that if you smoke cigarettes you will definitely get lung cancer. But this is not so. If you smoke cigarettes, your odds of getting lung cancer are only about 10:1.[36] So most members of the group (smokers) are unaffected by the factor in question (lung cancer). But even though your odds of getting lung cancer are low if you smoke (10:1), they would be even lower if you did not smoke. Thus, just because most members of the group (smokers) are unaffected by the factor (lung cancer), that does not mean that if you are affected by the factor (if you do have lung cancer) you are less likely to belong to the group. People with lung cancer are clearly much more likely to be smokers than people without lung cancer.

Analogously, just because most people who appear as apparitions died non-violent deaths, that does not mean that if someone died a violent death, they are less likely to be seen as an apparition. People who die violent deaths could be *more* likely to be seen as an apparition. And in fact, this is actually the case: One study in Iceland found that people who died violent deaths are more likely to be seen as an apparition than people who did not die violent deaths.[37] Just as people who smoke are unlikely to get lung cancer, people who die violent deaths are unlikely to be seen as apparitions, simply because a low percentage of people are seen as apparitions. But they are still more likely to be seen as apparitions than people who did not die violent deaths (of people who were seen as apparitions, 30% had died a violent death whereas only 8% of the general population had died a violent death). Hence, rather than being an argument against the apparition hypothesis, the fact that Jesus died a violent death could

---

36. See Rebecca Goldin, "Lung Cancer Rates: What's Your Risk?" http://stats.org/stories/lung_cancer_rates_mar08_06.htm.

37. Erlendur Haraldsson, "Experiences of Encounters with the Dead: 337 Cases," *Journal of Parapsychology* 73 (2009): 91-118 (104).

be cited as something which is more probable on the apparition hypothesis. We shall have to consider this possibility below.

Bayesian Conclusion: In light of the fact that this argument can be turned around and used as something more probable on ~h, we will put off our conclusion until we consider it under the arguments for ~h below.

5. The Duration of the Resurrection Appearances[38]

The Argument: In Dewi Rees's study, the spouses tended to see the apparitions over many years, but this was not so in the case of the resurrection appearances. Both Paul and Acts tell us they ceased. (Paul tells us Jesus' appearance to him was Jesus' last appearance (1 Cor 15:8) and Luke indicates the appearances ceased with the ascension.)

Bayesian Formulation: If Jesus rose from the dead (h) it is probable his appearances would have ceased after a short period of time. But if Jesus did not rise from the dead (~h) it is improbable his appearances would have ceased after a short period of time. (Or even if it is improbable that if Jesus rose from the dead his appearances would have ceased after a short period of time, this is even more improbable on ~h.)

Response: The first point to note is that though Rees's study found that when a person sees an apparition they tend to see it again, other studies have found that apparitions tend to be one time occurrences.[39] The reason why the studies conflict is probably because Rees's study was done on the elderly, whereas the other studies were done on the general population. Elderly people have more hallucinations than the population at large,[40] and that means one will find more reports of apparitions among the elderly (though not more reports of real apparitions). Thus we should not conclude that real apparitions are usually seen over a period of many years.

But further, the other half of the argument is factually wrong—for Jesus *was* seen over many years. Our sources indicate that post-mortem appearances of Jesus did not stop after forty days, nor did they stop at any point during the early days of Christianity. Acts tells us that after Jesus' ascension, and even after his initial appearance to Paul, he still appeared: He appeared to Stephen (Acts 7:55-56), and to Paul (Acts 18:9; 22:17-18). Likewise, though Paul tells us Jesus' last appearance was the appearance that converted Paul (15:8), he mentions a later appearance in which Jesus counseled him about his "thorn in the flesh" (2 Cor 12:7).[41] In fact, appearances of Jesus never

---

38. O'Collins, *Christology*, 99.

39. The Census of Hallucinations found 427 people reporting multiple hallucinations/apparitions, whereas about 1200 only reported one experience (Professor Sidgwick's Committee, "Report on the Census of Hallucinations," *Proceedings of the Society for Psychical Research* 10 (1894): 25-422 (42)).

40. G. Berrios and P. Brook, "Visual Hallucinations and Sensory Delusions in the Elderly," *British Journal of Psychiatry* 144 (1984): 662-664.

41. O'Collins himself has co-authored an article on the distinction between the earlier and later appearances, but he apparently does not see its relevance here: Daniel Kendall and Gerald O'Collins, "The Uniqueness of the Easter Appearances," *Catholic Biblical Quarterly* 54 (1992): 287-307.

stopped: They were reported in the writings of the Church Fathers, and they still continue today.[42]

Thus the appearances did not stop after forty days. The evidence does, however, indicate that the early Christians understood the earlier and later appearances as different types of appearances. At Jesus' ascension, the angels tell the disciples that Jesus will come back in the same way he has left (Acts 1:11); the implication is that Jesus will not be seen again until he descends on the Mountain of Olives (during Israel's apocalyptic battle against the nations surrounding it; see Zech 14:4, where we are told the Lord's feet will rest on the Mount of Olives). Hence, Luke very likely thinks the pre-ascension appearances are different from the post-ascension ones, since Jesus is not supposed to be returning until he descends on the Mount of Olives, so the post-ascension appearances must somehow not be a true return of Jesus. And though in 2 Corinthians 12:7 Paul mentions an appearance which took place after his initial one, in 1 Corinthians 15:8 he says Jesus' initial appearance to him was Jesus' last appearance, so he must have thought the appearances were somehow different.

As for what the distinction is, the following evidence indicates the distinction is that the first appearances were believed to be physical appearances, whereas the later ones were believed to be non-physical visions.[43] First, Stephen is the only one who can see Jesus in Acts 7:55-56 (if the others could see Stephen, they would surely not have stoned him). Second, Paul sees Jesus in a trance in Acts 22:17-18. None of the pre-ascension appearances involved a trance, but Daniel saw a vision in a trance (Dn 10:7), and in Daniel's case the others with him could not see the vision. Third, just as Paul sees Jesus in a trance and at night, he also sees a living Macedonian while in a trance and at night (Acts 16:9). Now, the Macedonian is clearly not there physically; he is in Macedonia. This is not a physical appearance, but an apparition of the living.

Given this distinction, some will say that the argument should simply be modified. If the early church believed Jesus' earlier appearances were physical, and his later appearances non-physical, we must find some way to account for that belief. And if no natural explanation can be found, we should conclude the earlier appearances really were physical (and hence Jesus really rose from the dead) and the later appearances really were non-physical.[44]

However, simply because the Christians believed there was such a distinction, this does not mean the distinction was real. Perhaps the Christians thought there was a distinction though there was not. Since we have seen apparitions can mimic

---

42. For contemporary visions of Jesus, see Philip H. Wiebe, *Visions of Jesus: Direct Encounters from the New Testament to Today* (Oxford: Oxford University Press, 1997). For visions of Jesus during the time of the Church Fathers, see David W. Bercot, *A Dictionary of Early Christian Beliefs: A Reference Guide to More Than 700 Topics Discussed by the Early Church Fathers* (Peabody, MA: Hendrickson, 1998), 674-75.

43. On the fact that this is the distinction, see Craig, *Assessing*, 51-52.

44. So Craig, *Assessing*, 290.

the appearance of a physical being, the early Christians easily could have thought the earlier appearances were physical though they actually were not.

Bayesian Conclusion: This argument is factually wrong since the resurrection appearances did not cease after a short period of time. And even if they had ceased after a short period of time, it is not clear that this would make them different from apparitions. And even if this does make them different from apparitions, there is no reason to think this is a difference which is more probable given h.

6. The Disciples Proclaimed the Resurrection[45]

The Argument: Most of the bereaved do not tell others about their bereavement experiences, but the disciples proclaimed the resurrection publicly and even dramatically changed their lives and created a whole new religious movement.

Bayesian Formulation: If h is true it is probable the disciples would have proclaimed the resurrection, but if ~h is true, it is improbable they would have.

Response: Clearly, this difference can be explained by the fact that the resurrection appearances took place in a different context than typical apparitions do. People who see apparitions today live in a culture where apparitions are considered by many to be signs of mental imbalance, and thus many people who see apparitions are reluctant to admit it.[46] But the disciples, besides living in a culture in which supernatural encounters such as apparitions were considered normal, misinterpreted (if the apparition theory is correct) this apparition for a resurrected person, and they thought that this person's resurrection heralded the eschaton. Naturally, their lives were transformed and they proclaimed the resurrection to the world.

Bayesian Conclusion: If h is true it is probable the disciples would have proclaimed the resurrection (since if Jesus actually rose from the dead, they would proclaim this). But if ~h is true, it is also probable the disciples would have proclaimed the resurrection (since ~h proposes Jesus' appearances as an apparition were mistaken for resurrection appearances, and the disciples would also have proclaimed the resurrection in this case).

7. Crisis Apparitions[47]

The Argument: All real apparitions are crisis apparitions. All real apparitions take place at the time the person whose apparition it is dies. But the resurrection appearances took place at the time of Jesus' death

---

45. O'Collins, *Christology*, 99; Licona, *Resurrection*, 636.
46. On this point, see Allison, *Resurrecting*, 271 n295.
47. Craig, *Assessing*, 293.

Bayesian Formulation: If Jesus rose from the dead, it is probable his appearances would be post-mortem, but if he was an apparition it is improbable his appearances would be post-mortem.

Response: In light of our examination of the apparition literature, this argument is clearly incorrect. Plenty of real apparitions take place well after the time the person whose apparition it is dies.

Bayesian Conclusion: If Jesus rose from the dead, it is probable his appearances would have been post-mortem. But if Jesus was an apparition, it is also probable his appearances would be post-mortem, since contrary to this claim, post-mortem apparitions are common.

Data Which Is More Probable on the Resurrection Hypothesis

We now come to the data which actually is more probable on the resurrection hypothesis. This is the most important part of our investigation, since this is where we will learn why the resurrection hypothesis is more probable than the apparition hypothesis. We will separate the data into data which comes from 1 Corinthians 15, data which comes from the Gospels if their general reliability is not accepted, and data which comes from the Gospels if their general reliability is accepted.

Data From 1 Corinthians 15:3-8

1. *Appearances to Large Groups*: Appearances to groups of more than four people are exceedingly improbable given the apparition hypothesis. I have reviewed a large number of cases of collective apparitions, and though I have examined over forty cases, I have not found a single well-evidenced case of an apparition which appeared to more than four people.[48] Thus the appearances to the Twelve (or technically the eleven; Judas

---

48. For a literature review of collective cases published up till 1933, see Hornell Hart and Ella B. Hart, "Visions and Apparitions Collectively and Reciprocally Perceived," *Proceedings of the Society for Psychical Research* 41 (1933): 205-249. This article presents twenty cases of collectively perceived apparitions of the dead or dying and nine cases of collective apparitions of unrecognized figures (many of whom may have been dead), as well as other types of collective apparitions. Collective apparitions typically appear to only two or three people. The only case in their collection of an apparition of a person who was dead, or possibly dead, and which appeared to more than three people is case t35 (this apparition appeared to four people).

Unless we count the apparition of Samuel Bull (see G.W. Balfour and J.G. Piddington, "Case of Haunting at Ramsbury, Wilts," *Journal of the Society for Psychical Research* 27 (1932): 297-304; cited by Hart and Hart on p. 220-21). But this case is highly likely to have been a fraud. First of all, the apparition engaged in long conversations, and, as we explained in chapter 3, this is a characteristic which is much more likely to be present if the case is fraudulent. Second of all, the witnesses endeavored to use the apparition as a reason to receive higher-quality housing. Making up a story about a ghost in an attempt to receive better housing is actually a not uncommon phenomenon (see Ian Wilson, *In Search of Ghosts* (London: Headline, 1995), 32-33).

was dead[49]), the 500, and all the apostles would be exceedingly improbable given the apparition hypothesis. However, these appearances are not exceedingly improbable given the resurrection hypothesis. For we know that Jesus, during his life, often gathered together with groups, especially the Twelve (presuming the Gospels are accurate in this regard, and most scholars agree that they are).[50] Thus it is plausible (though I would not claim probable—that is, not in terms of *absolute probability*) that after his resurrection Jesus would have the desire to appear to large groups, and especially to the Twelve. And in addition to having the desire to do so, he would surely have the power to do so, for a resurrected Jesus ought to have the power to do anything he desires (as long as it does not render the truth of Christianity obvious; this apparently being a limitation which God placed on Jesus' activities).[51] But an apparition of the dead, though it may have the desire to appear to groups, would not be very likely to have the power to do so. For, as we have said, apparitions rarely, if ever, appear to large groups, thus this is evidently a power which they lack.

Bayesian Formulation: If Jesus was raised from the dead, it is not exceedingly improbable that there would be appearances to large groups. But if Jesus was an apparition, it is exceedingly improbable that there would be appearances to large groups. Since collective apparitions which appear to more than four people are rare or non-existent in the apparition literature, the odds of such an apparition are exceedingly low, and so let us assign odds of 100:1 against. By contrast, it is plausible (that is, not exceedingly improbable) that Jesus would make appearances to large groups if he was raised from the dead, and so let us assign the odds of this as 10:1 against. In this case, the datum favors h by odds of 10:1 (100:1/10:1=10:1).

---

49. The fact that Paul refers to the Twelve does not necessarily mean he did not know of the death of Judas. Gary Habermas and Michael Licona give the analogy of the college basketball conference known as the Big Ten still being called the Big Ten even though there are now eleven teams (*The Case for the Resurrection of Jesus* (Grand Rapids, MI: Kregel, 2004), 303). And Dale Allison notes that Xenophon refers to a group called "the thirty" despite the fact that two of the members of the group had died and thus there were technically only twenty-eight. And he also notes that Octavian, Mark Antony, and Markus Aemilius Lepidus were referred to as the "triumvirate" even after one of them died (Allison, *Constructing Jesus*, 69).

50. On the historicity of the Twelve, see John P. Meier, "The Circle of the Twelve: Did It Exist during Jesus' Public Ministry," *Journal of Biblical Literature* 16 (1997): 635-72. Even if we cannot trust the Gospels in this regard, we ought to think it plausible that Jesus often gathered together with groups, because Jesus was a rabbi, and we know rabbis often taught groups (see e.g., H. L. Strack, and Gunter Stemberger, *Introduction to the Talmud and Midrash* (2nd ed.; ed. and trans., Markus Bockmuehl: Minneapolis: Fortress, 1996), 11).

51. We are here considering what is probable or improbable given h, and the skeptic may endeavor to object that our whole general portrait of the data is exceedingly improbable given h, because the main thing that we should expect, given h, is stronger evidence for the reality of Jesus' resurrection. If Jesus rose from the dead, such skeptics will say, God ought to have made the evidence obvious. This objection could be used against any evidence for any miracle, and it simply reduces to the problem of divine hiddenness: the question of why, if God exists, he does not make his existence obvious. We will not consider this quite large issue here (but see Jake H. O'Connell, "Divine Hiddenness: Would More Miracles Solve the Problem?" *Heythrop Journal* 54 (2013): 261-67).

2. The Appearances were Collective and Recurrent: This datum is improbable given the apparition hypothesis. An apparition which appears both recurrently and collectively is a quite uncommon find in the apparition literature, except in the case of haunted houses (by a case of a haunted house, I mean a case of appearances which are confined to one particular locale).[52] But for the following reasons, Jesus' appearances are unlikely to have been occurrences of a haunting apparition.[53] First, just like cases of typical apparitions, there are few, if any, cases of haunting apparitions which appeared to large crowds.[54] Second, if the appearances all took place in a particular locale, it is surely unlikely that by the time of the Gospels, the tradition would have been changed such that there were appearances in many different locales. This is especially unlikely given that we know both Judaism and paganism prized sacred sites.[55] Third, such an apparition would not leave behind an empty tomb. Fourth, many cases of hauntings involve physical phenomena (footsteps, chills, et cetera). If

---

52. More precisely, I am aware of some cases of non-haunting, collective apparitions which recurred one time (case t12 in Hart and Hart, "Visions and Apparitions," and the Whitman case discussed in chapter 3), and I am not aware of any non-haunting, collective apparition which recurred more than one time. 1 Cor 15:3-8 mentions six appearances of Jesus.

And in fact, even if we dispense with the collective element, it should still be recognized that any type of a non-haunting, recurring apparition which recurred as much as Jesus' appearances did is uncommon. (I cannot think of any such cases, but without more careful consideration of the question, I am hesitant to declare that they are exceedingly uncommon.) One might wonder whether recurring apparitions may be underreported in the literature, for there could be cases of recurring apparitions which the witnesses are not aware are recurring, because they do not know someone else saw the apparition. For example, Bob sees an apparition but does not tell anyone, and Joe later sees an apparition of the same person, but does not tell anyone. Bob and Joe have seen a recurring apparition, but neither knows this, since neither has said anything. However, although this problem could lead to some underreporting, it cannot account for the fact that recurring apparitions are considerably more likely to be haunting apparitions. If witnesses of haunting apparitions are likely enough to talk to each other, witnesses of non-haunting apparitions ought also to talk to each other enough. It may be argued that witnesses of haunting apparitions are more likely to talk to each other, because a haunting apparition is an apparition which takes place in the same locale, and witnesses of an apparition are more likely to talk to each other if they both frequent the same locale. This argument would be persuasive if witnesses of non-haunting, recurring apparitions tend not to talk about the experience very much. However, this does not appear to be the case. Many witnesses of crisis apparitions tell someone else about the experience even before they find out that the person died (Gurney found plenty of cases of this nature). Witnesses of collective apparitions often tell others about it (e.g., see the case of an apparition in a bedroom which we discussed in chapter 3), and so do witnesses of informational apparitions (e.g., see the case of the Blue Orchid, discussed in chapter 3).

53. For well-evidenced cases of hauntings, see: three of the cases related in chapter 3 (the Cornell case, the Cheltenham case, and the Lady in Grey); five of the cases summarized in Hart and Hart, "Visions and Apparitions," (cases p21, t23, s27, t33, and t37); W.D. Bushell et al., "Second Report of the Committee On Haunted Houses," *Proceedings of the Society for Psychical Research* 2 (1884): 137-51; Anonymous [Society for Psychical Research], "Haunted House," *Journal of the Society for Psychical Research* 12 (1910): 374-80; Alan Gauld, "The Haunting of Abbey House, Cambridge," *Journal of the Society for Psychical Research* 46 (1972): 109-123.

54. Hart and Hart's review of collective apparitions included haunting apparitions.

55. See the sources referred to in Daniel A. Smith, *Revisiting the Empty Tomb: The Early History of Easter* (Minneapolis: Fortress, 2010), 232 n55.

such phenomena were present at Jesus' appearances, this would have tipped off the disciples that a haunting was going on. The fact that they did not conclude a haunting was occurring indicates that such phenomena were not present. Fifth, the fact that the appearances began three days after Jesus' death is considerably more likely given the resurrection hypothesis. For few, if any, cases of hauntings begin shortly after the death of the person whose apparition it is.[56] Thus, it is exceedingly improbable that a haunting apparition would appear shortly after the person's death, haunting apparitions evidently lacking either the desire or (more likely) the power to appear shortly after death. But it is not exceedingly improbable that a resurrected Jesus would appear shortly after death, for there is no reason to think it exceedingly improbable that a resurrected Jesus would have both the desire and power to appear shortly after death. Sixth, haunting apparitions typically display a lack of awareness of their surroundings. If Jesus displayed a lack of awareness of his surroundings, it is difficult to see how the disciples could have thought he was raised from the dead.[57]

So what we must endeavor to address is the probability of a non-haunting, collective and recurring apparition. Since such apparitions appear to be exceedingly uncommon, let us assign this datum a probability of 1% given the apparition hypothesis. Now as for the probability of the datum given h, I believe there is a greater than 1% chance a resurrected Jesus would want to make collective and recurring appearances. It would not be a surprise if Jesus wanted to appear to his close followers, of which there were many (the Twelve, his family, and other followers, such as Mary Magdalene), but these people are not likely to have all been in one place at the same time, and so a single appearance to all of them would not be possible. Thus, we should not be surprised by recurring appearances.[58] And collective appearances are not surpris-

---

56. Is there any way that haunting apparitions which commence soon after the person's death could be underreported in the literature? There appears to be no reason to think so. If people are likely to report non-haunting apparitions which begin shortly after the death of the person, there does not seem to be any reason why they would be unlikely to report haunting apparitions which begin shortly after the person's death.

57. The skeptic might suggest that the first person to see the risen Jesus experienced an individual hallucination in which the hallucinated Jesus proclaimed that he was risen from the dead, and this individual hallucination was coincidently followed by real apparitions. Thus, the disciples' belief in Jesus' resurrection was caused by the individual hallucination rather than the real apparitions. But such a coincidence would be extremely improbable. Consider all of the failed apocalyptic movements which history has bestowed upon us—the movement of Sabbatai Sevi, the movement of Joanna Southcott, the Millerites, the Jehovah's Witnesses, and many others. (For a list of such movements, see https://en.wikipedia.org/wiki/List_of_dates_predicted_for_apocalyptic_events; for a discussion of some of these movements, see Allison, *End of the Ages*, 163-68; Allison, *Constructing Jesus*, 148-53.) This hypothesis would require that out of all these movements, in only one case did someone experience an individual hallucination proclaiming that the leader of the apocalyptic movement was raised from the dead, and only in this same case did real apparitions of the leader occur (for, outside of the resurrection appearances, we have no cases of such leaders being proclaimed raised from the dead, and we have no cases of real apparitions of such leaders). This is definitely unlikely.

58. Even if we concede that non-haunting collective apparitions which recur one time ought not to count for highly uncommon, we can still make our second argument by noting that non-haunting,

ing because, since these followers often gathered together (e.g., Jesus' brothers would often be with his mother, the Twelve would often be in a group), unless Jesus went out of his way to avoid collective appearances, it would not be a surprise if some of his recurring appearances were also collective.

Bayesian Formulation: If Jesus was an apparition, it is exceedingly improbable that his appearances would be both collective and recurrent. So let us assign this datum given ~h a probability of 100:1 against. But it is plausible that if he rose from the dead, his appearances would be both collective and recurrent. So let us assign the odds of getting the datum given h as 10:1 against. Thus the datum favors h by odds of 10:1.

Bayesian Update: 10:1 x 10:1 = 100:1.

3. *The Appearance to Paul*: The appearance to Paul does not seem exceedingly improbable given h. Such an appearance would certainly be likely to stop the persecution which Paul was carrying out (Gal 1:13), and so we should expect Jesus to have the desire to make such an appearance, and there does not appear to be any reason why he would not also have the power to make such an appearance. Hence the datum is not exceedingly improbable given h. However, the datum does appear to be exceedingly improbable given ~h, for cases of apparitions which appear to persecutors, or which make an appearance which is any way analogous to an appearance to a persecutor, are very uncommon.[59]

Bayesian Formulation: Let us suppose the odds of Jesus appearing to Paul given that he rose from the dead are 10:1, and the odds of Jesus appearing to Paul given that he was an apparition are 100:1. The datum supports h by odds of 10:1.

Bayesian Update: 100:1 x 10:1 = 1000:1.

An Analogy

Let us suppose that a New Year's festival is being held in Los Angeles, and thousands of people have decided to attend. While at this festival, someone discovers that his wallet has been stolen, and hence that a case of pickpocketing has occurred.[60] The police are endeavoring to find the culprit, and the first thing they must determine is whether the thief was an experienced pickpocket or an inexperienced pickpocket

---

collective appearances which recur as much as Jesus' appearances did are uncommon. It would not be a surprise if a resurrected Jesus wanted to appear to groups, and it would not be a surprise if he wanted to make more than two appearances. But, if non-haunting, collective apparitions which recur more than one time are highly uncommon, then a non-haunting, collective apparition which recurs more than one time must be construed as exceedingly improbable given ~h. And so the datum is highly improbable given ~h, but not so given h.

59. I am not aware of any cases of real apparitions which appear to a persecutor. The skeptic might suggest that an appearance to a persecutor could fit under some more general category. Although I am open to this possibility, I do not see any more general category under which it fits.

60. In real life, if someone discovers that his wallet is missing, possibilities other than pickpocketing must be considered. But, to keep the analogy simple, let us suppose that the police have somehow been able to rule out all non-pickpocketing hypotheses.

(let us suppose that the reason they wish to determine this is because they know that an inexperienced pickpocket is considerably easier to catch). How do they proceed? They endeavor to determine whether each piece of data is more probable given that the thief was an experienced pickpocket, or given that he was an inexperienced pickpocket. The first piece of data which they consider is the fact that the act of thievery took place in front of a large crowd. They know that an experienced pickpocket would not commit such an act in front of a large crowd, for experienced pickpockets know that they are considerably more likely to be caught if they perpetrate the act in front of a large number of witnesses, but an inexperienced pickpocket does not know this, thinking he can get away with it. In other words, an act of pickpocketing in front of a large crowd is plausible given an inexperienced pickpocket, but implausible given an experienced one. Hence, the police conclude that this datum is considerably more likely given the hypothesis that an inexperienced pickpocket committed the crime. Then they consider the second piece of data, which is the fact that, in addition to committing an act of pickpocketing which took place in front of more than one witness, the pickpocket also committed other acts of pickpocketing at this same festival (in other words, we have had an act of pickpocketing which was perceived collectively, and we have had recurrent acts of pickpocketing). The police know that this datum is considerably more likely given an inexperienced pickpocket than given an experienced one. For the police know that though it is plausible that an inexperienced thief would commit further acts of pickpocketing after having committed one in front of more than one witness, it is not plausible that an experienced thief would do this. For an experienced thief knows that if he has committed an act of pickpocketing in front of more than one witness,[61] there is a greater chance of being caught if he commits more acts of pickpocketing, because there is a greater chance that someone observed his first act of pickpocketing and so people may be on the lookout for him (most acts of pickpocketing are undetected at the time the act is committed, it is not noted that anything is awry until later on, when the victim discovers his wallet is stolen). But the inexperienced pickpocket does not know this. Finally, the police consider the third datum—the fact that the culprit (or at least, someone matching the description of the culprit)[62] later appeared in front of a police officer, a member of the group which is

---

61. Let us suppose that the experienced pickpocket would hardly ever commit an act of pickpocketing in front of a large crowd, but he sometimes commits an act of pickpocketing in front of a small number of witnesses. He knows that committing an act of pickpocketing in front of a large crowd would raise the odds too much that he will be caught. But an act of pickpocketing in front of a small crowd, though it raises the odds that he will get caught, does not raise the odds to too great of an extent (he cannot be extremely particular about when he commits an act of pickpocketing, because opportunities to commit such an act are hard to come by).

62. The analogy is not completely exact, for Paul knew for sure that the one who appeared to him was Jesus, but a police officer is unlikely to know for sure that a criminal has appeared before him. The criminal would not likely tell the police officer that he is a criminal, so all the police officer could be sure of is that someone matching the culprit's description has appeared to him (and, let us suppose for the sake of our analogy that the description was quite specific, not a general description would could

trying to catch the pickpockets. We know it is exceedingly improbable that an experienced pickpocket would do this, but is not implausible that an inexperienced one would do this (the inexperienced one might not realize that there is a good chance that someone has seen his act of pickpocketing, and so he does not expect that any description of him has gotten round to the police). Clearly, all the data points in the direction of an inexperienced pickpocket.[63]

Bayesian Conclusion for 1 Corinthians 15:3-8: Odds of 1000:1 in favor of h.

Sample Size

Before we move on, a point should be made concerning sample size. We found three pieces of data from Paul which are more probable given the resurrection hypothesis than given the apparition hypothesis. But since we have only a very small sample of Paul's knowledge of the resurrection appearances (he only spends five verses discussing them), Paul must of course have had more data than what he reveals in these five verses. But since in this small sample we have found only data which is more probable given the resurrection hypothesis, we should expect that if we had more of Paul's data, we would find more data which is more probable given h. For if Paul had primarily data which was more probable given ~h, or if his data was fairly evenly mixed, it is not likely we would only find data more probable on h in the small sample of his data we do have. Thus, though the probability of h is already high based on the amount of data we do have, we should expect that if we had more data from Paul, the probability of h would become even higher.

---

fit many individuals).

63. This same type of analogy can be made for the haunting apparition hypothesis. The point about the large crowds remains the same. In regard to haunting apparitions not commencing shortly after death, we might say that an experienced pickpocket does not often commit an act of pickpocketing shortly after the opening of the festival, because the experienced pickpocket knows that at the beginning of the festival, when people have not yet had much to drink, a victim of pickpocketing is more likely to notice the fact that he is being pickpocketed. But after the festival has gone on for a while, and many people have had a lot to drink, a victim is less likely to notice. However, the inexperienced pickpocket does not know this. With regard to the physical phenomena, we might say that when an act of pickpocketing is committed by an experienced pickpocket, it is often the case that physical evidence is left—namely, a burn mark in the victim's pocket—because an experienced pickpocket often uses a mechanical device to remove the wallet from the pocket. An inexperienced pickpocket, however, does not often do this, because he does not know how to obtain this device. Our points about the appearances being confined to a particular locale, and the empty tomb, and ghosts being unaware of their surroundings, could also be worked into the analogy, but this would make the analogy more complex. The essential point is that we look for evidence which is more probable given one hypothesis than given the alternative hypothesis.

Data Which Comes From the Gospels if Their General Reliability is not Accepted

The Empty Tomb (or Empty Burial Place): In chapter 4, we concluded that the only datum of the Gospels which can be accepted as historical if the Gospels are not generally reliable is the fact that Jesus' tomb (or burial place, if Jesus was buried in the ground) was discovered empty. If Jesus rose from the dead, the probability of getting an empty tomb is clearly 100%, since a resurrected person would necessarily leave behind an empty tomb. The probability of the empty tomb given the apparition hypothesis is very low: An apparition would not leave behind an empty tomb, because an apparition is a non-physical being, and hence if someone appears as an apparition, that is not going to have any effect on the whereabouts of their body.

However, the proponent of the apparition hypothesis would no doubt want to argue that Jesus' tomb became empty for some other reason, and then combine the apparition hypothesis with the hypothesis of a naturalistic explanation for the empty tomb (or rather, as I will explain, with the entire set of plausible naturalistic explanations). Now, in choosing a hypothesis for the empty tomb, the proponent of the apparition hypothesis would not be able to choose a hypothesis which would require that the appearances be explained by some other hypothesis than the apparition hypothesis. For example, he would not be able to entertain the hypothesis that the disciples stole the body, because that hypothesis requires that the appearances were a result of the disciples lying. And he would not be able to entertain the swoon hypothesis because that hypothesis requires that the appearances were the result of Jesus tricking the disciples into thinking he was resurrected. The proponent of the apparition hypothesis is thus constrained to those hypotheses for the empty tomb which are not mutually exclusive of the apparition hypothesis. And also, he is constrained to those hypotheses which are not so outrageous that their probability is negligibly low (for example, the hypothesis that aliens abducted the body or the hypothesis that the body spontaneously disintegrated). The available hypotheses would seem to be as follows: 1) the hypothesis that disciples of Jesus other than the main group of disciples stole the body (in this case, the appearances would not be a result of lies, because the disciples who witnessed the appearances would not be the same disciples who knew the body was stolen). 2) The hypothesis that sorcerers robbed Jesus' grave (we know that sorcerers did sometimes rob graves).[64] 3) The hypothesis that Joseph of Arimathea moved the body to another tomb.[65] Now if any of these hypotheses is true, they do of

---

64. On the possibility of grave robbery by sorcerers, see Richard C. Carrier, "The Plausibility of Theft," in Robert M. Price and Jeffrey Jay Lowder eds., *The Empty Tomb: Jesus Beyond the Grave* (Amherst, NY: Prometheus, 2005), 349-68 (350-51). For a response to the grave robbery hypothesis, see James Patrick Holding, "The Stolen Body Theory," in James Patrick Holding ed., *Defending the Resurrection: Did Jesus Rise from the Dead?* (Maitland, FL: Xulon: 2010), 390-98 (390-93).

65. Carrier has also made the most thorough case for this hypothesis: Richard C. Carrier, "The Burial of Jesus in Light of Jewish Law," in *Empty Tomb*, 369-92. For a refutation, see Glenn Miller,

course explain the empty tomb, but the problem for the skeptic is that none of these hypotheses has a very high probability.[66] In regard to 1), if disciples other than the main group of disciples stole the body, we would expect that they would have told the other disciples about this once the other disciples began to believe Jesus rose from the dead. And further, there is not any plausible motivation for why any of Jesus' disciples would want to steal the body. In regard to 2), although sorcerers did occasionally rob graves, this was a quite uncommon occurrence, and is thus improbable. (And it was probably even less common in Palestine than in the Roman world.)[67] And in regard to 3), there is not any plausible motivation for Joseph of Arimathea to move the body, and if he did, we would expect him to have produced it once the disciples began to proclaim the resurrection.

Bayesian Formulation: The probability of getting an empty tomb if Jesus rose from the dead (h) is 100%. The probability of getting an empty tomb if any of these other three hypotheses is true is also 100%, but since all of these hypotheses have significant problems, there is a low probability any of them is true in the first place. Let us assign each hypothesis a probability of 300:1 against. If the odds in the case of each hypothesis are 300:1 against, the odds that one of the three of them is true become 300:1 divided by 3 = 100:1 against. The odds of getting an empty tomb are thus 100 times greater (100:1 in favor vs. 100:1 against) on the resurrection hypothesis than on the apparition hypothesis. Hence the datum favors h by odds of 100:1.

Bayesian Conclusion for 1 Corinthians 15:3-8 Plus the Empty Tomb: 1000:1 x 100:1 = 100,000:1.

Data which Comes from the Gospels if their General Reliability is Accepted

1. The Physicality of Jesus' Appearances: Several facts indicate that the resurrected Jesus was physical, and physicality is clearly more probable on the resurrection hypothesis.

"Good Question: Was the Burial of Jesus a Temporary One Because of Time Constraints," http://christianthinktank.com/shellgame.html; and James Patrick Holding, "The Wrong Tomb Theories," in *Defending the Resurrection*, 399-407 (403-404).

66. For more complete refutations of naturalistic explanations for the empty tomb, see Craig, *Assessing*, 255-74; James D.G. Dunn, *Jesus Remembered* (Grand Rapids, MI: Eerdmans, 2003), 828-40; Dale C. Allison Jr., *Resurrecting Jesus: The Earliest Christian Tradition and its Interpreters* (New York: T&T Clark, 2005), 299-331

67. All of the texts cited by Carrier in the essay referred to above are from the Roman world. There is at least one Jewish text which mentions grave robbing sorcerers: Babylonian Talmud, Baba Bathra, 58a (the text presents a fictional story, but fictional stories can still reflect actual practices). But the reason I think grave robbing sorcerers were much less likely to be found in Palestine is because we have very few references to sorcerers in Palestine (no sources come to my mind except the one I just cited; I exclude references to sorcerers in the Old Testament, for just because sorcerers were common in Palestine in the Old Testament, that does not mean they were common during Jesus' time), but there existence in the Greco-Roman world is much more well documented: See Daniel Ogden, *Magic, Witchcraft, and Ghosts in the Greek and Roman Worlds: A Sourcebook* (Oxford: Oxford University Press, 2002).

First, a number of passages tell us that after Jesus' resurrection, he ate (Lk 24:41-43; Jn 21:15; Acts 10:41). Now it would not be surprising if a resurrected person ate, since a resurrected person is a physical being and a physical being can eat. But it would be surprising if an apparition ate, for an apparition is a non-physical being and thus should not be able to eat (and there are no accounts of apparitions which appear to contradict this claim).[68] Second, Jesus is touched (Mt 28:9; Jn 20:17). This is unsurprising on the resurrection hypothesis, but it is surprising on the apparition hypothesis, since apparitions are rarely touched.[69] Third, Jesus leaves a physical effect on the environment: John 20:7 tells us that his burial cloths were rolled up after he exited the tomb. As we explained in chapter 3, apparitions do not often leave effects on the physical environment. Fourth, Jesus calls attention to his crucifixion wounds (Lk 24:39-40; Jn 20:27), an action which is plausible on the resurrection hypothesis, but implausible on the apparition hypothesis since there are few, if any, cases of apparitions calling attention to ostensibly physical wounds.

Bayesian Formulation: If Jesus rose from the dead, it is highly probable that he would give evidence of being a physical being. But if Jesus was an apparition, it is exceedingly improbable he would give evidence of being a physical being since, as we have just explained, apparitions rarely give such evidence. Let us assign the odds that Jesus would give such evidence given that he was resurrected as close to 100%, and the odds he would do so if he was an apparition as 100:1 against. The datum thus favors h by odds of 100:1.

2. *The Length of Jesus' Appearances*: At least two of Jesus' appearances lasted a long time. At the Emmaus appearance, Jesus accompanies the Emmaus disciples for a seven mile walk. And in the appearance related in John 21, Jesus eats breakfast with the disciples and continues to converse with them after breakfast. Long appearances are exceedingly improbable given the apparition hypothesis, for apparitions rarely, if ever, last very long.[70] But long appearances are not exceedingly improbable given the

---

68. There are accounts of apparitions eating in ancient literature, but no accounts which could be argued to be historically reliable.

69. According to Hart, "Six Theories," 168, 8% of apparitions are perceived tactually. But it is almost always the apparition making contact with the percipient, not the percipient making contact with the apparition. G.N.M. Tyrell, *Apparitions* (New York: Macmillan, 1963 [1953]) tells us "in nearly all cases it is the apparition which touches the percipient."

70. No apparition in Hart's collection lasted more than a half hour (Hart, "Six Theories," 159). Erlendur Haraldsson, *The Departed Among the Living: An Investigative Study of Afterlife Encounters* (Guildford: White Crow, 2012), 210 reports the only case that comes to my mind in which the apparition lasted a long time and there is also some evidence that the apparition is real. However, the evidence is very weak: the identity of the apparition was established based on a very general description that could fit many people, and further, the individual who supposedly identified him could not remember this when questioned. In contrast to ostensibly real apparitions, and apparitions to psychologically normal people in general, note the long conversations carried on with the apparitions in three cases in which the witness appears to have been mentally imbalanced: William F. Matchett, "Repeated Hallucinatory Experiences as a Part of the Mourning Process among Hopi Indian Women,"

resurrection hypothesis, for if Jesus was really raised, it makes sense that he would want to appear to his followers at length in order to continue the fellowship he had with them before his death.

Bayesian Formulation: If Jesus was an apparition it is exceedingly improbable the appearances would have lasted a long time. But if Jesus was resurrected, it is not exceedingly improbable the appearances would have lasted a long time. Let us assign the odds of long appearances given that Jesus was an apparition as 100:1 against, and the odds of long appearances given that he was resurrected as 10:1 against. The datum favors h by odds of 10:1.

Bayesian Update: 100:1 x 10:1 = 1000:1. (We are considering for now only the data which comes from the Gospels if their general reliability is accepted, and so are not including for now the data of 1 Corinthians 15 or the empty tomb. This is why our calculation is restarting.)

3. *The Earthquake*: Matthew tells us there was an earthquake at the time of Jesus' resurrection (Mt 28:2). Now if Jesus was actually raised, an earthquake is not particularly surprising, for in the Bible earthquakes often occur in conjunction with divine activity (e.g., Isa 29:6; Ezek 38:19; Zech 14:5). But if Jesus was an apparition, God was not involved, and so we must postulate that the earthquake was a mere coincidence.

Bayesian Formulation: The odds of an earthquake just happening to occur on the day Jesus is believed to have risen from the dead are clearly very low. Suppose we assume there was an earthquake in Jerusalem once every 1000 days, and thus assign the odds of this datum on ~h as 1000:1 against. If the odds of God causing an earthquake to herald Jesus' resurrection are as low as 100:1 against, the datum still favors h by odds of 10:1.

Bayesian Update: 1000:1 x 10:1 = 10,000:1.

4. *The Angel*: Matthew also tells us that on Sunday morning, an angel rolled away the stone from the tomb (Mt 28:2). This is not especially improbable given h, for angels often aid God, and so it would not be surprising that an angel would participate in the event of Jesus' resurrection. By contrast, the apparition hypothesis would have to propose that the angel rolled back the stone even though Jesus was not actually about to come forth from the tomb. We do not have any reports in the apparition literature of angels rolling back stones, and thus this event is clearly improbable given ~h.

Bayesian Formulation: Let us suppose the odds of an angel rolling back a stone on h are 10:1 against and the odds of this on ~h are 100:1. The datum supports h by odds of 10:1.

Bayesian Update: 10,000:1 x 10:1 = 100,000:1.

Psychiatry 2 (1972): 185-94.

5. *Jesus Gives the Disciples the Holy Spirit*: In John 20:22, Jesus breathes on the disciples to give them the Holy Spirit. This is not exceedingly improbable given that Jesus rose, for if he had, the Messianic age had dawned, and an outpouring of the Holy Spirit was expected to occur during the Messianic age (Joel 2:29; Acts 2:16). But we have few, if any, reports of apparitions breathing on the witnesses.

Bayesian Formulation: Let us suppose the odds of Jesus breathing on the disciples given that he rose from the dead are 10:1 against, and the odds of him doing this given that he was an apparition are 100:1 against. The datum favors h by odds of 10:1.

Bayesian Update: 100,000:1 x 10:1 = 1 million:1.

6. *Jesus Displays ESP*: In John 21:6, Jesus knows where the fish are even though he could not know this by normal means, and in John 21:18-19, Jesus predicts Peter's death by crucifixion. Although apparitions sometimes present the percipient with information that could not have been known by normal means (that is what informational apparitions are), the information is typically[71] information which pertains to their death. Thus the probability of an apparition displaying the sort of ESP Jesus displayed is exceedingly low. But if Jesus was raised from the dead, it is not surprising that he would display this sort of ESP, for he had displayed it during his ministry (e.g., he knew Peter would find a coin in a fish's mouth (Mt 17:27); he knew Judas would betray him; and he knew Peter would deny him), and thus it is not surprising that he would display it after rising from the dead.

Bayesian Formulation: Let us suppose the odds of Jesus having this sort of ESP given that he was resurrected are 10:1 against, and the odds of this given that he was an apparition are 100:1 against. The datum supports h by odds of 10:1.

Bayesian Update: 1 million:1 x 10:1 = 10 million:1.

7. *Jesus Says He is Raised*: The most pressing problem for the apparition hypothesis is the fact that Jesus tells the disciples he is raised. Jesus tells the disciples he has risen from the dead, and in fact, even tells them he is not an apparition. Luke 24:46, "thus it is written, that the Christ would suffer and rise again from the dead the third day." Luke 24:44, "Why are you troubled, and why do doubts arise in your hearts? See My hands and My feet, that it is I Myself; touch Me and see, for a spirit does not have flesh and bones as you see that I have." And John 20:27, "Reach here with your finger, and see My hands; and reach here your hand and put it into My side; and do not be unbelieving, but believing." This data is clearly quite expected on the resurrection hypothesis but quite unexpected on the apparition hypothesis.

---

71. In Hart's collection, only 1% of apparitions had precognitive or retrocognitive features ("Six Theories," 168). But Hart does not cite the case or cases in his collection which illustrate this, so there is no way to know whether we can rule out naturalistic explanations in the case or cases in question, and thus we cannot know whether these features have actually been documented among apparitions.

Bayesian Formulation: To explain Jesus uttering these sorts of words if he was an apparition but was not trying to deceive the disciples (we will consider the possibility that he was trying to deceive the disciples when we consider the objective vision theory), the apparition hypothesis must propose some reason other than deception for why Jesus would claim that he rose from the dead. No plausible reason seems forthcoming. We could propose that Jesus was in a very confused state, and did not know what he was saying (perhaps one's mind becomes very foggy as one makes the transition to the spiritual world). Or, to anticipate an idea we will address more fully below, we could suppose that the disciples' minds somehow altered the message Jesus was trying to convey to them; Jesus was trying to say he was an apparition, but the disciples changed the message into a claim of resurrection. But there are no other cases of apparitions where the apparition mistakenly communicates the idea that he has risen from the dead. Thus even if apparitions are sometimes in a confused state, or even if the witnesses are able to alter an apparition's message to some extent, these phenomena would still leave Jesus' claim to be risen from the dead implausible given the apparition hypothesis. Thus Jesus saying these sorts of things is exceedingly improbable given ~h, but of course, highly probable given h, for a person who was actually raised from the dead would be expected to say so. Let us assign the odds of the data given ~h as 1000:1 against, and odds of the data given h as 100%. The odds are thus 1000:1 in favor of h.

Bayesian Update: 10 million:1 x 1000:1 = 10 billion:1.

Bayesian Conclusion for 1 Corinthians 15:3-8, Plus the Empty Tomb, Plus the Information Which We Can Get From the Gospels if the Gospels are Generally Reliable: 100,000:1 x 10 billion:1 = 1,000,000,000,000,000: 1 (i.e., 1 quadrillion to one).

Dependence Hypotheses

This calculation has assumed that all of the factors are independent. I have made this assumption because the factors do not seem to be related to each other at all.[72] For example, eating fish does not seem to be related to how long an appearance lasts. So there is no reason to think an apparition which eats fish is more likely to last a long time, or vice versa. Or again, earthquakes do not appear to be related to displaying ESP. So there is no reason to think an apparition which displays ESP would be more likely to coincide with an earthquake, or vice versa. The only thing which seems to bind the factors together is that they are all not exceedingly improbable if Jesus rose from the dead. However, there are two hypotheses of dependence which need to be considered. The first is the hypothesis that Jesus was trying to mislead the disciples into thinking he was raised from the dead. We will consider this hypothesis below when we look at the objective vision theory. But one other hypothesis of dependence

---

72. Except that we did find a relationship between recurrent and collective apparitions, and we addressed that.

could conceivably be proposed, and that is that the reason this apparition was able to do so many things an apparition does not usually do is because this apparition was a very powerful apparition, an apparition which was able to control the means by which apparitions get through to a greater extent than typical apparitions. If we hypothesize an extremely powerful apparition, then the factors would be dependent, because they all derive from the apparition's greater control of the laws of apparitions.

But there are two problems with this hypothesis. The first problem is that the resurrected Jesus does not merely do things which an apparition does not typically do; all of the things he does are more probable given that Jesus rose from the dead than given that he was an apparition. If Jesus was simply a more powerful apparition, he ought to have done other things which apparitions do not typically do besides just those things we should expect to find if Jesus rose from the dead. For example, suppose the apparition was more transparent than typical apparitions, glided through the air more often than typical apparitions, was invisible to some of the witnesses more often than typical apparitions, passed through matter more often than typical apparitions, or communicated telepathically more often. These are all characteristics which apparitions do not typically have (only a fairly low percentage of apparitions have them),[73] but which would be more probable given that Jesus was an apparition than given that he rose from the dead. If Jesus was an apparition with greater power, why did he only use his greater power to do things which a resurrected person would be more likely to do than an apparition, and never use his greater power to do things which an apparition would be more likely to do than a resurrected person? This would not make sense unless Jesus was trying to deceive the witnesses of his appearances. Thus this hypothesis does not predict the data well, because it cannot account for why Jesus does not do anything which is more expected if he was an apparition.

The second problem for this hypothesis is a problem we have encountered before, that is, the fact that Jesus did not tell the disciples he was an apparition. Surely an exceptionally powerful apparition, which was capable of all sorts of feats apparitions do not usually perform, would be capable of the simple feat of communicating to the disciples the fact that he was an apparition and not a person physically raised from the dead.

It should also be noted that even if I am mistaken in regarding all of the factors we have examined as independent, the entire case for the resurrection hypothesis would not topple. If I am mistaken only in the case of a small number of factors, the argument would only lose a slight bit of force. For example, if two of the factors which support h by odds of 10:1 were shown to be completely expected given one of the factors in the list, the strength of h would be reduced by odds of 100:1 (10:1 x 10:1). But even if the odds in favor of the resurrection hypothesis were reduced by 100:1, the

---

73. See Hart, "Six Theories," for all these characteristics. 2% of apparitions are transparent (168); 4% glide instead of walk (168); 14% are not seen by all present (159); 6% pass through matter (168); 4% communicate telepathically.

odds in its favor would still remain very high. And it should also be realized that dependence can reduce the evidential force of a datum without entirely taking away its evidential force. For example, suppose Jesus displaying his wounds has a probability of 100:1 given ~h if the datum is independent, but we think that given that Jesus ate fish, the datum has a probability of 50:1. The evidential force of Jesus displaying his wounds is reduced by half, but it is clearly not completely eliminated.

Objection: Apparitions and Cultural Variance

A possible objection to my argument concerns the possibility of cultural variance in regard to apparitions. We have determined the probability an apparition will have certain characteristics by considering the frequency with which apparitions that have been reported in contemporary times have had those characteristics. But isn't it possible that the frequency of characteristics of apparitions could vary across time and culture? Perhaps apparitions in Jesus' culture were different, and so perhaps the characteristics which we are unlikely to find when examining contemporary cases of apparitions would not be unlikely to be found if we examined cases of apparitions from Jesus' culture. For example, even though apparitions of today do not last a long time, perhaps apparitions in Jesus' culture did. Or, even though apparitions today do not appear to more than three people, perhaps apparitions in Jesus' culture did.

In response, we first have to admit that some characteristics of apparitions do vary depending on the time and/or culture. Consider the evidence of a study by Erlendur Haraldsson and Karlis Osis which compared deathbed visions in India to deathbed visions in the US.[74] They found significant variance in the case of a variety of factors. For example, in the US sample, 61% of the apparitions seen were female as compared to 23% in the Indian sample.[75] And in the US sample, 66% saw apparitions of the dead and 12% saw apparitions of religious figures, whereas in the Indian sample, 28% saw apparitions of the dead and 48% saw apparitions of religious figures.[76] However, Haraldsson and Osis also found evidence of cultural stability on a number of other factors. For example, though the two cultures varied in regard to what percent of apparitions were religious figures and what percent where deceased persons, if we add up the two categories, we find that the percentage of people who saw some type of apparition (either a religious figure or a deceased person) was 78% vs. 76%. Another close correlation concerned the percentage of apparitions which indicated that their purpose in coming was to take the witness away to death: this was 79% vs. 69%.[77] In

---

74. Karlis Osis and Erlendur Haraldsson, "Deathbed Observations by Physicians and Nurses: A Cross-Cultural Survey," *Journal of the American Society for Psychical Research* 71 (1977): 237-59; Karlis Osis and Erlendur Haraldsson, *At the Hour of Death* (3rd ed.; Norwalk, CT: Hastings House, 1997).

75. Osis and Haraldsson, *Hour*, 100.

76. Osis and Haraldsson, *Hour*, 93-94.

77. Osis and Haraldsson, *Hour*, 90.

addition, other studies have found close correlations on various other factors. For example, the percentage of apparitions that had died violent deaths in Erlendur Haraldsson's collection of apparitions from late twentieth century Iceland was very close to the percentage found by the Census in its study of the late nineteenth century UK: the numbers were 30% vs. 28%.[78] Another example is the percentage of the population which has seen an apparition. D.J. West replicated the Census on a smaller scale in 1948 and 1990. In the three studies, the percentage of the population which had seen an apparition was very close: 10%, 14%, and 11%.[79] (Although we should note that Ian Stevenson did not find any reports of apparitions in a culture in Lebanon.[80] Thus, it is possible the prevalence of apparitions varies. However, it is also possible that the reason Stevenson did not find any reports in this culture is because the subjects lied about not having seen apparitions. Apparitions did not fit into the group's worldview—the group believed that people are immediately reincarnated upon death, and thus souls are never disembodied and thus cannot appear as apparitions. Therefore, the subjects would have a motivation to lie about not having seen apparitions.[81])

Thus the evidence indicates that some characteristics vary and others do not. So the question is whether the specific factors I have cited above vary. There are three points to make in this regard. First, some of the data cited above as being improbable on the apparition hypothesis could not vary by the culture, because the data are not related to the characteristics of the apparitions: The empty tomb, the angel rolling away the stone, the earthquake, and Jesus telling the disciples he rose from the dead are clearly not facts which we could potentially be more likely to find in one culture rather than another.

Second, in the case of all the data improbable given ~h and probable given h I cite above, which are based on the frequency of certain characteristics among contemporary reports of apparitions (e.g., length of appearance, eating, the sort of ESP displayed by Jesus), the characteristics are unknown or rare (occurring less than 1% of the time) in all cases that have been collected in modern times, not just in a particular collection of cases (such as the Census or West's). (I base this judgment on my general knowledge of the literature, having read through thousands of accounts of apparitions.) Now the accounts collected in contemporary times have actually been drawn from a rather wide range of eras and cultures. We have accounts from the late 1800s to today, which means, as far as the question of time, any changes that have taken place over the course of the last 130 years ought to be evident to us. And the accounts have

---

78. Haraldsson, "Experiences of Encounters with the Dead," 107.

79. See n2 in chapter 1.

80. Ian Stevenson, *Cases of the Reincarnation Type: Volume 3: Twelve Cases in Lebanon and Turkey* (Charlottesville, VA: University of Virginia Press, 1980).

81. It is well known that people have a tendency to lie in order to give socially desirable answers. This is called "social desirability bias." See e.g., Anton J. Nederhof, "Methods of Coping with Social Desirability Bias: A Review," *European Journal of Social Psychology* 15 (1985): 263-80.

come from various different cultures and subcultures. The apparition accounts which the SPR collected in the late 1800s were collected almost entirely from members of the upper class, whereas accounts in more recent times have come primarily from average people. The subculture of upper class Victorian England was significantly different from the subculture of most average people today. Also, about 1000 of the 17,000 cases collected by the Census of Hallucinations were not drawn from England, but came from various other countries (Brazil, Austria, Germany, France, Italy, and Sweden).[82] Haraldsson's cases of apparitions were collected in Iceland from the 1970s until more recent times,[83] and Haraldsson has said that Iceland underwent significant cultural changes over the course of that time period.[84] Haraldsson and Osis's study of deathbed visions in India is also relevant. They did not report that any of their cases from India displayed any of the characteristics which I cited above as being rare or unknown among contemporary apparitions. Further, I have read through all of the accounts of apparitions published on the website adcrf.org, of which there are over twenty from non-Western countries (e.g., India, Pakistan, Jordan), as well as Charles Emmons's study of 146 apparition accounts from Hong Kong,[85] and do not recall seeing any accounts of apparitions with any of the characteristics in question. Thus I think the research which has been done on apparitions in different cultures is sufficient for us to conclude that the characteristics I cited above are very uncommon for apparitions regardless of the culture.

(I have at various points in this work cited a study by Hornell Hart entitled "Six Theories About Apparitions," which studied the frequency of various characteristics of apparitions. We can have a reasonable amount of confidence in the generalizability of this study's findings, because the study takes reports from a wide range of years instead of from one particular collection; it is a study of 165 cases of ostensibly real apparitions (104 apparitions of the dead, and 61 apparitions of the living) which appeared in the literature from about 1870-1950. But, except for the instances in which the study has been cited in the current section (the section entitled "Data Which is More Probable on the Resurrection Hypothesis,"), I cannot supplement the study's results by affirming that my general knowledge of the literature verifies that the characteristic is just as uncommon for apparitions not included in this study as for those included in it. In the case of all the characteristics I have cited in this section, the characteristics are rare (occurring less than 1% of the time) or unknown in all the literature I have read, and I can confidently claim that this is so, because it is not difficult to remember from one's general knowledge of the literature that a certain characteristic shows up rarely if ever. But with regard to characteristics which Hart

---

82. Sidgwick, "Census," 159.

83. Haraldsson, "Experiences of Encounters with the Dead."

84. Erlendur Haraldsson, "Psychic Experiences – Third of a Century Apart: Two Representative Surveys in Iceland," *Journal of the Society for Psychical Research* 75 (2011): 76-90.

85. Emmons, *Chinese Ghosts*.

found to be more common, (characteristics occurring 5%, of the time, 10% of the time, 20%, of the time, etc) it is not possible for me to say that the characteristic shows up with the same amount of frequency in the rest of the literature, for one cannot make a judgment on these sorts of numerical estimates in the way that one can if one is only being asked to judge whether a certain characteristic shows up rarely or never. However, Hart's study, since it covers a wide range of literature, is better than nothing, and thus is worth citing; but I do not think anything essential in this book hinges on frequencies for which I have had to rely solely on Hart's study.[86])

Third, if the frequency of some characteristics of apparitions were different during Jesus' time, we should not expect that the characteristics would differ in such a way that all the things which we should expect to find if Jesus was resurrected would also be things we would expect to find if he was an apparition in the ancient world. If all of the characteristics which are typically uncommon among apparitions in our day and probable given the resurrection, were common among ancient apparitions, it would look as if ancient apparitions were intending to mimic the appearance of someone physically raised. Thus even if some of the characteristics we have cited above would not be improbable given the apparition hypothesis in the ancient world, the odds are very low that all of them would be—unless ancient apparitions were trying to mimic the appearance of resurrected people, but that idea is itself extremely improbable.

Data Alleged to be More Probable on the Apparition Hypothesis

Before we look at the data which is potentially more probable given ~h, I should say that I am not going to consider here any data which has been alleged to be more probable given ~h but which I have already shown to be more probable given h. For example, the fact that the appearances were collective,[87] recurrent,[88] or that Jesus was seen by someone who did not know him in life (Paul).[89] Although these data have been argued to be more probable given ~h, I have already shown them to be more probable given h, and there is no need to repeat the same arguments given above.

1. Jesus is Unrecognized[90]

The Argument: It is a well-known fact that in some of Jesus' resurrection appearances he is not initially recognized as Jesus. In the Emmaus appearance, he accompanies two

---

86. I noted above that Emmons's study *Chinese Ghosts* contradicts Hart's in regard to the frequency of certain characteristics. But as I also noted, Emmons is not a study of real apparitions, thus we cannot be sure his findings would apply to such a study.
87. Allison, *Resurrecting*, 279.
88. Allison, *Resurrecting*, 279.
89. Allison, *Resurrecting*, 280.
90. Leslie D. Weatherhead, *The Resurrection of Christ: In The Light of Modern Science and Psychical*

disciples on a seven mile journey and explains the Old Testament prophecies to them, but they do not know who he is until the end of the journey. In John 20:14, Mary does not recognize him when he first speaks, and in John 21:12 we read, "Jesus said to them, 'Come and have breakfast'. None of the disciples ventured to question Him, 'Who are You?' knowing that it was the Lord." The implication is that there was some reason to doubt whether the figure they saw was Jesus. Now we must admit that in the case of John 20:14 and 21:12, there may very well be natural explanations for why Jesus was not recognized: Mary may not have recognized him because she was not facing him at first (the passage says that she recognized Jesus when she turned towards him), and the disciples may not have recognized him in John 21 because of the distance (Jesus was on the shore though they were in a boat some distance away). However, in the Emmaus account, there must surely be some supernatural or paranormal explanation for the non-recognition, for distance certainly cannot explain it (Jesus was within a few feet of them) and we can hardly suppose, as John Gill suggested,[91] that the two disciples, being exceedingly distraught over Jesus' death, kept their heads down the entire walk and never bothered to look at the face of the person walking with them.

The argument for the apparition hypothesis is that if Jesus was a physical being it would be rather peculiar for anyone to fail to recognize him, so perhaps this fact is better explained on the hypothesis that Jesus was not physical.

Bayesian Formulation: If Jesus was an apparition (~h) it is probable he would be unrecognized. But if he was resurrected (h), it is improbable he would be unrecognized. (Or even if it is improbable he would be unrecognized on ~h, it is significantly more improbable on h.)

Response: It is indeed the case that the non-recognition of Jesus is peculiar on the resurrection hypothesis. But what do we mean by peculiar? When we say that this or that fact is peculiar on some hypothesis we mean that the hypothesis gives us no reason to expect that fact; the probability of the datum given the hypothesis is not high; it is either low or neutral. However, if the datum has a low or neutral probability given one hypothesis, this is no mark against that hypothesis unless the probability of the datum given some alternative hypothesis is higher.

But in this case, the datum in question is equally peculiar on the apparition hypothesis. For though there is no reason to expect Jesus to be unrecognized if he was a physical being, there is also no reason to expect him to be unrecognized if he was an apparition; apparitions are typically recognized, just as physical beings are. Thus an apparition which is unrecognized is just as peculiar as a physical being which is unrecognized; the probability of getting the datum is therefore not high on either hypothesis, so the datum simply does not support either hypothesis.

Research (London: Hodder&Stoughton, 1959), 64.

91. John Gill, *Gill's Commentary* (vol. 5; Grand Rapids, MI: Baker, 1980 [1811]), 584.

We should say, however, that there is one reason for thinking the datum may be more probable on the resurrection hypothesis. Though the argument is not especially strong, it is at least worth noting.[92] Jesus, during his ministry, made a statement to the effect that at the resurrection people will be like angels (Mk 12:25). Now Jesus' non-recognition is clearly reminiscent of the hidden angel stories in the Old Testament and other Jewish literature, those stories in which an angel visits Earth and is not recognized as an angel until the end of his visit (such as the story of Sodom and Gomorrah, or Tobit). If the resurrected do become like the angels at the resurrection, perhaps they will take on this power of the angels to become unrecognized. However, the weakness of this argument is that Mark 12 does not tell us the details of exactly how human beings will become like angels, thus there is no guarantee that the power to become unrecognized is one of the ways in which we will become like angels. Thus, while Mark 12 might make Jesus' non-recognition more intelligible on the resurrection hypothesis, the passage is only suggestive.

(It should be noted that although Jesus was initially unrecognized at at least one, perhaps three of his appearances, this was certainly not so for all of the appearances, for there is at least one appearance in which Jesus must certainly have looked like himself. This is the appearance in Luke 24:36 in which the disciples fear Jesus is a ghost. If Jesus was mistaken for a ghost, he must have looked like his pre-resurrection self, for if he had looked different, the disciples would not have thought "this is the ghost of Jesus," since they would not have recognized him as Jesus. They would have thought "who is this figure that has appeared in the room?")

Bayesian Conclusion: Neither h nor ~h gives us much reason to expect Jesus to be unrecognized. Thus the datum is not any more probable on one hypothesis than on the other (or perhaps, given Jesus' words in Mark 12:25, the datum is very slightly more probable on h).

2. Jesus Can Appear and Disappear Suddenly[93]

The Argument: The resurrected Jesus does not enter or leave a room in the way a physical being typically does; he simply appears and disappears into thin air.[94] This

---

92. We might as well briefly mention that Michael Perry attempts to explain Jesus' non-recognition on the apparition hypothesis by citing a case in which a person saw an apparition and did not realize who the apparition was until after the appearance (Perry, *Easter Enigma*, 204-5). However, in the case in question, the reason the witness did not recognize the apparition is because, as the witness states, he did not get a clear look at it. This is not analogous to the resurrection appearances where the witnesses do not recognize Jesus despite having a clear look.

93. Montefiore, *Miracles*, 105; Allison, *Resurrecting*, 281.

94. However, contrary to the claim one will sometimes find in the secondary literature, there is no reason to suppose that the resurrected Jesus walks through a locked door in Jn 20:19. The text does not state that Jesus walked through a locked door, but only that the doors were locked and that Jesus appeared. Jesus could have accomplished this either by walking through a locked door or

is at the very least unusual, some would argue impossible, for a physical being. But though sudden appearances and disappearances are not typical for physical beings, they are entirely typical for apparitions. Apparitions typically enter or leave by appearing and disappearing into thin air.[95] Since apparitions usually act in this manner, whereas human beings rarely, if ever, do, we would seem to have a fact which is much better explained on the apparition hypothesis.

Bayesian Formulation: If Jesus was an apparition (~h) it is probable he would appear and disappear suddenly. But if he was resurrected (h) it is improbable he would do so.

Response: It first needs to be noted that though it is rare for a physical being to enter or exit by appearing and disappearing, Jesus is not a typical physical being, but a physical being who, after his resurrection, spends most of his time in heaven and only makes occasional trips to Earth. Thus the question is not "what is the probability a physical being will enter or leave in this manner?" but "what is the probability a physical being who must traverse between Earth and heaven will enter or leave in this manner?" One of the things BT tells us is that when a more specific reference class is found, the initial probability of a hypothesis changes. If we know Bob is a man in his sixties, the odds of him having heart disease are different than if we only know that he is a man (for more men in their sixties have heart disease than men generally). Likewise, if Jesus is a physical being who has to traverse between Earth and heaven, he belongs to a more specific reference class than "physical beings"; he belongs to the reference class of "physical beings who traverse between Earth and heaven." Now, though the probability that a physical being will appear and disappear is low (if we took a random physical being and were asked to bet on whether he had ever appeared and disappeared into thin air, we should certainly lay very low odds), the probability that a physical being who must traverse between Earth and heaven will do this is not low, but is in fact very high. For we need to ask the question: If a physical being did want to move back and forth between heaven and Earth, how would he do it? If heaven is indeed a parallel dimension rather than some physical place in our own dimension, the only way a person could enter that dimension is if he appeared and disappeared—since the person cannot be in both dimensions at once, when he enters one, he must no longer be visible in the other. (And even if heaven is some planet within our own dimension, then though it would not be absolutely necessary for a person to disappear in order to go there (he could instead ascend all the way up) it would still be likely that he would do so, because it would be quicker to go back and forth by materializing and dematerializing than by ascending and descending.) Further, apparitions actually illustrate this

by materializing, but given that throughout ancient Jewish literature beings from heaven appear by materializing and given that they never walk through solid objects, we should assume Jesus materialized here.

95. Hart found that 8% of apparitions leave by fading out, which means 92% leave by disappearing abruptly ("Six Theories," 168).

fact, because apparitions, presuming they are real, do enter and leave our dimension or planet by appearing and disappearing.

Thus if it is possible for a physical being to appear and disappear, and if Jesus was a physical being who had to travel between Earth and heaven, it is entirely to be expected that he would do so by appearing and disappearing (though he could also ascend, but there is no reason to expect he must ascend every time, and some apparitions also ascend).[96] Hence in Bayesian terms: The probability that Jesus would appear and disappear given that he was a physical being who must traverse between Earth and heaven is high, though the probability he would do so given that he was an apparition is also high.

But the question will then become whether it is possible for a physical being to appear and disappear, and some may also wonder whether the Gospel writers might have thought Jesus was non-physical because of his appearing and disappearing. A simple response to this is that if it is given that God created the world, then it is surely possible for him to move Jesus' body from one place to another, for if he created matter from nothing he can surely cause matter to pass from one place to another. And as for the beliefs of the Gospel writers, since they all relate an empty tomb, they must all have believed Jesus' body was physical.

But a more detailed response is as follows. There are three reasons to think the Gospel writers believed Jesus was a physical being despite the fact that he appears and disappears. And there are two reasons to think that a physical being can indeed appear and disappear in the way Jesus did.

In regard to the beliefs of the Gospels writers, first, even in his pre-resurrection body, Jesus can walk on water (Mk 6:45-52). This is an action which violates the laws of nature, and which would seem to be almost as indicative of non-physicality as appearing and disappearing. Yet the Gospel writers surely think that the pre-resurrection Jesus is a physical being.

Second, in Acts 8:39-40, Philip is miraculously transported from one place to another, which necessarily means he disappeared in one place and then appeared in another. Thus Philip, an ordinary human being, can appear and disappear just as Jesus did.

Third, in ancient literature there was a category of post-mortem beings known as revenants; these were not disembodied spirits, but reanimated corpses, akin to zombies. These reanimated corpses often appeared and disappeared suddenly, just as Jesus did, though they are clearly believed by the writers to be material beings.[97]

---

96. Hart, "Six Theories" (168) tells us 1% of apparitions rise into the air without physical support. He does not cite the case or cases in his collection which illustrate this, so I do not know how high into the air such apparitions have gone.

97. D. Felton, *Haunted Greece and Rome: Ghost Stories from Classical Antiquity* (Austin, TX: University of Texas Press, 1999), 28.

Of course, simply because the New Testament writers *believed* it was possible for a physical being to materialize and dematerialize, this does not mean that it is in fact possible. However, modern science agrees that this is indeed possible, hypothetically as well actually. First, physicists are agreed that it is hypothetically possible that a physical object could dematerialize and rematerialize. Physical objects are made up of smaller particles, and these particles move from one place to another, and it is possible (though exceedingly improbable without divine intervention) that all of the particles could move at once, in which case the entire object would be moved. Thus if all of the particles in Jesus' body suddenly moved from one place to another, Jesus' whole body would move from one place to another.[98]

Second, in an experiment at the California Institute of Technology, researchers were able to dematerialize a beam of light and rematerialize it in another place. Although a beam of light is not a human, it is still a physical object and thus science has accomplished the teleportation of matter.[99]

Bayesian Conclusion: If Jesus rose from the dead it is highly probable he would appear and disappear suddenly, and if he was an apparition it is also highly probable he would appear and disappear suddenly. Thus the datum has a high probability on both h and ~h.

3. A Spiritual Body not Made of Flesh and Blood?[100]

The Argument: There are two passages in Paul which could be taken to mean that Paul did not believe in a physical resurrection. In 1 Corinthians 15:44 Paul refers to the resurrected body as "a spiritual body." This has been interpreted by many to mean a non-physical body. And in 1 Corinthians 15:50 he tells us that "flesh and blood cannot inherit the kingdom of God," a statement which has been interpreted to mean that physical beings cannot inherit the kingdom of God.

Bayesian Formulation: If Jesus was an apparition (~h) it is probable that Paul would have referred to the resurrection body as a spiritual body and one not made with flesh and blood (though it is not necessarily probable he would have used these specific terms, it is probable he would have made some statements indicating that he thought the resurrection body non-physical). But if Jesus was resurrected (h) it is improbable Paul would have referred to the resurrection body with these terms (or used any other language which indicates the resurrection body is non-physical).

---

98. Craig, *Reasonable Faith*, 260-61.
99. See "Quantum Teleportation," http://www.its.caltech.edu/~qoptics/teleport.html.
100. Badham, *Christian Beliefs*, 32, 35; Perry, *Easter Enigma*, 108.

Response: We should first note that if the surface meaning of these texts is correct, they contradict the texts we examined in chapter 1 in which Paul clearly affirms belief in a physical resurrection, such as Romans 8:11 where Paul states that the Holy Spirit will give life to our mortal bodies, and 1 Corinthians 15:53-54 where he tells us our corruptible, mortal bodies must put on incorruptibility. However, once 1 Corinthians 15:44 and 15:50 are understood properly, it becomes clear that the surface meaning is not correct, and that they do not actually endorse a non-physical resurrection. With regard to Paul's reference to a "spiritual body," Paul does not mean a non-physical body; he means a body which is empowered by the Holy Spirit (a "Spiritual" body with a capital S). This is clear from the parallel between 1 Corinthians 15:44 and 1 Corinthians 2:15. In 1 Corinthians 2:15 Paul refers to the "natural person" and "Spiritual person." And in 1 Corinthians 15:44 he refers to the "natural body" and the "Spiritual body." Now in 1 Corinthians 2:15, Paul is clearly contrasting a person empowered by the Holy Spirit and a person not empowered by the Holy Spirit; he is not concerned with physical people and disembodied people. Hence given the parallel in expression, we can assume that Paul means the same thing in 1 Corinthians 15:44. He is contrasting a body not empowered by the Holy Spirit (our pre-resurrection body) and a body empowered by the Holy Spirit (our resurrection body). It becomes especially clear that this is so once we realize that Paul elsewhere says that the Spirit will raise us from the dead (Rom 8:11), and thus he clearly believes the Spirit empowers the resurrected body.

As for Paul's statement that "flesh and blood cannot inherit the kingdom of God," it is now widely agreed that the term "flesh and blood" does not mean literal flesh and blood, but is simply a figure of speech meaning human beings in their weakness.[101] In a number of texts from the same time period, the term flesh and blood bears this meaning. For example, Sirach 14:18, "Like abundant leaves on a spreading tree that sheds some and puts forth others, so are the generations of flesh and blood: one dies and another is born." Here the author clearly means human beings, and since he is discussing the transitory nature of human life, it is clear he means human beings in their weakness.

And in addition to these texts, there is a further reason why the expression "flesh and blood" should not be taken literally: The verb in the passage is in the singular.[102] That is, the passage reads "flesh and blood *is* not able to inherit the kingdom of God" rather than "flesh and blood *are* not able to inherit the kingdom of God." If Paul meant actual flesh and blood, he would have used the plural, since literal flesh and blood are two different things. Since he uses the singular, he must be referring not to literal flesh

---

101. The most thorough recent discussion of the meaning of this term is Andy Johnson, "On Removing a Trump Card: Flesh and Blood and the Reign of God," *Bulletin for Biblical Research* 13 (2003): 175-92.

102. Craig, *Assessing*, 102.

and blood, but to a single thing which can be referred to by this term, and that thing must be human beings.

Bayesian Conclusion: In these verses, Paul simply affirms that the resurrected body is empowered by the Holy Spirit and that human beings in their weakness cannot inherit the kingdom of God. It makes sense for Paul to speak this way if he thought Jesus was resurrected, but it also makes sense for him to speak this way if he thought Jesus was an apparition, so this data is not any more probable given h or given ~h.

4. Paul's Use of "Ophthe"[103]

The Argument: In 1 Corinthians 15:3-8, Paul uses the word "ophthe" ("appeared") in reference to Jesus' appearances ("he appeared to Peter"... "he appeared to the Twelve" ... "he appeared to a group of over 500..."). It has been argued that ophthe means a non-physical type of seeing, because it is used in reference to people seeing heavenly visions, and these visions seem to have been non-physical in nature. (We have mentioned Daniel 10:7 where Daniel's companions cannot see the vision he sees; and Acts 7:55-56 where Stephen sees Jesus but the crowd cannot see him.)

Bayesian Formulation: If Jesus was an apparition (~h) it is probable Paul would have referred to his appearances using the word ophthe. But if Jesus rose (h) it is improbable he would have used this word. (Or even if it is not probable that Paul would use this word if ~h is true, it is even more improbable he would use the word if h is true.)

Response: This argument is clearly fallacious because plenty of examples can be cited in which ophthe refers to the ordinary seeing of a physical object. For example, Genesis 46:29, "Joseph prepared his chariot and went up to Goshen to meet his father Israel; as soon as he appeared [ophthe] before him, he fell on his neck and wept on his neck a long time" and 1 Kings 18:1, "Now it happened after many days that the word of the LORD came to Elijah in the third year, saying, 'Go, show yourself [appear/ophthe] to Ahab, and I will send rain on the face of the earth.'" Hence the word ophthe can refer either to ordinary or non-ordinary seeing (it is as flexible as the English word "appear") and thus the use of this word is equally to be expected whether Jesus' body was physical or non-physical.

Bayesian Conclusion: Since the same word refers to both physical and non-physical seeing, and the New Testament writers would have to say Jesus was seen regardless of whether he was seen physically or non-physically, the fact that this word is used is highly probable on h and highly probable on ~h.

---

103. Weatherhead, *Resurrection*, 50-51.

5. Paul Equates the Other Appearances with His Own[104]

The Argument: In 1 Corinthians 15:3-8, Paul seems to equate the other appearances with his own, for he tells us that he has had an appearance of Jesus just as the others have. Now we know from Acts that Paul's appearance was visionary in nature: he sees a blinding light, and only he, not his companions, can see the figure. If Paul's appearance was visionary, and he has told us that the other appearances were like his own, then he has implied that the other appearances were visionary and hence non-physical.

Bayesian Formulation: If Jesus was an apparition (~h) it is probable Paul would equate the appearances with his own, since his appearance, being an appearance of a non-physical being, was an appearance of an apparition. But if Jesus rose from the dead (h) it is improbable he would equate the resurrection appearances with his own.

Response: There are multiple problems with this argument. First of all, Paul does not say that the other appearances were like his. He says that he has seen an appearance of Jesus and so have the rest of the disciples, but he says nothing about whether Jesus appeared to him in the same manner as he appeared to the others. In fact, the phrase "as to an abortion" (*ektroma*) indicates Paul knew there was something different about his appearance (though exactly what he meant by this word commentators do not agree).[105] Second, although Paul's appearance was different, it does not appear to be the case that Paul's appearance was visionary if by "visionary" we mean the appearance was only visible to Paul. Although only Paul sees Jesus, certainly the others present hear the voice,[106] and see the light, for they all fall down. This is in marked contrast to Daniel's vision and Stephen's vision in which the others present do not see or hear anything. The reason why only Paul saw Jesus is thus very likely not because only Paul was capable of seeing him, but because only Paul looked into the light. The light is described as "brighter than the sun" (Acts 26:13) and Paul is temporarily blinded after the appearance, though we are not told anyone else is blinded; thus the implication is that no one else looked into the light. If the others had looked into the light, they would have seen Jesus. Third, it is only from Luke's account in Acts that we know

---

104. Perry, *Easter Enigma*, 159. This argument has also been made on behalf of the idea that the early Christians thought the appearances were objective visions: Marcus J. Borg on pp. 132-33 of Marcus J. Borg and N.T. Wright, *The Meaning of Jesus: Two Visions* (San Francisco: HarperSanFrancisco, 1999).

105. One will find the meaning of this term discussed in commentaries on 1 Cor. It appears to be related to the fact that Paul became an apostle later than the other apostles.

106. Acts 22:9 appears to say that the others with Paul did not hear the voice, but the solution is that the word in question (*akouo*) does not necessarily mean "hear" but can also mean "understand." Thus the meaning of Acts 22:9 is simply that Paul's companions did not understand the voice. See Gleason L. Archer, *New International Encyclopedia of Bible Difficulties* (Grand Rapid, MI: Zondervan, 1982), 382.

anything about what Paul's appearance was like; but if we accept Luke's account of Paul's appearance it would be inconsistent not to accept his accounts of the other resurrection appearances. And in those appearances we find, as we saw above, various data not probable on the apparition hypothesis.

Bayesian Conclusion: If the data were actually as they are claimed to be—if Paul's appearance was visionary and if he intended to equate the other appearances with his own in terms of their mode—these facts would indeed be more probable on ~h than on h. However, all Paul in fact tells us is that he has seen Jesus and so have the other apostles. Since Paul would be expected to say this regardless of whether they saw Jesus physically or as an apparition, this datum is probable on both h and ~h.

6. Violent Deaths

The Argument: It is now time to return to a point raised earlier. Haraldsson found that people who died violent deaths are more likely to appear as apparitions. In 30% of the cases of apparitions he collected, the person whose apparition it was had died violently (by accident, murder, or suicide), though only 8% of the general population had died violently. The fact that Jesus died violently and people who die violently are more likely to appear as apparitions, would seem to help the apparition hypothesis.

Bayesian Formulation: If Jesus was an apparition (~h), then though it is not probable he would have died violently (since there is a 30% chance), it is more probable he would have died violently than if he was not an apparition (since if he was not an apparition there would only be an 8% chance).

Response: If Jesus was an apparition, there is a 30% chance he would have died violently (assuming for the sake of argument that all of the results of Haraldsson's survey of apparition experiences in late 20th century Iceland hold for all cultures and all times). So to take this away as evidence in support of ~h, we must show there is at least a 30% chance that if Jesus was resurrected he would have died violently. The way to do this is to note that the belief in Jesus' resurrection is intimately connected with belief in the idea that his death was an atoning death for the sins of the world. Without this death, the resurrection makes no sense theologically. Hence, the hypothesis "Jesus rose from the dead" entails the idea that he also atoned for our sins, and so a violent death is actually probable, or at least not especially improbable given h, since a violent death is not a surprise if Jesus needed to experience the worst depths of human suffering in order to atone for sin. Now, whether the doctrine of the atonement makes sense is a question that has to be considered as part of the initial probability, and if the atonement cannot survive scrutiny, the resurrection hypothesis will not be a posteriori probable (unless we formulated a version of the resurrection hypothesis which significantly differs from the one traditionally held by Christians). But we are here concerned only with the specific evidence.

Bayesian Conclusion: If Jesus was an apparition (~h), it is not exceedingly improbable he would have died violently, but if he was resurrected, an idea which entails the atonement, it is also not exceedingly improbable he would have died violently.

7. Jesus' Clothes[107]

The Argument: In John 20:6 we are told that Jesus' burial garments were still in the tomb when Peter and the Beloved Disciple inspected it. Thus when Jesus made his appearances he must have had new clothes. It has been argued that this makes more sense on the apparition hypothesis than on the resurrection hypothesis since the resurrection hypothesis requires that Jesus' new clothes were materialized, which requires another miracle in addition to the resurrection.

Bayesian Formulation: If ~h is true it is probable Jesus would have new clothes during his appearances. But if h is true it is improbable Jesus would have new clothes during his appearances.

Response: There is no reason why Jesus causing new clothes to materialize should pose a problem for the resurrection hypothesis. If God created the world, and thus caused all matter to materialize from nothing, it would obviously not be difficult for him to materialize clothes. In addition, if the Gospels are accurate (and this objection grants that they are, since it is only by assuming the accuracy of the Gospels that we can believe John's statement about Jesus' burial clothes), Jesus had materialized bread and fish at the miracle of the feeding of the 5000, so materializations would be nothing new for him.

But further, one fact makes it not only plausible but highly probable Jesus would materialize new clothes if he rose from the dead. His old clothes would be covered with blood from the crucifixion—would he want to exit the tomb in bloody grave clothes?

Bayesian Conclusion: If Jesus was an apparition (~h) it is highly probable he would have appeared with new clothes. But if he was resurrected (h) it is also highly probable he would have appeared with new clothes.

---

107. Weatherhead, *Resurrection*, 65; Montefiore, *Miracles*, 106.

8. The Disciples Doubt[108]

The Argument: Matthew 28:17 tells us that some of the disciples doubted at Jesus' appearance to the Twelve in Galilee ("When they saw Him, they worshiped Him; but some were doubtful"). Perhaps this doubting was because they doubted his physical nature.

Bayesian Formulation: If Jesus was an apparition, it is probable the disciples would doubt his physical nature. But if Jesus was resurrected, it is improbable the disciples would doubt his physical nature.

Response: If the disciples were indeed doubting Jesus' physical nature, this is certainly improbable on the resurrection hypothesis. However, it is highly conjectural to suppose that this is why the disciples doubted. Though why they doubted is not clear, there are various other possibilities.[109] Perhaps they doubted because Jesus looked different, as he did in the Emmaus appearance. Perhaps they doubted whether they ought to be worshipping him, because they doubted whether he was God. Perhaps they doubted whether he could really be raised, since a resurrection seemed unbelievable (especially if those doubting were not among the Eleven);[110] perhaps they thought he was an impostor.

Bayesian Conclusion: Since there is no reason to think the doubting concerned doubt about a physical resurrection, the doubting cannot be said to be high on the apparition hypothesis. But there is also no reason to expect doubting on the resurrection hypothesis, so it cannot be said to be high on the resurrection hypothesis either. And there are not any reasons why the datum should be regarded as improbable given either hypothesis. Thus the probability of the datum is simply neutral given either hypothesis.

9. Jesus Became a Spirit?[111]

The Argument: 1 Corinthians 15:45 tells us that whereas Adam became a "living soul," Jesus "became a life-giving spirit" and 1 Peter 3:18-19 tells us Jesus was "put to death in the flesh, but made alive in the spirit; in which also he went and made proclamation to the spirits now in prison." Since a spirit is an apparition, these passages mean Jesus became an apparition.

---

108. Badham, *Christian Beliefs*, 26; Allison, *Resurrecting*, 280.

109. See Licona, *Resurrection*, 358-62 for an overview of some of the possibilities.

110. This is grammatically possible. See Robert M. Bowman and J. Ed Komoszewski, *Putting Jesus in His Place: The Case for the Deity of Christ* (Grand Rapids, MI: Kregel, 2007), 294-96.

111. Badham, *Christian Beliefs*, 40.

Bayesian Formulation: If Jesus was an apparition (~h) it is probable he would be referred to as a spirit. But if he was resurrected (h) it is improbable he would be referred to as a spirit.

Response: In regard to 1 Corinthians 15:45, the proper translation is "Spiritual being," which is to say, a being empowered by the Holy Spirit, not a disembodied spirit. This is clear from the fact that the word in 15:45 which is typically translated "soul" is in fact the root word of the word translated "natural" in 1 Corinthians 15:44, and thus, a better translation of the word in 15:45 would be "natural being"; and the word translated "spirit" in 15:45 is in fact the root word of the word translated "Spiritual" in 1 Corinthians 15:44, so therefore, a better translation of that word is "Spiritual being." Just as in 1 Corinthians 15:44, Paul is contrasting something empowered by the Holy Spirit with something not empowered by the Holy Spirit. In 15:44, it is the body; in 15:45, it is the entire human person.[112]

In regard to 1 Peter 3:18-19, the prima facie meaning of this passage is certainly that Jesus became a spirit and that he then went and preached to the spirits of the dead in Hades. But in fact, this passage gives the wrong impression, for the passage does not actually mean Jesus became a spirit, and though 1 Peter 4:6 may refer to Jesus' preaching to the spirits of the dead, that is not the event which 1 Peter 3:18-19 refers to.

The phrase "made alive in the spirit," does not mean Jesus became a spirit. When the phrase "in the spirit" occurs in the New Testament, it means "in the power of the Holy Spirit." For example, Matthew 22:43, "Then how does David *in the Spirit* call Him 'Lord.'" Luke 2:27, "And he [Simeon] came *in the Spirit* into the temple." And Revelation 1:10, "I was *in the Spirit* on the Lord's day." Clearly, in none of these passages was the person an immaterial being. (Just as with 1 Corinthians 15:44 ("Spiritual Body"), the reason these passages are often misinterpreted is because "spirit" as in a disembodied soul, is confused with "Spirit" as in the Holy Spirit.)

As for the subsequent words about Jesus preaching to the spirits in prison ("in which also He went and made proclamation to the spirits now in prison, who once were disobedient, when the patience of God kept waiting in the days of Noah, during the construction of the ark"), for two reasons, it is clear these words do not refer to Jesus going to Hades to preach to the spirits of the dead. First, these spirits are referred to as disobedient. Why would Peter refer to these spirits as disobedient if he meant the spirits of the dead? For not all dead people were disobedient; many dead people were good people. Second, if Peter meant the spirits of the dead, why would he refer to those who were disobedient during the days of Noah? Not all dead people died then, so he cannot mean all the dead, and it does not make sense for him to single out the dead in Noah's time.

Thus, clearly the prima facie interpretation of this passage will not do. The passage does not have reference to the spirits of the dead, and if we want the passage to

---

112. On this text, see Licona, *Resurrection of Jesus*, 415-416.

make sense, we need to find a group of spirits other than those of the dead who were disobedient during the days of Noah and who were placed in prison. We find what we are looking for in 1 Enoch, where we are told that before the flood there were fallen angels (spirits) who were disobedient by intermarrying with the daughters of men, and that these angels were later imprisoned.[113] (Enoch's story is an expansion of the brief reference in Genesis 6:1-4 to the intermarriage between the "Sons of God" and the "daughters of men.") Thus these are the spirits Jesus preached to.

Thus this passage does not mean Jesus became a spirit and then went to free the spirits of the dead. It means Jesus was raised in the power of the Holy Spirit, and then preached to the fallen angels of Genesis 6.

Bayesian Conclusion: Since Paul's referring to Jesus as a life-giving spirit and 1 Peter's referring to the resurrected Jesus as empowered by the Holy Spirit does not mean Jesus became an apparition, these passages are not any more probable given that Jesus was an apparition (~h) than given that he was resurrected (h).

General Bayesian Conclusion

Since we have failed to uncover any data which is more probable given ~h than given h, we are left with the same conclusion we had after finishing our last section: the odds are 1 quadrillion to one in favor of h.

There is one other non-supernatural version of the apparition hypothesis to consider. But since we must invoke initial probability to analyze it, I will address it after addressing the objective vision theory.

The Objective Vision Theory

Now that we have considered the apparition theory as a naturalistic hypothesis, before we consider how the apparition theory would look if it is combined with the objective vision theory, we should first consider the objective vision theory by itself. The objective vision theory is the theory that Jesus appeared as a non-bodily apparition, but not according to the manner in which apparitions typically appear, but either because of a direct act of God, or because of Jesus' supernatural power.[114] The theory is clearly a supernatural hypothesis, since the apparition is brought about either by God himself or by miraculous powers which were bestowed on Jesus by God.

This theory, which has been fairly popular in the world of theology, would certainly seem attractive if we accepted the premises which its proponents have often accepted, those premises being: 1) the Gospels (including the story of the empty tomb)

---

113. See Donald P. Senior and Daniel J. Harrington, *1 Peter, Jude, and 2 Peter* (Collegesville, MN: Liturgical, 2003), 103.

114. See n25 in chapter 1 for proponents and critics of the objective vision theory.

are unreliable and thus there is no evidence the appearances were corporeal; 2) the earliest Christian belief, the one present in Paul's writings, is that the resurrection is not physical; 3) Paul equates the other appearances with his own visionary, non-physical appearance. Now if it is the case that Paul's appearance was an objective vision, and if he equated the other appearances with his own, and if he tells us the early Christians did not believe in a physical resurrection, and if the Gospels cannot be used to contradict any of this, then certainly the objective vision theory looks promising. However, we have argued above that each of these premises is wrong, and the only other arguments which could conceivably be given for the objective vision theory have already been dealt with under the data apparently more probable on the apparition hypothesis, since the same data generally supports both hypotheses, because both look for data indicative of non-bodily appearances (for example, Jesus' appearing and disappearing, or Paul's reference to a spiritual body).[115] Thus we are left with no positive evidence in favor of the objective vision hypothesis. But we do have arguments against it. First, the early Christians clearly believed the appearances were physical (this is so not only for the Gospel writers, but also for the Christians in Paul's time, as we explained in chapter 1), and second, the Gospels present us with much data indicating that the appearances were indeed physical (e.g., Jesus eating and saying he is resurrected). Hence the objective vision theory could only be maintained as an explanation if God deliberately misled the disciples, presenting them with data which led them to believe Jesus was resurrected though he was not. (And we do not even need the Gospel data to conclude that God would have to have given them misleading data. For from the fact that the Christians in Paul's time believed in a physical resurrection we can deduce that God must have given them some misleading data, even if we do not know what that data was.)

This question of whether God would mislead the disciples becomes not just one factor but the only factor relevant to whether or not the objective vision theory is true. And this is why we can address this theory and the combination objective vision/apparition theory so much more briefly than we did the apparition theory, for the only issue to consider is initial probability, and in this case, initial probability is a simple issue to consider.

One might be inclined to think that we should examine the specific evidence, that we should address the objective vision theory in the same way we addressed the apparition theory. That is, that we ought to address it by looking for data which is more

---

115. There are some arguments which will only work on one hypothesis or the other. For example, we saw how the argument that an apparition would mean God mislead the disciples does not work on the natural version of the apparition hypothesis, and the argument from violent deaths is based on Haraldsson's survey of natural apparitions and so Jesus' appearances must be non-supernatural apparitions for that data to be relevant. But it is the case that if one consults the works of proponents of the objective vision theory (see note above) one will find many of the same arguments cited, and I cannot think of any major arguments for the objective vision theory that have not already been dealt with under the apparition theory.

probable on the resurrection hypothesis than on the hypothesis that God misled the disciples. But this cannot be done. The reason this cannot be done is that if God did in fact intend to mislead the disciples, then any data which is probable on the resurrection hypothesis is just as probable on the hypothesis that God misled the disciples. For anything which a resurrected person can do to convince us he rose from the dead, a person who wants to trick us into thinking he rose from the dead can also do. (Unless he wants to do something which is beyond his power to do. Someone trying to trick us into thinking he is a police officer, for example, may not have the same kind of badge as a real police officer because he was unable to acquire such a badge. But since God is omnipotent he should not be limited in his ability at all.) If a real resurrected person would seem physical, so would someone trying to trick us into thinking he was resurrected. If a real resurrected person would eat food, so would somebody who is trying to trick us into thinking he was resurrected. If a real resurrected person would tell us he is resurrected, so would someone trying to trick us into thinking he was resurrected. In Bayesian terms:

It is probable a resurrected person would seem physical (h), but it is also probable a fake resurrected person would seem physical (~h)

It is probable a resurrected person would eat food (h), but it is also probable a fake resurrected person would eat food ~h).

It is probable a resurrected person would tell us he is resurrected (h), but it is also probable a fake resurrected person would tell us he is resurrected (~h).

Since the fake resurrected person is trying to trick us into thinking he rose from the dead, he will try to do everything which it would be probable for a resurrected person to do and nothing which it would be improbable for a resurrected person to do.

Hence, since both theories predict the same data, the specific evidence is equally well explained by both theories. In a case like that, it is necessary to turn to the initial probability. And the initial probability in this case simply reduces to this: We must ask whether it is more probable that God should lead us to believe that Jesus was raised because Jesus actually was raised, or that he should lead us to believe Jesus was raised because he wanted to trick us into thinking Jesus was raised. Now the argument that the objective vision theory would require deception on the part of God has been made many times before against this theory,[116] usually with the expectation that the skeptic will give up if he must postulate deception by God. But the skeptic, rather than giving up at this point, may want to know just why it is so improbable that God would mislead anyone.

Several points can be made concerning this. First, if one accepts the Bible's claims about God, obviously God is not in the habit of misleading people. For we are told: "God is not a man, that He should lie," (Num 23:19) and "it is impossible for God to

---

116. E.g., Alexander Balmain Bruce, *Apologetics; Or, Christianity Defensively Stated* (Edinburgh: T&T Clark, 1892), 393; James Orr, *The Resurrection of Jesus* (London: Hodder & Stoughton, 1908), 229-30; McGrew and McGrew, "Argument From Miracles," 627.

lie" (Heb 6:18). Second, even if the inspiration of the Bible is not accepted, there is also the innate feeling human beings have that God does not mislead people. (It is possible, after all, that God, in the sense of an all-powerful being, exists, but that God is not all good and likes to deceive people. But does not our innate sense tell us this cannot be so?) But even if one rejects this innate sense, there is still a purely empirical argument: We ought to presume God is honest until we have evidence to the contrary, because it is our experience of the world that the large majority of people are honest the large majority of the time, and thus if we meet someone we have never met before, we should presume that what they tell us is honest until we have evidence to the contrary. Hence if you are lost and you stop and ask someone for directions, though you know nothing about the person you ask (you have no specific evidence concerning their honesty), you believe they are telling the truth; you follow their directions. Hence even if we have no specific reasons to think God is honest, we should presume he is honest until we have evidence to the contrary, simply because God is a person and any statement from any person we assume to be honest until we have evidence to the contrary. To put this in Bayesian terms, since the large majority of statements from the large majority of people are honest, the initial probability that any given statement from any given person is honest is very high, and so if we have no specific evidence, we simply base our judgment on the initial probability. (Analogously, if I know 99% of people in a given village eat pizza, and I encounter a person from that village, I should believe that person eats pizza even if I have never seen him do anything to indicate he eats pizza.)

But we do need to note that there is at least one instance in the Bible in which it appears God does mislead someone. In the story in which God asks Abraham to sacrifice Isaac, it certainly seems that God misleads Abraham into thinking God wants him to sacrifice Isaac, even though it turns out this is not what God wants Abraham to do. Now one could respond that perhaps God was not misleading Abraham here, for though God asks Abraham to *offer* Isaac as a sacrifice, God never says that he will *accept* it. But now let us concede for the sake of argument that God does mislead Abraham in this passage. This still does not affect our argument, because it only shows that God, like most human beings we know, misleads people once in a while (and the story of Abraham only gives us grounds to think he may mislead us for a good reason, not for a bad reason—and if we think, as the author of Hebrews does (11:19), that Abraham expected God to raise Isaac from the dead, we realize Abraham was not in as much distress as is commonly supposed, and hence God misleading him does not seem as troublesome as it otherwise would). God misleading somebody one time does not give us any more reason to think God misleads people often, than the fact that your wife might mislead you once in a while should make you think she misleads you often. Even if we have found one example of God misleading someone, this still gives us no reason not to follow the line of thought above, which is that since the large majority of people only mislead other people rarely, and God is a person, the initial probability he is misleading me in any given instance is low, and thus in a case where I have no evidence one way or the other, I should simply play the initial probability and bet that God is not misleading me.

And we should also note that if God misled the disciples concerning the resurrection, then, being as the deception has not been corrected in 2000 years, and being as God allowed them to make this deception the central event of the Christian religion, God would have performed a much grander deception than in the case of Abraham. For in that case, he quickly enlightened Abraham as to the truth. Thus I do not think God misleading Abraham provides a precedent for the idea that God might mislead someone to the extent that the objective vision theory proposes he has misled us in regard to the resurrection. God deceiving Abraham to a minor extent does not provide us with any more reason to think he would perform a major deception than your wife deceiving you about how much she spent shopping should make you think she will deceive you about having cheated on you.

Thus if there is no evidence one way or the other as to whether God misled the disciples in this instance, we should assume he did not, and thus assume the resurrection hypothesis is the best hypothesis. However, we should mention here that Michael Perry, who recognizes that his combination apparition/objective vision theory requires deception on the part of God (we will explain below why the apparition/objective vision combination requires the same amount of deception as the objective vision theory by itself) proposes the following reason as to why God deceived the disciples: The common belief in the disciples' time was that an apparition was a lifeless shade, and therefore if the disciples knew Jesus was an apparition they would have believed he was a mere lifeless shade, and so God allowed them to think Jesus was resurrected in order to keep them from thinking he was a lifeless shade.[117]

But there are three problems with this argument. First, Perry supposes that God misled the disciples into thinking Jesus was resurrected in order to keep the disciples from misleading themselves into thinking Jesus was a lifeless shade. But why is mistakenly thinking Jesus was resurrected any better than mistakenly thinking Jesus was a lifeless shade? Second, there would not seem to be any difficulty in explaining to people of the first century that an apparition did not have to be a lifeless shade. Why would modern people be any better able to understand this concept than ancient people? Third, and most significantly, people of the first century actually did make this distinction, for contrary to Perry's claim, there were different conceptions of apparitions in the first century. Some apparitions were thought to be lifeless shades, but others were indeed believed to be the deceased persons in full vigor. For example, when the deceased Jeremiah is seen in 2 Maccabees 15:13-16, and the deceased Adam (11:4-11 Recension J) and Abel (12:3-13:5) are seen in the Testament of Abraham,

---

117. Perry, *Easter Enigma*, 194-96.

they clearly have all their wits and vigor about them; they are not like the shades of Sheol.[118]

A Resurrection and Objective Visions?

Before we consider the possibility of combining the objective vision theory and apparition theory, we should consider one variant of the objective vision theory. This is the idea that Jesus was indeed raised physically, but that when he appeared to the disciples, he did not appear with his physical body, but instead appeared as an objective vision. This scenario is certainly hypothetically possible, but it only makes sense if we think (as Pannenberg, one of its most well-known exponents, thought):[119] 1) there is evidence for the empty tomb (and hence Jesus was raised physically); but 2) there is no good evidence for the corporeality of the appearances (because the Gospels are unreliable); and 3) there is evidence the appearances were objective visions (the evidence of Paul's testimony). But we have seen that the Gospels are reliable and that Paul does not attest to objective visions. Suppose however, that we cannot use the Gospels as evidence and so we have only the empty tomb and the fact that Jesus appeared. In that case, we do not have any explicit statements from the earliest Christians that Jesus' *appearances* were physical; they are only explicit in telling us he was *raised* physically. However, even in this situation, there are still two reasons to think Jesus' appearances were physical rather than objective visions.

First, if a person is physical, we should expect that they will appear physically unless we have some reason to think otherwise. This is because our experience of physical beings tells us that physical beings appear physically the large majority of the time (the only exceptions are when apparitions of the living are seen, if one accepts the reality of apparitions), thus we should expect a physical being to appear physically unless there is evidence to the contrary. In Bayesian terms, the initial probability a physical being would appear physically is very high, so even if we have no specific evidence in a particular case, we should still assume they appeared physically, simply because of the initial probability. (One might object that I rejected the same type of argument when it was used on behalf of the apparition theory: the argument that since physical beings do not typically appear and disappear, Jesus appearing and disappearing indicates he was not a physical being. However, my methodology is not inconsistent. If Jesus was

---

118. On different types of apparitions in ancient literature, see Deborah Thompson Prince, "The 'Ghost' of Jesus: Luke 24 in Light of Ancient Narratives of Post-Mortem Apparitions," *Journal for the Study of the New Testament* 34 (2007): 287-301; Jake H. O'Connell, "Did Greco-Roman Apparitional Models Influence Luke's Resurrection Narrative? A Response to Deborah Thompson Prince," *Journal of Greco-Roman Christianity and Judaism* 5 (2008): 190-99. N.T. Wright, *Resurrection*, 32-84, has a thorough overview of the sources which do present apparitions as lifeless shades.

119. Wolfhart Pannenberg, *Jesus: God and Man* (Philadelphia: Westminster, 1982): The Gospels are unreliable (92), the other appearances were like Paul's, which was visionary (92-93), the appearances were objective visions (93-95), the empty tomb is historical (100-106).

a physical being, we should expect whatever is true of physical beings to be true of Jesus until we have evidence to the contrary. But in the case of Jesus' appearing and disappearing we had evidence to the contrary: We knew that Jesus was in a situation which physical beings are rarely in (the situation of having to traverse from Earth to Heaven), and this gave us reason to believe that what was ordinarily true of human beings was not true of Jesus in this case. But as to his appearing with his physical body, there is no evidence to the contrary.)

Second, since Jesus was the first fruits of those raised from the dead, we should expect that his appearances to the disciples would give them a taste of the resurrected life. But if the disciples were only seeing a non-bodily vision of Jesus, they were not encountering resurrected life during his appearances.

The Apparition Theory and Objective Vision Theory Combined

We have considered the apparition theory as a naturalistic hypothesis, but as I said, some writers have tried to combine this theory with the objective vision theory by postulating that though Jesus was an apparition, and hence generally followed the laws of apparitions, he was able, due to God, to control the laws of apparitions in a way that typical apparitions cannot, and hence his appearances sometimes departed from the laws. Thus, the various ways in which the resurrection appearances differ from typical apparitions are simply a result of the fact that Jesus was able to control these laws better. But the problem with this suggestion is that we have seen that the resurrection appearances do not merely differ from typical apparitions, but that they differ in just the manner we would expect them to differ if the resurrection appearances were appearances of a physical being—for we have seen that there is a large amount of data which is more probable given that Jesus was resurrected than given that he was an apparition. Hence if the combination apparition/objective vision theory is true, Jesus was not merely altering the laws of apparitions, but he was altering them in such a way that the apparitions mimicked exactly what we would expect to find if Jesus was in fact making physical appearances. Departing from the laws of apparitions in just the manner one would need to depart from them in order to mimic physical appearances is clearly an attempt to mislead the disciples into thinking the appearances were physical. Hence, this hypothesis reduces to a more specific version of the objective vision theory—Jesus follows the laws of apparitions to some extent (as opposed to the ordinary objective vision theory where we have no reason to think he follows them at all, because the appearances are entirely supernatural), but he still presents the disciples with data designed to mislead them into thinking he is physically raised. Therefore, this theory carries all of the same problems as the objective vision theory in its simpler form.

Bayesian Conclusion for the Objective Vision Theory and the Combination Objective Vision/Apparition Theory

Since the resurrection hypothesis, objective vision hypothesis, and objective vision/apparition hypothesis all predict the same data, the specific evidence is equally well explained by each hypothesis.[120] The question thus reduces to initial probability. If we think the probability God would actually raise Jesus from the dead is higher than the probability God would mislead the disciples into thinking Jesus was raised from the dead, then the resurrection hypothesis is the most probable of the three hypotheses.

Another Form of the Apparition Hypothesis

I said above that there was one other non-supernatural version of the apparition hypothesis to consider, but that it could not be addressed until after we addressed the objective vision theory, because in the case of this version of the apparition theory, initial probability is the essential consideration. This version of the apparition theory would make all of the data which is ostensibly more probable on the resurrection hypothesis, just as probable on the apparition hypothesis. Michael Perry proposed this version of the hypothesis as a way of explaining why Jesus tells the disciples he is not a ghost in Luke 24:39,[121] and as a way of explaining some other data as well (such as the appearance to Thomas). (Although Perry also proposed another, mutually exclusive way of explaining Jesus' words and other data seeming to be more probable given the resurrection—the hypothesis that this data was the result of deception; we already considered the deception hypothesis above.) Though Perry did not apply this hypothesis to all the data, he seems to imply it can be; and in fact it can indeed be applied to all of the data.

The version of the apparition hypothesis which I have reference to is a version which proposes that the way in which the witnesses perceive an apparition is not entirely a result of the apparition's efforts, but is either wholly or partially a result of the witnesses' subconscious minds. The partial version of this hypothesis would propose that apparitions are disembodied spirits communicating from the other side, but that when the disembodied spirit tries to communicate an image of itself to the percipients, the percipients do not accept that image exactly as it is; their subconscious minds alter that image to some extent, and so the image that is actually seen is a combination

---

120. More exactly, they all predict the same data in regard to that data which would give the appearance of having been raised from the dead; that is, any specific evidence which might be cited in support of the resurrection hypothesis is equally probable on any of the three hypotheses. But if one wanted to look for data to help us distinguish between the objective vision theory and objective vision/apparition theory, one could find such data: If the resurrection appearances generally possessed many of the characteristics as apparitions, this would support the combination hypothesis over the pure objective vision hypothesis, for if the appearances were purely objective visions we should not expect them to share many of the characteristics of typical apparitions.

121. Perry, *Easter Enigma*, 210-13.

of the mind of the sender and the mind of the receivers. This hypothesis can claim some support from a phenomenon that has been reported in some cases of reciprocal OBEs. A reciprocal OBE is an OBE in which the person having the OBE is seen as an apparition at the place where they experience themself having the OBE. (For example, Bob has an OBE in which he experiences himself as being in Sally's house, and Sally sees Bob as an apparition in her house at the same time Bob is having the OBE.)[122] In some cases of reciprocal OBEs, it appears that the manner in which the witness sees the apparition is partially determined by the mind of the witness. For example, in one case, the person having the OBE was in bed at night, but when the witness saw him, she did not see him wearing his nightclothes, as we would expect if the apparition was entirely a construct of the sender's mind (for the sender knew he was wearing his nightclothes); she saw him with his daytime clothes on.[123] Likewise, recall that in the Cornell apparition discussed in chapter 3, there were differences in the way the two witnesses perceived the apparition. So there is some merit to the idea that the witnesses might affect the way in which the apparition is seen.[124]

On the basis of this data, the proponent of the apparition hypothesis could propose that the reason we have so much data which we would seem more likely to get if Jesus was resurrected, is that the witnesses' subconscious minds, because of the fact that the witnesses thought they were seeing Jesus risen from the dead, fashioned the witnesses' perception of the apparition so that they would see the apparition doing many things which it would seem a resurrected person ought to do. Thus just as the witness in the case we just mentioned saw the apparition with his daytime clothes on even though the apparition was not trying to communicate this, so the witnesses to the resurrection appearances saw Jesus eating, showing them his wounds, telling them he was raised from the dead and so on, even though Jesus was not himself trying to communicate any of this.

There is also the full version of this hypothesis, which is based on the super-ESP theory of apparitions. Recall that the super-ESP theory of apparitions proposes that an apparition is entirely a construct of the witness's mind: It is not a disembodied spirit; it is a consciousless image created by the subconscious mind of the percipient, though it may present the percipient with information he did not previously know (information which the percipient's subconscious mind acquired by ESP), and even be seen by other people (because the percipient's subconscious mind may pass the image on to another person's subconscious mind). Now if the super-ESP theory of apparitions is correct, the hypothesis we are considering may seem even more plausible: If the apparition is wholly a construct of the percipient's subconscious mind, then why could

---

122. On reciprocal, and other evidential, OBEs see n112 in chapter 3.

123. For this case and one similar case, see Stephen E. Braude, *Immortal Remains: The Evidence for Life After Death* (Lanham, MD: Rowman & Littlefield, 2003), 268.

124. G.N.M. Tyrell made this concept a central aspect of his theory of apparitions (*Apparitions* (New York: Collier, 1963 [1953]).

the percipient's subconscious mind not fashion the apparition any way it wishes? If it could, then there is no reason the percipients' subconscious minds could not trick them into thinking a resurrected person had appeared.

If either form of this hypothesis is true, then since the minds of the percipients were trying to trick them into thinking Jesus was raised from the dead, then just as with the objective vision theory, all of the things which it would be probable for a resurrected person to do would also be probable for the apparition of Jesus to do.

But there are three problems with both versions of this hypothesis. First, since there is no other case on record displaying the characteristics the resurrected Jesus displayed, there is no other case in which the witnesses' minds were able to modify the information sent by a disembodied spirit, or to create an image wholesale, in the manner that this theory proposes the disciples did. Thus, although if we grant the premise of either version of the hypothesis (that the apparition image is a combination of the minds of the sender and receiver, or that the apparition image is entirely a construct of the witness's mind), it becomes *possible* this hypothesis is true, the hypothesis has an exceedingly low initial probability, because in the case of no other apparition have the witnesses' minds been able to create the type of image which the hypothesis proposes the disciples created in the case of the resurrection appearances. Second, in the case of some of the characteristics which the resurrection appearances displayed but which typical apparitions do not, the disciples would not even have known that apparitions did not usually display the characteristics, since no studies of the frequency of characteristics of apparitions had been done in the disciples' day. For example, the disciples could not have known that apparitions do not usually last a long time, or that apparitions do not usually display the sort of ESP Jesus displayed, or that apparitions are not usually collective and recurrent. Hence this hypothesis would have to postulate that the disciples acquired by ESP information which would in fact not be known to the rest of the world till the present time. This reduces the initial probability of the hypothesis even more. Third, Matthew's data about the guards seeing the angel roll back the stone and the occurrence of the earthquake cannot be explained by this hypothesis—unless the hypothesis proposed that the disciples were able to subconsciously project an image of an angel to the guards, and were able to subconsciously use psychokinetic powers to cause the stone to roll away and even cause an earthquake. But proposing this would reduce the initial probability even further. Hence this version of the apparition theory suffers the same problem as the objective vision theory: It can make the data probable given ~h only by drastically reducing the initial probability of ~h.

Appendix: The Prudence of Bayes' Theorem

Now that we have concluded our Bayesian analysis of the New Testament data, I would like to conclude with a cautionary note. Although it is always possible to evaluate data with Bayes' Theorem, I am not sure how often it would be prudent to do so. Of course, I have reference to a conscious use of BT, for any analysis of any data involves at least a subconscious use. But why might a subconscious use often be preferable? Because humans' minds have been constructed to use BT in a subconscious manner and this faculty of ours generally works quite well. A conscious and proper use of BT will work even better, but the question is whether a conscious use will always be a proper use. For in many cases, people may not understand how BT ought to be used consciously and the attempt to use it consciously may muddle the matter. In one real life court case, jurors with no previous experience in the use of BT were compelled to use it to determine a verdict.[125] This strikes me as not being a very good idea; conclusions which seem plain upon an ordinary examination of the facts may get rather mixed up when untrained individuals are compelled to translate them into the BT equation. One could suggest that the situation will be remedied if everyone has sufficient training in BT, but the question then becomes whether the use of BT will get us much further than we were before the application of BT. It seems to me that in the present case it has, for the stalemate surrounding the question of similarities and differences between the resurrection appearances and apparitions can clearly be broken once consequent probability has been considered consciously. But I do not think the conscious application of BT will always have such a positive effect. In many cases, we will not be able to see very much more than we could see when BT was being used subconsciously, and the little more we can see will not be worth the added time and effort. And as for how often the conscious use of BT will make a significant improvement, although I cannot be sure, if I had to bet, I would say that BT is not going to turn the world of religion upside down.

125. See http://en.wikipedia.org/wiki/R_v_Adams.

Appendix

Can the Historian Affirm that a Miracle Occurred?

THE HISTORIAN OF CHRISTIANITY faces a problem which historians in other disciplines do not often encounter: some of the sources with which he deals report the occurrence of miracles. Since Christian historians work with sources which report miracles, and since the sources are not so poor that the claims are obviously false, the logical course of action would seem to be to evaluate these claims. However, as many readers are likely aware, there is a widely held opinion that claims of miracles should be dismissed *a priori*, that it is impossible even in theory for a historian to affirm the occurrence of a miracle. There are various reasons given for this position, such as that miracles violate the laws of nature, that they represent a God of the gaps approach, or that they belong to the province of theology not history. After examining one preliminary issue, I will argue that a historian can affirm that a miracle occurred, because he can affirm that the two conditions necessary for a miracle to occur have actually occurred. That is, the historian can affirm: 1) that a violation of the laws of nature occurred, and 2) that the violation of the laws of nature was either directly caused by God (e.g., the Virgin Birth), or was caused by a person to whom God gave the ability to cause it (e.g., the miracles of Elijah and Elisha).[1] I will not argue that any particular alleged miracle has actually occurred, only that the evidence for any alleged miracle should be evaluated just as the historian would evaluate the evidence for any other alleged event.[2]

---

1. Miracles have traditionally been understood as violations of the laws of nature which are caused by God. Gary R. Habermas cites five prominent thinkers whose definition of "miracle" has included these two elements: Rudolf Bultmann, David Hume, Richard Swinburne, C.S. Lewis, and John McNaugher (PhD diss; Michigan State University, 1976; available at: http://www.garyhabermas.com/books/habermas_dissertation_1976.pdf 26-29). However, "caused by God" can refer to either a violation of a law of nature which was directly caused by God (e.g., the Virgin Birth) or a violation of a law of nature which was caused by a person to whom God gave the ability to cause it (e.g., the miracles of Elijah and Elisha), and consequently of which God was the indirect cause. Scholars have had both types of events in mind when they have referred to events caused by God.

2. Allow me to note some other sources which address the same general question as this essay (whether a historian can affirm that a miracle occurred) from a similar perspective: C. Stephen Evans, "Critical Historical Judgment and Biblical Faith," in Ronald A. Wells ed., *History and the Christian Historian* (Grand Rapids, MI: Eerdmans, 1998), 41-67 (54-67); Paul Rhodes Eddy and Gregory Boyd, *The Jesus Legend: A Case for the Historical Reliability of the Synoptic Jesus Tradition* (Grand Rapids, MI: Baker Academic, 2007), 39-90; William Lane Craig, *Reasonable Faith: Christian Truth and Apologetics*

APPENDIX: CAN THE HISTORIAN AFFIRM THAT A MIRACLE OCCURRED?

Preliminary Issue: The Burden of Proof

The preliminary issue which we must examine before we begin is the question of where the burden of proof lies. I maintain that the burden of proof lies on the one who argues that the historian *cannot* affirm that a miracle occurred, not on the one who argues that the historian *can* affirm that it occurred.

When a historian encounters a source which claims that a given event happened, the historian attempts to determine whether the alleged event actually happened. He will encounter lots of different kinds of events: one source might claim a flood happened, another that an earthquake happened, another that a battle happened. But whatever the purported event, the historian tries to determine whether it happened. Thus if someone wants to argue that there is some particular alleged event the actuality of which a historian should not even attempt to determine, the historian needs to be given a reason why. For in his experience, every event which he has examined has been one which he can, at least in theory, use historical criteria to evaluate. Thus every time he comes across in his sources an alleged event he has not looked at before, he is going to assume that, like all alleged events he has previously encountered, he can determine whether or not this event actually happened. Hence, if someone wants to argue that there is a particular alleged event (or particular kind of alleged event) which cannot be determined to have happened, the burden of proof is certainly on that person to show why this event is an exception. The historian will wait for the critic to provide some reason why he *cannot* evaluate the event; the historian will not think it incumbent upon him to provide a reason why he *can* evaluate it. Thus if the critic asserts that the historian cannot determine whether a miracle happened, the historian will wait for the critic to explain why he cannot determine whether a miracle happened. The critic maintains that this type of event is different from other events, but the critic cannot just assert this, any more than he can assert that volcanoes are not open to historical investigation. The default position is that a miracle, or any other purported event, is open to historical investigation; the burden of proof is on the critic to prove otherwise.

Objections to Miracles

The critic, of course, does have reasons, and the reasons have to do with the nature of a miracle. A miracle has traditionally been defined as an event which 1) violates the

---

(3rd ed.; Wheaton, IL: Crossway, 2008), 247-83; Michael R. Licona, "Historians and Miracle Claims," *Journal for the Study of the Historical Jesus* 12 (2014): 106-129. In addition, I should mention some of the most influential contemporary works on miracles, though these works are not as concerned with the historical aspect (they are more concerned with the theological and philosophical aspects): C.S. Lewis, *Miracles: A Preliminary Study* (2nd ed.; San Francisco: HarperCollins, 1960); Louis Monden, *Signs and Wonders: A Study of the Miraculous Element in Religion* (New York: Desclee, 1966); Richard Swinburne, *The Concept of Miracle* (London: Macmillan, 1970).

APPENDIX: CAN THE HISTORIAN AFFIRM THAT A MIRACLE OCCURRED?

laws of nature, and 2) is either directly caused by God (e.g., the virginal conception) or is caused by a human being to whom God has given the ability to violate the laws of nature (e.g., the miracles of Elijah and Elisha, and of Jesus). Thus there are two aspects to a miracle, and the critic can direct his argument at either one: He can either argue 1) that a historian cannot attempt to determine whether a violation of the laws of nature took place, or 2) that even if a historian can determine whether a violation of the laws of nature took place, a historian can neither determine whether God was the cause of the violation of the laws of nature, nor whether a human being who caused the violation of the laws of nature had been empowered by God to do so. Objections to miracles have been made on both fronts and we will consider them one at a time. First we will consider objections to the idea that a historian can affirm that a violation of the laws of nature occurred. Then, granting that violations of the laws of nature are possible, we will consider objections to the idea that a historian can affirm either that God was the direct cause of the violation of the laws of nature, or that the human being who caused the event was given the ability to do so by God.

Can The Historian Affirm That a Violation of the Laws of Nature Occurred?

Are The Laws of Nature Immutable?

One of the most common objections to the suggestion that miracles can happen is the idea that the laws of nature simply cannot be violated. They are inviolable: not only have they never been violated, but it is impossible in principle that they ever could be.[3]

This objection usually assumes that the immutability of the laws of nature is an assured result of modern science rather than a matter of dispute. But in fact, there is no consensus among scientists or philosophers of science on this question. (And it is debatable whether it is even a scientific question, or a purely philosophical one.) In fact, though we all have a general idea of what is meant by "the laws of nature" (something like "the way in which nature operates"), there is not even any consensus on precisely what a law of nature is—whether the laws of nature are descriptive, describing what does and does not happen in the world, or prescriptive, adjudicating on what can and cannot happen.[4] However, it is not necessary to reach agreement on

---

3. Spinoza is a well-known proponent of this argument: "On Miracles" in his *Theological-Political Treatise* (1670). Available at: http://www.jhom.com/topics/miracles/spinoza.htm. Mark Wm Worthing mentions some contemporary proponents of the argument, such as Stephen Hawking: "God, Process and Cosmos: Is God Simply Going Along for the Ride?" in Hilary D. Regan ed., *Interdisciplinary Perspectives on Cosmology and Biological Evolution* (Hindmarsh: Australian Theological Forum, 2002), 153-71 (160-63).

4. For an overview of contemporary thought about the laws of nature, see the entry for "Laws of Nature" in the *Stanford Encyclopedia of Philosophy*.

exactly what these laws are, in order to conclude that, whatever their exact nature, they are not immutable.

The idea that scientific laws are immutable is arrived at by induction. We have examined a great many events and they have all conformed to scientific laws, hence we conclude that all events conform to scientific laws. This is good methodology; we use it in all areas of life. The sun has come up every day, and so we assume it will come up tomorrow. It has snowed every winter (in certain parts of the world) and so we assume it will snow next winter. But the assumption we make—that what has been true of past experience will continue to be true of future experience—is one which can only be held with a degree of probability, not certainty. For sometimes what has always been true in the past does not continue to be true in the future. For example, suppose someone who has never watched a basketball game before watches a game on television and sees the players make ten free throws in a row. This person has never seen a missed free throw. But certainly he will be wrong to conclude from this that basketball players make 100% of their free throws. He should remain open to the possibility that the basketball players will eventually miss a shot (and in this case, that is surely what will happen).

This methodology should not only apply to basketball; it should apply to every other area of life, including miracles. If I encounter someone who claims to be able to change water into wine, I should judge this improbable, but there is no reason I should not invite him to demonstrate it, rather than dismiss it *a priori*. It is possible that though I have seen 1000 glasses of water and never seen one change into wine, the 1001st one might very well change into wine.

If someone did observe the transformation of water into wine, what should he conclude about the laws of nature? He can reach one of two conclusions—either the laws of nature have been violated or the laws of nature need to be radically reformulated so that the changing of water into wine is no longer considered a violation of the laws of nature. I will not render an opinion on which conclusion is better since this would require a detailed discussion of the nature of scientific laws—a matter on which there is no agreement—and since for present purposes the point is only a technical one. To those who specialize in studying the laws of nature, there may be a significant difference between actually violating the laws of nature and simply radically reformulating them. But the question currently under consideration is whether the historian can affirm that miraculous events—events typically considered violations of the laws of nature, such as changing water into wine, or raising the dead—have occurred. Hence, I use the term "violation of the laws of nature" to mean either a violation in the technical sense, or a radical reformulation. The question of whether such events actually constitute violations of the laws of nature or only radical reformulations of them is not essential to the concerns of this essay. The essential point is only that there is nothing about scientific laws which prohibits such events from occurring. The laws of nature give us grounds to think that such events have a low probability of occurring, but we should not rule them out absolutely.

It is by following the approach to induction that I have suggested, rather than the one which the critic of miracles proposes, that quantum mechanics was discovered.[5] Prior to the discovery of quantum phenomena, every event scientists observed could be predicted with certainty. If an apple is thrown into the air, there is not merely a probability it will come down—it will always come down. Thus when scientists began to study quantum phenomena, they assumed they would be able to predict the particles' behavior with certainty. They assumed that if a particle approached a barrier it would either always be stopped by or always not be stopped by the barrier, because such certainty had been true of every previous event they had witnessed. But, in fact, they discovered that they could only predict the particle's behavior with a degree of probability: sometimes it would be stopped by the barrier and sometimes it would not. Hence, the laws of nature were radically reformulated: It was concluded that only events taking place on the macroscopic level can be predicted with certainty, whereas events on the microscopic level can only be predicted with probability. If physicists had instead approached quantum phenomena with the mindset that the laws of nature are inviolable, they would never have been able to study quantum phenomena properly. Likewise, if we approach miracles with the mindset that the laws of nature are inviolable, we will not be able to study miracles properly.

Hume

The admission made above, that a violation of the laws of nature has a low probability of occurring, calls to mind David Hume's objection to miracles. Hume's argument runs as follows: A miracle, by definition, is an improbable event; miracles do not happen very often. But if it is improbable, how can we justifiably believe it happened? For it is always wiser to prefer a probable explanation to an improbable one.[6]

Hume's argument has exerted a considerable amount of influence on subsequent thought about miracles, but it is safe to say that our knowledge of probability theory renders the argument false.[7] The essential problem with Hume's argument is that it confuses initial probability with epistemic probability. The initial probability is the

---

5. I do not mean that physicists were consciously employing this methodology. Part of the task of philosophy is to identify thought processes that people employ without realizing they are employing them. For example, when philosophers propose criteria for evaluating hypotheses, such as explanatory scope and explanatory power, these are criteria which people use every day while evaluating hypotheses, but they do not usually realize that they are using them.

6. David Hume, *On Miracles* (1748). The arguments of Hume and also of Troeltsch (see next section) have been propounded by a variety of critics and responses to them can be found in a number of sources including: Craig, *Reasonable Faith*, 269-77; Eddy and Boyd, *Jesus Legend*, 39-90; Norman L. Geisler, *Christian Apologetics* (Grand Rapids, MI: Baker Books, 1976), 265-67, 301-303.

7. See S.L. Zabell, "The Probabilistic Analysis of Testimony," *Journal of Statistical Planning and Inference* 20 (1988): 327-54.

probability that a hypothesis is true prior to an examination of the evidence, whereas epistemic probability is the final probability, that is, the probability that a hypothesis is true subsequent to the examination of the evidence. For example, suppose I want to know the probability that a certain person, say Bob, got a royal flush at poker last week. Now, the odds of getting a royal flush are over 600,000:1, and if Hume's argument is applied consistently we will have to conclude that Bob did not get a royal flush, for a royal flush is an improbable event and it is therefore unwise to believe it happened. But after the evidence is examined, the probability that Bob got a royal flush may actually be very high. In this case, the evidence would consist of eyewitness testimony, and if we have no reason to believe the witnesses were lying or otherwise mistaken, then the epistemic probability that Bob got a royal flush is actually very high. The analogy with miracles is clear: Although the initial probability of a miracle may be very low, once we examine the evidence—which is usually the testimony of eyewitnesses (testifying either directly or indirectly, through their writings)—the probability that a miracle occurred may be very high. Probability theorists have built this reasoning into Bayes' Theorem, a mathematical theorem for determining the probability that an event occurred. Bayes' Theorem requires that an event's probability can only be determined by weighing the event's initial probability with the specific evidence for the event. The initial probability cannot simply be taken by itself, as Hume would have us do.

Troeltsch

Ernst Troeltsch's argument has also exerted considerable influence. Troeltsch appealed to the principle of analogy. He argued that in order to do history we have to assume that the world of the past operated in the same way as the world of the present. If some phenomenon does not take place today, we cannot affirm that it took place in the past, since we have no analogy for it. Troeltsch reasoned that if there is no analogy for a phenomenon, then we cannot make sense of it. Now this point is correct. An analogy involves identifying similarities, and if we encounter an idea which has no similarities at all to anything we have ever experienced, then we cannot make sense of it. But Troeltsch concluded—incorrectly—that since miracles do not occur today, we have no analogy for them, and so we cannot affirm that they took place in the past.[8]

The first problem with Troeltsch's argument is that it assumes that miracles do not take place today. But given the many miracle claims made in contemporary times, it is questionable whether this contention is true. If miracles occur today, Troeltsch's argument fails even if we grant Troeltsch's premise that a historian can affirm that an event took place in the past only if the same type of event occurs today.

---

8. Ernst Troeltsch, *Religion in History* (James Luther Adams and Walter F. Bense trans.; Minneapolis: Fortress, 1991), 11-32 (essay "Historical and Dogmatic Method in Theology" originally published in 1898).

But in fact, this premise is completely untenable. For in making his argument, Troeltsch misunderstands what an analogy is—he confuses analogy with identity. To say that two things are analogous is not to say that they are exactly the same, but only that they are similar in certain respects, while necessarily being dissimilar in other respects. No two events are exactly the same and if we could only affirm that an event took place in the past if the exact same event takes place in the present, we would never be able to affirm that any event took place. But if a past event need only be similar in certain respects to present events for us to affirm that it happened, then there is no problem with affirming that a miracle happened, since any miracle will be similar to some present event in certain respects. For example, a person walking on water is similar to a number of present day events: a person traveling on the water in a boat, a person floating on his back on the water, and a person walking on ice (frozen water). In all cases, the basic concept is the same: a person is suspended above water in some manner. So this is where the similarity lies. There are, of course, differences, but there are supposed to be differences when we are dealing with analogy and not identity.

This leads us to the most fundamental problem with Troeltsch's argument. Although he is quite right that if a concept is completely dissimilar to everything we have ever experienced, we will not be able to understand it, there is in fact no concept which is completely dissimilar to everything we have ever experienced. Whatever the concept is, no matter how unfamiliar, it will be similar in some respects to something which we have previously experienced. For if it was not, we could not understand it, and so we could not identify it as a concept. A unicorn, for example, is similar to a horse. Bigfoot is similar to a gorilla. The Loch Ness Monster is similar to various large sea creatures, such as whales and sharks.

The final problem with Troeltsch's argument is that it would require us to rule out *a priori* the Big Bang, the most popular explanation for the origin of the universe. For the Big Bang postulates creation out of nothing, an event which surely does not occur today, and which, if it did occur, could only be considered a violation of the laws of nature.

God of the Gaps

The "God of the Gaps" argument, unlike the two previous arguments, is not associated with any particular name, but it is surely one of the most common arguments against miracles. This is the argument that it is illegitimate to postulate a supernatural or paranormal explanation because science has again and again eliminated such explanations, and thus any supernatural or paranormal explanation will eventually be replaced with a natural explanation. The ancient Greeks used to think that thunder was caused by Zeus, but modern science has shown that it is really caused by the expansion of air that occurs following a bolt of lightning. Even Newton, one of the greatest of modern scientists, fell prey to the God of the Gaps approach: he supposed

God was necessary to account for the force of gravity, but scientists today have no trouble explaining this phenomenon naturalistically.[9]

The answer to this argument is that even though modern science has been able to show that some phenomena which were once thought to have a supernatural explanation actually have a natural one, if there are still other phenomena for which a supernatural explanation seems preferable, we should continue to prefer a supernatural explanation for these phenomena. We should not simply hope that science will someday discover a natural explanation. It is illogical to argue that simply because science has shown that *some* phenomena which were once thought to have a supernatural explanation actually have a non-supernatural explanation, therefore science will eventually show that this is true of *all* phenomena. Such an argument is analogous to arguing that because *some* murderers have been exonerated by DNA evidence, therefore *all* murderers will eventually be exonerated by DNA evidence—that because science has found a non-murder explanation for *some* murder cases, science will eventually find a non-murder explanation for *all* murder cases. Perhaps science will eventually show that all alleged miracles are false and that all alleged murderers are innocent, but a hypothesis can only be based on the data available at the moment. It is always possible a hypothesis will have to be discarded when more data is available. Of course, for a miraculous explanation to be accepted, it must be shown that this is indeed the best explanation of the current data. But it is not permissible to argue, as the God of the Gaps argument does, that even if a miraculous explanation does seem to be the best explanation of the data it should not be accepted.

The Paranormal and the Miraculous

I have distinguished between two aspects of a miracle—the fact that it is 1) a violation of the laws of nature, and the fact that it is 2) either directly caused by God or caused by someone to whom God gave the ability to cause it—and I have alluded to the possibility that an event could be a violation of the laws of nature without the second condition being fulfilled. It may be wondered what type of event this could be. I have in mind a so-called paranormal event. Paranormal events furnish a definitive argument in favor of the historian's ability to affirm that a violation of the laws of nature occurred.

Paranormal events occur outside of any religious context, but if they really happen they certainly constitute violations of the laws of nature (in the sense explained above—if paranormal events occur they require that either the laws of nature were actually violated or that they must be radically reformulated).[10] Some ostensibly para-

---

9. Paul C.W. Davies, *The Mind of God: The Scientific Basis For a Rational World* (New York: Simon& Schuster, 1992), 76.

10. Not all so-called paranormal events require violations of the laws of nature or radical reformulations of them. Phenomena such as bending metal with the mind, clairvoyance, and predicting

normal events take place spontaneously; they are not under anyone's control (e.g., Near Death Experiences, or apparitions). But more pertinent to the present topic is the fact that some people claim to be able to produce paranormal phenomena on demand. Psychics have claimed to be able to bend metal with their minds, predict the future, and communicate with the dead. All of these things—if they really occur—constitute violations of the laws of nature. But very few would argue that such claims should be rejected *a priori*; rather, they should be tested. If a psychic claims to be able to bend a spoon with the power of his mind, he should be asked to do so under properly controlled conditions. Indeed, many have been tested, though none have ever passed the tests successfully: The James Randi Educational Foundation has for some years offered one million dollars to anyone who can demonstrate any paranormal power under properly controlled conditions.[11] But the point for our purposes is not that any of the purportedly paranormal events are real, but only that it is possible in theory to prove that they are; the evidence can be evaluated.

If it is possible to evaluate the evidence that some person living today has paranormal powers, then it is possible to evaluate historical evidence that some person in the past had these powers. For any evidence we have at the present time will eventually become historical evidence. Eventually all of the eyewitnesses will die and all that will remain will be documents, primarily written records, and subsequent generations will have to base their belief in the reality of the paranormal phenomena on this historical evidence. If we would expect subsequent generations to analyze what is to us contemporary evidence but will be to them historical evidence, then to be consistent we must be willing to evaluate the evidence from ages past.

Conclusion

So there seems to be no reason why a historian cannot consider historical evidence that a violation of the laws of nature occurred. If sources claim Jesus walked on water or rose from the dead, there is no reason why the historian cannot evaluate these claims. However, the historian may wish to eschew the theological aspect. He may wish to separate the two aspects of a miracle and hold that while he can affirm that a violation of a law of nature took place, he cannot affirm that God had anything to do with it. Maybe God was involved with the events, or maybe—as would be the case if the paranormal events discussed above really happened—the events have nothing to do with God; it is for the theologians to decide. This approach would only be an

---

the future would require this, but phenomena such as Bigfoot and aliens would not: previously unknown ape creatures or extraterrestrials would fit into the natural universe just fine. When I use the term "paranormal" in the text, I am referring to the types of paranormal phenomena that do constitute violations of the laws of nature.

11. It should be noted that the failure of subjects who claim to be able to produce paranormal phenomena on demand does not necessarily lead to the conclusion that paranormal phenomena which take place spontaneously are not authentic.

extension of one that is already quite popular in scholarship: The position of many scholars is that while a historian cannot affirm that a miracle took place, he can affirm that an event took place which people at that time interpreted as a miracle.[12] Hence, although we cannot say that Jesus' miracles were real miracles, we can say that Jesus did things which his contemporaries believed were miracles. From this it is a short step to arguing that since a historian can affirm that a violation of the laws of nature took place, he can affirm that some event was a violation of the laws of nature, but he cannot affirm that God had anything to with it.

If this essay succeeds only in persuading historians that they can affirm that a violation of the laws of nature took place, it will have accomplished something. But I wish to go further and argue that a historian can affirm that God was the cause of the violation of the laws of nature. That is, the historian can affirm either that 1) God was the direct cause of the event or 2) the event was caused by someone who was given the ability to perform the event by God.

Can the Historian Affirm that God was the Cause of a Violation of the Laws of Nature?

If the historian is asked to determine whether God was the cause of a violation of the laws of nature, he is only being asked to determine 1) whether a conscious being was the direct cause of an event (such as the Virgin Birth; God caused this directly). Or: 2) whether a conscious being gave someone the ability to perform a certain action (as in the case, for example, of Elijah. God gave Elijah the ability to perform violations of the laws of nature; God did not perform them directly). Historians frequently affirm that both types of events occurred. For example, when a historian affirms that Caesar crossed the Rubicon, he affirms that a conscious being, Caesar, is the direct cause of an event; Caesar's conscious decision to cross the Rubicon is the most immediate cause of why he crossed the Rubicon. And if a historian affirms that a person who had stopped breathing began to breathe again after a doctor gave him CPR, he affirms that a conscious being (the doctor) gave someone the ability to perform some action (breathe). Likewise, if the historian affirms that a child was able to chop down a tree because his father gave him an ax, the historian affirms that a conscious being (the father) gave someone the ability to perform some action (chop down a tree). Thus *a priori*, it does not seem that the historian is being asked to do anything unusual when he is asked to evaluate whether God caused a violation of the laws of nature.

But if the conscious being in question is God, does that make a difference? Does that mean that the matter falls outside the province of history and within the province of theology? The answer is that there is no reason why the provinces should not sometimes overlap: some topics belong to both theology and history.

---

12. See e.g., John P. Meier, *A Marginal Jew: Rethinking the Historical Jesus: Volume 2: Mentor, Message, and Miracles* (New York: Doubleday, 1994), chapter 17.

Appendix: Can the Historian Affirm that a Miracle Occurred?

In general, different disciplines study different subjects, but sometimes different disciplines study the same subjects. In such a case, if an expert in one discipline is studying a question, it may be that he cannot answer the question without taking into account the work of the experts in another discipline. For example, if the question is whether depression has a physical or psychological cause, there will be two types of experts addressing the question: psychologists and neurobiologists. If the psychologist wants to discover the answer to the question, he has to consider the arguments of neurobiology; he has to consider himself competent to evaluate the arguments of the neurobiologists. And the neurobiologist cannot answer the question with his data alone; he has to evaluate the arguments of the psychologists.[13]

I do not know of any disciplines which are truly mutually exclusive, where it is impossible even in theory to have a problem which requires insight from both disciplines to solve. In fact, the Writing Center of the University of North Carolina at Chapel Hill tells us that religious studies frequently overlaps with other disciplines: "religious studies is a deeply interdisciplinary field," and the professor may require students "to use theories and methods drawn from many other departments, programs, and curricula of study." These statements are followed by a list of about two dozen subjects which religious studies students may be required to interact with, subjects as diverse as Art, Ecology, Music, Political Science, and Psychology.[14]

There is no reason why theology and history should be the exception to the rule that subjects may overlap; the burden of proof is certainly on those who suggest that it is. If the historian is concerned with trying to determine whether a conscious being is the direct cause of some action or whether a conscious being gave somebody the power to perform some action, and the conscious being is God, and it is the task of the theologian to tell us what God is like and what sort of actions he is likely to perform, then we have the same situation as we do when the psychologist and neurobiologist are both studying depression. The historian should consider the work of the theologian and attempt to answer the question. (If the objection is made that different theologians, particularly those from different religions, will give the historian different answers, the response is simply that the historian will have to decide which theologians he agrees with. Different neurobiologists may have different ideas as to the role of the nervous system in depression. The psychologist will have to decide which neurobiologists he agrees with.)

---

13. On the intersection between psychology and neurobiology in the study of depression, see Stephan J. Claes and Charles B. Nemeroff, "Corticotropin Releasing Factor (CRF) and Major Depression: Towards an Integration of Psychology and Neurobiology in Depression Research," in Jozef Corveleyn, Patrick Luyten, and Sydney J. Blatt eds., *The Theory and Treatment of Depression: Towards a Dynamic Interactionism Model* (Leuven: Leuven University Press, 2005), 227-252.

14. "Religious Studies," http://www.unc.edu/depts/wcweb/handouts/religious_studies.html. This source does not affirm that *theology* overlaps with all these disciplines. The source draws a distinction between theology and religious studies—religious studies being the study of religion from a non-faith, neutral perspective. I am not sure which subjects the authors would suggest theology overlaps with. But I am citing the source only to illustrate the general point that subjects very frequently intersect.

However, there are cases in which the historian will have to refrain from making a judgment because he does not consider it possible to acquaint himself with the other discipline to the extent that he needs to in order to make an informed judgment. In the case of depression, the psychologist may be able to acquaint himself with the narrow area of neurobiology which is required to understand the limited number of issues from this field which bear on the psychologist's question. But if he has to acquaint himself with large areas of this field, or with areas of this field which are particularly esoteric to him, he may decide that he cannot acquaint himself with this field sufficiently, and so he cannot answer the question. So while a historian may decide that he can in principle affirm that a miracle occurred, he may also decide that in the case of some particular miracle, the theological issues are too complicated for him to reach a judgment. Historians will differ on whether or not this is the case, depending on their knowledge of theology and depending on which theological issues are pertinent to the issue in question. But there is no reason in principle why the historian should not evaluate the theological data when studying a miracle, in the same way that the psychologist evaluates the neurobiological data when studying depression.

Objections: The Nature of Faith, the Laws of Nature, and Competing Miracle Claims

I have argued that the historian can in principle affirm that God caused a violation of a law of nature, but there are two particularly common objections that must be considered. There is also an in practice objection to consider, an objection which argues that though it is theoretically possible to affirm that a miracle occurred, in practice it is not possible. Since this particular in practice objection attempts to rule out not just the reality of one particular miracle, but all miracles, it approaches the status of an in principle objection and so it should also be considered here.

Faith

The first in principle objection runs as follows: The teachings of religion are matters of faith. By definition, they cannot be proved. We can either believe something because of the evidence, or we can believe it by faith. And since religion is concerned with faith, we have to accept religious beliefs, including the belief that miracles happen, by faith. As Alan Segal says: "[faith] does not depend on rational argument. If it did, it would be reason, not faith."[15] Likewise, according to Steven Pinker: "faith is believing

---

15. Alan F. Segal, "The Resurrection: Faith or History?" in Robert B. Stewart ed., *The Resurrection of Jesus: John Dominic Crossan and N.T. Wright in Dialogue* (Minneapolis: Fortress Press, 2006), 121-39 (137).

in something without good reasons to do so."[16] And according to Ronald Hendel: "facts are facts, and faith has no business dealing in the world of facts."[17]

The definition of "faith" that is presupposed by this argument is belief in the absence of evidence, or so-called "blind faith." I am not sure how this definition of faith arose, but it must be of fairly recent origin, since it is not the Biblical definition or the historical definition. The Biblical writers clearly speak of people having faith even though those people have been provided with very compelling evidence. In Romans 4:1-25, Paul explains that Abraham had faith, but Paul also tells us this faith came about in response to hearing the audible voice of God, surely compelling evidence (God is said to have told Abraham: "In you will all the nations be blessed"). (Whether or not Abraham really did hear God's voice, the point is that Paul thought he did, and so Paul thought Abraham had compelling evidence on which to base his faith.)[18] The author of Hebrews gives us a long list of people who had faith, such as Noah, Abraham, Moses, and Samson (Heb 11:1-40). But all of these people had been given compelling evidence of the existence of God. Noah and Abraham heard God's voice, Moses performed miracles by God's power, Samson was given supernatural strength by God. (Again, whether these things really happened, all that is important for our purposes is that the author of Hebrews believed they did.)

With regard to the historical definition of faith, it is unquestionably the case that most theologians throughout the church's history have not considered evidence to be incompatible with faith. Many theologians have appealed to evidence to support Christianity, principally the evidence of miracles and Messianic prophecy.[19]

The conception of faith as belief in the absence of evidence is also not the only conception of faith current in our own day. Merriam-Webster online (based on the Merriam-Webster Collegiate Dictionary) provides three religion related definitions of the word "faith," two of which make no comment on the role of evidence in faith ("belief and trust in and loyalty to God"; "belief in the traditional doctrines of a religion"), and only one of which excludes evidence ("firm belief in something for which there is no proof") (http://www.merriam-webster.com/dictionary/faith.)

---

16. Steven Pinker, remarks in a discussion at Harvard University, quoted by Lisa Miller, "Harvard's Crisis of Faith: Can a Secular University Embrace Religion Without Sacrificing its Soul?" *Newsweek*, February 11, 2010. Available online at: http://www.newsweek.com/2010/02/10/harvard-s-crisis-of-faith.html.

17. Ronald S. Hendel, "Farewell to SBL: Faith and Reason in Biblical Studies," *Biblical Archeology Review* 36.4 July/August 2010.

18. It is clear that first century Jews believed the Scriptures narrated actual events. For example, Josephus, a Jewish historian who wrote in the first century CE, considers the Flood to be a real event, noting other historians who mentioned it (*Antiquities of the* Jews 1.3.6), and he even goes so far as to say that he has seen the very pillar of salt which Lot's wife was turned into (1.11.4).

19. See the many theologians discussed in Avery Cardinal Dulles, *A History of Apologetics* (2nd ed.; San Francisco, CA: Ignatius Press, 2005).

The Laws of Nature

A second objection is, like one of the objections considered above, based on the laws of nature. The objection in this case is not that the laws of nature *cannot* be violated, but that God *would not* violate them. The argument is that it makes little sense for God to violate his own laws. If he established these laws, then it seems strange, perhaps wrong, for him to violate them. According to David Strauss, the idea that God would violate the laws of nature is "irreconcilable with enlightened ideas of the relation of God to the world."[20] William Lane Craig tells us that Voltaire "said that it was absurd and insulting to God to think that he would interrupt the operation of 'this immense machine,' since he designed it from the beginning to run according to his divinely decreed, immutable laws."[21]

The problem with this objection is that it confuses the laws of nature with human laws. Human laws are established to guard against wrong: we make it against the law to do something wrong, so violating a human law is wrong (presuming the law is just). But the laws of nature have nothing to do with right and wrong. Rather, they are concerned with the way nature operates. When we refer to the laws of nature, we only mean that this is the way nature operates; we do not mean that it would be wrong for nature to operate differently. There is therefore nothing wrong with God temporarily causing nature to operate differently, especially if he has a reason for doing so (such as to give evidence of his existence). If the term "violate" connotes the wrong idea, then we can simply say that God alters or changes the laws of nature.

Miracles in Other Religions

The third objection, the in practice one, concerns the matter of miracle claims in different religions.[22] The argument is that different religions claim miracles in support of their teachings, but different religions teach contradictory things, and since they cannot all be true, no miracle can be taken to support the truth of a particular religion. (If this argument is successful, the notion that miracles are actually examples of paranormal phenomena will seem more plausible.)

The flaw in this argument is that simply because there are miracle claims in more than one religion, it does not follow that there are equally well-supported miracle claims in more than one religion. Only in the case of Christian miracles is the evidence not extremely weak. The Gospels date forty-seventy years after Jesus' death, Paul's epistles date even earlier than the Gospels, and Paul knew some of the eyewitnesses.[23]

---

20. Strauss, *The Life of Jesus Critically Examined*, 843.
21. Craig, *Reasonable Faith*, 249.
22. This is another argument popularized by David Hume in *On Miracles* (1748).
23. At various points in his epistles, Paul mentions his acquaintance with the eyewitnesses (see especially Gal 2:11-13).

By comparison, the earliest sources reporting miracles by Muhammad and Buddha date to hundreds of years after their deaths and have no eyewitness support. The first biography of Apollonius, a wonder worker who is supposed to have flourished in the first century CE, was not written until 125 years after his death.[24] Practitioners of Eastern religions who claim to be able to perform miracles have been exposed as frauds.[25] In short, miracle claims in every other religion are either too far removed from the eyewitnesses to be taken seriously, or can be explained by some natural explanation such as fraud.[26]

(Although I do not think that there is any evidence for the reality of any miracle claims outside of Christianity, if there was such evidence, it would not immediately follow that miracles are events which do not have anything to do with God. We would have to choose between that option and several other options. For example, perhaps some miracles are greater than others, and the true religion can be determined by which religion has the greatest miracles.[27] Or if religious pluralism is true, perhaps God has some reason for allowing miracles in different religions. Or if miracles are performed on behalf of different gods, perhaps polytheism is true—perhaps different gods do exist.[28])[29]

Conclusion

I have made the case that a historian can affirm that a miracle occurred because he can affirm that a violation of the laws of nature occurred and that God was the cause of the violation of the laws of nature. Since the historian should assume he can affirm that any type of event occurred until it is shown otherwise, the burden of proof is on the critic to show that violations of the laws of nature are an exception, and the arguments

---

24. For a thorough evaluation of non-Christian miracle claims, see Monden, *Signs and Wonders*, 254-95.

25. See e.g., Erlendur Haraldsson and Joop H. Houtkooper, "Report on an Indian Swami Claiming to Materialize Objects: The Value and Limitations of Field Observations," *Journal of Scientific Exploration* 8 (1994): 381-97.

26. Of course, one cannot have a comprehensive knowledge of every miracle claim in every religion, or even of every published claim, but it can be stated with confidence that every non-Christian miracle claim which is frequently cited in conjunction with this particular argument is not as well-evidenced as the Christian miracle claims.

27. A possibility suggested by Gary R. Habermas, *The Risen Jesus and Future Hope* (Lanham, MD: Rowman and Littlefield, 2003), 95.

28. A possibility suggested by Richard Swinburne, "Miracles," *Philosophical Quarterly* 18 (1968): 320-28.

29. There is one other in practice objection which deserves brief mention: that the ancients were stupid and gullibly accepted alleged miracles with no attempt at critical investigation. This is certainly not true of Jesus' time, the time period during which we have the best attested miracle claims. The ancients during Jesus' time were more critical than during any period of history before the Enlightenment. This has been demonstrated by Glenn Miller's examination of the ancient sources: "Were the Miracles of Jesus Invented by the Disciples/Evangelists?" http://christian-thinktank.com/mqfx.html.

for the critic's position fail. The question of whether God was the direct cause of a violation of the laws of nature is no different from a question historians routinely ask: whether a conscious being was the direct cause of some action. And the question of whether God gave somebody the ability to perform a violation of the laws of nature is also no different from a question historians routinely ask: whether a conscious being gave a person the ability to do some action. Thus a historian should assume he can affirm that either God is the direct cause of an event or that God gave a person the ability to perform some action; the burden of proof is again on the critic to show otherwise. The arguments of the critic in this case also fail. Hence, since a historian can affirm that the two conditions required for a miracle to occur actually occurred, a historian can affirm that a miracle occurred.

A final question to address is whether the historian is still acting as a historian when he evaluates whether God was the cause of an event. Is he still a historian or has he become a theologian? The analogy, again, is that of the psychologist and the neurobiologist who are both studying depression. Does the psychologist become a neurobiologist when he is studying the area of neurobiological literature relevant to the subject of depression? Or is he still acting as a psychologist when he makes a judgment on neurobiological issues? While there is a sense in which the psychologist becomes a neurobiologist (if by "neurobiologist" we mean "someone who studies neurobiology"), he is still a psychologist since he is still concerned with a psychological question: what the cause of depression is. Likewise, though a historian in a sense becomes a theologian when he studies theology, he is still a historian since he is still concerned with a historical question: whether a conscious being was the cause of an event (directly, or indirectly through a human). The historian who examines whether a miracle occurred is thus both a historian and a theologian. He is a historian because he is studying a historical question; but the question cannot be answered without also studying theology. Analogously, when the psychologist studies depression, he is a psychologist because he is studying a psychological question; but the question cannot be answered without also studying neurobiology. There is no reason why theology and history, like psychology and neurobiology, should not sometimes overlap. Theology is a very broad field; it is the study of Christian doctrine (or, according to some definitions, the study of Christian doctrine from the viewpoint that the doctrines are true).[30] History is the study of past events. These definitions are not mutually exclu-

---

30. "Theology" is a flexible term. The two most common definitions of theology are "the study of Christian doctrine" (or the study of religious doctrines generally, but it is Christian doctrine, and thus Christian theology, which is most relevant to this article), and "the study of Christian doctrine from the viewpoint that the doctrines are true." (I do not mean that these exact definitions are widely used, but that they encapsulate the two most common ideas that people refer to by the word "theology.") Francis Schussler Fiorenza tells us that "the nature and method of theology are issues about which much diversity exists in the history of Christian thought," and that there are varying definitions of theology: "*Theology* is often used as an umbrella term to cover all the theological disciplines. Yet the term also denotes a specific discipline known as systematic theology. . . *Theology* is also often used in contradistinction from religious studies. . . Yet 'religious studies' and 'theological studies' are sometimes

sive—it might be a Christian doctrine that a past event occurred (the Nicene Creed affirms the historicity of the Virgin Birth, the crucifixion, and the resurrection). If the definitions are not mutually exclusive, why should the fields always stay separate? Psychology is the study of the mind and behavior, and neurobiology is the study of the nervous system. These definitions are not mutually exclusive—it might be that actions of the nervous system affect the mind and behavior; and, in fact, this is what occurs in depression. In this case, the fields do not stay separate. Depression is considered a proper subject of psychology even though it also requires one to study neurobiology, and miracles should be considered a proper subject of history even though they also require one to study theology.

---

used interchangeably" ("Systematic Theology: Task and Methods," in Francis Schussler Fiorenza and John P. Galvin eds., *Systematic Theology: Roman Catholic Perspectives: Volume 1* (Minneapolis: Augsburg Fortress 1991), 1-88 (6-7)). Despite the confusion, the central points for our purposes are clear: In order to affirm that a miracle occurred, the historian has to affirm that God was the cause of an event. Affirming that God was the cause of an event is typically considered theology. But the historian can affirm that God was the cause of an event and still be doing history, even though he will also be doing "theology" on most definitions of theology.

www.ingramcontent.com/pod-product-compliance
Lightning Source LLC
Chambersburg PA
CBHW081417230426
43668CB00016B/2268